Dillon John Talbot

Travels Through Spain

Dillon John Talbot

Travels Through Spain

ISBN/EAN: 9783744759960

Printed in Europe, USA, Canada, Australia, Japan

Cover: Foto ©Andreas Hilbeck / pixelio.de

More available books at **www.hansebooks.com**

CHARLES the III.^d KING of SPAIN &c.
In the Robes of the New Order of Carlos Tercero.
from the Original Picture of Antonio Velasque.

TRAVELS THROUGH SPAIN,

WITH A VIEW TO ILLUSTRATE

THE NATURAL HISTORY

AND

PHYSICAL GEOGRAPHY OF THAT KINGDOM,

IN A SERIES OF LETTERS.

Including the most interesting Subjects contained in the Memoirs of

DON GUILLERMO BOWLES, and other SPANISH WRITERS,

INTERSPERSED WITH HISTORICAL ANECDOTES.

ADORNED WITH COPPER-PLATES AND A NEW MAP OF SPAIN:

WITH

NOTES and OBSERVATIONS relative to the ARTS, and descriptive of MODERN IMPROVEMENTS.

Written in the Course of a late Tour through that Kingdom

By JOHN TALBOT DILLON, Knight and Baron of the SACRED ROMAN EMPIRE.

Lo unico a que puede aspirar, es a la gloria de ser el primero que ha intentado una descripcion fisica de este pais.
DON GUILLERMO BOWLES.

LONDON:
Printed for G. ROBINSON, No. 25, PATERNOSTER-ROW;
And PEARSON and ROLLASON, in BIRMINGHAM.
M.DCC.LXXX.

To
The Right Honourable
THOMAS LORD GRANTHAM,
Late
His Majesty's Ambassador at the Court of
MADRID.
This Work is most respectfully INSCRIBED.
By His Lordship's
most obliged, and
most humble Servant,
John Talbot Dillon.

PREFACE.

AT my return from Italy, in the year, 1778, I once more visited Spain, and traversed the whole kingdom (a). This journey afforded me the greater pleasure, from not only being versed in the Spanish language, but having made many friends and acquaintance during my former residence in that kingdom, besides, being no stranger to their manners and customs; which circumstance greatly contributed to increase my amusement, and render my travels far more agreeable than they would have been to a person in a less eligible predicament.

On my arrival at Madrid, the ingenious and elaborate work of Don Guillermo Bowles (b), first fell into my hands. This valuable treatise is designed as an introduction to the *Natural History and Physical Geography* of the kingdom of Spain, for the execution of which the author was very well qualified, having been employed many years by his Catholic Majesty in visiting mines and other purposes tending to the improvement of that kingdom, in different branches of mineralogy, and other useful arts. Upon the perusal of this production, it occurred to me, that at a period when *Natural History* is so much cultivated, a more perfect acquaintance with a country, which had hitherto in this respect almost escaped philosophical enquiry, would meet the approbation of an English reader; more especially as we might be induced to expect from such a writer, abundant variety of accurate information, that could not be offered by any common investigator: particularly when the many inconveniencies of bad roads, and other embarrassments, that offer themselves perpetually in those kingdoms are considered. I have therefore availed myself of this work as my chief guide, with respect to the principal objects of natural history, without being a mere copyist in every minute detail; but on the contrary, such original remarks are offered as I flatter myself will not be unacceptable to the candid reader.

We are informed by Mr. Bowles, that having casually (in 1752) met with at Paris, Don Antonio de Ulloa, now an admiral in the Spanish fleet, he was induced by this gentleman to enter into the service of Spain, and that he soon after set out for that kingdom to receive his instructions, and to put them into execution. In this commission he was associated with Don Joseph Solano, who in 1773, was appointed governor of St. Domingo; Don Salvador de Medina, who died at California, whither he went to make observations upon the transit of Venus; and Don Pedro Saura, an advocate of Madrid. The two former gentlemen were naval officers and well known by their literary abilities and travels.

The first object that engaged Mr. Bowles's attention was an inspection into the quicksilver mine of Almaden, in La Mancha, at that time greatly neglected, though a place of the utmost

(a) This was my third voyage to Spain.
(b) Introduccion a la historia natural y a la geografia fisica de Espana, por Don Guillermo Bowles. Madrid, 1775, 4to.

consequence

iv   PREFACE.

consequence to the Spaniards, as they extract from the cinnabar ore of that mine, the major part of the quicksilver that is requisite for the working of their silver mines in America.—Mr. Bowles relates that he set out for Almaden on the 17th of July, 1752, and having with great attention visited the mines, he offered new proposals to the Spanish ministry, in which was contained a more eligible process than that which had been adopted for extracting the quicksilver, which was certified by experiments made on the spot, in the presence of the king's officers, which received the approbation of government, and served to fix him in their service. Several years after this first expedition he continued his progress through most of the provinces of Spain, of which he has given rather a desultory, though curious account, which he laid before the public, and published at Madrid in 1775, dedicated to his catholic majesty Charles the third.

In the letters which I now present to the public, I have included most of the observations and remarks of Mr. Bowles in the course of his various journies, from the year 1752 down to the present time, which were read with great applause by the Spaniards, and bought up with such eagerness, that in 1778 no copies were to be found. A translation was soon after made into French by the viscount de Flavigny, who has every where literally followed the original text, without any additional note or observation (a) : in the progress of a work of so extensive a nature, which comprises such a variety of subjects, we could not reasonably expect that Mr. Bowles, as a foreigner, and more particularly at his advanced age, could set before the public, in the metropolis of Spain, so elaborate a performance, without the assistance of a native perfectly acquainted with his maternal language, till now so little introduced in philosophical researches, though extremely copious and expressive.

Accordingly we find no less a person in the literary world than the ingenious and erudite Don Nicholas de Azara, the present Spanish agent at the court of Rome, the reviser of this work; but notwithstanding this extraordinary assistance, there remain many obscure passages in different parts of the text, which necessarily render an exact translation extremely difficult, as well as tedious and disagreeable. Some passages are merely local, and would therefore afford little or no entertainment to an English reader. We find moreover, that in his introduction he is compelled, from a deficiency of expression applicable to his subject, to enter into tedious details. The ambiguity of the Spanish language perplexes him, and throws a cloud over his meaning. After this he further tells us, that he confines himself to no kind of order or method; one chapter treats of Valencia, the next of Aragon, another of Biscay, Catalonia, or the Escurial, and what is somewhat singular, the thirtieth chapter presents us with his first journey from Bayonne into Spain. Judging it expedient to avoid such confusion, I have endeavoured to arrange his materials in a proper manner; and have accordingly divided this work into two parts. The first comprises the journey to Madrid, by the way of Navarre, then I enter into a description of the northern parts of Spain, which includes many remarkable objects in Castile, Aragon, and Biscay. In the second part, departing from Madrid, I tra-

(a) Introduction a l'histoire, naturelle et a la geographie physique de L'Espagne traduit de l'original Espagnol de Guillermo Bowles, par le Vicomte de Flavigny. Paris, 1775. 8vo.

verse

PREFACE. v

verse the provinces of Estremadura, Andalusia, Grenada, Murcia, Valencia, and Catalonia; and though many of these districts have been the immediate objects of my observation, I ingenuously acknowledge that the chief remarks, with regard to the natural history of those provinces, are from Mr. Bowles's valuable memoirs; where I have differed from him in opinion, my objection is thrown into a note; and where I judged extraneous matter was introduced, it is suppressed; upon the whole, if I can derive the merit of giving these sheets an English dress, or afford any kind of novelty by enlivening the text, I shall be satisfied in having compassed my design; more especially, if the literati should indulge me with the opinion, that I have offered them any thing deserving their attention, which has not appeared before in print, occasioned by the dearth of research in a country so rich nevertheless in materials, that Mr. Bowles justly calls it "A Virgin Land."

There are, I flatter myself, some parts of this book, which cannot, in any respect, be considered as borrowed from Mr. Bowles's work; in those parts the historian and the antiquary may probably meet with such detached pieces, as have hitherto escaped their observation. I must acknowledge that I am likewise indebted to the works of the celebrated Don Antonio Ponz, secretary to the royal academy of San Fernando at Madrid, whose travels through Spain have met with universal applause and recommended him to the royal favour. As the extensive circulation of Ponz's works induced Mr. Bowles not to quote from them, I have been prevailed upon to avail myself of them, judging they would be agreeable to the English reader, and have endeavoured to blend the quotations with the text, in such a manner as I deemed would render them the most acceptable; my design being merely intended as an essay to afford a guide to future assemblies. It is offered to the public in the flattering expectation that it may stimulate more capable travellers to investigate the subjects it treats of with greater judgment and accuracy. A summary account of the mineral waters of Trillo is introduced with a similar view. It is selected from the judicious treatise of Dr. Ortega, F. R. S. and I am indebted to the observations of the late Don Joseph Quer, his Majesty's Surgeon, for what is offered on the virtues of the Perennial leaved Strawberry tree.

If it should be urged that I have taken too great liberties with Mr. Bowles's text, let it be remarked, I have invariably prefixed his name at the head of each letter, any part of the contents of which is borrowed from him, to acknowledge fairly my obligation. I have likewise endeavoured to do justice to his ideas as far as the great variation of idioms would allow; it being as distant as possible from my intentions to depreciate in the smallest degree, the extraordinary merit, which must impartially be ascribed to his uncommon talents. To what I have said I must subjoin that it never was my intent to produce a translation of his book; of which many curious pieces are omitted relative to *Marina*, the Mexican mines, and other miscellaneous matter. On the whole I have aimed at catching the quintessence of his book. I have ventured to communicate it to my countrymen for their instruction, benefit, and entertainment. How far I have succeeded, I leave to the candid, the intelligent reader; but shall venture to say with Wentworth Dillon, Earl of Roscommon,

The

PREFACE.

*The genuine sense intelligibly told,
Shews a translator both discreet and bold.*

It now behoves me to apologise for the many defects and imperfections that will present themselves to the eye of criticism in the course of perusing this work. Should my style appear cold and inanimate when I climb the bleak snowy mountains of Aragon and Biscay, how much more must I dread languor and torpidity in the fruitful plains of Andalusia and Granada; or, amidst the flowery lawns of captivating Valencia. But thus situated at the bar of criticism, I trust myself to the candour of my jury, the impartial public; let me plead in defence of any defects in language, a long absence from my native country, which however afforded me great satisfaction, more particularly at the Court of Vienna, from the extraordinary favours I had the honour to receive there, from two successive emperors.

It yields me a most flattering retrospect to repass in my memory, the various friendly offices I received from many distinguished persons, during my tour through different parts of Spain, and also the assistance of some of my friends in England, in the execution of this design. I hope my learned friend, Dr. Withering, will please to accept my sincerest acknowledgments for his very liberal assistance and obliging revision of this work. I am further particularly indebted for many communications to a Gentleman, whose long residence in Spain, gave him the best opportunities of information, equal to his kind disposition to promote literary researches there, and to whose friendly assistance the first historian of the age has expressed such particular obligations.

The reader need not be surprised that I have not engaged in politics, naval or military operations; they were foreign to my subject, which leads not to speak of fleets or armies, or the efforts of contending princes, no more than of national characters. The researches of nature alone, and the admiration of providence in their discovery, afford an ample field for the philosophic traveller! If I have sometimes expatiated on the qualities or excellence of Spanish productions (a), I hope, nevertheless, it will not be thought, that I mean to lessen or feel less warmth for the innumerable advantages of my own country, wherein, if we have not the rich fruits of the southern climes, we enjoy so many other essential benefits, superadded to the greatest abundance of every necessary, every conveniency of life, as cannot fail, from our insular situation, to render us a most happy people. Thus even supposing for a moment we grant to other nations every advantage of a luxuriant climate, or that the Spaniard lives in ten degrees of more indulgent skies;

*'Tis Liberty that crowns Britania's isle,
And makes her barren rocks, and her bleak mountains smile.*

ADDISON.

Birmingham, April 15, 1780.

(a) Even the great Linnæus, speaking of the natural advantages of the climate of Portugal has said, Bone Deus! Si Lusitani possent sua bona naturæ, quam infelices essent, plerique alii, qui non possident terra s Exoticas. See Linnæus in epistola die. 12 Februarii, 1765.

TABLE of CONTENTS.

PART I.

CH.		PAGE
I.	DIVISION of the kingdom of Spain.	1
II.	Itinerary from Bayonne to Pamplona, and from thence to Madrid. A mine of sal gem at Valtierra described.	6
III.	Natural history of the grana kermes, or scarlet grain.	18
IV.	The method of making salt-petre in Spain.	32
V.	Of the Merino sheep.	46
VI.	Inconveniencies arising from the Merino sheep and the partial laws of the Mesta.	57
VII.	Miscellaneous observations made at Madrid, with some account of the royal cabinet of natural history.	66
VIII.	Description of the palace and gardens of Aranjuez.	81
IX.	The baths and mineral waters of Trillo.	89
X.	The royal seat and gardens of St. Ildefonso.—City of Segovia.	108
XI.	Departure from Madrid for the city of Burgos.	115
XII.	Remarkable objects on the road from Burgos to the provinces of Alaba and Guypuscoa, as far as Irun, the last town on the frontiers of Spain towards France.	127
XIII.	Of the iron ore of Mondragon in Guypuscoa and famous Toledo blades.	134
XIV.	Environs of Reinosa, source of the river Ebro.—Intended canal of Castile.	140
XV.	Natural history of the Spanish plant gayuba, or perennial leaved strawberry-tree.	145
XVI.	Description of the lordship of Biscay and its products.	151
XVII.	Reflections on the genius and character of the Biscayners.	162
XVIII.	Description of the town of Bilbao and manners of the inhabitants.	172
XIX.	Strictures on the injudicious method laid down in the Spanish ordinances for the propagation of timber.	178
XX.	Description of the iron mines and forges at Sommorostro in Biscay.	187
XXI.	Observations on the copper mines of La Platilla in the lordship of Molina.	196
XXII.	The source of the Tagus and its environs described.	205
XXIII.	Mine of cobalt in the Valley of Gistau, in the pyrenees of Aragon.	211
XXIV.	Observations on an alum mine near the town of Alcaniz, in the kingdom of Aragon.	220
XXV.	Remarkable depository of fossil bones, near the village of Concud in Aragon.	224

PART II.

CH.		PAGE
I.	DON Guillermo Bowles inspects the quickfilver mine of Almaden, by order of government.—His new method of extracting the quickfilver from the ore of that mine.	231
II.	Itinerary of Don Guillermo Bowles continued from Almaden to the city of Merida in Estremadura.	249
III.	Natural history of the locusts that ravaged the province of Estremadura, in the years 1754, 1755, 1756, and 1757.	256

CONTENTS.

IV. Of the barren and wretched district of Batuecas in Estremadura.	270
V. The convent of Juste in the Vera of Plasencia, famous for the retreat of the emperor Charles V.	278
VI. Further observations made by Don Guillermo Bowles, in the course of a tour from Almaden to the silver mine of Guadalcanal.	284
VII. Description of the famous silver mine at Guadalcanal in Estremadura.	289
VIII. Remarkable objects in the course of another tour from Guadalcanal to the city of Seville.	301
IX. Extraordinary qualities of the river Tinto and copper mine of that name, in its neighbourhood.	310
X. A tour into the kingdom of Jaen, the lead mine of Linares, unfortunate fate of Macias the poet.	316
XI. Journey from Merida to Malaga.	324
XII. The country described between Malaga and Cape de Gat.	333
XIII. Excursion from the city of Granada to Cordova and Anduxar in Andalusia.	341
XIV. Observations made in a progress from Cadiz to Carthagena.	348
XV. The face of the country described between Carthagena and Alicant.	358
XVI. Road from Alicant to the city of Valencia.	367
XVII. Observations made in the city of Valencia and its environs.	374
XVIII. Journey from Barcelona to the mountain of Montserrat.	381
XIX. Singular mountain of fossil salt near Cardona in Catalonia.	390
XX. Observations on the roundness of pebbles in the beds of rivers.	395
XXI. Describing the hot wells at Caldas in Catalonia, and those of Caldetas, near the city of Mataro.	405
XXII. Remains of antient volcanos in Spain.	409
XXIII. Return to Valencia and Castile.—Mine of salt gem at Minglanilla.—Source of the river Guadiana.—Mine of antimony near Santa Cruz de Mudela in La Mancha.	414

LIST of PLATES given in this WORK.

FRONTISPIECE, Charles the IIId. king of Spain, in the robes of the new order of Carlos Tercero, instituted the 19th of September, 1771.
Figure of Minerva with dedication, before the preface.
Map of Spain to face letter the first.

Plate I. The arbutus uva ursi, to face	Page 21
II. The great ant bear	76
III. The crested falcon	80
IV. Arch of Fernan Gonzales, in Burgos	121
V. The cathedral of Burgos	125
VI. Tower and giralda of Seville	308

The tail-piece, a landscape, exhibiting a view of the Spanish gennet and lizard, with different trees and plants, such as the palm, scarlet oak, Indian fig, aloe, vine, &c.

VII

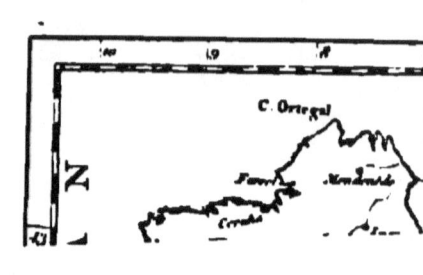

TRAVELS through SPAIN;

WITH A VIEW TO ILLUSTRATE THE
NATURAL HISTORY AND PHYSICAL GEOGRAPHY
OF THAT KINGDOM.

PART I.

LETTER I.

Division of the kingdom of SPAIN.

THE dominions of Spain are generally classed by their writers in the following order. The kingdom of Spain, consisting of Old and New Castile; the kingdoms of Leon, Aragon, Navarre, Granada, Valencia, Galicia, Seville, Cordova, Murcia, Jaen, and Majorca; the principalities of Asturias, and Catalonia, the provinces of Estremadura, Guipuscoa, and Alava, and the lordships of Biscay, and Molina: they are bounded by the Cantabrian ocean, or bay of Biscay, on the north, by the Pyrenean mountains and the Mediterranean towards the east; by the streights of Gibraltar and the Mediterranean, which divide it from Africa, on the south, and by the great Atlantic ocean on the west: lying between 36 and 43 degrees of north latitude, and between 8. 22. longitude, reckoning from the island of Ferro, the most western of the Canary islands (a). The Pyrenean mountains are the highest in Spain, extending from the ocean to the Mediterranean, several others branching out, as from their root, such as mount Idubeda now called Montes de Oca, the Orbion, Moncayo, the Puerto de Pajares, or pass from Castile to Asturias, the Puerto de Guadarrama, which separates the two Castiles, that of Molina, of Cuenca, of Consuegra, of Alcaraz, of Segura, of Cazorla, and the Montes Marianos now called the Sierra Morena (b): the Puerto del Rey (c),

(a) Descripcion de la provincia de Madrid, por Thomas Lopez. Madrid, 1763, 12mo.

(b) *Sierra* is a general name in Spain for all wild districts whose rugged appearance seems to resemble the notches of a saw (which is *Sierra* in Spanish.) Of these places the Sierra Morena in Andalusia is one of the most extensive and bleak. Translated literally it answers to our English word, Black-Heath.—The inhabitant of such a country is called *Serrano*, and if the district is small, it is called *Serrania*.

(c) The word *Puerto* is applied to passes from one province to another where duties are paid. I could not help smiling to read in a modern geographer, that *Orduña*, (because there is a *Puerto* there) has a good harbour, when it is an inland city seven leagues from Bilboa. J. Barrow's geog. dict. 2 vol. ful. 2d edition revised and corrected, 1763.

At many of these *Puertos* there are ludicrous duties established, as for example, at the *Puerto del Rey* in Sierra Morena a singular toll is paid for monkies, parrots, negroes, and guittars unless played upon at the time : married women unless in company with their husbands or producing certificates ;—viz. for any monkey, parrot or singular bird, one *real vellon*; a guittarre, one *peseta*; any drum, unless the king's, one *peseta*; a woman as above described, one *real vellon*; a travelling mule, one *quarto*.

which

which commands the communication between Castile and Andalusia, and the Puerto del Muradal, where lies that famous pass called las Navas de Tolosa, celebrated for the victory obtained there in 1212 over the king of Morocco, and other passes of less note.

Amongst the rivers, the Ebro has its source near Fontibre, six leagues from Aguilar del Campo, passes by Logrono, Viana, Calahorra, Tudela, Zaragossa, Mequinenza, and Tortosa, and a little lower falls into the Mediterranean at the Alfaque islands.

The Guadalquivir has its source in the Sierra de Segura, passes by Beas, Baeza, Andujar, Cordova, Loxa and Seville, and enters the ocean at San Lucar de Barrameda, receiving in its course the waters of the rivers Guadalbullon and Genil.

The Tagus rises in the Sierras near Albarracin, passes by Zurita, Aranjuez, Toledo, Almaraz, Alcantara, Abrantes, Santarem, and Lisbon, where it is three miles broad and enters the ocean, having the tide as high as Santarem, and receiving in its course the waters of the Jarama, Manzanares, Guadarama, Alberche, and others.

The Guadiana rises about four leagues from Montiel in the Laguna Ruydera, and after running under ground appears again near Damiel at the lakes or lagunes called *Ojos de Guadiana* " the Eyes of Guadiana," then passes by Calatrava, Ciudad Real, Medellin, Merida, Badajoz, and Ayamonte, where it falls into the ocean, after running for some time in Alentejo, in Portugal, and separating that kingdom from Spain, having Castro Marin of Portugal on the west, and Ayamonte on the east.

The Duero rises in the Sierra of Orbion and passes by Soria, Almazan, Osma, San Estevan de Gormaz, Aranda de Duero, Roa, Simancas, Tordesillas, Toro, Zamora, Miranda de Duero, Lamego, and enters the ocean at Oporto, receiving the rivers Eresma, Adaja, Pisuerga, Ezla, Agueda, and others.

The Minho has its source in Galicia near Castro del Rey. It runs South West and passes by Lugo, Orrense and Tuy, after which it divides Galicia from Portugal, and falls into the Atlantic at Caminha.

Other smaller rivers are also worthy of notice such as the Segura, Guadalaviar, Lobregat, Caya, Vidaso, Tinto, Guadalate, &c.

Spain may be said to enjoy a temperate and healthy air, neither so cold as the northern regions, nor so burning

ing as the scorching heats of Africa, and abounds in cattle, game, fowl, corn, wool, silk, wax, honey, excellent wine, brandy, oil, and sugar, all kinds of fruit and pulse, aromatic herbs and plants, the finest of oaks, quarries of marble, alabaster, jasper, and other precious stones; mines of silver, lead, copper, iron, mercury, antimony, and cobalt: in short every natural advantage tending to the pleasure and happiness of mankind.

The territories of Spain are said to contain 25,000 square leagues (a). According to returns made to the Count de Aranda in 1768, the general population of the whole, including the Canaries and Mediterranean islands, amounted to about nine millions of souls. In the year 1778 it was further calculated to be between ten and eleven millions, and supposed to be increasing.

(a) The Spanish league is 7680 varas. 17 Spanish leagues make one degree, equal to 20 French leagues.
Three Castilian feet make one vara of Castile, whose length is about 33 inches English.

LETTER

LETTER II.

Itinerary from Bayonne to Pamplona, and from thence to Madrid. A mine of sal gem at Valtierra described.

QUITTING Bayonne I proceeded on my journey towards Spain (*a*), and travelling through an uneven country, I began to perceive a species of slaty stone which announced the vicinity of the Pyrenees about half a league distant. The environs of Anoa are mountainous. The farmers manure the ground with lime to sow maiz or Indian corn, laying on a greater quantity for wheat, without which it yields nothing, which proves the necessity of this method to cherish and expand the tough and cold soil in mountainous countries.

Half a league from Anoa a rivulet forms the boundary between France and Spain. The country is covered with fern, which they cut and heap in piles, till it rots and serves for manure. In the arable land, and where cattle have grazed, there are two kinds of mint, ground ivy, and other usual plants. You next pass a Carthusian

---

(*a*) The itinerary of Mr. Bowles is supported in this letter, with respect to natural history, and further illustrated with the historical part not mentioned by that writer.

convent

convent at the foot of a high mountain chiefly of quartz (a), whose summit is a rock of purplish sand, and from thence descend to the first village in Spain called Maya, seated in a valley where they have good crops of maiz and turneps, and whose soil though not calcareous produces equally the same kind of plants. Such as the elder, henbane, nightshade, swallow wort, figwort, thorn-apple, hawthorn and bullace tree. After passing the village of Elizondo and traversing the vale, I ascended a mountain of blueish lime rock with fine beech towards the top, its sides lined with many other trees, such as elder, hawthorn, and holm. This mountain is one of the highest in this country; but in speaking of the plants found here, I only mean such as are seen in that part still uncultivated, for where the ground has been opened, and near the inn called Venta de Belate, not far from the top of the mountain, being accessible to animals, the following plants are to be seen, celandine, mint, cuckow-flower, crowfoot, plantain, sowthistle, figwort, archangel, dock, arsmart, and two sorts of maidenhair on the walls, from whence I judge that if a house was built on the highest and most barren mountain, and the ground manured with the dung of animals, we should soon perceive the same plants that are observed in the neigh-

(a) Quartz is a hard vitrifiable stone, something intermediate betwixt rock crystals and flints or opake vitrifiable stones, well known to metallurgists, mineralogists, and miners. According to Cronsted, it is easier to be known than described.

bourhood

bourhood of villages and in plains, and that it is not a good rule to judge of the height of a mountain by the appearance of plants, if no diſtinction is made between the ſpontaneous ones and the others, elſe we might conclude that the little hill of Meudon near Paris is as high as the Pyrenees.

From the Venta de Belate it is an eaſy deſcent into another vale well cultivated with vines and corn, which extends as far as the city of Pamplona, capital of the kingdom of Navarre. In this vale there is a wood of ſtately oaks, with plenty of box, thorntree, wild roſes and other common plants of cultivated countries. You keep conſtantly on the borders of a rivulet running amongſt round ſand-ſtone of a purple colour, ſimilar to thoſe on the other ſide towards France. I ſaw the following plants in the plains of Pamplona, on the ſide of the roads, in the fields and the vineyards; two ſorts of eringo, one called the hundred headed ſort, and the other with large leaves, poppy, dockweed, white horehound, vipergraſs, elder, white gooſegraſs, devilſbit, cinquefoil, croſswort, henbane, tutſan, agrimony, teaſel, hawthorn, reſt harrow, crowfoot and bullace.

In this plain it is clearly ſeen how the limy rock decays, for in an almoſt perpendicular fiſſure above an hundred feet high, the earth which at firſt ſight and even

to

TRAVELS THROUGH SPAIN.

to the touch appears to be clay, is nothing more than limy earth, mixed with a small portion of clay, the result of rotten plants as I experienced with the acid I always carry with me whenever I travel. The same sort of earth of a blueish colour is found near Pamplona, but harder, and so very hard in a hill opposite to the city, as to deserve the name of stone, disposed in strata with the same obliquity as the fissure abovementioned, all which proves the decomposition of the rocks.

Leaving Pamplona I traversed a champaign country for two leagues and a half to the mountain opposite, which having passed, a variety of cultivation takes place. Some limy rocks are so barren, that nothing is to be seen but butchers broom, a few oaks, juniper, and lavender, for two leagues and a half further, when I arrived at the city of Tafalla; then passing an extensive plain full of aromatic plants, had five leagues to Caparroso. This plain may be thrown into four divisions, the first from Tafalla being olive trees, the second vineyards, the third corn-fields, and the fourth barren, except a few olive trees and some corn-fields near Caparroso, where a hill divides the plain, and now and then, the rounded purple stone shews itself again the same as in France.

From Caparroso I crossed a high hill where any miner might mistake the strata of gypseous stone which is only one or two inches thick, for spar, but you may dig as deep as you please, and never find any thing but gypsum, which is very seldom seen where there is mineral. The country, is every where barren and miserable, a perfect desert without water, and nothing but rosemary, lavender, and a few starved oaks. After quitting this wretched district a fertile plain opens to the eye, supplied by wheels with water from the Ebro, and here I saw the tamarisk, which is a beautiful plant when in flower.

From Caparroso it is four leagues to the Ebro in a plain bordered by a chain of hills from east to west, composed of limy earth mixed with gypseous stone, sometimes in strata, granulated, or in masses, white as snow. This chain extends about two leagues, and towards the middle, where it is the highest, stands the village of Valtierra: about half way up, there is a mine of fossil common salt, which being transparent and resembling chrystal, goes by the name of Salgem, and is seen above ground where the shaft is made at the entrance of the mine. About twenty paces within, one observes that the salt, which is white and abundant, has penetrated into the very beds of gypseous stone. This mine may be about four hundred paces in length, with several lateral shafts, upwards of eighty paces, supported by pillars of salt, and gypsum, which the miners have very judiciously left at proper distances, so that it has all the appearance of a gothic cathedral. The salt follows the direction

direction of the hill, inclining a little to the north, like the strata of gypsum, being comprised in a space about five feet in height without variation, and seems to have corroded several beds of gypsum, and marl, and insinuated itself into their place, though much of those substances still remain.

At the end of the principal shaft, the miners have carried out a branch to the right, where the saline bed appears to have followed exactly the inclination of the hill, which in that part is very perpendicular: this stratum of salt descends to the valley, and goes on to the opposite hill; which regularity destroys the system of those who pretend that sal gem is formed by the evaporation occasioned by subterraneous fire. If this was the case, the beds would not be undulated in this manner, resembling those of coal at Chamond, near Lyons, in France, or those of asphaltos (*a*), in Alsace, that follow the elevation and declivity of the hills or vallies, the bi-

---

(*a*) *Asphaltos* or *Jewish bitumen* is so called from the lake Asphaltites or dead sea in Judea, which rises up in the nature of a liquid pitch, and floats upon the surface of the water like other oleaginous bodies, and is condensed by degrees through the heat of the sun; the Jews formerly used it to embalm their dead. The Arabs gather it for pitching their ships, but Europeans use it in medicinal compositions, especially in theriaca, or Venice treacle, as also a fine black varnish, in imitation of that of China. Rolt's dict. of commerce. London, 1761.

The origin of bitumens is an interesting question, concerning which naturalists are not agreed, some imagining that they essentially belong to the mineral kingdom, and others that they proceed originally from vegetable substances; we must allow this latter opinion to be the most probable, &c. See dict. of chemistry, translated from the French. London, printed for T. Cadell, 1777.

B 2   tumen

tumen often floating on the water when it meets with it.
I am of opinion that salt grows in the mine like minerals, that coal is the product of fossil wood, as appears from such remnants as are found in the mines (*a*), and that the asphaltos is produced by the water of some spring. I examined attentively these strata of salt, comparing them with the matter in which they are embedded. I observed the roof to be of gypsum with aromatic plants, then two inches of white salt, separated from the gypsum by a few threads of saline earth, then, three fingers breadth of pure salt, with two of stone salt, and a coat of earth, next another blueish bed, followed by two inches of salt; and lastly, other beds alternately of earth, and chrystaline salt to the bed of the mine, which is gypseous stone undulated like the rest, descending to the valley, and rising on the opposite hills. The strata of saline earth are of a dark blue, but those of salt, are white. This mine is of a great elevation with respect to the sea, for you always go up hill to it from Bayonne, excepting those casual descents which are inseparable from mountainous countries.

(*a*) It has been asserted that coals being sometimes produced from clay saturated by petroleum, may be found in any place or situation where clay or argillaceous flate is to be met with, in ancient simple or modern stratified mountains, as well as on, and in volcanic mountains, and that henceforth coals will not be considered as constantly produced from trees, plants, and forests, buried by inundations, though many coal mines may have had such an origin. See Ferber's mineralogical history of Bohemia, page 508, note 3, prefixed to Baron Born's travels through Transilvania and Hungary, translated by R. E. Raspe, London, 1777.

It

It is a continual afcent from Valtierra to Agreda, the firſt town in Caſtile, on the top of one of the higheſt mountains in Spain called Moncayo, whoſe rocks ſo decompoſe into earth, as to be covered with plants, deſerving the attention of a botaniſt, from the great variety thence afforded in the vegetable kingdom. From Agreda the country is well cultivated to Hinojoſo, without any trees or plants, as far as Almeriz, and forwards to Almazan, on the banks of the Duero: examining this diſtrict, which produces wheat and barley, I diſcovered lime rock at a few feet from the ſurface, which for a great extent has an outward coat of ſandy ſoil, with quartz and ſand ſtone totally different from the bottom, which gives it the appearance of a foreign matter brought from a diſtance. The phænomenon is ſingular, and thoſe who are fond of hypotheſes have here an ample field to employ their imagination.

Leaving Almazan you riſe upon an eminence which affords an extenſive proſpect, the country at a diſtance having the appearance of a plain, the eye not being able to catch the many irregularities of ground. After ſome leagues of uncultivated land, the country improves; three leagues and a half further, I came to Paredes, and croſſing a barren plain arrived at Baraona, then paſſing over the ſteep hill of Atienza, the confines of the two Caſtiles,

Caſtiles, I came in five hours to Xadraque, and four leagues further, to Flores; about half way, there is a place where there are hills with great clefts. One evidently ſees they were cauſed by the rains which carry away the limy earth, and that all that country had been a plain, for the parts that remain without gullies, have a bottom of hard rock, and in proportion as the water makes its way through, they form gullies; I ſaw ſome juſt beginning, with a likelihood of riſing into hills in the courſe of twenty years; from whence I conjecture, that if ſome hills give way, and crumble into plains, others, in the courſe of time by the motion of waters, gradually form themſelves into mountains.

In paſſing this road, you go through a wood of ſcarlet oak, whoſe leaves are covered with the gall inſect, and on coming out of the wood, find a well cultivated country with vineyards, corn fields, and plenty of thyme, lavender, ſantal, and ſage; then paſs by the village of Hita at the foot of a pyramidical hill, rearing its lofty creſt above the others, like a great rock in the ſea, with an old Mooriſh caſtle on its ſummit.

Having croſſed the river Henares you enter a fertile plain with a great deal of ſmall grained ſandy pebble. It is remarkable that on entering New Caſtile, ſtone of this kind is always found, even in hills of limy earth:
after

after passing a range of cultivated hills I arrived at the famous city of Alcala de Henares, with an university founded in 1499, by that great statesman Cardinal Ximenez de Cisneros, who also endowed it with a good library, and printed here, at his own expence, the first polyglot bible, known by the name of Complutensian. The university is a handsome structure, Ximenes is buried in the church with an elegant monument, by Dominico of Florence. The medaillon of the Cardinal has been removed from the tomb into the library. Before I leave Alcala, let me entertain you with a story related by the witty Don Antonio Ponz, secretary of the royal academy of San Fernando, at Madrid, in his tour through Spain, who, visiting the convent of San Diego, belonging to the Franciscans, thus expresses himself; "I could not swallow two pills that my conductor endeavoured to ram down my throat, which, for his part, he seemed to have very easily digested. He shewed me a picture of St. Jerome in a cardinal's robe, and a red hat, which is quite out of character, and wanted to persuade me it was a portrait of Cardinal Wolsey; after that would make me believe it was valued at fifteen thousand dollars (£. 2500) though I was startled at the sum, I did not choose to displease the person who was doing me a favour. I must not forget to tell you I also saw, in a chapel, on the altar of St. Francis, the head of that saint in clay, painted to imitate nature. I do not know what

what you will think of the manner in which I was assured it was made; a potter had placed his vessels in the oven to be baked, and behold one of them came out changed into this head! you may believe it if you please; many believe it at Alcala! for my part, as I know no other circumstances of this miracle, and have no other authority than that of my guide, with his tale about the fifteen thousand dollars, I am rather suspicious (a)."

Alcala is only six leagues from Madrid, and belongs to the Archbishop of Toledo; it gave birth to Miguel Cervantes de Saavedra, the celebrated author of the much admired romance of Don Quixote (b). The country

---

(a) Viage de España par Don Antonio Ponz, tom 1, Madrid, 1776.

(b) Miguel Cervantes de Saavedra was born at Alcala de Henares the 9th of October 1547, and died at Madrid the 23d of April, 1616. The same nominal day as his illustrious contemporary Shakespear.

There is such a variety of matter and so many beautiful passages and allusions in Don Quixote, that it is impossible to travel through Spain, without their frequently occurring to the mind. Don Guillermo Bowles has occasionally quoted him, and I hope I may be allowed the same liberty. This book is one of those capital pieces only understood by those who can read him in the original. We may now soon expect a new and classical edition of Don Quixote printed in England in the original Spanish, illustrated by annotations and extracts from the historians, poets and romances of Spain and Italy, and other writers ancient and modern, with a glossary and indexes, by the Reverend John Bowle, M. A. F. S. A. See letter to the Rev. Dr. Percy concerning a new edition of Don Quixote, by the Rev. John Bowle, M. A. F. S. A. London printed for B. White, 1777.

Besides the advantage of having a more perfect and accurate text than has ever yet appeared, this is a work of such magnitude as will reflect infinite honour on the erudition and taste of the ingenious editor; how singular a pleasure to the admirers of Cervantes in general! how great the surprise to the Spaniards! when they behold one of their favorite characters so nobly emblazoned by an Englishman.

around

around is bleak, owing to the fingular averfion which the Caftilians have in general to the planting of trees. Nothing further occurs between this place and Madrid, the environs of which will be defcribed on another occafion.

LETTER III.

Natural history of the Grana Kermes, or scarlet grain.

AMONGST the various and valuable productions with which the beneficent hand of nature has enriched the dominions of Spain, the *Grana Kermes* is chiefly deserving of attention. This valuable production had been considerably neglected in that kingdom since the importation of cochineal from America; however, the royal Junta de Comercio, or board of trade at Madrid, having an eye to the further advantages to be drawn from this precious article, gave orders a few years ago to Don Juan Pablo Canals, director general of the madder and dyes of Spain, to report the state of this product; and to him I am indebted for the present information on this subject(a).

The grana kermes is the *coccos baphica* of the Greeks; the vermiculus, or coccum infectorium of the Romans; and the kermes, alkermes, of the Arabs; being the ingredient with which the antients used to dye their gar-

---

(a) Memorias que de orden de la real junta general de comercio y Moneda se dan al publico sobre la Grana Kermes de España. Por Don Juan Pablo Canals y Marti. Madrid, 1768.

ments

ments of that beautiful grain colour, called coccinus, coccineus, or cocceus, different from the purpura of the Phœnicians, which at firſt had been obtained from that teſtaceous fiſh, called the murex (*a*). But in courſe of time the purple colour and other tints having been more eaſily effected by means of the kermes, the murex was neglected on account of the expence, and the kermes we are now ſpeaking of, was introduced; which giving a ſtronger and brighter colour, was univerſally adopted, and ſupported its reputation for ages, till the diſcovery of America; as is evident from the many old tapeſtries, damaſks, and velvet hangings, ſtill preſerved in cathedrals, which ſeem yet to retain their primitive luſtre and brightneſs (*b*).

In the reign of Lewis the fourteenth, Giles and John Gobelin, in the year 1667, under the patronage of Col-

---

(*a*) Tyrioque ardebat murice lana. Virg. En. lib. 4.

Though the dye obtained from the murex was thought to have been loſt, it ſeems to be known on the coaſts of England, France, Spain, and the Weſt Indies, though neglected on account of the great trouble and expence. See Padre Feijoo Theat. critico, tom 6, diſc. 4. According to Gage, they find a ſhell fiſh in the ſeas of the Spaniſh Weſt Indies, which perfectly reſembles the antient purpura, and in all probability is the ſame. Cloth of Segovia dyed with it, uſed to ſell for 20 crowns the ell, and none but the greateſt Spaniſh lords wore it. Don Antonio de Ulloa alſo gives a particular account of this fiſh, and the uſe made of it in America. See gentleman's magazine, for October and November, 1753.

(*b*) This was the colour called *carmeſi*, by the Spaniards; *cramoiſi*, by the French; and *crimſon*, by the Engliſh.

bert, introduced the secret into France of dying woollen of that beautiful scarlet called after their name, which was done with the kermes that had been long in use in Flanders, where many old pieces of tapestry, though above two hundred years old, had scarcely lost any thing of their bloom. But cochineal, being now introduced into the dyehouse, so called from the latin word coccinella, as a diminutive of coccum, and giving that brightness to scarlet, at first called Dutch, and afterwards Paris scarlet, the invention of which, according to Kunkel, is owing to Kuster, a German, by means of a solution of tin in aqua regia; the kermes then began to decline, and yield in its turn as the murex had done before, of which Colbert makes a particular complaint, in his general instructions to the dyers of France, in the year 1671 (*a*). Insensibly, the kermes was totally laid

---

(*a*) As the Phœnicians neglected the antient purple, and gave a preference to the scarlet, whose colour is less costly and more beautiful; just so, the French have forsaken our scarlet for that of the Dutch. This new-invented colour was at first in esteem on account of its brightness; but being less durable than that of France, and under a notion that they were both equally liable to spots, they were soon laid aside, which occasioned the downfal of our most valuable cloth manufactures, where this colour was so much in use, particularly amongst our nobility, that few were without a scarlet cloak of cloth, much preferable to those of Barracan now in fashion, which are of foreign manufacture, less becoming, and also dearer, if we consider the short time they last. Chap. 304. " Again in the next chapter :" Therefore, to reinstate our cloth manufactory and vermilion dye, (the kermes) it should be introduced amongst the nobility and army as the noblest of colours, most suitable to their rank; besides cloth being more serviceable, either of this, or any other colour, than those flimsy Barracans, we import from abroad. General instructions of Colbert, 1671.

aside,

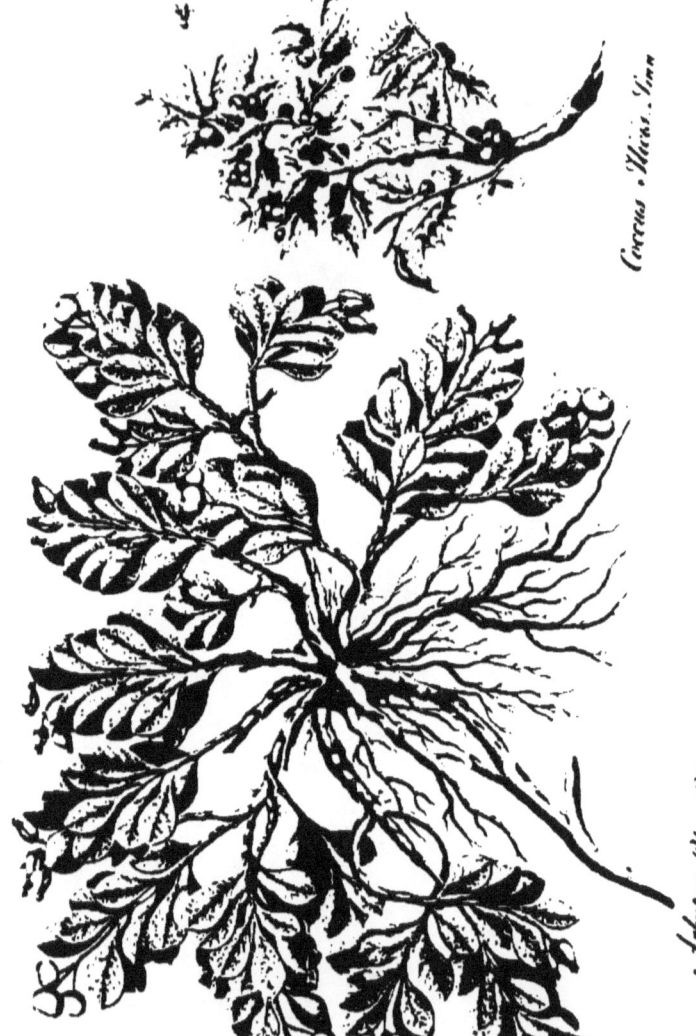

aside, and cochineal made use of, not only in yarns, but also in silk; this new method being every where in fashion, except at Venice, and in Persia, for scarlet, and in other parts of the east for crimson.

The ancients thought the kermes was a gall-nut on account of its figure and size, not being larger than a juniper berry, round, smooth, glossy, and rather black, with a cinereous down. It is found sticking to the branches, or tender leaves of the oak called in Spain *coscoxa*, a derivative of the latin word cusculium, the coccus ilicis of Linneus, likewise called *carrasca* in Spanish, from the Arabic word *yxquerlat*, softened afterwards to *escarlata*; being the smallest species of oak, the same which Caspar Bauhine and other botanists call ilex aculeata cocci-glandifera (*a*).

This tree, whose height is about two or three feet, grows in Spain, Provence, Languedoc, and along the

(*a*) According to Pliny, the term cusculium is derived from a Greek word, signifying to cut the excrescencies, as it happens on this occasion with respect to the kermes.

Clusius says, Hispanis major frutex qui grandem fert *carrasca* dicitur, qui vero coccum gignit *coscoxa*. Caroli Clusii rariorum aliquot stirpium per Hispanias observatarum historia, Antuerpiæ, 1576.

It is still called scarlet grain by the dyers, under the notion of being a grain of seed, though the very name in Arabic, signifies little worms.

Roderic, archbishop of Toledo, who finished his history of Spain in 1243, seems to have coined the latin word *scarlatum*, to express this colour. Tunc comes Petrus Assurii indutus scarlato et insidens equo albo, &c. Rod. Toletani de rebus Hispanicis, lib. vii. cap. 1.

Mediterranean

Mediterranean coaſt; alſo in Galatia, Armenia, Syria, and Perſia, where it was firſt made uſe of. Dioſcorides ſays it grows plentifully in Armenia, and without particularizing other places, mentions what grows there to be better than that of Spain, which proves its high eſtimation in thoſe days; moreover confirmed by Pliny, who, ſpeaking of that which grew near Merida, adds, " Coccum Galaciæ rubens granum aut Circa Emeritam Luſitaniæ in maxima Laude eſt." Lib. 9. cap. 41. For which reaſon the Romans obliged the Spaniards, according to the ſame writer, to pay their tribute in this article (a).

Joſeph Moya, a Catalan writer of the laſt century, publiſhed a treatiſe entitled *Ramillet de Tinturas*, dedicated to the city of Barcelona, under the feigned name of Pheſio Mayo. He ſays, the Kermes is common all over Spain, principally in that part of Aragon bordering on Catalonia, in Valencia, and in the biſhopric of Badajoz in Eſtremadura, as likewiſe in Setimbre of Portugal, where it is the beſt, and equal to the kermes of Galatia and Armenia. Mr. Hellot of the French academy of ſciences, in his Art of Dying, chap. 12. ſays it is found in the woods of Vauvert, Vendeman, and Narbonne; but more abundantly in Spain, towards

(a) Book 16. chap. 8.

Alicant,

TRAVELS THROUGH SPAIN.

Alicant, and Valencia. It not only abounds in Valencia, but alfo in Murcia, Jaen, Cordova, Seville, Eſtremadura, la Mancha, Serranias de Cuenca, and other places.

In Xixona and Tierra de Relleu, there is a diſtrict, called De la Grana, where the people of Valencia firſt began to gather it, whoſe example was followed all over Spain. It has, ſome years, produced thirty thouſand dollars (£5000 -) to the inhabitants of Xixona. In the Year 1758, there went out of that town, Relleu, Buſſot, Caſtilla, Ibi, Tibi, Unil, Santa faz, Muchiamel, and San Juan de la Huerta de Alicante, above a thouſand perſons to gather the kermes, which was afterwards ſent to Alicant, where it was put into caſks for exportation, being chiefly ſhipped for Genoa and Leghorn, paſſing from thence to Tunis. In the ſame year, 1758, they gathered about 300 arrobes of kermes at Xixona, which ſold for about twenty-four dollars (£4 -) the arrobe (a), with about ſix per cent. duty and ſhipping charges, till on board. In the kingdom of Seville it is put up to public ſale and is generally bought by the people of the neighbourhood, who ſell it again for exportation to the merchants of Cadiz.

(a) An arobe is 25 ℔. Spaniſh weight; 100 ℔. Spaniſh weight equal to 97 ℔. Engliſh.

Both

Both antients and moderns seem to have had very confused notions concerning the origin and nature of the kermes; some considering it as a fruit, without a just knowledge of the tree which produced it; others, taking it for an excrescence formed by the puncture of a particular fly, the same as the common gall observed upon oaks. Tournefort was of this number. Count Marsigli, and Dr. Nisole, a physician of Montpelier, made experiments and observations, with a view of further discoveries, but did not perfectly succeed. Two other physicians at Aix, in Provence, Dr. Emeric and Dr. Garidel, applied themselves about the same time, and with greater success; having finally discovered that the kermes is in reality nothing else but the body of an insect transformed into a grain, berry or husk, according to the course of nature; whose history I shall now briefly relate:

The progress of this transformation must be considered at three different seasons. In the first stage, at the beginning of March, an animalcule, no larger than a grain of millet, scarce able to crawl, is perceived sticking to the branches of the tree, where it fixes itself, and soon becomes immoveable; at this period it grows the most, appears to swell and thrive with the sustenance it draws in by degrees: This state of rest seems to have deceived

deceived the curious obferver, it then refembling an excrefcence of the bark; during this period of its growth, it appears to be covered with a down, extending over its whole frame, like a net, and adhering to the bark: its figure is convex, not unlike a fmall floe; in fuch parts as are not quite hidden by this foft garment, many bright fpecks are perceived of a gold colour, as well as ftripes running acrofs the body from one fpace to another.

At the fecond ftage in April, its growth is compleated, its fhape is then round, and about the fize of a pea: it has then acquired more ftrength, and its down is changed into duft, and feems to be nothing but a hufk, or a capfule, full of a reddifh juice not unlike difcoloured blood.

Its third ftate is towards the end of May, a little fooner or later, according to the warmth of the climate. The hufk appears replete with fmall eggs, lefs than the feed of a poppy. Thefe are properly ranged under the belly of the infect, progreffively placed in the neft of down, that covers its body, which it withdraws in proportion to the number of eggs: after this work is performed, it foon dies, though it ftill adheres to its pofition, rendering a further fervice to its progeny, and fhielding them from the inclemency of the weather or the hoftile attacks of an enemy. In a good feafon they multiply exceedingly, having from 1800 to 2000 eggs, which produce

duce the same number of animalcules. The ancients knew them to be insects, for Pliny says, " Coccum ilicis celerrime in vermiculum se mutans." Lib. 24. sect. 4. When observed with the microscope in July or August, we find that what appeared as dust, are so many eggs, or open capsules, as white as snow, out of each of which, issues a gold coloured animalcule, of the shape of a cockroche, with two horns, six feet, and a forked tail.

Mr. De Reaumur has placed the kermes in the class of gall insects, on account of the analogy in their mode of propagation, and immoveable form, continuing even after death, like the other species of this class, found upon different trees, appearing only like galls, or excrescences, to the most accurate naturalists: Therefore they could not be more properly named, than gall insects. There are of them of different shapes and sizes, but that of the *coscoxa* or *carrasca* (the kermes) is of a spherical figure, about the size of a juniper berry. It is found most plentifully on the oldest and lowest trees, and when the kermes are gathered near the sea, they are larger and give a brighter colour than those in any other places.

There are several species of galls discovered on different trees, and plants of Spain, though they only make use of those gathered on oaks, either for dying, or any other purposes; such are those, from the Levant called

called Aleppo galls, which were generally made ufe of, till it was difcovered by frequent experiments, that the new ingredient called dividivi was preferable, being a fruit from the province of Carracas, and Maracaybo, in South America.

The great myftery which hitherto had not been difcovered, by thofe naturalifts who knew how to diftinguifh the gall infect, from the galls, was to inveftigate their mode of propagation: Mr. de Reaumur affures us, that from frequent obfervations it appeared to him, that there are both male and female, but that fome which are extremely fmall, transform themfelves into gnats, while others, growing larger, depofit their eggs, without any transformation; from which, and their analogy with the others, he concluded, that the fmall gnats with wings, though large in comparifon with their body, and ftriped with a beautiful crimfon, were the males of the gall infect, which he obferved with the help of a microfcope, feeing how they fecundate the females, before they affume a globular form towards March; but this happens when it is fcarcely ever noticed, and in fo fingular a manner, that a common obferver would never imagine fuch an event to have happened, or, even fuppofe, that the males which he faw frifking about, had the leaft connection with the females; but on the contrary, were fmall gnats which accidentally light upon the fame boughs;

boughs; if to this observation we add, that as the new kermes which come forth in June, remain small without engaging our attention till March ensuing, when they begin to swell without any appearance of animal life, it will not be thought so extraordinary, that they have been generally held as a vegetable production. In Languedoc, and Provence, the poor are employed to gather the kermes, the women letting their nails grow for that purpose, in order to pick them off with greater facility.

The custom of lopping off the boughs is very injudicious, as by this means they destroy the next year's harvest. Some women will gather two or three pounds a day, the great point being to know the places where they are most likely to be found in any quantity, and to gather them early with the morning dew, as the leaves are more pliable and tender at that time, than after they have been dried and parched by the rays of the sun: strong dews will occasionally make them fall from the trees sooner than usual: when the proper season passes, they fall off of themselves, and become food for birds, particularly doves. Sometimes there will be a second production, which is commonly of a less size with a fainter tinge. The first is generally found adhering to the bark, as well as on the branches and stalks; the second is principally on the leaves, as the worms choose

that

that part where the nutritious juice preferves itfelf the longeft, is moft abundant, and can be moft eafily devoured in the fhort time that remains of their exiftence, the bark being then drier and harder than the leaves.

Thofe who buy the kermes to fend to foreign parts, fpread it on linnen, taking care to fprinkle it with vinegar, to kill the worms that are within, which produces a red duft which in Spain is feperated from the hufk. Then they let it dry, paffing it through a fearce, and make it up into bags. In the middle of each its proportion of red duft put in a little leather bag alfo belongs to the buyer, and then it is ready for exportation, being always in demand on the African coaft.

The people of Hinojos, Bonares, Villalba, and other parts of the kingdom of Seville, dry it on mats in the fun, ftirring it about, and feparating the red duft, which is the fineft part, and being mixed with vinegar, goes by the name of *Paftel*. The fame is done with the hufks; but thefe have but half the value of the duft.

There is no doubt, but if this branch of induftry was more clofely attended to, there is yet room for improvement, and the kermes would give a brighter colour, fimilar to that obtained from the cochineal, likewife an infect found in the Mexican woods on a plant called nopal

by

by the Americans, and *tuna* by the Spaniards; being the opuntia maxima folio obtufo rotundo of Sir Hans Sloane, and the cactus opuntia of Linneus.

It is remarked that thofe plants which are cultivated by art, give a much finer cochineal, known by the name of meftica, fo called from the quantities collected of it in the diftrict of Meteca, in the province of Honduras (*a*).

But neither the cochineal, the kermes, or any fimilar production, would afford that beautiful colour, were it not for the falts employed in the lye by the dyers, to bring it to perfection. Mr. Maquer in his art of dying filks, affures us, that the white tartar employed for crimfon colours, gives by means of its acidity, that brilliancy to cochineal, and that though other acids might produce the fame effect, it would not be with fo much fuccefs. Mr. Goguet, in his " origin of laws, arts and fciences," tells us, the ancients ufed a great deal of falt, to make their dyes folid, and permanent, fupplying the place of our chemical preparations by other fecrets unknown to us. Plutarch, in the life of Alexander the Great, mentions, that conqueror having found in the treafures of the king of Perfia, a prodigious quantity of purple ftuffs, which though they had lain by above one hundred and

---

(*a*) See fecond memoir of Mr. de Reaumur, tom 4.

ninety

ninety years, still preserved their lustre, because they had been prepared with honey; behold, says Mr. Goquet, a secret unknown to us! but if we reflect for a moment, that honey is a vegetable salt, like sugar, we shall find it to be the same as tartar, which is no more than an essential salt of wine; so that the salts employed by the ancients, were equivalent to those used at present in the dye-house. Probably the salts of fruits have the same effect in the manner they are used in Persia for dying of silk, where, instead of tartar and honey, they use the pulp of red melons, well dried, mixed with allum, barilla, and other salts.

The kermes of Spain is preferred on the coast of Barbary, on account of its goodness. The people of Tunis mix it with that of Tetuan, for dying those scarlet caps so much used in the Levant. The Tunisians export every year above one hundred and fifty thousand dozen of these caps, which yields to the Dey a revenue of one hundred and fifty thousand hard dollars, (£33,750—) per annum for duties; so that, exclusive of the uses and advantages of kermes in medicine, it appears to be a very valuable branch of commerce in Spain, and there is still sufficient encouragement to use every effort for its improvement.

LETTER

LETTER IV.

The method of making Saltpetre in Spain.

IN the year 1754, I received orders (*a*) from the ministry to inspect into several saltpetre works, as well as into the making of gunpowder, which having complied with, the following reflections occurred to my mind.

All the professors of chemistry I had conversed with, either in France or in Germany, laid down as a fixed principle, that there are three mineral acids in nature: that the vitriolic, is the universal one, belonging to metals, from whence the other two arise. That the nitrous is second in activity, and belongs to the vegetable kingdom, and the marine being the weakest of all, is homogeneous to fish. They do not include the animal acid, which united with the phlogiston (*b*), forms the phosphorus. I was further taught, that the fixed alkali of salt-

---

(*a*) Don Guillermo Bowles.

(*b*) By phlogiston, chemists mean the most pure and simple inflammable principle, concerning which there are a great variety of opinions and doctrines, supported on the one hand, and controverted on the other with equal ingenuity, by chemical writers.

petre,

petre, did not exist purely, and simply in nature, but was generated by fire, and when they found saltpetre, to be dug out of the earth naturally in the East Indies, they thought to save the difficulty, by saying it proceeded from the incineration of woods, which had impregnated the earth, with this fixed alkali, the basis of saltpetre; so that I had been led to believe, it was formed by certain combinations, that took place in the act of combustion; but I soon found my error, when I had had seen the method of making saltpetre in the different provinces of Spain. I have now evident proofs that the basis of nitre really exists in the earth and in plants, the same as in the *Soda* of Alicant. Let these learned gentlemen come to Spain, they may convince themselves of this truth, and see saltpetre with its alkaline basis, in the manufactures of Castile, Aragon, Navarre, Valencia, Murcia, and Andalusia, where it is made without the assistance of vegetable matter; sometimes throwing in a handful of ashes of matweed, merely to filter the lye of earth, and though they often meet with gypseous stone in the neighbourhood of their works, yet they make excellent saltpetre by boiling the lixivium of their lands only, in which they do not find an atom of gypsum; consequently they have gunpowder in Spain, without being indebted for its fixed alkali, to the vegetable kingdom, and without the visible or sensible conversion of the vitriolic acid of gypsum into the nitrous.

Having thus difcovered in Spain a perfect fixed alkali in the earth, I purfued my obfervations on other falts, and vegetable productions, and after many reflections and experiments, I difcovered that fimilar fixed alkalies, many oils, and neutral falts, proceed from different combinations of the air, earth, and water, with fuch matters as the air conveys in a diffolved ftate, and that thefe three elements, rifing, falling, and meeting, combine together, and form new bodies in the organs of vegetation.

Thofe who are verfed in phyfics, agree, that all the fubftances of the very globe we inhabit, confift of the combinations of fire, water, earth, and air; why then deny them the power of combining, in the living organs of plants? when we fo often perceive in them, the faculty of changing, and transforming productions in the kingdom of nature. In proof of it, we find that many cruciformed plants give by analyfis, the fame volatile alkali as animals, notwithftanding that their tubes are fimilar to the eye, with thofe that give acids.

Some plants have their roots fo fmall, and yet their branches, leaves and fruit fo ponderous, that it appears impoffible, fo inconfiderable a root fhould draw fufficient nurture out of the earth for fuch various purpofes. It feems therefore, that the ambient air, containing many

diffolved

diffolved bodies, penetrates into the plants, and combines in the vegetative tubes, forming thofe fubftances difcovered by analyfation.

I have frequently feen water melons in Spain weigh from twenty to thirty pounds, with a ftem of only two or three ounces, fo great was the increafe of the fibrous and tubulous fubftance of thofe plants, owing to the watery particles they imbibed from the air. It fhould feem then, that many plants draw their principal fupport from the air, water, and a fmall portion of earth, combined by the imperceptible labour of the vegetative tubes, and veffels of air, which convert thofe matters into the products we contemplate, and tafte; many plants producing all thefe effects in water only, and we find that mint, and other odoriferous plants whofe roots grow in water, and in the air, give the fame fpiritus rector, and oils, as thofe that grow in the earth.

Botanifts know very well that thofe aquatic plants that fpring up from the bottom of waters have with a very trifling deviation, the fame properties and qualities in the frozen regions, as in fultry and parching climates, and, that their acrimony, caufticity, infipidity, and coolnefs, are invariable.

The experiments made by Van Helmont on the willow tree, making it grow in water, and a fmall portion of dried earth,

earth, shew how much air, and water, added to the internal labour of plants, contribute to vegetation.

In the memoirs of the French academy of sciences, we find experiments of a celebrated chemist, to prove the existence of three neutral salts, in the extract of borrage. If he had gone further, and proved that one of these three salts, existed in the earth, which produced the borrage, he would have illustrated the system of physics, and cleared up the point I am speaking of. The same memoirs mention another academician, who reared an oak for many years, only with water, the consequences of which speak for themselves.

There are millions of firs about Valladolid, and Tortosa, replete with turpentine, and growing in a small portion of earth, and great quantity of sand, in which it would be difficult to prove that the thousandth part of the turpentine, so plentifully produced by these trees, had existed; of course, it must be owing to channels of air, connected with the tubes of vegetation.

The conductory vessels of the wormwood of Granada, convey a bitterness to the very juice of the sugar cane, which grows by its side: the soil of the king's botanic garden at Madrid, is of one equal kind, for all the different plants that are reared there, yet some produce a wholesome fruit, while others near them, are poisonous;

and

and one, with fixed alkali, will thrive close to another, full of volatile alkali. (a).

The mountains and vallies of Spain, as well as the gardens, are full of aromatic plants, yet I do not know that any body has ever extracted by analysis, any aromatic water, or volatile oil, from any uncultivated land. The variation of soil, or culture, may alter the form of plants, change the lustre of their drapery, or give additional flavour to their fruit, but it can never change their essence, and nature. In proof of this, it is known, there is only one indigenous tulip in Europe, (I found it in flower near Almaden,) it is small, yellow, and ugly, appearing only in the spring. Gardeners may invent modes of cultivation, try all the climates of Europe, they may produce larger tulips with brighter colours, but they all will be inodorous, and the little tulip of Spain, will give by analysis, the very same product as the most superb of the east, whose beautiful garment in common with other gay flowers, is owing to the phlogiston in the organs of vegetation, and not to iron as

---

(a) Just as Shakespear has emphatically said:

    The strawberry grows underneath the nettle,
    And wholesome berries, thrive and ripen best
    Neighboured by fruits of baser quality.   *Hen. 5th.*

has

has been thought. This phlogiston is manifest by analysis in the leaves, where the least atom of iron has never been discovered.

There are many lands in Spain which naturally produce salt-petre, sea-salt, and vitriolic salts; but the plants which grow spontaneously in those soils, give by analysis the same product as those of their species in gardens, where there never was any appearance of salt-petre, sea-salt, or vitriolic acid.

Analize as often as you please, those plants so numerous near iron mines, whose roots penetrate into the very ore, or those that grow in ferruginous and superficial earth. I am sure you will not collect from their roots, branches, ashes, extracts, or oils, more iron, than what is found in the same species of plants that spring up in places without the least communication with any such minerals.

Whatever efficacy there may be in culture, and manure, to remove, absorb, and open the pores of the earth, enriching the watery particles, that rise in the vegetative tubes, conveying new substances which contribute to that perfection, we observe, from the soil, and which they lose when transplanted, yet they still at-

tain

tain various substances of vegetation from the air, which chemists may look for in vain in the earth (*a*).

Many plants are emollient in the spring and summer, and astringent in autumn and winter. Their mucilaginous quality admits of alteration in the tubes, and the combination of earth, air, and water, engenders a vitriolic acid (*b*), just as the alkali and the leaves receive colour from the phlogiston; from whence I conceive the reason of the nitrous soil in Spain, abounding with such a prodigious quantity of fixed natural alkali; which calls to my mind what is fondly advanced by the adepts, "That some lands have the natural properties of loadstone to attract peculiar substances from the air."

It is certain then, that plants have proper tubes to attract the elements, and form a natural fixed alkali, and have peculiar separate principles which only combine by the means of fire in the act of combustion to form that artificial fixed alkali I had been taught to believe was the only one that existed in nature.

(*a*) The ingenious author of this reasoning does not seem to be aware, that it would be equally fruitless to look for these substances in the water, or in the air. It is true that we cannot extract turpentine from the sand, or from the earth, in which the fir trees of Valladolid and Tortosa grow; but it is equally true, that we cannot extract it either from the air, or from the water of those countries.

(*b*) The existence of vitriolic acid in vegetables has not yet been proved.

Perhaps

Perhaps the foda and falicornia may thrive better when nurtured by falt water, but it is no lefs certain that the alkaline bafis of common falt is found formed in thefe two plants, and in many others as well as in the barilla, which is fowed in many parts of Spain, where they make as good foap as that famous fort at Alicant made with foda and falicornia. With refpect to neutral falts, there are at leaft five fubftances, in which they are found, viz. earth, plants, falt water, mineral, and artificial fubftances.

After this digreffion, let us now fee how faltpetre is generally made in France and in Spain, I fay nothing of England or Holland, becaufe they make none, importing what they want from the Eaft Indies, where it is found naturally in the earth, as in Spain, where I have feen faltpetre made with the lixivium of nitrous earth, collected in places where perhaps there never was a tree nor a plant.

In Paris they have feventeen faltpetre works: every thing that is carried on there, as well as in other parts of the kingdom, is done according to royal ordinances, in the manner I am going to relate: The rubbifh and filth of old houfes is carried to the works, and pounded with hammers; the duft is then put into cafks, perforated at bottom, the aperture covered with ftraw, to
give

give a free paſſage to the liquor. Water is then poured on this duſt, which in its paſſage carries away all the ſaline matter. This impregnated matter is called a lye, which if they were at that period to boil, would produce ſaltpetre of a greaſy nature; to remedy this, they purchaſe the aſhes of all the wood fires in Paris, from which they alſo draw a lye that is mixed with the former, then boil up the whole (*a*). In proportion as the water evaporates, the common ſalt which cryſtalizes when hot, ſoon falls to the bottom of the cauldron, and the ſaltpetre, which only cryſtalizes when cool, remains diſſolved in the water. They draw off this water, loaded with ſaltpetre, into other veſſels, and place it in the ſhade, where the nitre cryſtalizes. This is called ſaltpetre of the firſt boiling, having ſtill ſome remains of common ſalt, earth, and greaſy matter, incorporated with it; it is conveyed to the arſenal to be properly refined, being boiled over again, and left to cryſtalize two or three times, or more if found neceſſary; by which means it is cleared of all its impurities, and becomes perfectly adapted to the making of gunpowder and the other uſes to which it is applied in the arts; but for medical purpoſes, it muſt undergo another purification. Thoſe who

---

(*a*) The fact ſeems to be this; the ſalt they obtain from the lye of the rubbiſh, is a nitre with an earthy baſis, the fixed vegetable alkali procured from the wood aſhes is then added; this alkali precipitates the earth from the nitrous acid, and taking its place, forms true ſaltpetre.

are curious of being more exactly informed, may find a very accurate account of these works in the memoirs of the academy of sciences by Mr. Petit, to which I refer them.

In Spain, where a third part of all the lands, and the very dust on the roads in the eastern and southern parts of the kingdom, contain natural saltpetre, I have seen them prepare it in the following manner.

They plough the ground two or three times in winter, and spring, near the villages. In August they pile it up in heaps of twenty and thirty feet high: then fill with this earth a range of vessels, of a conic shape, perforated at bottom, observing to cover the aperture with matweed and a few ashes, two or three fingers deep, that the water may just filter through. They then pour on the water, (sometimes without putting any ashes); the lye that results from this operation is put into a boiler. The common salt, which as we said before precipitates, and crystalizes when warm, falls to the bottom of the cauldron in a proportion of 40 lb. to a quintal of materials (*a*); then the liquor is poured into buckets placed in the shade, where it shoots, and crystalizes into salt-

---

(*a*) The Spanish quintal is 100 lb. weight, and about 93 lb. English. The arrobe of Madrid is 25 lb. Spanish, and four arrobes make one quintal.

petre.

petre. The great quantity of common salt which accompanies the nitre, makes me think, that the marine acid with its bafis, is converted into nitre. The fame earth, deprived of its nitrous quality by this procefs, is again carried back to the fields, and expofed to the elements, by which means in the courfe of a twelvemonth, affifted by the all-powerful and invifible hand of nature, it again becomes impregnated with a frefh fupply of nitre, and what is ftill more furprifing, and cannot be obferved without admiring the wonderful works of the omnipotent creator, the fame lands have produced time immemorial an equal quantity of faltpetre; fo that if the fupreme power was to annihilate all the factitious faltpetre of France, and Germany, Spain alone could fupply the reft of the world, without the aid of a fixed alkali, afhes or vegetables, if public œconomy joined hands with induftry, and affifted in bringing thefe great points to perfection. I once afked one of thefe people the reafon of that conftant production of faltpetre, but his only anfwer was, "I have two fields, I fow one with corn, and "have a crop, I plough the other, and it furnifhes me "faltpetre."

This faltpetre thus cryftalized is fimilar to that of Paris of the firft boiling. In Spain they only boil it once more, and it becomes perfect, and proper for making of gun-powder, aqua fortis, and other purpofes of the fhops.

shops. Its bafis placed in a cellar, attracts the dampnefs of the air, lofes its activity, and forms a fixed alkali, which mixed with the vitriolic acid, forms a vitriolated tartar, a certain proof that the nitrous air of Spain is natural and perfect in itfelf, without the affiftance of any fixed alkali whatever(*a*.)

I fhall not dwell upon the proportion of faltpetre, fulphur, and coal, ufed in the making of gunpowder; as it depends upon experience, and is generally known. I was prefent at the proofs made by the king's officers in Granada, to afcertain whether the powder had the qualities required, in order to be admitted or refufed, but I do not think thofe proofs were to the purpofe, as new made powder perhaps may throw a ball to the diftance required; yet to form a true judgment of its real quality and goodnefs, it fhould be tried in different places and climates, and at various feafons of the year; for I am convinced that the gunpowder which would come up to the ftrength required by the king in the dry and warm climate of Andalufia, would be found deficient in the damp and moift air of Galicia, which fhews how little

---

(*a*) However incredible this account of Mr. Bowles may appear to an Englifh chemift, it would be rather rafh to deny the truth of it, particularly as he obferves that the bafis of the nitre thus produced is a fixed alkali, and united with the vitriolic acid, forms vitriolated tartar. But if there is no deception in the cafe, the fpontaneous production of the vegetable fixed alkali in a place where no vegetables grow, is a fact altogether new, and worthy of a further examination.

such

such experiments are to be depended upon. Of all the inventions I know of for this purpose, the least imperfect is that of Mr. Darcy, a design of which may be seen in the first volume of Mr. Beaume's treatise on chemistry.

When the Count de Aranda was director of the engineers, I remember an old officer of artillery informed me that in the last wars in Italy, he had seen barrels of gunpowder, that were good in the morning, and bad the next night: This did not surprize me, knowing the variations of weather, and the effects of dampness piercing through the casks and damaging the powder, so as to render it unfit for service, for which reason every precaution should be taken to guard against these inconveniences (*a*).

(*a*) This is the substance of Mr. Bowles's discourse. Some observations of his relating to the qualities of salts are omitted, as those subjects are treated of with greater exactness by modern chemists, to which the reader is referred.

It is likewise unnecessary to expatiate upon, or point out the properest methods of preserving gunpowder, so well known in this country, and with respect to the force of fired gunpowder, a late publication gives us the most curious and ample information, viz. "The force of fired gunpowder and the initial velocity of cannon ball, determined by experiments, from which is also deducted the relation of the initial velocity, to the weight of the shot and quantity of powder. By Charles Hutton, master of the military academy of Woolwich, which gained the prize medal of the Royal Society." Phil. transact. for 1778, vol. lxviii.

LETTER

LETTER V.

Of the Merino Sheep.

THE wools of Spain form a confiderable branch of our commerce with that country. It has even been faid that their fine quality was originally owing to a few Englifh fheep fent into Spain, as a prefent by our Henry the fecond, or according to others, by Edward the fourth, in 1465, but without entering into fruitlefs inveftigations of an event fo remote, and of fo little confequence, I fhall confine myfelf to fpeak of thofe remarkable fheep known in Spain by the name of *Ganado Merino*, " The Merino flocks," and defcribe the conftant method of conducting thofe numerous tribes from the northern to the fouthern provinces, to which they attribute that peculiar fine quality of the wool, which has rendered it fo famous all over Europe (*a*.)

(*a*) Though this account of Spanifh fheep appeared in the gentleman's magazine for 1764, and in other publications, yet as I am informed it came originally from Mr. Bowles, I have again inferted the fubftance of his difcourfe, in juftice to its original author, with fome further illuftrations relating to the wool of Spain, not mentioned by that writer.

There are two forts of sheep in Spain, some that have coarse wool, and are never removed out of the province to which they belong, and others, that after spending the summer in the northern mountains, descend in the winter to the milder provinces of Estremadura, and Andalusia, and are distributed into districts, which go by the name of *Merindades*. These are the Merino sheep, of which it is computed there are between four and five million in the kingdom (a). The word Merino, signifies a governor of a province. The Merino mayor is always a person of rank and appointed by the king. They have a separate jurisdiction over the flocks in Estremadura,.

	Sheep.
(a) The duke of Infantado's flock about	40.000
Countess Campo de Alcofe Negretti	30.000
Paular, and Escurial convents, 30.000 each	60.000
Convent of Guadalupe	30.000
Marquis Perales	30.000
Duke of Bejar	30.000
Several flocks of about 10.000 each	100.000
All the other flocks in the kingdom together, on an average about	3.800.000
	4.120.000

In 1778, the wool of Infantado was 9285 arrobes in the greafe, and Negretti nearly the same. Wafhed wool coarse and fine together, worth at an average, eight and a half rials vellon per lb. (about 2s) exclusive of duties which are 10 per cent. on exportation.

There is a curious discourse on the wools of Spain in the second volume of the Spanish correspondence of lord Sandwich, lord Sunderland, and sir William Godolphin, in a book entitled, Hispania illustrata. London, 1702.

which

which is called The *Mesta*, and there the king in person is Merino mayor (*a*).

Each flock consists generally of ten thousand sheep, with a *Mayoral* or head shepherd, who must be an active man well versed in the nature of pasture, as well as the diseases incident to his flock. This person has under him fifty inferior shepherds, and as many dogs, five of each to a tribe. The principal shepherd has a hundred pistoles (about £75.) and a horse every year. The other servants have 150 rials for the first class (£1. 13s. 9d.) 100 rials for the second class (£1. 2s. 6d.) 60 rials for the third class (13s. 6d.) and 40 rials, or nine shillings for the other attendants. Each of these has an allowance of two pounds of bread a day, with the same quantity of an inferior sort for the dogs. They are likewise permitted to keep goats, and a few sheep, of which they have the meat, and the lambs, provided the wool remains for the master. They may do what they please with the milk, of which they seldom make any advantage. In the months of April and October, each shepherd has 12 rials given him (about 2s. 9d.) as a perquisite previous to his journey.

Though these flocks divide and separate themselves over several provinces of Spain, it will be unnecessary to

---

(*a*) There is a supreme council at Madrid called *Consejo de Mesta* which takes cognizance of all matters relating to sheep, wool, shepherds, pastures, woods, and all concerns that belong to royal seats and parks.

relate

relate what paſſes in each, their government being ſimilar and uniform. The places where they are to be ſeen in the greateſt numbers are in the Montana and Molina de Aragon in the ſummer, and in the province of Eſtremadura in the winter. Molina is to the eaſtward of Eſtremadura, the Montana is to the north, and the moſt elevated part of Spain; Eſtremadura abounds with aromatic plants, but the Montana is entirely without them.

The firſt care of the ſhepherd in coming to the ſpot where they are to ſpend the ſummer, is to give to the ewes as much ſalt as they will eat; for this purpoſe they are provided with 25 quintals of ſalt for every thouſand head, which is conſumed in leſs than five months; but they eat none on their journey, or in winter. The method of giving it to them is as follows. The ſhepherd places fifty or ſixty flat ſtones about five ſteps diſtance from each other; he ſtrews ſalt upon each ſtone, then leads his flock ſlowly through the ſtones, and every ſheep eats at pleaſure. This is frequently repeated, obſerving not to let them feed on thoſe days in any ſpot where there is lime-ſtone. When they have eaten the ſalt, they are led to ſome argillaceous ſpots, where from the craving they have acquired, they devour every thing they meet with, and return again to the ſalt with redoubled ardour (a).

(a) Mr. Bowles obſerves, that if the diſtrict is limy or marly, the ſheep eat leſs ſalt in proportion to the lime they find, and aſking the reaſon of one of the ſhepherds, was told, it pro-

At the end of July each shepherd distributes the rams amongst the ewes, five or six rams being sufficient for an hundred ewes. These are taken out of flocks where they are kept apart, and after a proper time are again separated from the ewes.

The rams give a greater quantity of wool, though not so fine as the ewes, for the fleeces of the rams will weigh twenty-five pounds, and it requires five fleeces of the ewes to give the like weight. The disproportion in their age is known by their teeth, those of the rams not falling before the eighth year, while the ewes, from their delicacy of frame or other causes, lose theirs after five years.

About the middle of September they are marked, which is done by rubbing their loins with ocre diluted in water; some say this earth incorporates with the grease of the wool, and forms a kind of varnish, which protects them from the inclemencies of the weather; others pretend that the pressure of the ocre keeps the

_{ceeded from their grazing in cornfields, on which occasion the illiterate shepherd seemed to relate the fact though ignorant of the cause, which was, according to Mr. Bowles, " from the salt all limy matter abounds with, and partaken of by cattle, either in licking the stones, or communicated by vegetation to grass; for which reason, their appetite is not so keen for any salt that is offered them;" however we cannot admit this to be the true cause, as chemists are now well assured that lime does not contain any salt whatever.}

wool

wool short, and prevents it from becoming of an ordinary quality; others again imagine, that the ocre acts in the nature of an absorbent, and sucks up the excess of transpiration, which would render the wool ordinary and coarse.

Towards the end of September these Merino flocks begin their march to a warmer climate; the whole of their route has been regulated by the laws and customs, time immemorial. They have a free passage through pastures, and commons belonging to villages, but as they must go over such cultivated lands as lie in their way, the inhabitants are obliged to leave them an opening ninety paces wide, through which these flocks are obliged to pass rapidly, going sometimes six or seven leagues a day, in order to reach open spots less inconvenient, where they may find good pasture, and enjoy some repose. In such open places they seldom exceed two leagues a day, following the shepherd and grazing as they move on. Their whole journey from the Montana, to the interior parts of Estremadura may be about one hundred and fifty leagues, which they perform in about forty days.

The first care of the shepherd is to lead them to the same pasture where they have been the winter before, and where the greatest part of them were eaned; this is no difficult task, for if they were not led there, they will discover

discover the ground, by the great sensibility of their olfactory organs, to be different from that which is contiguous; or were the shepherds so inclined, they would find it no easy matter to make them go further. The next business is to order the folds, which are made by fixing stakes, fastened with ropes one to the other, to prevent their escape, and being devoured by the wolves, for which purpose the dogs are stationed without. The shepherds build themselves huts with stakes and boughs, for the raising of which as well as for fuel, they are allowed to lop off a branch from every tree. This law is the cause of so many trees being rotten and hollow, which grow in those places frequented by these flocks.

A little before the ewes arrive at their winter quarters, it is the time of their eaning, at which period the shepherds must be particularly careful. The barren ones are separated from the others, and placed in a less advantageous spot, reserving the best pasture for those that are fruitful, removing them in proportion to their forwardness: the last lambs are put into the richest pasture, that they may improve the sooner, and acquire sufficient strength to perform the journey, along with the early ones.

In March the shepherds have four different operations to perform with the lambs, that were eaned in the winter; the first is to cut off their tails, five fingers below

the

the rump for cleanliness; the second is to mark them on the nose with a hot iron; next they saw off the tips of their horns, that they may not hurt one another in their frolicks; finally they castrate such lambs as are doomed for bell-wethers, to walk at the head of the tribe; which is not done by any incision, but merely by squeezing the scrotum with the hand, till the spermatic vessels are twisted like a rope, and decay without further danger.

In April the time comes for their return to the Montana, which the flock expresses with great eagerness, by various movements and restlessness, for which reason the shepherds must be very watchful, lest they make their escape, which often happens when proper care is not taken, and whole flocks have sometimes strayed two or three leagues while the shepherd was asleep, as on these occasions they generally take the straightest road to the place which they came from.

The first of May they begin to shear, unless the weather is unfavourable; for the fleeces being piled one above the other, would ferment in case of dampness, and rot; to avoid which, the sheep are kept in covered places to shear them more conveniently; for this purpose they have buildings that will hold twenty thousand at a time, which is the more necessary, as the ewes are so delicate,

that

that if immediately after shearing they were exposed to the chilling air of the night, they would certainly perish.

One hundred and fifty men are employed to shear each thousand sheep. Each person is reckoned to shear eight sheep a day, but if rams, only five, not merely on account of their bulk, and greater quantity of wool, but from their fickleness of temper, and difficulty to keep them quiet, the ram being so exasperated, that he is ready to strangle himself, when he finds he is tied; to avoid which, they endeavour by fair means and caresses to keep him in temper, and with much soothing, and having ewes near him, they at last engage him to stand quiet, and voluntarily suffer them to proceed.

On the shearing day the ewes are shut up in a large court, and from thence conducted into a sudatory, which is a narrow place, where they are kept as close as possible, that they may perspire freely, in order to soften the wool, and make it yield with more ease to the shears. This is particularly useful with respect to the rams, whose wool is more stubborn. The fleece is divided into three sorts; the back, and belly, give the superfine, the neck and sides give the fine, and the breasts, shoulders and thighs, give the coarse wool.

The sheep are then brought into another place and marked, examining those without teeth, which are destined

tined for the slaughter-house; the healthy are led to graze, if the weather permits, if not, they are kept within doors, till by degrees they are accustomed to the air. When they are permitted to graze without being hurried, they select and prefer the finest grass, never touching the aromatic plants, though they find them in plenty, and if the wild thyme is entangled with the grass they separate it with great dexterity, avoiding it on every occasion, moving eagerly to such spots as they can find that are without it.

When the shepherd thinks there is a likelihood of rain, he makes proper signals to the dogs to collect the flock, and leads them towards shelter; on these occasions the sheep not having time to chuse their pasture, pick up every thing they meet, thyme, rosemary, and every herb indiscriminately, even poisonous ones; such as henbane, poppy, and hemlock, particularly soon after they are sheared. Were they to take a fancy and give a preference to aromatic plants, it would be a great misfortune to the owners of beehives, as they would destroy the food of the bees, and occasion a disappointment in the honey and wax. They are never suffered to move out of their folds till the beams of the sun have exhaled the night dews, nor do they let them drink out of brooks, or standing waters, where hail has fallen, experience having taught them, that on such occasions

they

they are in danger of losing them all. The wool of Andalusia is coarse, because their sheep never change climate like the Merino flocks, whose wool would likewise degenerate, if they were kept at home; and that of Andalusia would improve, were they accustomed to emigrate.

Between fifty and sixty thousand bags of washed wool are annually exported out of Spain. A bag generally weighs eight arrobes or 194 pounds English. About twenty thousand bags of this wool are sent annually to London and Bristol worth from £30. to £35. each ; so that we have one third of the produce, and of the best sort. The wool of Paular, which is the largest, though not the best, is reserved for the king of Spain's manufactures. The common and shooting dresses of the royal family of Spain and their attendants, are made of the cloth of Segovia, from whence our English nobility, in Henry the VIIth's time were supplied with fine cloth (*a*).

The crown of Spain receives annually, by all duties together on exported wool, near sixty millions of reals vellon per annum. (£675,000.)

(*a*) Breadth of Spanish cloth made at Segovia 1 3-4ths vara, or 57 3-4ths inches English.

LETTER

LETTER VI.

Inconveniencies arising from the emigrations of the Merino sheep, and the partial laws of the Mesta.

YOU desire my opinion (a) concerning the Mesta, but I have nothing to add to what I have frequently mentioned to you, on a subject not easily reduced into the compass of a letter; however I shall once more lay before you those observations that have engaged me to entertain the notions I have formed to myself concerning the Mesta.

This appellation has corruptly crept into our language, and been applied to sheep, when in reality it had no other signification, than a mixture of grain, and feed, such as barley, beans, oats, lentils, &c. nor was any such name as the Mesta flocks known in Spain before the days of king Alfonso El Ultimo, when English sheep were first

---

(a) This letter was written by the late ingenious Padre Sarmiento, to Don Antonio Ponz, and is dated Madrid, 12th Sept. 1765, and published by Ponz, in his eighth volume of Viage de Espana, Madrid, 1778. It shews how far the spirit of improvement has extended, and reached even within the gloomy walls of convents, and as it gives a lively idea of the spirit of the times, I thought it would perhaps be more acceptable to preserve it in its original form.

brought into Spain in the Spanish caracks. It was then that the office of judge of the Mesta had its rise according to the Bachelor Fernan Gomez de Ciudad Real, in his 73d epistle. The aforesaid king Alfonso introduced these foreign valuable sheep called Marinas, and not Merinas, according to the vulgar opinion; in the same manner as his present majesty, Charles the third, has lately introduced at the Casa del Campo(a), some goats from Angora, so valued for their hair of a fine white, almost like silk, the breed of which might easily be propagated, as the district they come from, is in a parallel latitude with Spain.

A few years after this event relating to the English sheep, our kingdom was desolated by an universal pestilence, which in 1348 ruined Spain and part of Asia; and in 1350 carried off king Alfonso. The dominions of Spain suffered infinitely on this dismal occasion, insomuch that since the universal deluge, there is no instance of an equal calamity, for it wasted the country, and swept away two-thirds of the inhabitants. Spain became depopulated, and husbandry seemed to be lost. The many rural churches in the centre of the kingdom, are proofs of this terrible havock, that ruined whole villages, of which *Etiam periere ruina*. Thus four or five villages, perhaps of two hundred families, were destroyed, and

(a) A royal seat near Madrid.

the country changed into a swamp or a heath, open to any invader, and free to the first comer, who was willing to take possession. The whole territory was afterwards claimed by the adjacent more fortunate villages, from whence we may account for the present amazing jurisdiction of some villages, which includes a space of fourteen leagues in circumference; insomuch that in places where before this fatal event, there were three or four populous parishes, there is now only one lonely parish thinly inhabited by people in distress; others were totally destroyed, nothing remaining but the steeples which are called rural churches.

These churches, or at least these steeples, seem still to be crying out like Æacus in Ovid to Jove his sire, on a similar event, "*Aut mibi redde meos, aut me quoque conde Sepulchro.*" The doleful condition of these miserable wretches will strictly bear the comparison. The pestilence it is true lasted only a few years, but their misery has continued above four centuries.

It is to this calamitous time we must attribute the origin of the Mesta. The English sheep were first brought into the mountains of Segovia, without the least ideas of the Mesta or of Estremadura. It was the great space of uncultivated land and the want of husbandmen that encouraged both shepherds and cattle to stray beyond their boundaries,

boundaries, and to wander into diſtricts where no impediments occurred to their progreſs, making a caſual uſe of the lands without the leaſt thought of proper cultivation, as that would require more hands than they were able to furniſh; and on this occaſion they firſt introduced that barbarous method of ploughing with mules, by which they only juſt ſcratched up the ground.

Thus what was ſo imperfectly tilled, and much more left entirely uncultivated, remained for the purpoſe of grazing for foreign cattle, to the great prejudice of agriculture. Eſtremadura is a province of Leon, and not of Caſtile; the natural remedy for theſe misfortunes was immediately perceived by the Portugueſe, though the Caſtilians would not underſtand it, ſome being warped by their avarice, under a fond notion of having large tracts of land although barren, and others by the flattering idea of poſſeſſing numerous flocks, as if agriculture had been loſt. The laws therefore that were made by Ferdinand King of Portugal deſerve to be written in letters of gold, one of which was; "That no perſon who was not an huſbandman or his ſervant, ſhould keep ſheep either for himſelf, or for others; and if any other perſons were deſirous of having them, they muſt oblige themſelves to cultivate a certain portion of land, under the penalty of loſing their cattle if the regulation was not exactly complied with." By this ſingular and moſt excellent law, many defects of the Meſta could be remedied, both in reſpect to the ſheep, and the ſhepherds, who without cultivating a foot of land uſurped ſo conſiderable a diſtrict, in a manner ſo prejudicial, to the induſtry of the farmer.

It is ſhameful to obſerve in Spain, a continuation of the barbarous cuſtoms of the Saracens, who totally neglectful of agriculture, wander with their cattle over the depopulated plains of Arabia and Lybia. When the induſtrious Moors poſſeſſed Eſtremadura, they turned the whole province into a garden, replete with inhabitants, as appears by the numerous armies they brought into the field againſt the Chriſtians. They did not ſend their flocks to Caſtile, nor the Spaniards come with theirs into Eſtremadura, for the Meſta was unknown.

This expreſſion therefore is not circumſcribed to the ſole mixture, or variety of cultivation, but comprehends grazing, united with farming, ſince the practice of both properly combined, conſtitutes the true farmer, who without ſome cattle, will ever be poor. The method obſerved by the Romans, in allotting a certain number of head of cattle of the larger and ſmaller ſort, in proportion to a given quantity of land, evinces the propriety of ſimilar laws in Portugal, as well as the indiſpenſable connection of theſe branches of rural œconomy.

Some

Some perhaps will not believe, that the depopulation of Spain proceeds from the Mesta, as there are waste provinces to be found where the Mesta is unknown. But I must answer them in general terms, that where there is no Mesta, every part is populous, as for instance, Galicia, Asturias, the Montana, and Biscay; to which may be added, Navarre, Catalonia, and Valencia. The Mesta not only depopulates Estremadura, but also the kingdoms of Leon, and Castile, where the sheep destroy the country in their passage, preventing the farmers from inclosing their lands, according to their natural rights, as well as the civil and national laws, which permit those inclosures where happily the Mesta does not prevail.

To return to the state of population. The Roman empire, according to Riciolus, was supposed to contain four hundred and ten millions of people. In the days of Tertullian not a foot of land was uncultivated. Solinus says of Spain, " *nihil otiosum, nihil sterile est.*" Estremadura contains two thousand square leagues of land. The most moderate calculation admits of a thousand persons to each square league; then Estremadura would admit of two millions of inhabitants, which allowing four persons to a family, would make five hundred thousand families; but Ustariz (*a*) only allows to Estremadura sixty

(*a*) Theoria y practica de commercio y marina, por Don Geronimo de Ustariz, Madrid, 1742. This curious book has been translated into English. See Ustariz's theory and practice of commerce, by Kippax. London, 1751.

thousand

thousand families; and the number is now thought to be less. Consider then the disproportion, and what prejudice the country receives from the Mesta. Galicia, where there is no Mesta, and only sixteen hundred square leagues, has above a million of inhabitants. So much concerning population, the life of a state, when idleness is banished, and industry encouraged. With respect to cattle, Galicia has more than Estremadura. Ustariz says that about four millions of sheep go into Estremadura: In Galicia they have not flocks of thirty and forty thousand head, possessed by one person contributing nothing towards agriculture; he that has forty or fifty sheep is a Crœsus, but the poorest of farmers have at least five and twenty head of different kinds. Few reflect, that in a state, a great many small portions are of much more consequence than a few large divisions, though consisting of infinite numbers.

Other advocates for the Mesta extol the value of the wool, and tell us it is an active commerce, but Ustariz shews, that foreigners only pay us at par, for the wool in the fleece, and have a profit of four to one in vending their manufactures. The way to form an active commerce of our wool, and our silk, of which we have such plenty, would be to work it ourselves, and prohibit all foreign importations.

The

The culture of filk is of no prejudice to agriculture like the Mesta; a manufacture of filk would be of more advantage to Estremadura, than all the flocks of the Mesta together. Ustariz computes the Mesta to employ forty thousand people, destined by nature for agriculture; therefore, as each person could till land enough to produce 50 fanegas of corn(*a*), would they not be better employed in raising two millions of fanegas of corn, either at home or in Estremadura, than in leading such a wandering life in idleness and poverty? In Galicia they are not burthened with such swarms of vagabond strollers with their dogs, nor are they pestered with wolves; one little girl while she is spinning can overlook the domestic œconomy, and have an eye to the whole flock of the family, when the plains of Estremadura are ravaged, and laid waste by the locust. Ask these partisans of the Mesta, whether their sheep ever go into battle, or render any public service to their country? I know you have read the memorial of complaints made by the province of Estremadura against the Mesta; though they still suffer this inconvenience in the interior parts of the kingdom, they ought to be more cautious on the frontiers towards Portugal, to prevent bad

(*a*) Fanega is a corn measure in Spain, five of which make an English quarter of eight bushels.

consequences

consequences in case of a sudden invasion. I should be glad to know how many head of cattle are maintained in Madrid, for I know their provision is not brought from the mountains, or pastures, but from cultivated plains. Finally, I shall always be of opinion that except some spots reserved for the royal chace, and the diversion of our sovereigns and their illustrious line, all the rest should be cultivated, as in the days of Tertullian, that each farmer should inclose his lands, and that the same should be allotted to them for tillage, in proportion to their abilities, allowing a certain number of cattle, corresponding to the extent of the farm. Then, for the greater advancement of agriculture, the cultivators of land should form a body politic, with power to enact wholesome laws, and regulations, for the encouragement and benefit of husbandry. The Mesta people did so and had a confirmation of their laws from Charles 5th, in 1544, but with this condition, of their not being prejudicial to a third person. Let Estremadura answer, whether this is the case? and let the farmers then give their opinions. But I must insist with Solinus, that in Spain, no part where there is a possibility of avoiding it, should remain *otiosum neque sterile (a)*.

(a) Ever since the accession of the house of Bourbon to the throne of Spain, the extension of commerce, and the improvement of agriculture have been primary objects. The Real Junta de Commercio, or Board of Trade, was first erected by Philip the 5th, on the 15th of May, 1707. Many new regulations have been made for the benefit of commerce and agriculture,

LETTER VII.

Miscellaneous observations made at Madrid, with some account of the royal cabinet of Natural History.

THE town of Madrid is now become the capital of the monarchs of Spain, situated in the center of their dominions, and from one of the filthiest places imaginable, is at present on a par for cleanliness with se-

since his present majesty's arrival from Naples at Madrid, which was on the 9th of December 1759. For the greater encouragement of agriculture, all the old laws relative to corn were repealed in 1765, and the embarrassments with which they were clogged, totally removed; new laws more favourable to industry, were enacted, and a spirit of freedom and liberty introduced in the commerce of grain, in order to give every encouragement to the farmer. To improve the minds of the people, Academies were erected in Madrid, Valladolid, Seville, Valencia, and Barcelona, besides many literary societies in different parts of the kingdom, particularly one at Madrid, with the noblest of titles " Los Amigos del pais," The Friends of their country, in which every subject is to be considered, tending to the advancement of arts, manufactures, and commerce; and the better to convey these ideas to the public, the art of printing has been particularly attended to, and brought to very great perfection; however as all those literary establishments are still in their infancy, time only will discover their intended effects. The new roads through the kingdom form a principal branch of modern improvement, and for the better compleating the same, they have been again put under the direction of the general post office, by a royal decree of the 8th October, 1778, with new revenues assigned for the purpose; but with respect to the want of inns, and conveniencies for travellers, Don Antonio. Ponz, in his last volume insists, that every thing that has, or can be said, on the subject, is still short of the truth. " La verdad es, que en quanto a la penuria que se padece en esta materia, qualquiera se quedara corto por mucho que diga." Viage de España, tom. 8. folio. 212. Madrid 1778.

veral

TRAVELS THROUGH SPAIN. 67

veral principal cities of Europe, being likewife well paved and lighted, but in refpect to population, it is far inferior to London, Paris, or Naples. *(a)* Madrid is in a high fituation, all the rivers and brooks in its neighbourhood fall into the Tagus, whofe waters roll down to the ocean. The Guadarama mountains, to the north weft of the town, are covered with fnow feveral months of the year, which added to the piercing north

(a) The following table publifhed at Madrid for the year 1778, will fhew the prefent ftate of population in that town.

Parifhes.	Marriages.	Births.	Deaths.
St. Mary	13	41	28
St. Martin	343	930	338
St. Gines	74	308	108
St. Lewis	107	139	79
St. Jofeph	114	212	121
St. Nicholas	7	12	15
St. Saviour	9	11	13
St. John	2	17	15
Holy Crofs	86	208	108
St. Peter	13	30	14
St. Andrew	108	311	109
St. Michael	18	87	30
St. Juft	213	703	248
St. Sebaftian	341	801	277
St. Iago	18	71	42
	1466	4031	1577

There died this year in the parifhes and in the three hofpitals 3483 perfons, without reckoning infants, and thofe who died in communities, nunneries, and the other hofpitals of the court; and there have been 4372 births, including the foundlings baptifed in St. Gines.

This year 611 infants have been brought to the royal foundation of *La Inclufa* for foundlings, of which 341 have been baptifed in the parifh of St. Gines. Kalendario manual, y Guia de forafteros en Madrid para el ano de 1778.

winds, that reign in the winter, renders it exceffively cold, while in fummer the fouthern and wefterly blafts are generally attended with dampnefs and rain. Travellers have told us, the air is fo fubtle that if a dead dog was thrown into the ftreets over night, he would not have a bit of flefh on his bones in the morning, but this is a fable, as it is a known fact, that dead dogs and cats lie in the ftreets continually, as well as dead mules, clofe to the road fide, for days together, without any fuch effect.

Hiftorians relate that King John 2d being in Madrid, in 1434, it began to rain and fnow on the 29th of October, and never ceafed till the 7th January following, infomuch that feveral houfes were deftroyed, and the inhabitants reduced to the greateft diftrefs for want of provifions; a report having been fpread that the King intended to alienate the town, the inhabitants petitioned the King not to defert them, which finally terminated in a royal edict of the 30th of May 1442, by which it was ordained that neither the town or its jurifdiction, could ever be alienated.

The principal ftreets of Madrid are paved with cut flint, the others with pebbles, found in the neighbourhood, the cut flint on account of its fharpnefs is very inconvenient to foot paffengers, and the flat pavement near the houfes is too narrow. The town is well fupplied

plied with water, and there are conduits in the principal streets; that called del berro, in the neighbourhood of the town, is constantly drank by the royal family wherever they are. The bread is white and good, and when the barrenness of the country all round is considered, the *plaza mayor* or principal square, where the market is kept, is extremely well supplied with all manner of provisions.

Mr. Bowles has observed that if that celebrated professor Mr. Henckel, had come to Madrid, he would soon have been convinced of his error, in saying that " flint was not to be found in strata and only in detached lumps, or in masses, for here he would find all the environs replete with strata of flint; and moreover not a house or a building, but what has been constructed with lime made from flint (*a*), which serves also for fire arms, as well as for the pavement. In some places pieces are

(*a*) It is allowed that nature by some process unknown to us, seems to change limestone into flint, but this change once made, we cannot by calcination or any other known means convert flint into lime : It is true that flint may be calcined, and then it loses its flinty appearance, becomes white and may by a superficial observer be mistaken for lime, but it will not unite with an acid, it will not dissolve in water, it will not make a cement; in short it does not possess any of the distinguishing properties of lime. There are in this island beds of limestone stratified with layers of flint, and it is probably the case with these hills near Madrid; so that they get flint and limestone from the same quarry.

I am indebted to an ingenious friend since my return to England for this observation, and as I had not an opportunity of ascertaining the point to satisfaction with respect to those places near Madrid, I have related the circumstance as stated by Mr. Bowles, with hopes that some future traveller in Spain may be inclined to examine that ground more minutely.

found

found of it full of a species of agate, streaked with red, blue, white, green, and black, that take a very good polish, but these colours are accidental, and disappear by calcination. No acid will dissolve it, or cause any effervescence; when calcined, it burns in the water with more violence than true limestone, and mixed with the pebble or coarse sand near Madrid, makes an excellent material for building, though it does not answer so well with the fine sand of the river. It is impossible to fuse this flint alone, or any other found in limy or argillaceous earths, no more than the different kinds of agates, cornelians and rock crystal, but they calcine by themselves; that is are turned into lime and fuse very well mixed with the fixed alkali of *Barilla*, or with lead, the easiest to fuse of all metals, and change into the English flint glass, which is by far the best hitherto known. Many naturalists, according to Mr. Bowles have followed this erroneous opinion respecting flint, and amongst the rest Mr. de Reaumur. Linneus in his Systema Naturæ, says, " *Silex nascitur in montium cretaceorum rimis, uti quarzum in rimis Saxorum*," but we have only to open our eyes, to be fully convinced of the fallacy of this assertion, when we contemplate the numerous beds of flint near Madrid, and in different parts of Spain, and Italy, separated from all cretaceous matter. The abate Fortis, in his late travels into Dalmatia, found the flint there, quite different from the descriptions of former naturalists,

naturalists, and adds, " I have often seen the flint in the very act as I may say of passing from the calcareous state to the siliceous, and particularly I have often found flint envelloped in volcanic matter. I have formed a series of these progresses, which I have shewn to some of my friends (a)."

In the environs of Madrid there are above two hundred villages, but few can be seen on account of the inequality of the ground, the country being broken up by continual gullies, and various changes of aspect, occasioned by torrents, and other casual accidents, in a country little cultivated, and abandoned to every vicissitude of season. Near the town they chiefly sow barley, and here and there have some trifling vineyards. Their tillage is much the same as in Old Castile, that is, just to scratch up the earth and scatter the seed at random, then to cover it over with a similar indifference, and wait for the coming of the poor labourers from Galicia, to get in their harvest. The farmers pretend that if they were to make use of a stronger plough, they should have less corn. Mr. Bowles next reproaches the Spaniards for passing over in silence their countryman Don Joseph Lucadelo, a gentleman of Aragon, who had invented a curious plough much esteemed by foreign nations, who had taken the merit of the invention to themselves,

(a) Travels into Dalmatia by the abate Fortis, translated into English. London, 1778.

themselves, suppressing the name of the ingenious Spaniard; but this person, whose name was Joseph Lucatelli, was a native of Carinthia, one of the provinces of the house of Austria, who having made his experiments before the emperor Leopold in 1663, at the castle of Laxemberg, near Vienna, obtained a certificate of its utility from the imperial court, and then came to that of Madrid, and performed other experiments equally successful at the Buen Retiro, in the presence of Philip the 4th, from whom he obtained an exclusive patent for the sole vending of his plough for 24 reals plate in Europe, (about 11 *s*.) and 32 reals plate (about 14 *s*. 6*d*.) in America, of which a printed account was published by Lucatelli, at Seville, in 1664. A model of this plough was sent by Lord Sandwich, then ambassador at Madrid, to John Evelyn, Esq; who presented it to the royal society, with a letter describing its use, which was inserted in the philosophical transactions of the 23d of February, 1669-70, and the model deposited in Gresham college.

Nothing can be more bleak and dismal than the general aspect of the country round the seat of its monarch, with a great want of trees, to which the Castilians have such a dislike, from a false notion that they increase the number of birds to eat up their corn; as if this reason would not hold good in other countries, where shade is not so necessary, as it is in Castile, to support

the

the moisture of the soil; or that it was ever an objection in Valencia, a kingdom so fertile and wooded: the Castilians not reflecting; that the seeds of plants, and leaves of trees, afford nurture for insects, and birds, and prevent them from destroying the grain as they do in Castile, for want of other food; besides the advantage of screening the earth in hot weather, and preserving a due moisture after dews and rain; for without their aid, the scorching beams of the sun parch up the earth, and render it unfruitful; so that what little comes up is devoured by birds, in a climate where nature seems to have designed it should be otherwise; for the climate of Madrid is not in itself averse to the propagation of trees, as may be seen by the public walks, and modern improvements and plantations. The old historians speak particularly of the woods, and of their advantageous situation for forest beasts, as appears from a book written by king Alfonso el ultimo, called *Libro de Monteria del Rey Don Alonso*, in which that monarch extols the country near Madrid, for its shady situation and extensive woods, well adapted for hunting the stag, wild boar, and even of bears (*a*).

(*a*) Libro de Monteria por G. Argote de Molina 1582. This curious book was drawn up by the particular command of King Alfonso; Argote de Molina being only the editor. It contains three books, and is very serviceable for the right understanding the geography of Castile, and Leon in those days. Besides particular directions for breaking of dogs, and training them properly, there is a circumstantial detail of the various woods, and situations, proper for venary, and forest beasts, understood under the title of *Monteria*, such as the bear,

I shall not particularize the various improvements that have taken place of late years; however the new regulations and extension of commerce with their American colonies, are worthy of notice, particularly the open and free trade with each other granted in 1764, to the provinces of Peru, New Spain, Guatimala, and kingdom of Granada, in America. In order to render this plan more compleat, and facilitate the intercourse with Europe, eight packet boats for conveying letters were built at Coruna, one to sail the first day of every month, with a mail for the Havana. Accordingly the first packet named the *Cortes*, sailed for the Havana the 1st of November, 1764. Five packet boats were established to sail from the Havana to Vera Cruz, from whence a post road was made as far as Mexico, with its necessary branches, and communications, with the different provinces; so that letters come every month from those distant places, and often sooner, than from European courts. At Porto Rico, four galliots were established for the correspondence of Terra Firma, and Peru, receiving the letters brought by the Coruna packet boats, and bringing back the answers, by which means they receive letters from Carthagena, and Santa Fe, as quickly as by

stag, wolf, and wild boar, which sport was the delight of Spanish princes, while they disregarded the beasts of the chace, such as the buck, fox, marten, and hare. His present Catholic majesty takes great pleasure in shooting wolves and wild cats.

the Havana. Two galliots were likewife ftationed at Carthagena, for the correfpondence between Porto Bello and Panama. To extend this advantage further to the fouthward, fix packet boats were appointed in 1767, to fail from Coruna to the river of Plate, and city of Buenos Ayres, from whence fix expreffes were to proceed annually with the letters for Peru and Chili, and other provinces of thofe extenfive dominions; all which has been conducted with fo much activity and fpirit, that communications have been opened over the famous *Cordillera* of Chili, between that kingdom and Peru, and a regular poft for letters kept up, in the moft remote jurifdictions; where, before that period, even the very idea or name of a poft-office was unknown. For the conducting of which, the general poft-office have 25 veffels; viz. 14 from the Coruna to the Havana, Montevideo and Buenos Ayres; 5 from the Havana to Vera Cruz; 4 from Porto Rico to Carthagena; and 2 from Carthagena to Porto Bello.

The Royal cabinet of natural hiftory, at Madrid, was opened to the public by his majefty's orders in 1775; a handfome houfe having been purchafed, of which the firft floor was appropriated for the royal academy of San Fernando, and the fecond for the purpofe of receiving an ample collection of natural curiofities, which had been collected in Paris by Don Pedro Davila (a) a native of Peru, which his majesty has accepted of, and appointed him director thereof; and was also at the charge of bringing them from Paris. Every thing is ranged with neatness and elegance, and the apartments are opened twice a week for the public, besides being shewn privately to strangers of rank.

The collection of beasts and birds, at present is not large, but may be supposed to improve apace, if they take care to get the productions of their American colonies. They have the skeleton of an elephant that died lately at Madrid; also a little American ox stuffed, called Zebu, by Mr. de Buffon, and Zebulo by the Spaniards. The great Ant bear from Buenos Ayres, the Myrmecophaga Jubata of Linneus, called by the Spaniards *Oso Palmera*, was alive at Madrid in 1776, and is now stuffed and preserved in this cabinet. The people who brought it from Buenos Ayres, say, it differs from the ant-eater, which only feeds on emmets and other insects; whereas this would eat flesh, when cut in small pieces, to the amount of four or five pounds. From the snout to the extremity of the tail this animal is two yards in length, and his height is about two feet. The head very narrow, the nose long, and slender. The tongue is so singular, that it looks more like a

(a) See catalogue des curiosités du cabinet de Davila. 3 tomes, avec figures. Paris, 1767.

a worm,

Ursa Palmara Hymenopelaga Inlula Sam
The GREAT ANT BEAR — from BUENOS AYRES.

a worm, and extends above sixteen inches. His body is covered with long hair, of a dark brown, with white stripes on the shoulders; and when he sleeps he covers his body with his tail.

The mineral part of the cabinet, containing precious stones, marbles, ores, &c. is very perfect. Amongst other curiosities they have a grain of gold of 22 carats, which weighed sixteen marks, four ounces, four ochavos, Spanish weight, found in California, and sent by the viceroy of Mexico as a present worthy of his majesty's acceptance (a); also several curious specimens of silver ore, from the Guadalcanal mine in Estremadura, of that sort called *Rosicler*.

Specimens of Mexican and Peruvian utensils, vases, &c. in earthenware of that kind, which the Spaniards call *Barro*, wretched both in taste and execution. Some productions likewise of Otaheite, which the Spaniards call amath.

A curious collection of vases, basons, ewers, cups, plates, and ornamental pieces of the finest agates, amethysts, rock crystals, &c. mounted in gold, and enamel;

(a) A curious treatise, now very scarce, was published at Mexico, by the viceroy, in June 1771, intitled Noticia Breve de la Expedicion Militar de Sonora y Cinaleo, fu Exito felix y ventajoso estado, en que por consequencia de ello se ha puesto ambas provincias. See a further account of this expedition in Robertson's history of America. Note LXV, vol. 9.

set with cameos, intaglios, &c. in an elegant taste, and the most delicate workmanship, said to have been brought from France by Philip the fifth. There is likewise a valuable collection of books and prints daily adding to the cabinet by the said Don Pedro Davila.

Were painting and sculpture my objects, this would be the place to describe the many fine pictures in the royal palace and in the noblemen's houses at Madrid; but I pass them over in silence the more readily, as modern travellers have described the most beautiful of these pictures. I shall just observe that a late writer who spent some time at Madrid, speaking of the church of the visitation, called *Las Salesas*, where the late king Ferdinand and his queen are interred, tells us, that at the principal altar, there is a fine copy of Raphael's transfiguration; whereas it happens to be a good picture of the visitation, in allusion to the name of the church, and done by Francisco de Muro at Naples. It is true a most excellent copy of Raphael's transfiguration may be seen at another church belonging to the convent of St. Teresa, placed there by the founder, the Prince de Astillana, who considered it as an original of Raphael, and valued it at ten thousand pistoles (about £7000). It is supposed to have been done by Julio Romano, the ablest and favourite scholar of Raphael. The same writer speaking of the pictures in the palace

of

of Buen Retiro in the saloon, named *De los Reynos*, calls one picture " Santa Cruz succouring Geneva"; whereas it is the surrender of Genoa to that officer, being placed amongst other historical pieces of the times, which are termed by him, "Scripture subjects of the old testament."

That beautiful equestrian statue of Philip the 4th, by Tacca of Florence, which stands in a little flower garden of the Retiro, is worthy of the highest admiration. The attitude of the horse is surprisingly bold, with both his fore feet in the air; and was imitated from a picture of Velasquez, sent to Italy for that purpose. When seen by the Florentine artists, they all agreed it was impossible to execute it; however Tacca with the assistance of Galileo happily applied the principles of equilibrium, and succeeded beyond expectation. This unfortunate artist died soon after of grief from the treatment he received from the grand duke's minister, concerning this statue, but his eldest son Ferdinand came to Madrid, and fixed the parts together, which were three in number, and placed the statue properly. Six hundred and fifty six quintals of 128 lb. of metal each, were employed in the casting. Its height, including the pedestal, is 84 palmos (19 feet 9 inches English) (a). In an inventory of the effects of the Retiro, it was valued at forty thousand pistoles (£. 28.000) an enormous sum, and

(a) A Spanish palmo eight inches and a quarter.

much

much more than it could ever have coſt. It was propoſed a few years ago to remove this ſtatue to ſome more conſpicuous place, but it is ſaid to have been objected to, by the then prime miniſter Marquis de Grimaldi, alledging that they muſt not pay any attention to the houſe of Auſtria, but he would have no objection if the head of Philip could be changed, for that of Charles the third.

Tacca alſo finiſhed the equeſtrian ſtatue of Philip the third in the Caſa del Campo, left imperfect by John de Bologna, at his death, and was brought to Madrid in 1616, by Antonio Guidi, brother in law to Tacca, attended by Andrew Tacca, another brother of the ſculptor, who brought with him the gilt metal crucifix fixed on the altar of the Pantheon at the Eſcurial. The mention of the Retiro has naturally led me into the agreeable gardens of that palace, and to the menagerie, where, amongſt other curioſities, they have a creſted falcon from the Carraccas. This curious bird, which is about the ſize of a turkey, raiſes his feathers on his head in the form of a creſt, and has a hooked bill; the lower mandible rather ſtraight; his back, wings, and throat are black, the belly white, the tail diſtinguiſhed by four cinereous, and parallel ſtripes, and is an undeſcript bird not taken notice of by Linneus.

LETTER

The CRESTED FALCON From the CARRACCAS, alive in 1778, in the Menagerie of Buen Retiro, at Madrid.

LETTER VIII.

Description of the palace and gardens of Aranjuez.

THE royal seat of Aranjuez, seven leagues distant from Madrid, and to which a most noble road has lately been made, is delightfully situated at the conflux of the rivers Tagus and Jarama; which run through the gardens, and add new beauty to this charming spot, where art and nature seem to go hand in hand with the most pleasing and rural simplicity. On one side, fine avenues of stately oaks and lofty elms, convey the truest ideas of magnificence, while they afford the most reviving shade; on the other, the sudden transitions to lawns and wilderness, the cascades of water breaking through the thickets, the tuneful songs of numberless birds, sheltered in these cool recesses, the occasional appearance and passage of the monarch, attended by the grandees of his kingdom; all these objects united, and concentered in one point, fill the imagination with pleasing ideas, and impress the mind of a traveller with a thousand agreeable sensations, particularly in the spring, when every thing is in high bloom and perfection, and engage him to look at Aranjuez as one of the most beautiful places in Europe.

The whole of these gardens may be thrown into three grand divisions, distinguished by the names of *La Huerta Valenciana* (a), *Los Delcites*, and *El Cortijo*. In the Huerta Valenciana, agriculture and gardening are carried on in the same manner as in that fruitful province, and they plough with horses. In the Cortijo they use oxen, as in Andalusia; and in other places they scratch up the ground with mules as is still practised in some parts of Spain. Which ever way one looks round, a constant variety pleases the eye and enraptures the mind. At one moment the sturdy buffalo moves before you, drawing his heavy burthen; soon after, the slow camel with his ponderous load; while the swift Zebra with his striped garment frisks over the plains. If you approach the farm, every object of convenience is consulted, and in the dairy every degree of neatness. The Dutch cow enjoys a luxuriant pasture, the brood mares greatly enliven the landscape, and the stables are filled with the most excellent horses. An immense nursery furnishes all manner of trees and plants, a cedar of Libanus, which

---

(a) By the term of Huerta is understood that kind of inclosure we call an orchard, but with a greater variety of cultivation. When they speak of an ornamented flower garden near a palace or nobleman's house, the Spanish term is *jardin*, the same as in French.

about twenty years ago was only a twig, is now thirty feet high: the garden called the *Isla* is particularly beautiful and rural. The Judas tree, which the Spaniards call *Arbol de Amor*, being happily difperfed there, has a very good effect early in the fpring, when covered with flowers without a fingle leaf; the banks of the Ifla are further enlivened by elegant yachts, for the amufement of the royal family. The fine avenue which alfo ferves for a public walk, called *Calle de la Reyna* has nothing equal to it at Verfailles. The extenfive flower garden on one fide, renders the walk extremely pleafant in an evening; and were I to mention the quantities of flowers and fruit, it would require many details. A great many elms and oaks have been planted this year, (1778) faid to be 101.000, which muft likewife include vines, olives, fhrubs, &c. They have lately begun to cultivate pine apples, unknown in every other part of the kingdom.

At the noon-tide hour, when the frefhnefs of the morning is paft, the fhady walks near the palace then become an object of fingular luxury, as well as the elegant fountains, whofe fportive waters give fuch a coolnefs to the air. Whoever has enjoyed the agreeable moments that pafs in pleafing converfe under thefe fhady bowers, will furely be charmed with their admirable effect, independent of every idea of modern improvements

ments, or criticifm upon fountains and water works. The nightingale and cuckow are heard here the latter end of April. That elegant bird the bee eater, called by the Spaniards *Abejaruxo*, the merops apiafter of Linnæus, which our travellers tell us comes no further South than Andalufia, is known not only to breed at Aranjuez and live there all the year round, but is alfo found at St. Ildefonfo, which is 20 leagues more to the northward. The golden thrufh is alfo feen here, a beautiful bird with a bright yellow plumage, the icterus of Edwards, called *oropendula* by the Spaniards, and *l'auriot* by the French, the oriolus of Catefby and Linnæus. Amidft the great variety of birds in thefe woods, there is one about the fize of a cuckow, called *Pito*, of a beautiful purple. Such a diverfity of objects could not fail to excite the genius and fire of the Spanifh writers; for my part I willingly join with that elegant poet Don Gomez de Zapia, who has fo naturally defcribed them, in a poem, of which the following lines are the beginning:

> En lo mejor de la felice Efpana
> Do el Rio Tajo tertia fu corrida,
> Y con fus criftalinas aguas bana
> La tierra, entre las tierras efcojida,
> Efta una Vega de belleza eftrana!
> Toda de verde yerba entretejida,
> Donde natura y arte en competencia,
> Lo ultimo pufieron de potencia (a).

(a) Parnaffo Efpanol Tom 3. Madrid 1773.

The Palace being an old building with several additions is more in the style of a hunting seat, as Philip the second designed it, than of a royal mansion, nor is there any thing very particular in the apartments, to take off from the enjoyment of so many fine objects abroad. The new wings to the Palace are finished; in one is a play house, and in the other a chapel. Part of the cieling of the former was painted by Mengs, who is now (1779) at Rome painting a holy family for the principal altar in the chapel.

There are seven fine pictures of Luca Jordano in the apartment called *El Cabinete Antiguo*, and six others in that *de los Mayordomos*; particularly one, is universally admired, in which a number of beasts are represented listening to Orpheus, and seeming to be struck with the melody of his lyre. The portraits of the grand Duke and Dutchess of Tuscany by Mengs, are in a new apartment called the king's dressing room. In the chapel, over the great altar there is a fine picture of the Annunciation by Titian, presented by him to Charles the fifth, and brought from the convent of Juste after the death of that Emperor. The Porcelain Cabinet where there are several large pieces of the king's own Manufactory, is also an object of curiosity to a traveller. In a word, this charming place is highly indebted to Charles the third for bringing the whole to its present state of beauty, and making the new road from Madrid, and the noble stone bridge over the Jarama: if the design is continued of planting trees on each side of the road, it will add greatly to its magnificence.

A topographical plan of Aranjuez and the improvements there, has been executed by Don Domingo de Aguirre, captain of engineers, in sixteen sheets, and the views in eight more. In short, these rural places have so many charms, that they cannot fail of pleasing every fancy, and meeting universal acceptation, as Lupercio Leonardo de Argensola has happily expressed it, in a little poem in praise of these gardens.

> Qualquiera aqui su condicion aplica,
> Aunque su origen trayga de otra parte,
> Do el sol menos, o mas se comunica!

But this is only to be understood with respect to the proper season of the year, suited to its situation, for as it lies in a bottom surrounded with mountains, the air is of course confined, which added to the great quantity of water, and numerous plantations, makes it agueish when the hot weather begins, for which reason the court generally removes about the end of May, and goes soon after to St. Ildefonso, which is a very high situation amongst the mountains of Guadarrama, where they

they begin a new spring and breathe a clear refreshing air during the scorching heats of summer.

Great quantities of liquorice grow wild near the road between Aranjuez and Toledo, as well as on the banks of the Tagus, where one also finds those curious reeds made use of by the Romans for writing, and celebrated by Martial, in an epigram addressed to Macer, who had been pretor in Spain.

> Nos Celtas, Macer, et truces Iberos,
> Cum desiderio tui petemus,
> Sed quocumque tamen feretur, illic
> Piscosi Calamo Tagi, notata
> Macrum, pagina nostra nominabit,   Lib. x.

The castle of Aceca dependent on the jurisdiction of Aranjuez though kept in good order, is more taken notice of on account of its former reputation, and antiquity, than from any other circumstance. Its district is supposed to have belonged formerly to a colony of Jews from Toledo, and so named from *azeba* in Palestine peopled by Joshua (a). There is no doubt that the Jews were in great repute in Spain in the early ages, insomuch that in 686, under the gothic king Ervigius, they had the boldness to assert, and endeavoured to persuade the king, that the Messiah was not come. Their de-

(a) Kings. Book 1. chap. 17.

scendants several years afterwards propagated fables, to prove their great antiquity in Spain, and in order to lessen the reproaches thrown on them by the Spaniards, they gave out, that they were not descended from those Jews who crucified our Saviour (*a*).

(*a*) Sandoval, bishop of Pamplona, relates, that when king Alfonso conquered the city of Toledo, he found it full of Jews, who shewed to that monarch two letters in Hebrew and Arabic, sent from the synagogue of Jerusalem to that of Toledo, giving them an account of Jesus Christ, and asking their opinion whether they should put him to death; also the answer of the Toledo Jews, dissuading them from it. These letters were ordered to be translated from Hebrew into Arabic by Galifre king of Toledo, and into Latin and Spanish by king Alfonso, and were preserved in the archives of Toledo till 1494. They were translated by Julian, archpriest of St. Just, and were afterwards in several hands. The answer of the Spanish Jews is dated Toledo 14th of the month Nisan, era of Cæsar 18, and of Augustus Octavianus 71. I know nothing further concerning the authenticity of this letter, says the bishop of Pamplona, than that it was found in the archives of Toledo, and in the same style and language in which I have given it. Historia de los Reyes de Castilla y Leon por Don fr. Prudencio de Sandoval obispo de Pamplona. En Pamplona 1615.

LETTER

LETTER IX.

Description of the baths and mineral waters of Trillo.

NO country abounds so much as Spain with hot baths and most excellent mineral waters, and they are now beginning to investigate their qualities. Those of Trillo have of late particularly engaged the attention of government, and we have been more accurately informed of their virtues and properties. The village of Trillo, in New Castile, is seventeen leagues from Madrid, by the new road lately made to that place, situated on the north banks of the Tagus, two leagues south of the city of Siguenza. The village of La Puerta is about a league to the eastward, and the town of Gualda much about the same distance to the westward. The country is hilly, and affords little corn or fruit, some few vineyards, and plenty of game. The Tagus abounds in fish, such as trout, eels, and barbel; has a stone bridge of one arch over it, of a solid structure, and considerable antiquity, being there when the first investigations were made about this place in 1558(a). A little river runs

(a) Particular mention is made of Trillo by Ambrosio Morales. Antiquedades de las Ciudades de Espana. Alcala de Henares, 1575.

from Cifuentes, which enters the Tagus at Trillo, and was once famous for its curious water mills, for sawing of timber brought down by the stream, which was the chief branch of industry of the inhabitants; but in the year 1710, on the 30th of December, they were visited by 1400 of the English army then serving in Spain, in favour of the archduke of Austria, who having staid there seven days, raised considerable contributions, and were succeeded by 8000 Portuguese their allies, under the Count de Atalaya, who ravaged the country, and pillaged the place: of the three saw mills, only one was left standing, which has since become useless. The inhabitants dwindled in numbers, and the few that remained, from a state of affluence and ease, experienced the extremity of poverty and distress; though in a situation, where the climate is remarkably temperate, the air pure, provisions plentiful, their mutton singularly excellent, and a fine spring of soft water runs near the village.

The baths are up the river on the opposite side of the Tagus, about the distance of a mile, with an agreeable road to them, made from the foot of the bridge, with an avenue of trees, through a pleasant district, well shaded with wood, where the warbling of nightingales, and the musical notes of various other song birds, delight the invalid, and welcome his approach to these salutary baths. Inns are now building for the reception of company,

pany, and every effort is made for the convenience of the infirm. The waters have been analyzed with exactness, a deputation having been appointed by command of the king, to conduct every thing with the utmost formality, under the direction of Don Miguel Maria de Nava, Dean of the council and chamber of Castile, assisted by Dr. Casimir Ortega, F. R. S. and royal professor of Botany at Madrid, who has published the proceedings of this assembly held at Trillo; and from his elegant treatise I have selected the following information (a).

These baths are situated at a small distance from the banks of the river, in a meadow, at the brow of a hill, which by its situation to the eastward, affords a refreshing shade the greater part of the morning. The baths are divided in the following manner.

Los Quatro Banos, called the king's bath, divided into four separate baths, all equally commodious, and handsome, with their proper appertenances.

(a) Tratado de las Aguas Termales de Trillo escrito de orden del Rey por el Dr. Casimiro Ortega, Madrid, 1778.——The ingenious and learned Dr. Ortega was in England a few years ago, and is well known to several gentlemen in this country. Besides the waters of Trillo, those of Ribas, at a small distance from the mountain of Nuestra Senora de Nuria, near the Pyrenees of Cataluna, are greatly resorted to in the spring, and autumn, for gravelly complaints, as is also the fountain of Paterna, in the Alpujarra mountains of Granada, called "*Aguas agrias*," "Acidulous waters."

The Countess's Bath, so named after the lady of the Count de Cifuentes, who is lord of the place, is close to the river, but judiciously built and remarkably solid, to resist every impulse of the stream, and equally decorated with every convenience and advantage.

The bath of the *Piscina* is about four hundred paces from the king's bath, and has acquired this appellation from being chiefly made use of, by the poor, who are most subject to cutaneous complaints, for which purpose this bath is remarkably efficacious. A dwelling-house is now building for the use of the bathers, with every distribution of apartments and convenience, requisite for a place of this nature : also, for a greater embellishment of the baths, they have planted round them that beautiful and odoriferous tree sent thither from the royal botanic garden at Madrid, by the name of robinia pseudo acacia. In Spanish *falso aromo*. (The false acacia.)

Dr. Ortega, after referring us to Macquer, and other eminent chemists, who all agree, that the analysis of waters, is the most difficult operation of chemistry, as it tends to discover that union, which nature by slow and secret steps, forms in water, and other substances, in its most occult and abstruse motions ; proceeds to his analysis of the waters of Trillo, after some strictures and criticisms on the writings of Dr. Limon Montero, on the mineral waters of Spain, published at the close of

the

the last century, intitled "Espejo Cristalino de todas las Aguas Minerales de Espana." And after denying them any nitrous, aluminous, or sulphureous qualities, as asserted by Dr. Limon, he closes his analysis with the following corollary:

"That these waters participate of five substances, two volatile, and three fixed; viz. a phlogistic vapour, extremely anodyne, penetrating, and friendly to the nervous system; of a moderate quantity of gas, calcareous earth, common salt, and selenetic salt; and that to each pound of water of sixteen ounces, one may calculate twenty-five grains and an half, of fixed principle. This computation was made on a considerable evaporation of water, of about a quintal (*a*), which was judged to be the best method, as less liable to errour, than those experiments with small quantities. It was also considered, that of the twenty-five grains and an half, of fixed principle, corresponding to each pound of mineral water, near fourteen grains are common salt, about three of selenetic salt, and about eight and an half, of absorbent earth; which for greater exactness we shall express in this manner;

  13 $\frac{707}{1000}$ grains common salt.
  2 $\frac{215}{1000}$ grains selenetic salt.
  8 $\frac{478}{1000}$ grains absorbent earth.

(*a*) A Spanish quintal 97 pound English.

The same proportions, with a very trifling deviation, were also found by Don Manuel Joachim Enriquez de Paiva, royal demonstrator of the chemical laboratory at Coimbra in Portugal.

Dr. Ortega observes, that the lightness of this water is so great, as even to enter into competition with that of distilled water, the purest we know of; therefore its effects will be the more easily accounted for: that the heat of the water, does not equal that of the blood, in a person in good health, and comes near to that tepid degree, prescribed by the physicians in artificial baths.

The bath of the princess is the most efficacious, or at least abounds most with phlogiston, and of course is better suited to those disorders where the efficacy of this principle is desired. The king's bath, and that of the countess have scarcely any phlogistic vapour, which variety makes them still more pleasing to the bathers, and applicable to different complaints; while the Piscina bath abounds chiefly with phlogiston, and is admirably suited to the disorders of the poor, as already observed: finally the two principles of gas, and of phlogiston, are of so volatile a nature in these waters, that a remarkable difference is observed betwixt the well, and the bath, by those who drink them immediately from the spring,

spring, or at a distance; which shews how much it evaporates by carriage; for which reason it should not be filled in earthen pitchers, but only in bottles or flasks, well corked, and carefully sealed. This is the substance of a public oration pronounced by Dr. Ortega, before a numerous assembly at Trillo, and afterwards published by authority of the council at Castile, in virtue of their decree for that purpose, bearing date the 11th of April 1778, to which are added a few trifling cases, with that of the dean of the council, Don Miguel Maria de Nava, at the head of them, who found great benefit from these waters, and presided at this pompous assembly, attended by the Count de Cifuentes, a grandee of Spain, and many other noblemen and gentlemen of rank, as well as several eminent physicians, surgeons, and apothecaries, who all concur in the praises of Trillo, and set their names to the facts there related.

I shall only select one case, inserted by Dr. Ortega, and taken by him verbatim from Dr. Mendoza, physician at Cifuentes, written at Trillo so early as the 18th of July, 1714, adorned with a copper-plate, representing the virgin Mary as protectress of the waters, being one of the first cures, which brought them into repute.

" A friar

"A friar of the congregation of St. Philip De Neri, was troubled with ulcers in his legs, the remains of a malignant eryfipelas, and an abfcefs in the bone of the right clavicle, which having been opened by the perfon who attended him, terminated after a long and painful procefs, in a fiftula. An ill-conditioned abfcefs of a great fize, was difcovered at the fame time, fituated on the laft right rib, which was deemed very dangerous to open. He had alfo a tumour feated in the right axilla, another on the left hand, and others on the fhoulders, a pain in the fide, a hectic fever, fhortnefs of breath, painful refpiration, and a fallow complexion, with conftant faintings and vapours, which flew to the head, and often occafioned a fyncope. Having fuffered thus, for two years, and all the remedies having failed, which are called human, he came to Trillo, drank the waters, ufed the baths, and voided a great deal of fand. The ulcers being healed, though for fome time the hectic did not fubfide, he returned the following feafon to repeat the ufe of the waters and baths; and was perfectly cured, fo as to go home without a fiftula, tumours, or pain in the fide; his refpiration recovered, with a healthy and florid complexion; and finally with fo much natural vigour, that even the iffues which he had been advifed to have made, could not be kept open, notwithftanding

" withstanding every endeavour for that purpose. The
" witnesses of this case were Dr. Aquenza, Dr. Porras,
" and the king's first surgeon Monsieur Legendre."

I now close this narrative with a list of such plants as
Dr. Ortega tells us he found in the environs of Trillo (a).

ACER Monspessulanum	*Montpelier maple*
Achillea ageratum	*Sweet maudlin milfoil*
* Achillea millefolium	*Milfoil yarrow*
* Adiantum capillus veneris	*True maiden hair*
* Agrimonia eupatorium	*Common agrimony*
* Agrostemma githago	*Corn cockle*
Allium descendens	- - - - *Garlic*
Allium victoriales	*Broad leaved garlic*
Allium paniculatum	- - - - - -
Alsine segetalis	*Corn chick weed*
Althæa cannabina	*Hemp leaved marsh mallow*
* Althæa officinalis	*Common marsh mallow*
Alyssum saxatile	*Yellow mountain madwort*
Anagallis monelli	*Blue flowered Pimpernel*
Androsace maxima	*Androsace with the largest empalement*
Anemone hepatica	*Single hepatica*
* Anthyllis vulneraria	*Double headed ladies finger*
Antirrhinum bellidifolium	*Daisie leaved snap dragon*

(a) Those marked with an asterisk are likewise natives of this country, the English names of which are adopted from " A Botanical arrangement of all the vegetables naturally growing in Great-Britain, with descriptions of their genera and species, according to the system of the celebrated Linnæus, &c." By William Withering, M. D. Birmingham, 1776.

Antirrhinum junceum	Rush leaved snap dragon
* Antirrhinum majus	Snap dragon toad flax
Antirrhinum saxatile	Snap dragon
Aphyllanthes Monspelliensis	- - - - - -
Apium petroselinum	Common parsley
* Aquilegia vulgaris	Common columbine
* Arbutus uva ursi	Perennial leaved strawberry tree
Aristologia longa	Long birthwort
Aristologia pistolochia	Scallop leaved birthwort
Asclepias nigra	Black swallow wort
* Asparagus sativa officinalis	Cultivated sparagus
Asparagus silvestris	Wild sparagus
* Asperugo procumbens	Goosegrass madwort
* Asperula cynanchica	Squinancy woodroof
* Asplenium ceterach	Common spleenwort
* Asplenium rutamuraria	White spleenwort
* Asplenium trichomanes	Green spleenwort
Atractyllis cancellata	- - - - Distaff thistle
* Bellis perennis	Common daisy
Berberis dumetorum	- - - - Barberry
Biscutella didyma	Buckler mustard with a double orbicular pod
* Borrago officinalis	Common borrage
* Bryonia alba	White briony
Buplevrum frutiscens	Shruby thorough wax
Buplevrum rigidum	- - - - Hare's ear
* Buplevrum rotundi folium	Round leaved thorough wax
* Buplevrum tenuissimum	Fine leaved thorough wax
* Buxus sempervirens	Tree box

* Campanula

* Campanula rapunculus	*Rampion bell flower*
Campanula stricta	*Bell flower with a stalk branching at the bottom*
Catananche coerulea	*Blue candy lion's foot*
Caucalis grandiflora	*Bastard parsley*
* Centaurea calcitrapa	*Starry knapweed*
* Centaurea cyanus	*Blue bottle knapweed*
* Centaurea nigra	*Black knapweed*
Cheiranthus tristis	*Stock gilly flower*
* Chenopodium murale	*Sow bane bite*
* Chlora perfoliata	*Yellow centaury*
* Chrysanthemum leucanthemum	*Daisy goldins*
* Cichorium intybus	*Wild endive*
* Conium maculatum	*Spotted hemlock*
Cistus albidus	*- - - - Cistus*
Cistus incanus	*Honey leaved cistus*
Cistus fumana	*- - - - - -*
* Cistus marifolius	*Hoary cistus*
Cistus populifolius	*Poplar leaved cistus*
Cistus umbellatus	*- - - - -*
Clematis viorna	*Virgin's bower*
Cleonia Lusitancia	*- - - - -*
Colutea arborescens	*Common bladder sena*
* Convallaria polygonatum	*Odoriferous bellwort*
Convolvolus terrestris	*Bindweed*
Coris Monspelliensis	*Montpelier coris. We have no English name for this plant.*
Coronilla coronata	*Jointed bodied coluthea*
Coronilla juncea	*- - - - Coluthea*
Cotyledon Hispanica	*- - - - -*

Croton

Croton tinctorium
Cynoglossum cherisolium
* Cynoglossum officinale — Stinking hound's tongue
Cytisus argenteus — Low silvery cytisus

* Daphne Thymelæa — Spurge laurel, or mezereon
* Daucus carota silvestris — Wild carrot
Daucus visnaga
Dictamnus albus — White fraxinella
Digitalis obscura — - - - Foxglove
* Dipsacus silvestris — Clothiers teazle

Echinops sphaerocephalus — Greater globe thistle
* Echium vulgare — Common vipergrass.
Ephedra destachia — Shruby horsetail
* Epilobium hirsutum — Hairy willow herb
* Equisetum fluviatile — River horsetail
* Equisetum palustre — Marsh horsetail
Erigeron tuberosum — - - - -
* Erysimum Barbarea — Rocket wormseed
* Euphorbia characias — Red spurge

Ficus carica — Figtree
* Fraxinus excelsior — Common ash
Fumaria enneaphylla — Nineleaved fumitory
* Fumaria officinalis — Common fumitory

* Gallium uliginosum — Marsh goosegrass
* Gallium aparine — Cleaver's goosegrass
* Gentiana centaurium — Centaury gentian
* Geranium cicutarium — Hemlock leaved cranesbill

* Geranium

*Geranium sanguineum	*Bloody cranesbill*
Geum montanum	*Mountain avens*
*Geum urbanum	*Avens bennet*
Globularia spinosa	- - - - -
*Glechoma hederacea	*Groundivy gill*
Glycyrrhiza glabra	*Smooth liquorice*
*Gnaphalium luteo album	*Jersey cudweed*
*Hedera helix	*Common ivy*
Hedysarum humile	- - - - -
Heliotrophium vulgare	*Common turnsol*
*Herniaria hirsuta	*Rough rupture wort*
Hieracium multicaule	- -·- - *Hawkweed*
Hieracium murorum	*Golden hawkweed*
*Hieracium pilosella	*Mouse ear hawkweed*
*Hippocrenis comosa	*Tufted horse shoe*
Hyssopus officinalis	*Common hyssop*
*Humulus lupulus	*Brewer's hop*
Illecebrum paronychia	*Spanish knot grass*
Inula montana	*Mountain elecampane*
Inula oculus christi	- - - - *Elecampane*
*Iris pseudoacorus	*Yellow flag*
Jasminum fruticans	*Shrubby yellow jessamine*
Juglans regia	*Wallnut*
*Juncus acutus	*Marine rush*
Juniperus oxycedrus	*Great Spanish juniper*
Juniperus Phœnicia	*Phœnician juniper*
*Juniperus communis	*Common juniper.*

Lavandula

Lavandula spica	Spike lavender
*Lepidium latifolium	Pepper ditander
Lepidium nasturtium aquaticum	- - - - ditander
*Ligustrum vulgare	Common privet
Linum gallicum	- - - - flax
Linum narbonense	- - - - flax
Linum suffruticosum	Shruby flax
Lithospermum fruticosum	Shruby gromwell
Lonicera caprifolium	White honeysuckle
Lotus dorycinium	- - - - Birdsfoot trefoil
Lotus siliquosus	- - - - - -
Lotus tetragonolobus	- - - - - -
Lysimachia ephemerum	- - - - Loose strife
*Lysimachia vulgaris	Yellow loose strife
Malva sylvestris	Common Mauls
Malva tournefortiana	- - - - - -
Medicago polymorpha orbicularis	- - - - -
*Mentha aquatica	Water mint
*Mercurialis annua	French mercury
Mercurialis tomentosa	Woolly mercury
Mespilus amelanchier	Alpine vespillus
Nigella arvensis	- - - - Fennel flower
*Oenanthe fistulosa	Water dropwort
Olea Europaea	Olive
Ononis mitissima	Smooth restharrow
Ononis natrix	Yellow restharrow
*Ononis spinosa	Thorny restharrow
Ononis tridentata	Three thorned restharrow

Ononis

Ononis viscosa	Clammy restharrow
*Ophrys spiralis	Triple twaye blador
*Origanum vulgare	Wild marjoram
*Orobanche major	Great broom rape
*Papaver rhæas	Corn poppy
*Parietaria officinalis	Wall pellitory
*Pedicularis sylvatica	Common louse wort
Phillyrea angustifolia	Narrow leaved phillyrea
Phlomis herba venti	Herbaceous Jerusalem sage
Phlomis lychnitis	- - - - -
Physalis alkekengi	Winter cherry
Pistacia terebinthus	Common turpentine tree
Plantago albicans	White plantain
*Plantago major	Great plantain
*Plantago maritima	Sea plantain
Plantago psyllium	Branching plantain
Plumbago Europæa	Common leadwort
Polygala Monspelliaca	Montpelier milkwort
*Polygonum convolvulus	Binding snakeweed
*Polygonum persicaria	Spotted snakeweed
*Populus alba	Abele poplar
Portulaca oleracea	- - - - purslaine
*Potentilla verna	Spring cinquefoil
*Poterium sanguisorba	Burnet ironwort
Prunella hyssopifolia	Hyssop leaved selfheal
Prunella laciniata	Jagged selfheal
*Prunella vulgaris	Common selfheal
Psoralea bituminosa	Three-leaved Jupiter's beard
Punica granatum	Pomegranate

Quercuo

Quercuo ilex	Evergreen oak
*Ranunculus acris	Upright crowfoot
Reseda luteola	Dyer's yellow weed
Reseda phyteuma	Rampion yellow weed
Rhamnus alaturnus	Alaturnus
Rhamnus catharticus	Purging buckthorn
Rhamnus pyrenaicus	---- Buckthorn
Rhus coriaria	Myrtle-leaved shumach
Rosmarinus officinalis	Common rosemary
Rubia tinctorum	Dyer's madder
*Rumex acutus	Sharp pointed dock
Ruta graveolens	Broad leaved rue
Ruta linifolia	Narrow leaved rue
*Salix rosmarini folia	Rosemary willow
*Salix helix	Rose willow
Salvia ceratophylla	------
Salvia officinalis	Garden sage
Salvia sclarea	Clary sage
Salvia viridis	Green sage
*Sambucus ebulus	Dwarf elder
*Sambucus nigra	Common elder
*Samolus valerandi	Pempernel marshwort
Scabiosa integrisolia	---- Devilsbit
Scabiosa stellata	Starry devilsbit
Scorzonera Hispanica	Scorzonera
*Scrophularia aquatica	Water figwort
Scrophularia canina	Dog's figwort
*Sedum album	White stonecrop
*Senecio vulgaris	Common groundsel

" Serapias

*Serapias longifolia	*Long leaved helleborine*
Sideritis hirsuta	*Hairy trailing ironwort*
Sideritis incana	- - - - -
Sideritis scordivides	- - - - -
*Silene nutans	*Nottingham catchfly*
*Solanum dulcamara	*Woody nightshade*
Solanum lycoperficon	*Love apple*
*Solidago virga aurea	*Common golden rod*
*Sonchus alpinus	*Blue sowthistle*
*Sparganium erectum	*Great bur reed.*
Spartum scoperium	*Common broom*
*Spiræa filipendula	*Dropwort meadowsweet*
*Stachys alpina	*Mountain clownheel*
*Statice armeria	*Seathrift*
*Stipa capillata	*Fine feathergrafs*
*Stipa pennata	*Downy feathergrafs*
Symphytum tuberofum	*Comfryl*
Telephium imperati	*True orpine*
Teucrium capitatum	- - - - *Germander*
*Teucrium chamædrys	*Wall germander*
*Teucrium chamæpitys	*Ground germander*
Teucrium pseudochamæpitys	- - - - *germander*
*Teucrium scordium	*Water germander*
*Thalictum flavum	*Common meadow rue*
Thymus alpinus	*Mountain thyme*
Thymus mastichina	*Maftick thyme*
Thymus zygis	- - - - *thyme*
Tordilium apulum	*The leaft hartwort of Apulia*
*Tragopogon porrifolium	*Purple goatsbeard*

O   Tribulus.

Tribulus terrestris	Caltrop with chick leaf and prickly fruit
*Trifolium melilotus officinalis	Melilot trefoil
*Trifolium pratense	Honeysuckle trefoil
*Triglochin maritimum	Spiked arrowgrass
*Triglochin palustre	Marsh arrowgrass
*Tussilogo farfara	Coltsfoot butter bur
*Ulmus campestris	Common elm
*Valeriana calcitrapa	Valerian with leaves, like those of the star thistle
*Veronica anagallis aquatica	Pimpernel speedwell
*Veronica beccabunga	Brooklime speedwell
*Veronica hederifolia	Ivy leaved speedwell
*Verbascum Thapsus	Great mullein
*Verbena officinalis	Common vervain
*Viburnum lantana	Pliant meal tree
*Vinca major	Greater periwinkle
*Viola odorata	Sweet violet

Besides the above spontaneous plants, the following are cultivated in gardens;

Amygdalus persica	Peach tree
Cratægus oxyacantha	White hawthorn
Prunus domestica	Plumb prune
Prunus cerasus	Black cherry prune
Pyrus communis	Pear apple
Pyrus cydonia	Quince
Vitis vinifera	Vine

☞ Since the environs of Trillo had induced Dr. Ortega to give a catalogue of plants in that neighbourhood, it insensibly engages me to add a few words respecting the study of botany in that kingdom, which hitherto had made so little figure as to draw down very pointed reflections from Linnæus, who says, " Hispanicæ floræ nullæ nobis innotuerunt adeoque plantæ

Carthamus tinctorius	*Bastard saffron*
Linum usitatissimum	*Common Flax*

plantæ istæ rarissimæ in locis Hispaniæ fertilissimis minus detectæ sunt. Dolendum est, quod in locis, Europæ cultioribus tanta existat nostro tempore barbaries botanices! paucissimas istas plantas, quæ nobis in Hispania & Portugalia constant, debemus curiosæ classi iii. Tournefortio et paucis aliis." Linn. biblioth. botanica, part vii. florillæ § viii. Hisp. pag. 96. which tended greatly to raise the emulation of the Spaniards; and while that celebrated botanist was taking measures to obtain a permission for one of his pupils to travel through Spain, he received a message from the Spanish ambassador at the court of Stockholm, which greatly surprised him, as it intimated the desire of his Catholic majesty to have a botanist recommended by Linnæus. This appears to have been owing to some English gentlemen then at Madrid, and among them Robert More, Esq; F. R. S. who dining with the prime minister Don Joseph de Caravajal, had been asked their opinion of Spain by that minister, who perceiving that the remark of Linnæus was not without foundation, and being informed that a Spanish flora would turn out as new as it was rich, determined that his country should soon be free from such a reproach; this was afterwards communicated to Linnæus by Mr. More in his tour through Sweden, and accounted for the application above-mentioned. Peter Lœfling, the favorite scholar of Linnæus, was accordingly fixed upon for this expedition, and was received in Spain in the most gracious manner. His surprise was great to find many lovers of botany at Madrid, particularly Don Joseph Ortega, secretary to the physical academy, Don Juan Minuart, chief apothecary to the armies, Don Joseph Quer, first surgeon to the king, who had a splendid botanical garden, and a most elegant collection of plants, Don Christoval Velez, apothecary of the college of physicians, who was possessed of a choice collection of botanical books, with a grand hortus siccus, and had drawn up a flora Madritensis. Lœfling was greatly caressed by these gentlemen, and in return paid a handsome compliment to each, by calling four new plants after their names. Linnæus has taken these names into all the subsequent editions of his *genera* and *species plantarum*, and into the last edition of his *systema naturæ*. Lœfling staid about two years at Madrid, making occasional excursions, during which time he collected above 1300 distinct species of Spanish plants. By orders of the court he embarked at Cadiz, in the year 1754, for South America, where he unfortunately died, 22d Feb. 1756, and Linnæus published his letters. See Iter Hispanicum, Holmiæ, 1758; and a further account of Peter Lœfling's life and botanical writings, in the 2d vol. of Bossu's travels in Louisiana, translated by J. R. Forster, F. A. S. London, 1771.

LETTER X.

The royal seat and gardens of St. Ildefonso, with some account of the city of Segovia.

WHOEVER has seen the gardens of Aranjuez will not think it extraordinary that the sovereign of Spain should have another agreeable seat in the fertile dominions of his crown, but when a traveller has crossed the craggy and bleak mountains of Guadarrama, it will be a matter of singular surprise to behold one of the most dreary rocks embellished with an agreeable villa, where the mines of Mexico have been lavished to effect the alteration; such is the royal seat of St. Ildefonso; for in few parts of the world, the powers of art have been more strenuously exerted to correct the rugged state of nature, and convert a horrid rock into a sumptuous garden, decorated with beautiful fountains, throwing up water to a great height, like those of Versailles; while a variety of trees, brought from different parts of the world, furnish shady walks, in a spot unfavourable by nature to all kind of vegetation; shewing to what the art of man can attain, and fully evincing the efforts of Philip the Vth. who at the

the expence of millions of dollars changed a barren and solitary mountain, into one of the most desirable spots in his kingdom; yet not without those inconveniencies which all the power of art cannot conquer; for on account of its lofty situation, the night air, even after the hottest summer's day, is so piercing, that it makes precaution necessary, to guard against its sudden and pernicious effects. In other respects nothing can be more reviving during the summer heats, than the shade of these gardens, invigorating the languid courtier, whose spirits are further revived by the coolness of the groves, added to the most limpid water that eyes can behold, in some places flying up into the air, to an immense height, in others rolling down in torrents, which, when catched by the rays of the sun, seem like so many sheets of liquid silver, of a most amazing brightness. As the cold air of this place keeps every thing back, the king finds a new spring after he has left Aranjuez, while his subjects are dying with heat at Madrid. The earliest fruits are but just ripe in August at St. Ildefonso, carnations and roses then adorn the parterres; September is the season for strawberries, raspberries, currants, and barberries; and snow lies on the mountains till the beginning of June. Many springs run down from the summit, and sides of the mountains, and are collected into a considerable bason at the upper end of the garden, to which they have given the name of *El Mar*,

" the

" the fea ;" from whence they are diftributed to all the different fountains and water works, the whole garden being on a flope, about two miles in circumference. Other fprings with two brooks, form the little river Erefma, abounding in falmon trout, where the king often diverts himfelf with fifhing, under the fhade of thickets, beautifully variegated by the pencil of nature.

The dreary mountain at the top of thefe gardens, is a kind of rock compofed of clay and fine fand, which by degrees crumbling and mixing with rotten leaves and roots, forms that light coat of earth, which juft covers the rock, and gives nurture to the firs and other trees and fhrubs. The foot of the mountain is of granite, and ferves for building, fometimes for mill-ftones, though rather too foft for this purpofe, ftanding in need of frequent repairs. They get vegetative earth on the North fide, about a hundred paces from the green rails of the flower garden, which being further cherifhed by manure, is laid a foot high on the rock, and by dint of cultivation and care, they are enabled to raife flowers and fruits, whofe roots hardly touch the barren foil of the place.

Mr. Bowles informs us, That when the late queen mother lived at St. Ildefonfo, the Infant, Don Lewis, her fon, had an aviary in the gardens, filled with a great
variety

variety of beautiful birds; one place was allotted for woodcocks, where they lived for several years. In the middle of their cage a channel of spring water was introduced, which kept up a constant freshness of verdure; a fir tree, stood in the centre, surrounded with shrubs, and they were daily supplied with fresh clods of turf, full of worms, which, though they hid themselves ever so much therein, the bird would instantly discover by the smell, and driving in his long bill bring them immediately out, then raising his head towards the sky, and extending the worm gently the length of his bill, would let it slide down softly, without any appearance of deglutition; all which was performed with the utmost facility, as if totally unemployed, without ever missing its aim, and should the woodcock be killed at that moment, these nauseous worms would immediately contribute towards the forming a delicious repast at the most elegant tables.

The palace of St. Ildefonso has a noble collection of excellent pictures. In the gallery there are many fine statues bought at Rome, out of the collection of queen Christina of Sweden; amongst which the groupe of Castor and Pollux sacrificing, and a fawn, are undoubtedly the most beautiful. The statues in the garden are chiefly of marble of Granada, some few of marble of Carrara: there is nothing else remarkable except the

fine

fine looking glaſſes made in the king's glaſs houſe at St. Ildefonſo, which ſupplies all the palaces ; they have here the largeſt tables perhaps in the world for running plate glaſs. The greateſt being 145 inches by 85, and its weight 405 arrobes. The ſmaller is 120 inches by 75, and weighs 380. This curious art was firſt invented by the Sieur Abraham Thevart, who propoſed it to the court of Verſailles in 1688, and is performed much like the caſting of ſheet lead by the plumbers, by which means they are enabled to make glaſſes of double the dimenſions of thoſe, by the Venetian method of blowing, beſides other improvements.

At a ſmall diſtance from the palace, at a place called the *Mato*, near the powder magazine, there is a vein of quartz, which appears above ground, running from South to North for about half a league, till it enters and loſes itſelf in the oppoſite mountain. A piece of this quartz, of about ſix pounds, being cut, ſeemed very curious, being half tranſparent, and almoſt as fine as rock cryſtal, having a kind of ſtripe, four fingers broad, between two coats, of a darker quartz. On following this vein ſeveral pieces of the ſame quartz appeared covered with rock cryſtal of a milk colour, forming thoſe veins called by miners, " noble veins." Mr. Bowles acknowledges he did not more particularly examine, or make any eſſay in this place ; and yet he tells us, us, he conjectures, and infers that it is an unwrought mine of gold.

The environs of St. Ildefonso and particularly the foot of the mountain are covered with a remarkably fine sort of grass, to which they give the name of *cosquilla*, from its effect of tickling the hand when touched. The root is about eight inches long, cylindrical, and about the size of a pin, diminishing towards the point; in the middle of this root, which is smooth, the stem springs up, bearing small capsules at their points, inclosing the seed; in many places, and particularly at Segovia, they make use of it at Christmas for ornaments in the churches, to imitate verdure; also little brooms are made with it to sweep away dust; it likewise grows in abundance in the plain of Olmedo, and is seldom to be seen elsewhere.

It is only a few hours ride from St. Ildefonso to the city of Segovia. The naturalist will meet with many objects of curiosity in the environs of this city, observing its different species of marble, granite, limestone, clays, and three sorts of sand (*a*). It's famous Roman aqueduct remaining so perfect to this day, will prove the solidity of its materials, more effectually than

---

(*a*) Mr. Bowles enters into many details respecting the variety of sand, clays, &c. in the environs of Segovia, which, not being considered as universally interesting, are omitted.

P   long

long diſſertations. Monſieur Seguier's method of diſcovering the inſcription on the *Maiſon Quarree* at Nimes, the invention of which is originally due to that celebrated antiquary, Monſ. Peyreſc, might likewiſe ſerve to diſcover that, which was formerly on the aqueduct of Segovia, for the place of the inſcription, marks, and holes of the letters, are yet very viſible (a). This place is much dwindled at preſent from what it was formerly. The cathedral is handſome and has been lately repaired; the mint in this city only ſerves for copper: gold and ſilver are coined at Madrid and Seville. The alcazar or caſtle is curious and in a fine bold ſituation. The unfortunate Duke de Ripperda was confined here, they ſhew you the dark room, from whence he made his eſcape, and the broken lock on the door is ſtill in the ſame ſituation.

(a) The little ſquare in Segovia, from whence you have a principal view of the aqueduct, is called El Azoguejo de Segovia, as a diminitive of the Arabic word Zocq, which ſignifies a ſquare or a market-place. This place is mentioned in Don Quixote, and ignorant tranſlators, becauſe the Spaniſh word *azogue* alſo ſignifies quickſilver, call this place the Quickſilver Houſe of Segovia. Palpino, in his Spaniſh dictionary tells us, without any authority, that a market is ſo called, becauſe the people in it are continually moving like quickſilver.

LETTER

LETTER XI.

Departure from Madrid for the city of Burgos.

ON leaving Madrid, to go into Old Castile, the first grand objects which strike the eye of a naturalist, are the mountains of Guadarrama, that divide the two Castiles; you leave the famous Escurial on the left, and following the new road, ascend these lofty mountains, whose tops, and particularly where the marble lion stands, are chiefly covered with fern, which is common here, though scarce in other parts of this country. From the highest part of the road, there is an extensive prospect of Old Castile, which is more elevated than New Castile, and forms a spacious plain not unlike a great sea. An easy descent leads to the *Hermita del Christo del Caloco*, where grey and blue marble is dug out of the adjacent mountain, and is found almost close to the road. The mountain terminates at Villacastin, but the grand plain only commences at Labajos, where they sow the peas called *Garbanzos* in a fine blackish soil, but they are not equally tender and large every year, no more than at Salamanca or Zamora; for though the land is good for this

this fort of pulfe, its fuccefs depends much upon the weather.

A new bridge has been lately built over the river Almarza, whofe banks are lined with poplar and elm; half a league further there is another plain, without a single tree, but water is found at two or three feet depth; fo that a very flight plough anfwers the purpofe, it being fufficient to tear away the weeds, to fecure a good crop of wheat; this is generally the cafe in Caftile, where they have fine harvefts without being obliged to wait for rain to fow their corn, the vicinity of of water and ftrong dews being fufficient to fertilize the foil, the reverfe of what happens in the fouthern parts, where the water is deep under ground, the foil dry and tough, and ftrong ploughs muft be ufed; befides waiting for rain, or an appearance of its falling, otherwife the grain hardens, and is in danger of being devoured by birds, infects, or rats. In thefe plains, the villages are numerous, as well as the vineyards, the foil is fandy, and yet, by means of the nearnefs of water, produces plenty of fhumach; every houfe has its garden, and the fides of the road are chequered with the lychnis, and oak of Jerufalem. Though the plain I have juft mentioned is of about eight leagues extent, without the appearance of a fpring, or a brook, the inhabitants drink the waters of wells and cifterns, with-

out

out any bad confequences, or being troubled with agues, as the water does not ftagnate, but has a current near the furface, and regains from a higher region, what it lofes by evaporation. This accounts for their having fuch fine grafs and pafture in Caftile, and fo many herds of cattle, with fuch a variety of game, birds, and wild and domeftic animals.

Near Valladolid there are groves of fir trees terminated by an extenfive plain, covered with green wormwood, oak of Jerufalem, and thyme, of that beautiful fort called thymus legitimus Hifpanicus. The city of Simancas (a) appears on the left, about two leagues diftance, as you enter the once famous city of Valladolid,

(a) The records of the kingdom having been found to be in great confufion, and a large collection of valuable papers difcovered at Valladolid, Philip II. ordered his chief architect, Juan de Herrera to conftruct proper apartments at Simancas for their prefervation, and they were difpofed of in nine grand divifions, or apartments, accordingly. In the ftrongeft, called the Cubo, were thofe relating to Granada, Indies, right to Naples, Navarre, Portugal, Vicariate of Siena, monarchy of Sicily, eftablifhment of the inquifitioo, wills of kings, capitulations of peace with France, with Moorifh kings, with the Houfe of Auftria, marriages of Catholic kings, grants of military orders, and ftate papers from the time of Ferdinand V. all which are preferved in wooden cafes fixed in the wall. In the year 1598 the king vifited them. All the proceedings relating to the imprifonment and death of Don Carlos his fon, were depofited here in a trunk, carefully locked. Another apartment was built for accounts, and other office papers; in another were papers relating to royal palaces, law fuits, grants, knights of military orders, and Indies; another for records of corporations; and in another the memorials and letters of kings, princes, and ftates, concerning Flanders, fince the rebellion. Vida de Philipe IId. Por Luis Cabrera de Cordova. Madrid, 1619. The American papers alone fill the largeft apartment of this *Archivo*, and are faid to compofe 873 large bundles. The profpect of fuch a treafure had excited the moft ardent curiofity of the elegant hiftorian of America, but the profpect of it was all that he enjoyed. Preface to Dr. Robertfon's hift. of America.

fituated

situated on the banks of the Pisuerga. This large city, exclusive of colleges and some churches that have good remains of gothic architecture, now only exhibits the dismal remains of its former grandeur; and the palace where Philip the second was born, has nothing but bare walls, where bats and spiders quietly inhabit the mansions of the great Emperor Charles, and the Philips his progeny.

Every thing is barren with dreary aspects of flat topped, barren sand hills as far as Caveron, where they have vineyards and make a tolerable light red wine. Leadwort is common on the side of the road, whose leaves pounded, are said to be good against the gangrene. The vineyards are numerous, near the town of Duenas (a), which belongs to the Duke of Medina Celi. The plain extends to Rodrigo, whose environs produce a little lavender, two sorts of shrubby Jerusalem sage, with a sage leaf, and meadow ragwort, which are the only plants the country affords. All the territory of Campos is so bare and destitute of trees, that the inhabitants are obliged for fuel, to burn vineflocks, straw,

---

(a) A Spanish proverb says, "*Ruyn con ruyn que assi se casan en Duenas*—Mean with mean, for thus they marry in Duenas." In 1506, Ferdinand of Aragon, after the death of his wife Queen Isabella, of Castile, was married here a second time to the Lady Germana de Foix, daughter of John de Foix, viscount Narbonne, by Maria, sister to Lewis 12th of France. This match having been made by the political Ferdinand, to cement his union with France, might perhaps displease the Castilians, and have given rise to the proverb. At present Duenas seems ill prepared for such splendid guests, and indifferently provided, even to celebrate the nuptials of a reputable Grazier.

dung, and the few aromatic shrubs they can find; their kitchens are like stoves, and they sit round them on benches, giving to these wretched hovels the emphatic name of *Glorias*. A solitary elm or a walnut tree now and then appears near a church, a sure sign that water is not far from the surface, and that its roots have partaken of it. When this happens, independent of every vicissitude of weather and climate, other trees would thrive in like manner, and the country might be rendered shady and pleasant, instead of being the most desolate in Europe; but it is no easy matter to conquer prejudices, or dissuade the Castilians from that erroneous notion, that an increase of trees would only augment the number of birds to eat up their corn, and devour their grapes.

On approaching the hills, the pebbles which had almost disappeared, shew themselves again, encreased both in number and bulk, and although from Labajos they were scarce larger than oranges, they are now double that size, and rounded, which the others are not, covering the tops of the hills: it is somewhat singular, that these stones, which are of a fine sandy grain, and are found every where in this province, should be of the very identical sort and colour, as those of La Mancha, Molina de Aragon, and other parts of Spain.

The country from hence to Burgos, produces plenty of wheat, and some flax; the road is a continual though gentle ascent, with much conglutinated sand stone, of which there is a sort near Burgos, so firmly conglutinated with small pebble that it forms a marble like the *Breccia*(a), and takes a good polish, specimens of which may be seen in the choir of the cathedral of Burgos. The environs of this ancient city are remarkably pleasant, and shady, with many beautiful avenues; the hills are no longer flat-topped, but have a chearful appearance; the waters are pure and salubrious, the rivers abound with trout, eel, and cray-fish. Though the air is sharp and rather piercing, it is esteemed very healthy, and Castile may justly be reckoned the country of partridges, hares, rabbits, and lamb. They do not sow their wheat before August, nor are grapes ripe before that time. The wild thistle with yellow flowers, is seen every where near the roads, and plenty of meadow sweet.

The city of Burgos is situated on the side of a hill, at the bottom of which, the river Arlanzon washes its walls, and has three stone bridges over it. The cathedral is a magnificent gothic structure, and one of the finest in

---

(a) The breccia silicia is the plumb pudding stone. This stone is of a very elegant appearance, when cut and polished; it is found in England. See Essay towards a system of mineralogy, by Axel Fred. Cronsted; second edition. London, 1772. Sect. CCLXXIII.

6. 3 c.5
1261

Plate IV. ARCH of FERNAN GONZALEZ in BURGOS.

Spain. The city is well inhabited by ancient nobility, and was formerly the refidence of their kings. It gave birth to that illuftrious hero Fernan Gonzales, and near the place where his houfe ftood, a triumphal arch has been erected to his memory at the expence of the city, with the following infcription :

FERNADO GONSALVI CASTELLÆ ASSERTORI. SVÆ ÆTATIS PRÆSTANTISSIMO DVCI MAGNORVM REGVM GENITORI SVO CIVI INTVS DOMVS AREA SVPTV PVBLICO AD ILLIVS NOMINIS ET VRBIS GLORIÆ MEMORIĀ SEMPITERNAM.

The parifh church of Santa Gadea (St. Agatha) more ancient than the cathedral, is remarkable for being the place, where that renowned champion Ruy Diaz de Bibar alfo a native of Burgos, commonly called the *Cid Campeador*(a), obliged king Alfonfo the 6th, before he was proclaimed, to fwear three times publicly, that he had no concern in the murder of the late king Sancho his brother, at the fiege of Zamora, where he was treacheroufly flain by a Spanifh knight, whofe name was Helicl Alfons, though he is ufually called Velido Dolfos. The words of this extraordinary oath were as follows,

You come to fwear, that you had no hand in the death of my lord the king, that you neither killed him, nor gave counfel therein.

(a) The title of Cid is derived from an Arabic word which fignifies Lord. See Don Quixote. It muft have been common in thofe days, for in the Spanifh chronicles, it is fometimes given to Jews.

The king and his nobles anfwered, *Amen.*

If otherwife, may you fuffer the fame death as that of my lord; may a villain kill you, let him not be a gentleman, nor born in Caftile, but come from foreign parts, nor be of the kingdom of Leon.

The king and his nobles anfwered, *Amen.* (a)

After this ceremony, Alfonfo was folemnly proclaimed king of Caftile, Leon, Galicia, and Portugal, in the prefence of the infanta his fifter, and the prelates, and nobles of his kingdom.

As Burgos was formerly a place of fo great importance in the affairs of Caftile, it is impoffible to look with indifference on thefe venerable remains, or view its magnificent cathedral, without calling to mind fome particular period of its ecclefiaftical hiftory; none feems more ftriking, than when the fon of a Jew was raifed to that fee, and became one of its moft illuftrious prelates.

(a) At the fecond time of tendering the oath the king changed colour, and at the third he was greatly difpleafed, faying, "Rodrigo Diaz why do you prefs me fo hard and make me fwear to-day, when you will come to kifs my hand to-morrow;" to which that warrior replied, "Yes, Sir, if my fervices are properly confidered, for in other kingdoms, knights are alfo rewarded, and you muft do the fame, if you mean to retain me in your fervice;" which fpeech the king never forgave, and foon after ordered him to retire out of the kingdom, allowing him only nine days for that purpofe. The Spanifh chronicles are full of the achievements and feats of the *Cid*. He died in 1099, and is buried in the church of St. Pedro de Cardena, near Burgos, where his memory is held in the higheft veneration.

Such

Such was *Paulus Burgenfis*, whose extraordinary elevation is worthy of notice. This great man was the son of a rich Jew at Burgos, of the tribe of Levi, whose name is not mentioned in history. In the year 1376 Paulus married Joanna, of the same tribe as himself, by whom he had four sons and one daughter. Gonzalo, his eldest, bishop of Plasencia and Siguenza, Alfonso, who succeeded his father in the see of Burgos; Pedro, Alvaro, Sancho, and Maria, who all at the conversion of the father, took the name of *Santa Maria*, and when Paulus was made bishop of Carthagena, they assumed the sirname of *Carthagena*.

Paulus had been for many years firmly attached by education, and principle to the Jewish religion, and being a man of great learning, enforced his opinions with vehemence. At this time the Jews professed their religion publicly in Spain, and held offices of trust and emolument. At the age of forty, Paulus Burgenfis embraced the Christian religion, and on the 21st of June, 1390, was publicly baptised in the cathedral, by Don Garci Alfonso de Cobarruvias, treasurer of the church, whose coat armour was assumed by Paulus, in memory of this event, which was a *lilly argent, in a field vert*. desiring to have the name of Paul in baptism, from his particular attachment to the sacred writings of that great apostle, of whom he used to say, " Paulus me ad fidem convertit.

Pauli mihi indebile nomen una cum caractere affignari depofco."

His two fons were baptized at the fame time, his eldeſt being eleven, and the youngeſt only two years of age. His father had been dead fome time in the Jewiſh religion, and his mother ſtill continued fo with remarkable ſteadineſs, though ſhe yielded at laſt to the arguments of her fon, but his wife was inflexible; for which reafon the marriage was diſſolved, and Paulus took upon him the clerical habit, purfued his ſtudies with new zeal, and foon after went to Paris, where he received the degree of maſter of arts, and continued writing to his late wife, ufing every argument to convince her of the fublime truths of the Chriſtian religion, in which at laſt he had the happineſs to fucceed. He then ſet out for Avignon, was made archdeacon of Trevino, in the fee of Burgos, and a canon of Seville. At the age of fifty-two king Henry the third of Caſtile, appointed him biſhop of Carthagena, and he became fo great a favorite with that monarch, that he made him chancellor of the kingdom, one of the executors of his will, and tutor to his fon and heir, John, then only two years of age, and afterwards king of Caſtile: finally Paulus was nominated to the fee of Burgos with univerſal approbation, which he refufed for a twelvemonth, but at laſt acquiefced, and took poſſeſſion of, in 1415, being ſixty-five years of age.

After

Plan V.

After the ceremony was performed in the cathedral, he was received with great splendour in his palace, by his mother, his late wife, and all the nobility. He was a rigid perfecutor of the Jews, whom he not only inveighed against in his writings, but used all his endeavours to strip of their privileges; if he did not always succeed, he obliged them however to dwell by themselves, in particular parts of the town, and his pupil, King John, drove them out of his kingdom (*a*); amongst the many treatises published against them by the bishop of Burgos, the most remarkable was one intitled "Scrutinium scripturarum," reprinted at Burgos in folio, in 1591. At last, this venerable prelate, worn out with old age and infirmity, was named Patriarch of Aquileia, and had the satisfaction to see his son Alfonso, dean of St. Jago succeed to him in the see of Burgos, and then closed his career in the eighty-third year of his age. Alfonso was equal to his father in virtue and learning. He went ambassador to Portugal, to treat about a peace with Castile, and was afterwards sent in the same character to the Emperor Albert. He finished the beautiful spires of the cathedral of Burgos, and Æneas Sylvius

(*a*) England was the first country that expelled the Jews (in 1181, the 19th of Edward 1st.) They had a similar fate in France much about that time; Spain banished them next, and afterwards Portugal. Oliver Cromwell permitted them to return to England, and the generality of Christians now treat them with more moderation. The popes receive them in Rome, and they sleep in tranquility close to the shrine of St. Peter; but the Spaniards and Portuguese still look on that dispersed people with an universal and national abhorrence.

(afterwards

(afterwards Pope Pius 2d.) ſtiles him, " Deliciæ Hiſpaniarum Burgenſis." He made an attempt, at the council of Baſil, to ſupport the precedency of the kings of Caſtile, before the kings of England, on which occaſion he publiſhed his treatiſe, entitled *El tratado de las ſeſſiones*. He alſo wrote many works on hiſtorical ſubjects; in a word, he lived in ſuch high eſtimation, that when Pope Eugenius, heard that the biſhop of Burgos intended to come to his court, he publickly declared in a full conſiſtory of cardinals, " That if Alfonſo of Burgos ſhould ever come to ſee him, he ſhould be in a manner aſhamed, to ſit in the chair of St. Peter (*a*)."

(*a*) Eſpaña Sagrada por Fr. Henrique Flores. Tom 26. Madrid, 1771.

LETTER

LETTER XII.

Remarkable objects on the road from Burgos to the provinces of Alaba and Guypuscoa, as far as Irun, the last town on the frontiers of Spain, towards France.

YOU no sooner quit Burgos, than new objects appear worthy of attention; for, in crossing an extensive plain, the gum-bearing cistus is seen in great plenty (a); it is an evergreen, with long, narrow, leaves, gummy and glossy; the flower is inodorous, and composed of five white petals, of the size of a common rose; each petal having a little purple spot on the tip of it. The old branches distil a liquid matter, which the heat of the sun condenses into a white sugary substance, like a piece of gum, of the size of one's finger, and yields a true manna; it is gathered and eat greedily by shepherds and boys. The Spaniards were little apprised of the advantages to be drawn from this plant, till of late years, when, on the representation of the royal college of physicians at Madrid, in 1752, orders were given to two of its members, to make a

(a) The cistus ladaniferus of Linnæus.

further

further investigation of this production; these were Don Joseph Minuart, and Don Chriftoval Velez, the former went into the mountains of Avila, and the latter, into several districts of Andalusia; it was found that Spain alone could procure manna sufficient to supply all Europe, equal in goodness to that of Calabria, in the kingdom of Naples; for not only an incredible quantity of it, was gathered in the parts abovementioned, where it is formed about the dog days, but likewise in the mountains of Asturias, Galicia, Cuenca, Aragon, and Catalonia, though no use had hitherto been made of it (*a*).

The defcent to Monafterio leads to a valley fertile in corn, soon after the district of Bureba begins, which is a champaign country, and populous, with numerous gardens, well stocked with fruit trees. Near Bribiefca they manure their land with a sort of white marl, of a

(*a*) Manna is a medicinal drug, of great use in the modern practice, as a gentle purgative, and cleanfer of the first passages, and is now become a confiderable article of trade. It may be reckoned among the number of gums which exfuding from the juice of a tree, and mixing with some faline particles of air, is condenfed into those flakes in which it is brought to England. The manna of Calabria is not gathered from the ciftus, but from the branches of the ash tree; and we are assured by Robert More, Esq; of Linfley, in the county of Salop, that the Neapolitans have many ways of counterfeiting the several appearances of manna, and that the most common, is with Glauber's salt, and sugar, with a small mixture of manna. It yields to his Sicilian majesty so large a revenue, and he is so jealous of it, that during the season, the woods are guarded by soldiers, who even fire upon people, that come into them, and the stealing of the liquor is death. "See the method of gathering the manna in the kingdom of Naples, in Rolt's dictionary of commerce."

bluei{h}

blueish cast; marl, being in its nature, a compound of different properties of argillaceous, and calcareous earths, is of great use in agriculture; it is sometimes soft, at other times hard, like stone, or slate, but generally crumbles by exposure to the air. The strongest sort, which abounds with clay, cannot be so proper for the argillaceous, and stony land of Biscay; but when the soil is light, calcareous, and spungy, not retaining the water, or too much worn out by cultivation, then a clayish marl will be of service, to procure the additional substance required; and if the land is stiff clay, a calcareous quality is most proper, as it always contains some sand, which helps to loosen the soil, and will give it fertility for a number of years.

The road to Pancorvo traverses calcareous mountains, forming part of those called " Los Montes de Oca," by which the Pyrenees are joined to the northern mountains of Spain. The town of Pancorvo lies in the narrowest part of a valley, closed in by these high hills, having a brook where there is excellent trout. The new road has been cut through the rock, which formerly offered the most horrid aspect to the traveller, threatening, as it were, every moment, to fall on his head, but now is safe and commodious, the passage having been considerably widened. The new road from Bilboa reaches as far as

Pancorvo, a diſtance of ſeventeen leagues, over a continual chain of mountains.

The boundaries of Old Caſtile are at Miranda de Ebro, three leagues beyond Pancorvo, where there is a bridge over the Ebro (a); on the other ſide of which, the province of Alaba begins, whoſe inhabitants have likewiſe made a fine road at their own expence, to the confines of Guypuſcoa. The road continues almoſt to Vitoria, bordering on the river Zadorra, in which the water lilly grows plentifully. The hills are of ſmall, and various coloured calcareous ſtone, conglutinated together: the plants are the arbutus uva urſi, or perennial leaved ſtrawberry tree, box, thorny furze, thorny reſtharrow, the kermes oak, and many ſorts of orchis. The firſt village in the province of Guypuſcoa, is Salinas, ſo called from its briny ſprings, which they evaporate with a boiling heat, and make ſalt. It is remarkable, that ſuch ſprings in France, and Lorraine, are always in vallies, but in Spain are conſtantly found on the tops of mountains, or in elevated places. This juſt mentioned, is on a very high hill, with numerous petrefactions of ſhells, in a kind of blueiſh marble, veined with ſpar, which has been uſed in making the road. This hill of Salinas is the higheſt part of Guypuſcoa.

(a) This bridge, which had been ſo much damaged, and part of it carried away by inundations, when Mr. Swinburne paſſed this way, and was obliged to go over in a ferry, was entirely repaired when I went over it in July, 1778.

From

From hence, it is four leagues to Mondragon, so famous for its iron mine in this neighbourhood, of which I shall speak more particularly hereafter. From Mondragon it is a journey of six leagues to Legaspia, passing by a forge on the banks of the river *Onate*, where they mix the ore of two mines, viz. that of Somorrostro in Biscay, noted for the flexibility of its metal, with the ore of this neighbourhood, which being more abundant and hard, takes forty hours in roasting, and is then fused once without any castina (*a*), getting at each fusion a quintal of iron, following the same method observed with the iron of Somorrostro, as will be described in a subsequent letter.

Onate is a populous and affluent town ; the church, the colonade, and statues of the college, are of sand-stone, full of Mica (*b*); the soil of the hills, and vallies, is a tenacious clay, formed by the total decomposition of the sand-stone, slate, and rotten vegetables. The

---

(*a*) Castina is a hard calcareous stone, of a whitish grey, used in forges, where iron is fused, in order to absorb the sulphureous acid, that mineralizes the iron, and renders it brittle.

(*b*) Mica, the glimmer, daze, or glist. See Cronstedt's mineralogy, sect. xciii. London, 1772. Mica, or talk, is an earthy or stony substance, consisting of thin, flexible, shining plates; micas have a soft touch, resembling that of unctuous substances. They are not soluble by acids. They are incapable of eliciting sparks when struck by steel, as flints do, for which reason they are called *Apyri*, that is, without fire; nor do they form a tenacious talle with water, as gypsum does. Mica is therefore neither a calcareous, siliceous, argillaceous, nor gypseous earth.——

farmers

farmers used to manure it with lime, to loosen the strength of the clay, and absorb its acid, but they now begin to use marl.

It is five hours and a half from Legaspia to Villafranca, passing by Villareal, where the houses are of sand-stone. They prune the oaks every where in this country, in the same manner as the mulberry trees in Valencia, that they may throw out more branches, to make charcoal for the forges, and they cut them every eight or ten years, as in Biscay. There are few springs in all these hills, though it so frequently rains, owing to the tenacity of the soil, which impedes the filtration of the water, so that they are obliged to drink melted snow from the mountains, yet without being troubled with the full-throat, so often attributed to this cause, though more probably arising from obstructions in the glands for want of perspiration (*a*). Two thirds of the inhabitants of this province, pass the days and nights in their smoaky cabins, without chimnies, affirming, that the closeness, and smoak, are conducive to health, as they dissipate

---

(*a*) An ingenious traveller lately returned from Switzerland informs us, that he had been at several places where the inhabitants drink no other water than those of rivers and torrents which descend from the *Glacieres*, and yet are not in the least subject to the full throat; so far from it, he had been told, snow water was esteemed a preservative, as well as the clear air of the mountains, and that they had been observed to diminish in elevated places, though always increased in the vallies, when once they had begun.—Sketches of the natural, civil, and political state of Switzerland, by Will. Coxe, A. M. London, 1779.

dampness

dampness, and promote perspiration. The inhabitants are certainly not only robust, but are even seldom troubled with rheums: they are moreover chearful and sociable, having nothing of that shyness observed in the meridional provinces.

From Villafranca (*a*), it is three leagues to Tolofa, one of the three principal cities of Guypufcoa, and from hence the road continues in sight of St. Sebastians, and Pafage, to Irun, the last town in Spain. Near this place the river Bidasoa enters the ocean, dividing Spain from France, and at a small distance from its mouth, the island of Pheasants is remarkable for having been the place where the Pyrenean treaty was concluded, in 1660, between cardinal Mazarin, on the part of France, and Don Lewis Mendez de Haro y Guzman, on the part of Spain, and the match was agreed upon, between Lewis XIV. and Dona Maria Teresa, daughter of Philip IV. mother to the Dauphin, and grand-mother to the Duke of Anjou, afterwards Philip V. of Spain, father to his present Majesty Charles III.

(*a*) Neither Legafpia, Onate, Villareal, Villafranca, nor Irun, are to be found on the well-engraved map of Spain, by Thomas Lopez, in 1770, who is geographer to the king, and of the academy of St. Ferdinand, and dedicates it to the Prince of Afturias, saying of this map, that it is, " conftruido con lo mejor, que ay impreffo, manufcrito, y memorias de los naturales;" but on the " mapa de las carreras de poftas de Efpana," dedicated to Charles the 3d, by Don Ricardo Wall, in 1760, and engraved by the faid Thomas Lopez, I find Villafranca, Tolofa, and Irun, but not Legafpia, Onate, or Villareal.

LETTER

LETTER XIII.

Of the iron ore of Mondragon, in Guypuscoa, with some account of the famous Toledo blades, so greatly valued formerly in England.

I Shall now relate some particulars concerning the famous iron mine of Mondragon, which is about a league distant from the town of that name, in Guypuscoa. It is called, by the Spanish miners, "*Hierro Elado*," frosen iron, is found in a red clay, and produces natural steel, with this remarkable circumstance, that it is not to be met with any where else in the kingdom (*a*). They even preserve to this day, a traditional story that this ore was used for those famous swords, which Catherine of Aragon, made a present of, to her consort, our Henry the VIIIth; some of which still remain in re-

(*a*) Steel, considered chemically, is nothing else than iron reduced by art to a particular state, which occasions some changes in its properties, but these properties are essentially the same as those of iron; that is, iron and steel are not two different metals, but the same metal, in two different states. Steel may be made by fusion or cementation: the first method is used to convert iron into steel, immediately from the ore, but more frequently from crude, or cast iron; but all ores of iron are not used indifferently, for this purpose, because some of these, which are therefore called *ores of steel*, are much fitter than others, to furnish good steel, and the steel extracted from them is called *natural steel*. Dictionary of chemistry, London, 1777.

pute in the highlands of Scotland, being suitable to their dress, and are called *Andre Ferrara*, the name of the maker, which is marked on the blades. The famous Toledo blades, those also of Zarragossa, called *Del Perrillo*, mentioned in Don Quixote (a), and others, were also supposed to be made of the ore of this mine, which gives forty per cent. metal, though rather difficult to fuse: good steel may be obtained from it with very little trouble, because the iron has in itself the proper disposition to receive in the forge, the necessary phlogiston to make excellent blades, but without cementation it perhaps may not answer for files, or razors. These blades were generally broad, to wear on horseback, and of great length, suitable to the old Spanish dress, but this being altered at the beginning of this century, when the duke of Anjou ascended the throne of Spain, the French swords were introduced with their dress, which even now is commonly called in Spanish, a military dress, *vestido de militar*, in opposition to the long black cloak universally worn there before

(a) These swords were called *Del Perrillo*, from the figure of a little dog on the blade; Cervantes endeavours to heighten the courage of Don Quixote, when he attacked the lion in the cage, by adding, "That his sword was of the common sort, and not so sharp as those famous ones, with the Perrillo mark." *Tu magnanimo! con sola una Espada, y no de las del Perrillo cortadoras.* Don Quixote, part II; cap. 70. Madrid, 1771. The Zarragossa artists had three distinct marks on their blades; viz. *El Perrillo*, a little dog; *El Morillo*, a Moor's head; and *La Loba*, a wolf. Swords with the *Loba* mark, have the name of Andre Ferrara on them, and are not uncommon, at this day, in England. They shew a sword in the small armoury of the tower of London, with the name of Andre Ferrara, and no other mark, which was taken in the Scotch Rebellion in 1715.

that

that epocha. So' that the old Toledo blades fell into difufe, and the manufacture declined; but his prefent majefty has again encouraged it, and a new manufacture has been lately fet up, by his orders, at Toledo, for the ufe of the troops, and they are faid to be as well tempered as the old ones, and are able to bear moft extraordinary proofs; but thefe are not made of the ore of Mondragon. There are various opinions relating to the old blades, we have been fpeaking of; fome fay, they were only tempered in winter, and when taken out of the forge, for the laft time, were vibrated in the air, in the coldeft weather; others relate, that they were heated till they acquired that colour, the Spanifh artifts call cherry, and then, were fteeped in a tub of oil, or greafe, for a moment or two, then plunged, in the fame manner, in warm water, all which was done in the depth of winter: others will have it, they were made of the natural fteel of Mondragon, with a lift of common iron in the middle, to make them more flexible, and then tempered in the common way, in the winter feafon. Such are the prevailing opinions about the blades of Mondragon, which are certainly excellent; but as to the prefent workmen of Mondragon, or in any part of Guypufcoa, they are yet unacquainted with the fecret of converting iron into fteel, or tempering it properly, and even in the making of tools, are far inferior to the artifts in England: it is fomewhat particular,

particular, that to this very day, they have no other word in the Spanish language, for a bickhorn, or a bench vice, than *Vigornia*, the Latin name for the city of Worcester, thought to have been once famous for works of that kind (*a*). As many of the most capital workmen of Toledo, quitted that city, on the decline of their trade, and settled in different parts of the kingdom, where they supported the reputation of their art; and as their blades have since been dispersed all over Europe, those who are curious in these matters, will, perhaps, not be displeased to see a list of their names; as by this means they may know them, whenever they fall in their way.

Bilboa	Pedro de Lagaretea
Orgaz	Pedro Lopez
Lisbon	{ Melchior Saanz
	Juan Martinez Machacha
	Sebastian Hernandez
Seville	{ Pedro de Lezama
	Juan Martinez el Mozo
	Francisco Alcocer
Madrid	{ Dionisio Corrientes
	Antonio Ruiz
Cuenca	{ Julian Garcia
	Andres Herraez
Valladolid	Juan Salcedo
Calatayud	{ Luis de Nieva
	Andres Munester

(*a*) Tesoro de la lengua Castellana per el licenciado Don Sebastian de Cobatruvias Orozco. Madrid 1611.

Cordoba

Cordoba	Alonso Rios
Zaragossa	Julian de Rey
San Clemente	Lopez Aguado
Cuellar,	⎧ Bartholome de Nieva
and	⎨ Calcado
Badajoz	⎩ Campanero

The following workmen still remained in Toledo.

Zamorano
Thomas de Ayala
Juan de la Horta
Francisco Ruiz, and sons
Juan de Vargas
Juan de Luizalde
Francisco Lardi
Andres Garcia
Heras, father, son, and grandson.
Alonso de Sahagun and sons
Fernandez
Martinez

Any old blades found with these last names, may be undoubtedly considered as true Toledos, and executed by the most capital artists. Cervantes further relates that Ramon de Hoces was famous at Seville for making of poinards. *Debia der fer el tal puñal de Ramon de Hoces el Sevillano* (a.) Nor should I forget the famous *Montante* of Spain (b), a huge weapon, used with both hands, at once

---

(a) Don Quixote, tom 3, page 293. Madrid, 1771.

(b) Cobarruvias gives to the word Montante, an Italian derivation, "Montante, espada de dos manos, arma de ventaja y conocida, de *Montar* palabra Italiana que quiere decir, subir, o

so well described by Milton, speaking of Michael's sword:

> "With huge two-handed sway
> "Brandish'd aloft, the horrid edge came down,
> "Wide wasting."   PARAD. LOST, Book vi.

In the king's armoury at Madrid, besides many curious and compleat suits of armour, they have a fine collection of antique swords, amongst the rest, they shew those, said to have belonged to Pelagius, to the Cid, and Bernardo del Carpio; also the sword of king Francis 1st, and that of John George, duke of Saxe-Weimar, taken from him by Charles 5th, at the battle of Horlingen. The swords of the Cid, and Bernardo del Carpio, were made at Zaragossa, but that of Francis, at Valencia, as was also the sword, likewise in this armoury, of that famous hero Garcia de Paredes, with his name on the blade, and on the other side "plus ultra operibus credite." Though these details may perhaps be considered of very little moment, it was not so with our ancestors, who set a high value on these Spanish blades, particularly the Toledos, as may be collected from various passages in our favourite writers, Shakespear, Johnson, and Butler.

porque el montante excede la estatura del hombre o porque se juege por lo alto.—Tesoro de la lengua Castellana, por Don Sebastian de Cobarruvias. Madrid, 1611. This curious book may truly said to be a treasure, according to his title, for those that study the Spanish language, and are desirous of understanding the true spirit and sense of its most difficult words, though the witty Quevedo passes rather a severe censure on it, in his novel intit'led, *Cuento de Cuentos*, adding, Tambien se ha hecho tesoro de la lengua Española donde el papel es mas que la razon, obra grande, y de erudicion desaliñada.

LETTER

LETTER XIV.

Environs of Reinosa, source of the river Ebro, and intended canal of Castile.

THAT part of Spain called "Montana de Burgos," may be thrown into two grand divisions. The first takes in all that space from the highest part of the mountains, to the Bay of Biscay, and the other, the space extending from the same height towards Castile. The highest part of these mountains, is that intermediate situation between Santander, and Burgos, it being a continual ascent of fourteen leagues from Santander to Reinosa, descending afterwards from thence, as far as Burgos. The source of the Ebro is within half a mile of Reinosa, and runs easterly, till it falls into the Mediterranean, while the Pisuerga runs into the Duero, whose course is westerly, and empties itself in the ocean; from whence it may be inferred, that Reinosa divides the waters between the two seas, and is therefore one of the most elevated districts in Spain, as well as the coldest, its lofty mountains raising their heads as high as the line of congelation, being constantly covered with snow. The soil of Reinosa produces the best oaks in the kingdom,

dom, equal to any in Europe, and some thousands of them, are occasionally felled for the service of the navy. Good oaks will not succeed so well in a rich limy soil, abounding with moisture, but require on the contrary, that it should be of an argillaceous nature, stiff and compact, as well as dry, where they suffer no injury from dampness, and thrive by slow and proper gradations. The soil of Reinosa is in general, composed of sandy rock, mixed with quartz, as large as chesnuts, cemented in the rock in the same manner as in the warm climate of Granada. About a league to the north of Reinosa there is a very high mountain called Arandillo, whose summit is at present so much decomposed, as to form an extensive plain where there is very good grass. The people of the country, say there was formerly a town here, and the quantities of loose stones still remaining, seem to confirm the report. The nature of this mountain is singular, its basis being of gypseous stone, its summit of sand stone, and its centre of limestone, with large impressions of cornu ammonis, and several scallop shells fixed in the rock. On the road to Reinosa, black marble veined with white is seen in great quantities; the same may be observed at the *Puerto* between Aspeitia, and Vidana, where there is a mountain of similar marble, from top to bottom. Two leagues to the southward of Reinosa, there is another high mountain, with an hermitage at the top, where there is great plenty of bilberry whortle,

whortle, the vaccinium of Linnæus (a); and to the westward, there is a height where great numbers of Roman coins have been dug out, which indicates its having been formerly a Roman colony: near this place several large lumps of emery are seen above ground, fixed in the sand stone (b).

The famous river Ebro, which once served as a boundary between the Carthaginians and Romans, has its source in a little valley at a small distance to the eastward of Reinosa, and proceeds from a copious spring at the foot of an ancient tower, called *Fontibre*; at a few paces from hence, its waters turn a mill, and abound in excellent trout, and plenty of cray fish; in passing by Reinosa, it is encreased by the waters of several other brooks, and springs; two leagues lower, it runs by the narrow pass of Montesclaros, receives different supplies in the course of its passage through the vallies, is considerable when it comes to the confines of Alava, and after traversing many open and fertile districts, passes by the city of Tortosa, where there is a bridge of boats over it, and then falls into the Mediterranean at the Alfaque islands, but on account of its many rocks, and shoals is not navigable higher than Tortosa, and even so far, only for small craft.

(a) Vint idea of Gerard and Ray.
(b) A more particular account of emery will be given in the second part of this work.

There is a small briny lake near the source of the Ebro, where they might obtain salt, as is done near the source of the Tagus, in the same manner as in Guypuscoa already mentioned. In winter this lake is covered with wild ducks, and other aquatic fowl; the country is well provided with game, they have partridges and quails in abundance, as well as hares, and in the mountains there are bears. The meadows are covered with usual plants, such as round birthwort, squinancy berries, yellow weed, parsley leaved vervain, privet, and cockscomb; but of the aromatic sorts, none but pennyroyal. Beech trees are common hereabouts, bearing the mast, which is a kind of a triangular seed in form of a nut, or rather an acorn, containing a whitish oleaginous pith, of an agreeable taste, but the inhabitants are ignorant of the method of drawing oil from this fruit, as in France: they gather it in the same manner as they do acorns, in Eſtremadura, getting up into the trees and ſtriking them with poles, and use it to fatten the swine. When put under the press and formed into cakes, it makes an excellent fodder for cows, on being mixed with water, and is of great service when they cannot go into the fields on account of the snow (a). The intended ca-

(a) An attempt was made some years ago to introduce the extraction of beech oil in England, and a patent was granted for that purpose, but it did not succeed, the country people choosing to keep their mast to fatten their swine, rather than sell it to answer the purposes

nal of Castile, is to begin at the village of Olea, near Fontibre, about a league and a half from Reinosa, is to pass by Comesa, Cabria, Villaescusa, Estrecho del Congosto, Mave, Villella, Estrecho de Nogales, Herrera de Pisuerga, Osorno, Fromista, Convento de Calahorra, and Grijota ; where it is to meet the branch of Campos, that is to come from Medina de Rio Seco, then to continue by Palencia, Duenas, Venta de Trigueros, and La Verucla, and enter the river Pisuerga, below Valladolid ; by which means, it will communicate with the Duero, and meet another branch, which is to begin at Segovia, and pass by Hontenares, Bernaldos, Nava de Cocos, Olmedo, Mata-pozuelos, and villanueva de Duero ; but when all this will be executed, those who have travelled through Spain, and observed the slow progress of all public works, may form a tolerable judgment, so that this grand improvement with many other projects, of a less solid foundation, may be said to be yet closely enveloped, and hidden in the bosom of time.

and private views of any Individual.—Rolt's dict. of commerce. London, 1761.—The nuts, when eaten, occasion giddiness, but when well dried, and powdered, they make wholesome bread. They are sometimes roasted and substituted for coffee. The poor people in Silesia use the expressed oil, instead of butter.—Dr. Withering's botanical arrangement, &c.

LETTER

LETTER XV.

Natural history of the Spanish plant Gayuba, or perennial leaved strawberry-tree.

THE Spanish plant gayuba, having been described by the late Don Joseph Quer, surgeon to his Catholic majesty, and first professor of botany in the royal garden at Madrid, I shall lay before my readers a summary of his treatise (*a*), with the observations which occurred to him in the course of his practice, respecting this plant.

The gayuba, or arbutus uva ursi, of Linnæus (*b*), is indigenous to Spain, for though it grows in Italy and

---

(*a*) Dissertacion physico botanica sobre la passion nephritica, y su verdadero especifico, la uva ursi, o Gayuba. Su autor Don Joseph Quer Cirujano de S. M. Consultor de sus reales exercitos, academico del Instituto de Bolonia, de la real medica matritense y primer professor de botanica del real jardin de plantas de Madrid. Madrid, 1763.

(*b*) Uva ursi. Clus hist. 63. Hispanic 79, k Tournefort inst. R. II. 599. Class xx. Tabern Icon 1080. Boerhaave Ind. A. 11. 119. Scheucha Itin vii. 500. Vitis Idæa foliis carnosis, et veluti punctatis, five Idæa Raiiis Dioscoridis, C. B. Pin 470. Raii hist. 11. 1489.
Radix Idæa putata et uva ursi I. B. i. 523. Idæa Radix Lugd. 193.
Uva ursi Galeni Clusio. Park, 1458.
Vaccinia ursi, five uva ursi apud Clusium Ger. 1330. Emac 1416.
Arctostaphylos. Siegesb. flor. 13.
Arbutus caulibus procumbentibus, foliis integerrimis. LINN, H. cliff. 163.
Officin. Vitis Idæa.
In Spanish Gayuba.

T other

other southern climates, it is found in none so common as in that kingdom. Don Joseph Quer discovered it near the Escurial, and on the hills of Buytreras, on the mountains of Manzanares, in different parts of the Alcarria (a), such as the district of Lupiana, mountains of Buen Dia, Albalete de Zorita, Fuente Novilla, and other places: it is particularly common near all the villages, and lands, belonging to the extensive Serrania of Cuenca, all the stony mountains of the lordship of Molina, and near the source of the Tagus. In Aragon, on the mountains of Daroca, *Puertos* of Atea, and Acere, on the mountains of Burgos, and Leon, and county of Niebla, and Carrera de Leon, from Contorno de Villalmanso, to Cogollos; and from Manciles, to Villadiego, as you go from Burgos to Cervera, in so copious a manner, that the place is called *Gayubal*: also on the skirts of the Pyrenees of Catalonia, in Biscay, and Navarre, and in the kingdoms of Granada and Valencia; insomuch that the before-mentioned professor adds, that he does not recollect ever to have gone upon a botanical party, without seeing it. It is so universally known in Spain, that it has its particular names in almost every province, as for example:

In Castile, Alcarria, and lordship of Biscay, *Gayubas*
In Leon, - - - - - - - - - - *Agauja*
In Bureba, - - - - - - *Gaulla*

(a) A populous district is so called, when consisting of villages, farms, and rural improvements.

In Rioja,	*Avuguas*
In Asturias, the fruit is called	*Rebellones*
In Albalate de Zoritæ,	*Aguavillas*
In the Villages of the Alcarria, indifferently,	{ *Gayuberas* { *Gaubillas*
In Utiel, Partido de Requena,	*Galluva*
In Real de Manzanares,	*Uba dus*
In Catalonia	*Buxarolla*.

The great variety of these names shew, how universal it is all over the kingdom, and proves what little dependance is to be had on the relations of travellers, who only see the high roads, and never deviate from them, to inspect into remote places: even Clusius, the most intelligent, and curious of those writers, tells us, he only saw it at the Venta del Baul, when it can be made appear, that in all those parts of Spain, which he traversed, it grows in great quantities; and were all the uncultivated places to be mentioned, where the Gayuba is found, particularly, such as are called *Rubiales*, it would form a list of almost all the stony and uncultivated places in the kingdom. It is perennial and an evergreen, flowers in March, and April, and the berries are ripe in September, and October. The leaves are narrow, rounded at the extremity, and contain only one fibre. The berry is as large as the kernel of a hazle nut. Its singular mode of multiplication is curious, proceeding from the old branches, which trailing on the ground and gently rising, throw out new roots, which maintain its brothers, though the fire should be cut off, or decay; it is pleasing to observe a shoot of two or three plants adorned with stems and branches, with others issuing from them, so that one plant occupies a great space of ground, covered with its green foliage and red berries; but what makes this plant more worthy of attention, is its excellent qualities in calculous cases, being in a manner an *unique* in those cases, where every other specific has its contraindication, while this admits of no kind of danger, nor has ever been complained of by those who have written concerning it; and none of those who used it by the advice of Don Joseph Quer, and acknowledge themselves to be perfectly cured, have ever complained of the least inconvenience, though some were not wanting, who remarked its effects with the greatest exactness; suspecting, that its singular efficacy in the cure of the stone, might perhaps hide other obnoxious qualities, which however the most accurate scrutiny has not been able to discover.

The method generally used, says professor Quer, in administering this simple remedy, is to give the powder of the leaves only, or a decoction in water. Foreigners frequently use the first method, and I have chiefly followed the latter, though I have observed the like good effects from both. When the berry is perfectly ripe, which

which is upon its acquiring a red colour like coral, it is given in powders from ten grains to a fcruple, or half a dram, and from half a dram to one or two drams. The root when in decoction, according to Chriftian Hermann, from half a dram to two drams: the fame with the leaves, or in an infufion, and about a handful, or handful and a half of the leaves or more, and in powder from half a fcruple to a dram; but according to my conftant practice, I have fixed the dofe to two drams of leaves in a pound of water, and when in powders, I always give a dram, becaufe a lefs quantity only excites pain, and does not come up to the defired effect. It fhould be ufed, three or four times a day in the paroxyfm, taking a copious draught of the decoction, and if it feems more palatable to a delicate ftomach to fweeten it with fugar, it may be done, but muft be continued for weeks and months. When the pains have ceafed, one dofe given daily two hours before breakfaft will be fufficient, obferving the ufual diet, in which cafe it may alfo be efteemed an excellent prefervative, without being repugnant to thofe few convivial hours which may fall to the lot of the wifeft of men.

It appears to be particularly ufeful in fcorbutic cafes, from the teftimony of two learned writers of the faculty, Marcus Mappi, and J. Chriftian Hermann, in the *biftoria plant. Alfat.* written by the former, and after his deceafe publifhed by the latter, where it is faid, " Baccæ maturæ hyemis.

hyemis tempore acefcunt; valde gratum habent faporem, fub nive vigent et confervantur diu, in locis feptentrionalibus, maxima copia crefcunt, et cum aliis ibidem crefcentibus, adæquatum et fufficiens remedium fcorbuti præbent, annotante id etiam Joanne Frid. Bachftrom, qui etiam horum myrtillorum rubrorum ingentem vim in iftis locis provenire confirmat, provido omnis neceffitatis humanæ numinis beneficio."---Pag. 331.

In the year 1734, after the conqueft of Naples, continues Don Jofeph Quer, I returned to the court of Madrid, and practifed in my profeffion, and prefcribed the gayuba, whofe virtues were unknown, though in many provinces, they were well acquainted with the name of the plant. In 1762, I gathered it at Fuente Novilla, to have it delineated; in many places, the country people were furprifed to fee me take notice of it, when according to their notions it was fo pernicious to children, who eat of its berries. I prefcribed it to a patient, ordering him to boil two drams of the leaves, in a large veffel of water, which had the happieft effect. By this means I introduced the ufe of it at court, and believe I was the firft in Spain who adminiftered it. In further proof of its efficacy, I fhall add, that the illuftrious Senor Lupia bifhop of Leon, having applied in feveral places, as well abroad as in Spain, for a remedy for a nephritic complaint, they fent him a plant from Rome, with the name of *Buxarola*, whofe virtues, as well as name, were totally
unknown

unknown to us, yet the vegetable exifts in great quantities, and is known in the kingdom of Leon by the name of Agauja.

In the year 1740, being at Barcelona, I went on a botanical party, to vifit the famous mountain of Montferrate, in company with that celebrated botanift Don Juan Minuart, profeffor of botany of the royal garden, and we fpent two and twenty days in that excurfion; my friend was much troubled with nephritic complaints, which were extremely painful, particularly at that moment when we were at the very fummit of the mountain, from whence he found the utmoft difficulty to defcend; luckily we met the gayuba on that very fpot, and when he had reached the convent, he had the moft violent fymptoms of his complaint, therefore I immediately ordered the following decoction:

R. Gayuba leaves - - 2 drams
   Camomile flowers - 1 dram
   Refined nitre - - 1 fcruple.

In a proper veffel, boiled in a pound of water, and left to fimmer, over a flow fire, the veffel kept covered, and when removed, not to be fhaken; the above to be drank lukewarm, adding half an ounce of refined fugar, and to be taken twice a day; that is, in the morning early, fafting, and in the evening, by which method the fits ceafed, and the patient continued it,
during

during the courfe of our tour, with the moſt happy effects, having been enabled to complete his refearches with comfort and eafe.

Thus far our author, who enters into many details, relating to nephritic complaints, and their method of cure, amongſt the antients and moderns, adding alfo the practice of Dr. de Haen, of Vienna, with refpect to this plant; but as it is fo well known to our phyficians in England (a), I have only made ufe of the hiſtorical part of his narrative, paſſing over fome trifling reflections on the fyſtem of Linnæus, with which he did not feem to be perfectly acquainted; we ſhall therefore the lefs regret his Spaniſh Flora, which he had begun, but only lived to finiſh the letters A, B, and C; and from fo injudicious a method of treating this ſcience, his more enlightened fucceffors will probably never be tempted to continue it.

(a) "Arbutus uva urſi, the perennial leaved ſtrawberry-tree, the ſtems trailing leaves very entire, cup purple, bloſſoms white. In the Highlands of Scotland, and in Wales, upon the mountains. The berries are infipid, pulpy, and mealy. The plant is much ufed in Sweden to dye an aſh colour, and to tan leather. Half a dram of the powdered leaves, given every, or every other day, hath been found ufeful in calculous cafes. It was firſt ufed for this purpofe at Montpelier, and afterwards Dr. de Haen, at Vienna, relates feveral cafes in which it proved of the greateſt fervice; its fuccefs in England has been uncertain, fometimes the patients found no relief, but though their complaints rather aggravated, than alleviated; whilſt in other calculous and nephritic cafes, the fymptoms have been almoſt entirely removed. Perhaps, upon the whole, we ſhall find it no better than other vegetable aſtringents, fome of which have long been ufed by the country people, in gravelly complaints, and with very great advantage, though hitherto unnoticed by the regular practitioners"—Botanical arrangement of all the vegetables growing in Great Britain, &c. by William Withering, M. D. Birmingham, 1776.

LETTER

LETTER XVI.

Description of the lordship of Biscay, and its products.

THE lordship of Biscay is a mountainous country, about twelve leagues in length, from east to west, and eight from north to south, consisting entirely of hills, and mountains, of various dimensions, most of which are cultivated to the very summit, the vallies being checquered as well as the hills, with villages, farms, arable land, and pasture; the whole with such infinite variety and beauty, as to form a delightful landscape, with the most pleasing and romantic aspects the mind can conceive: the surface of earth generally lies over masses of stone, or detached rocks, limestone, sandy or grit stones, and sometimes valuable marble of various colours, particularly that dark grey inclining to black, streaked with white. The pillars in the king's chapel at Madrid, are of this sort, and come from Manaria; at other times, the surface extends over iron mines, though that of Somorrostro, is the most considerable, and employs the greatest number of forges.

Many of these mountains, consist of hills piled up upon each other, like that of Gorveya, which takes five hours to ascend; its summit affords a beautiful plain, with abundance of pasture, where the herds of Biscay, and Alaba remain for some months. Amongst other plants, it produces the *Ribes*, or black currant, whose leaves have a flavour of pepper, and are reckoned useful in gouty complaints. Near Durango the hills are bare, and from their steepness, very difficult to ascend. *Serantes*, near Portugalete, is another high hill, in the form of a pyramid, and being seen at a great distance, is a good land mark for mariners, sailing into the river of Bilbao: from its shape it seems as if it had been a volcano; many have erroneously taken it, for the mine of Somorrostro, but this is at a league distance. There are other mountains of half a league or a league in length, with craggy peaks, whose sides nevertheless admit of cultivation, and dwellings, such as that of *Villaro*; others are low and flat topped, covered with earth, having farms and habitations, besides wood for charcoal, and even meadows for pasture, extending to their summit, but none yield products in proportion to their surface: for the vegetative system rising in a perpendicular line, an oblique superficies cannot support more trees or plants than a plain of equal basis; as on a triangle one cannot raise more perpendiculars, than such as fall on its immediate basis.

Small

Small rivers and brooks issue from the crevices and clefts of these mountains; from Gorveya there run four, which uniting with that from the great mountain of Orduna, added to other torrents bursting through gullies where there is no water in summer, serve to form the river of Bilbao: these are so tremendous in winter, when swelled by heavy rains, as even to threaten the town with destruction, if they unfortunately met the tide at high water; the inhabitants are often alarmed in this manner, and it is common with them to go about the streets in boats at this season of the year.

If we except the ploughed fields, and the bare tops of some jagged mountains, all the rest are covered with woods, either for timber, or charcoal; some are natural, such as the holm, and arbutus, others are sowed, or planted, particularly oaks, which grow very fast. Where there are no woods, and a good depth of soil, it produces impenetrable thickets of the shrub called *Argoma*, as well as Cantabrian heath(a), and fine gorze. Higher up, where there is less earth, the sides of the hills, and the vallies, have plenty of grafted chesnuts, which the Hamburgh ships carry away in great quantities from Bilbao. The apple tree seems here to be in its natural soil, and thrives admirably without cultivation; the whole country pro-

(a) Erica cantabrica flore maximo foliis myrti, subtus incanis. Ray's Syn. 471.—— Andromeda Daboecia. Linn.

duces varieties of this fruit, but those of Durango are the best. Renets are common of two or three sorts; cherry trees grow as high as elms, at *Gordejuela*. They have excellent peaches, which they call *pavias*, with this remarkable circumstance, that they are never grafted, or improved by any particular culture (*a*). Those of Aranjuez are of this kind, but have not their flavour nor mellowness. Of pears they have great variety, and also those choice sorts, as the beurre, fondante, doyenne, and bergamotte; besides abundance of figs, nuts, and currants; and though the country does not produce rasberries naturally, it abounds with excellent strawberries, as well as all manner of garden plants, greens, and pulse in perfection. Their onions are remarkably sweet; Galicia furnishes them with turneps for cattle, and they have the small ones for the kitchen; their cows and oxen are small, but stout and robust: goats they had better be without, as great care must be taken to prevent them from destroying the trees: sheep they have none, and indeed it would be a difficult matter to hinder them from continually entangling themselves amongst the thickets. They have six or seven sorts of grapes, of which they make the *Chacoli* wine; all spots are not

(*a*) The French distinguish peaches into two sorts, viz. pavies and peaches. Those are called peaches which quit the stone, and those whose flesh adheres closely to the stone, pavies, which are more esteemed in France than the peaches, though in England the latter are preferred by many.—*Miller*.

equally

equally favourable; however the vineyards are numerous about Orunda and Bilbao, and form the principal revenues of the country gentlemen; but as the prices are fixed, and no foreign wine can be introduced nor sold by the publicans, while their own vintage is selling, they are more eager to increase the quantity than meliorate its quality, for which reason it is in general bad; besides, they make their vintage too early, which gives a sharpness to the wine, and deprives it of body; and being unskilful as well as careless, mixing the rotten and sour grape with the rest, Chacoli is a very poor wine. Their whole vintage will not suffice for four months confumption, and the deficiency must be made up from the province of Rioja, which occasions a saying, " That all the iron of Bifcay is swallowed down in foreign wine, by the natives." Even Englishmen and Germans, are people of great sobriety, compared with many Bifcayners, yet drunken men are feldom feen in the streets, because they are accustomed to eat heartily in these drinking entertainments; both men and women breakfast, dine, eat in the evening, and sup very plentifully; and yet enjoy excellent health.

Most of the mountains of Bifcay, and Guypufcoa, are of an argillaceous substance, the stone decomposes very little, or resolves into earth, though calcareous stone is abundant,

abundant, and in many parts they have manured for ages paſt with lime, yet it has cauſed very little alteration; the argillaceous ſubſtance ſeems to abſorb the calcareous, mixed with it, for though lime is the beſt ingredient to looſen the argillaceous particles which cling to the roots of delicate plants, and hinder them from penetrating further, and alſo to correct the acid, and convert it into more tractable land, yet thoſe of Biſcay ſtill preſerve their tenacity; that were it not for extraordinary labour, they would only produce thickets of bruſh wood, and briars: to prevent which, they turn up the earth with iron prongs, which inſtrument they call *laya*. Three or four labourers unite together, for one alone would make no progreſs; by this means they ſeperate large pieces of turf, which are turned upſide down; then another perſon comes, and in the trench which they have made, cuts away the weeds and roots, and the turf is next broke with the ſpade, and the winter froſt detaches it ſtill more. This operation is termed *Layar*.

In ſpring they draw a harrow over it with oxen, then ſeparate it ſtill more with another harrow; if all this will not do, they beat it with wooden mallets; then with a ſpade they dig holes in ſtraight lines, at two feet diſtance from each other. In every one of theſe, they ſow three or four grains of maiz, a few ſeeds of pumpion, ſome kidney beans, and peas, then filling the hole with manure, they cover it over with earth

Between

Between September and October the ears of maiz are ripe, and they cut the plant close to the ground, leaving the root to serve as manure. The cattle eat the leaves; and the stalks being trod under foot, serve likewise for manure. After the corn is sowed, they slightly turn the earth, during the winter, with a long and narrow spade, to break it more effectually, and loosen the strong substance; this they call *sallar*. In May or June they do the same once more, to destroy the weeds, which would otherwise stifle the grain. Their harvest time is in August, and they leave the stubble till winter, for pasture, when they again renew the work of the laya. This may be done continually with land contiguous to a farm, which partakes of its manure, or has lime thrown over it; but the lighter soil is generally left fallow, a twelve month; some soils are so soft and flexible, as not to require a stronger plough than is used in Castile; but in such they only sow wheat, and as tractable land is scarce, they break up the sides of the mountains, which, having little depth, will not bear large trees, and are generally covered with furze; for this purpose they inclose, with a hedge, the ground to be broke up, turn up the earth with a spade, cutting turf four inches deep, entangled with weeds and roots; after these roots are thoroughly dried, in July or August, they pile the turf in the form of a pyramid, setting fire to the whole, and covering it with earth to prevent

vent inflammation, so that the earth may be burned in the same manner as charcoal. They spread out this burned turf, which acquires the colour of brick-dust, then till the land and sow their corn; the three first years they have a plentiful harvest of wheat, the fourth they sow barley, and the fifth flax; then the land begins to wear out, the hedge is taken down and it affords tolerable pasture till its surface gets covered with brambles and weeds. All this hard labour is necessary to oblige this stubborn soil to maintain such numbers of people, who like to live well, and stand in need of good food, to support such constant fatigue; even all this will not do, they are still forced to get corn from Castile, or elsewhere, but they always prefer that of Castile, as better though dearer. In the same manner they depend on their neighbours for other kinds of food, as in so close a country, covered with woods, little is left for grazing; nevertheless they eat better meat than their neighbours, as their cattle are stall fed in the winter.

Game would be plentiful if there were not so many sportsmen, though they do not want for partridges, and their quail are the best in all Spain. In marshy places, they are well stocked with wild ducks, woodcocks, and snipes. In the plains they have hares, but no rabbets, nor any deer, nor roebucks, which last the Spaniards call *corzo*, as coming originally from Corsica; as they give

the

the name of *galgo* to a greyhound, having firſt had them from Gaul, as Martial ſays,

"Leporemque læſum Gallici canis dente."
Lib. iⱨ. Epig. 47.

The woods are not without wild boars; and Don Manuel de las Caſas who had been miniſter of Marine at St. Sebaſtians, killed a very large lynx, (lupus cervarius) in that part called *las encartaciones* (a); but the common wolf is ſcarce, there being ſo few ſheep to entice them, and the country ſo fully inhabited by which means they are immediately diſcovered and killed. Hardly once in an hundred years one meets with a bear, though ſo common in the mountains of Leon and Aſturias, which form a chain jointly with thoſe of Biſcay; but they have plenty of foxes, to the great annoyance of their houſewives, from the havock they make amongſt the poultry. Their ſea-ports are well ſupplied with fiſh, every ſort being better and firmer in the ocean than in the Mediterranean, ſo that without having a very nice palate, it is eaſy to diſtinguiſh a bream of Biſcay from one of Valencia. Oyſters and other teſtaceous fiſh they have likewiſe in great plenty, and that delicate fiſh called *Sardina*, in ſuch numbers, that you may buy a hundred for the value of a halfpenny.

(a) The name of Encartaciones is given to a certain number of villages in the mountains of Burgos near Biſcay, where they enjoy the ſame franchiſes and privileges as the people of that lordſhip.

LETTER XVII.

Reflections on the genius and character of the Biscayners.

THE Biscayners give the name of republicks to the different jurisdictions in their provinces, all which, except Orduna, their only city, and a few towns, are composed of hamlets, and lonely houses, dispersed up and down, according to the convenience of situation, in so close and intersected a country. However their houses have every advantage of distribution, consisting of a principal story, besides the ground floor, for offices, with an appendage of stables, granaries, outhouses, courts, cellars, and gardens; with orchards, meadows, and often corn-fields, contiguous to the building, with chesnut groves, and other improvements to the very foot of the mountains. Nothing can be more pleasant to the traveller, than to see houses and gardens during the whole course of his progress, particularly from Orduna to Bilbao, an extent of six leagues, which seems like one continued village. The upper part of the houses were formerly of wood, but the new ones are of stone, and one seldom sees an empty house, or any fallen in ruins; on the contrary, many new ones, both large and convenient, are constantly building; from whence

whence it appears, that though population cannot well be confiderably encreafed, while new branches of induftry are not introduced, all the land being occupied, it feems, rather to augment, notwithftanding the many emigrations; and though fome women emigrate likewife, few remain at home without hufbands. Thefe difperfed families may be held as the moft antient in Spain, and the country is indebted to them, for population and culture. In the Bifcay language they are called *Ecbejaunas*; that is, lords of tenements, whofe anceftors have poffeffed them time immemorial, and will probably continue fo for future ages, as felling or mortgaging is held in great difrepute. Such lands as belong to rich families, are let out to others, and as they lie under their eye and infpection, the whole is attended to, with the utmoft activity; the parochial church ftands in the centre of the parifh, which, if too extenfive, has a chapel of eafe, for the conveniency of the parifhioners; many of whom repair to thefe churches from very great diftances, in the fevereft weather. Their antiquity may be traced from their dedications, which are generally to the Bleffed Virgin, to St. John, or the apoftles and faints of the Primitive Church; and their livings muft be comfortable, from the decent appearance of their paftors.

Not only Bifcay, Guypufcoa, and Alaba, but alfo the mountains of Burgos, are full of gentlemens feats, known by the name of *Solares*, or *Casas Solariegas* worthy of much veneration from their antiquity; the owners of these are distinguished by the title of *Hidalgos de Casa Solar*, or *de Solar Conocido*—" Gentlemen of known property;" the most honourable appellation in Spain. They are generally strong, plain structures, with square towers; but many of the towers have been destroyed; and in the modern repairs, they have followed the fashion of the times.

The head of the family is called *Pariente Mayor*, and is greatly respected by all the collateral branches; some of these are of such high antiquity, as to be thought to have dwelled there before the establishment of Christianity, in that country, since their ancestors were the founders of the churches, had the patronage of them, and were known so far back as four centuries ago, to have, even then, been time immemorial, in receipt of the tythes; others, without any patronage, are deemed equally antient; many are so far reduced as to be obliged to cultivate their estates, with their own hands, yet will not yield to the others, in nobility and descent, alledging that, though some branches have been more enriched by fortunate events, yet they are all equally sprung from one common ancestor. Their names have undoubtedly passed in a lineal succession, from a more antient date than the ages of chivalry, the establishment

ment of coat armour, or of archives, and records; to which they pay little attention, as of no importance to illuſtrate their quality, the poſſeſſion of one of theſe houſes, or the conſtant tradition of being deſcended from a former poſſeſſor, being more than ſufficient to enoble their blood; many ſuch having ſhined in the annals of Spain, by the nobleſt deeds, which have immortalized their names more than their ancient deſcent. Theſe have ſettled in different parts of the kingdom, while the head of the family has continued at home, in a ſtate of ſimplicity, ploughing his fields, and inſpiring his children, with ſentiments ſuitable to the heroical ages: the daughters are brought up in a different manner from moſt other parts of the world; here the moſt opulent do not diſdain the management of houſhold affairs, and every branch of domeſtic œconomy, with a noble ſimplicity, that ſeems to recall thoſe glorious ages of which Homer has ſung. Whoever looks for innocence, health and content, will find it amongſt the inhabitants of Biſcay; and if they are not the richeſt, they may be well deemed the happieſt of mankind (*a*).

It is pleaſing to behold with what affability the rich demean themſelves towards thoſe who are leſs ſo than

---

(*a*) Mr. Bowles relates, that the moſt opulent families make no ſcruple to bake, brew, dreſs victuals, and waſh linen. For my part I cannot ſay I obſerved theſe circumſtances amongſt the opulent Biſcaypers, though I often experienced their open-hearted hoſpitality and benevolence.

themſelves,

themselves, being obliged to this condescension from the natural spirit, and pride of the people, added to their education and notions of freedom. Unaccustomed to brook the least scorn, or to comply with that submissive behaviour so usual from the poor to the rich, in more refined and opulent kingdoms; yet the common proverb of Castile, *Pobreza no es vileza*, "Poverty is not a blemish," has no sway here, for such are their notions of labour, and industry, that their spirit makes them consider it, as an indignity to beg; and though the women are generally charitable, which cannot fail to attract mendicants, yet these are most commonly strangers.

The country people wear brogues, not unlike those of the highlands of Scotland, tied up with great neatness, being the most useful for a slippery and mountainous country. When they are not busy in the fields, they walk with a staff taller than themselves, which serves them to vault over gullies, and is an excellent weapon in case of assault, with which they will baffle the most dextrous swordsmen; they wear cloaks in the winter, the pipe is constantly in the mouth, as well for pleasure as from a notion that tobacco preserves them against the dampness of the air; all this, joined to their natural activity, sprightliness, and vigour, gives them an appearance seeming to border on ferocity, were it not the reverse of their manners, which are gentle and easy,

when

when no motive is given to choler, which the least spark kindles into violence.

It has been observed, that the inhabitants of mountains are strongly attached to their country, which probably arises from the division of lands, in which, generally speaking, all have an interest. In this, the Biscayners exceed all other states, looking with fondness on their hills, as the most delightful scenes in the world, and their people as the most respectable, descended from the *aborigines* of Spain. This prepossession excites them to the most extraordinary labour, and to execute things far beyond what could be expected, in so small and rugged a country, where they have few branches of commerce: I cannot give a greater proof of their industry, than those fine roads they have now made from Bilbao to Castile, as well as in Guypuscoa and Alaba. When one sees the passage over the tremendous mountain of Orduna, one cannot behold it without the utmost surprize and admiration.

The manners of the Biscayners, and the ancient Irish, are so similar on many occasions, as to encourage the notion of the Irish being descended from them. Both men and women are extremely fond of pilgrimages, repairing from great distances to the churches of their patrons, or tutelary saints, singing and dancing, till they almost

drop

drop down with fatigue. The Irish do the same at their *patrons*. The *Guizones* of Biscay, and the *Boulamkeighs* of Ireland are nearly alike: at all these assemblies, they knock out one another's brains, on the most trivial provocation, without malice or rancour, and without using a knife or a dagger. In both countries the common people are passionate, easily provoked if their family is slighted, or their descent called in question. The *Chacoli* of Biscay, or the *Shebeen* of Ireland, makes them equally frantic. In Ireland the poor eat out of one dish with their fingers, and sit in their smoaky cabbins without chimnies, as well as the Biscayners. The brogue is also the shoe of Biscay; the women tie a kercher round their heads, wear red petticoats, go barefoot, in all which they resemble the Biscayners, and with them have an equal good opinion of their ancient descent: the poor Biscayner, though haughty, is laborious and active, an example worthy to be imitated by the Irish.

So many concurring circumstances support the idea of their having been originally one people. It cannot be denied, but that the old Irish, whether from similitude of customs, religion, and traditional notions, or whatever else may be the cause, have always been attached to the Spaniards, who on their side, perhaps from political views, have treated them with reciprocal affection, granting them many privileges, and stiling them even *Oriundos*

TRAVELS THROUGH SPAIN.

in their laws, as a colony descended from Spain; yet, with all these advantages, if we except those gallant soldiers who have distinguished themselves in the field wherever they have served, few Irish have made a conspicuous figure in Spain, or have left great wealth to their families (*a*).

The King of Spain has no other title over these free people, than that, of Lord of Biscay, as the kings of England formerly held over Ireland; they admit of no bishops, nor of custom houses in their provinces, and as they pay less duties than the king's other subjects, they were not included in the late extensions of the American commerce; however, they content themselves with that renown which they have acquired for themselves and their issue, insomuch that upon only proving, to be originally belonging to that lordship, or descended from such in the male line, lawfully begotten, they are entitled to claim public certificates, or executory letters, termed *Cartas executorias,* expressive of their being *Hidalgos de*

(*a*) Another instance in which the Irish seem to have closely imitated the Spanish customs, is in the taking of snuff, of which Mr. Howel, who was in Spain in 1620. and went soon after to Ireland, gives us the following account, at an early period, after the first introduction of snuff into Europe: "The Spaniards and Irish take it most in powder, or smutchin, and it mightily refreshes the brain, and I believe there is as much taken this way in Ireland, as there is in pipes in England. One shall commonly see the serving maid upon the washing-block, and the swain upon the ploughshare, when they are tired with labour, take out their boxes of smutchin, and draw it into their nostrils with a quill, and it will beget new spirits in them, with a fresh vigour to fall to their work again."—Epistolæ Hoelianæ London, 1726.

Sangre, or " Gentlemen of blood;" their nobility having been confirmed to them, by the kings of Castile and Leon, lords of Biscay, in the plenitude of their power.

The most lofty Castilians have constant rivals for antiquity and descent in the inhabitants of Biscay, Asturias, and the mountains of Leon: thus, in Don Quixote, Dona Rodriguez, the duenna, speaking of her husband, says, he was as well born as the king, because he came from the mountains. *Y sobre todo Hidalgo, como el Rey, porque era montanes* (a).

Impressed with these flattering ideas, the high-minded Biscayner leaves his native soil, and repairs to Madrid. Conscious that his blood is pure, uncontaminated with mixtures of Jewish, or Mahometan race, he raises his hopes on honest industry, and sobriety, fulfilling his duties with zeal, and submission; he often meets with relations in affluence, and sometimes rises to the highest employments. It should seem that some such character must have offended the immortal Cervantes, from his pointed reflections in his celebrated romance of Don Quixote, where he says that, " an express being arrived " with dispatches of moment directed to Don Sancho " Panza, governor of the island of Barataria, into his own " hands, or those of his secretary, which being given to

(a) Don Quixote, part 2. tom. 4. cap. ci. Madrid, 1771.

" read

"read to the major domo, by Sancho; the imaginary
"governor aſked, Who here is my ſecretary? To which
"one preſent anſwered, *I, ſir, am the perſon, becauſe I
"can read and write, and am moreover a Biſcayner.* With
"this addition, replied Sancho, you are fit to be a ſecre-
"tary, even to an emperor" (*a*).

(*a*) Don Quixote, part 1. tom. 4. chap. c. Madrid, 1771.

LETTER XVIII.

Defcription of the town of Bilbao, and the manners of its inhabitants.

THE town of Bilbao, on the banks of the river Ybaizabal, is about two leagues from the sea, and contains about eight hundred houses, with a large square by the water side, well shaded with pleasant walks, which extend to the outlets, on the banks of the river, with numbers of houses and gardens, which form a most pleasing prospect, particularly as you sail up the river; for, besides the beautiful verdure, numerous objects open gradually to the eye, and the town appearing as an amphitheatre, enlivens the landscape, and completes the scenery.

The houses are solid and lofty, the streets well paved and level; water is conveyed into the streets, and they may be washed at pleasure, which renders Bilbao one of the neatest towns in Europe. Coaches are not in use, by which means, inequality of wealth is not so perceptible, exterior ostentation is avoided, and the poor

man

man walks by the fide of the rich, with equal eafe and content.

The air is generally damp, covers iron with ruft, deftroys furniture in the upper apartments, extracts the falt out of dried fifh, and multiplies flies beyond meafure, yet the town is remarkably healthy, and its inhabitants enjoy, to a great degree, the three principal bleffings of life, perfect health, ftrength of body, and a chearful difpofition, attended with longevity; in proof of which, though the town is very populous, the hofpital is frequently empty, and in the nine months, that Mr. Bowles refided there, only nine perfons were buried, four of which were above eighty. Every day one may fee men above that age walking upright, in chearful converfe with youth. Burning fevers, which the Spaniards dread fo much and call *tabardillos*, are not known here, and they are feldom troubled with agues. What is then the reafon that Bilbao, on the fide of a river, in fo damp a fituation, and chiefly built on piles, like the cities in Holland, fhould be fo remarkably healthy, with every indication againft it? I fhall endeadeavour to account for it.

The adjacent mountains ftop the clouds that arife from the faline vapours of the ocean, rains are frequent, but they are feldom without a fea breeze, or a land wind;
the

the current of the air being thus continually ventilated, never leaves the moist vapours at rest, and prevents their forming those putrid combinations, which heat generally occasions, on stagnated waters; thus the vicinity of the sea, the rains, and more than all, the strong currents of air, are the physical causes of its salubrity at Bilbao, as on the contrary, the continued heat which rarifies the exhalations of such rivers as have a slow motion, as well as the stagnated waters in ponds or lakes, where there is great heat in the air, and little wind, will be the causes of putrifying the vapours, and bring on fevers and other distempers. For this reason, the inhabitants of La Mancha are so subject to agues, and use as much bark as in Holland, because the air has little motion in summer, notwithstanding the country is open, and the surface is dry. In the same manner, a new house is dangerous to dwell in, where the damp vapours are confined, though one may sleep very safely in the deepest gallery of a mine, if the air has a free circulation.

To these favourable circumstances, the Biscayners owe their good spirits, freshness of complexion, and chearful disposition. In other countries, women are oppressed with the slightest fatigue; here they work as much as the strongest men, unload the ships, carry burdens, and do all the business of porters. The very felons, confined to hard labour in the mines of Almaden,

do

do nothing in comparison with these females; they go bare footed, and are remarkably active, carrying burthens on their heads which require two men to lift up. The wife yields not in strength to the husband, nor the sister to the brother, and after a chearful glass, though heavily loaded, they move on with alacrity, returning home in the evening, without the appearance of lassitude, often arm in arm, dancing and singing to the tabor and pipe.

Their music is defrayed at the expence of the town, after the manner of the antient Greeks. On holidays they play under the trees in the great square; the moment they begin, the concourse is great, men, women, and children, of all ages, are engaged at the same time, down to the very infants. The dances, are active, suitable to their strength, but divested of indecent attitudes or gestures. These surprising women, though constantly exposed to the air, have good complexions, with lively eyes, and fine black hair, in which they pride themselves greatly, and braid to uncommon advantage. Married women wrap a white handkerchief round their heads, so knotted, as to fall down in three plaits behind, and over this the Montera cap. They have a haughty look, and work in the fields like the men; their language is the *Bascuense*, which, without doubt, is original, and as antient as the peopling of the country,

being

being totally diſtinct, and without any connection with any Spaniſh dialect; thoſe who underſtand it, aſſure us it is very ſoft and harmonious, as well as energetic (a).

A general neatneſs prevails every where in the town of Bilbao. The ſhambles is a Tuſcan building, in the centre of the town, with an open court and a fountain in the middle; nothing can be more cleanly or better contrived, free from all bad ſcents, or any thing diſguſting as it is copiouſly ſupplied with water to carry away every thing offenſive. The meat is delivered ſo freſh and clean, as not to require being waſhed, as practiſed in other parts of Spain, which deprives it of its ſubſtance and flavour; the veal is white and delicate, and the poultry excellent: the woods afford plenty of birds, be-

---

(a) In the mountains of Biſcay and Navarre, the Spaniſh language, or romance, is neither ſpoken or underſtood.

See the following books.

De la antigua lengua, poblaciones, y Comarcas de las Eſpanas en que de paſo ſe tocan algunas coſas de la Cantabria por Andres de Poza —Bilbao, 1587, 4to.

El impoſible vencido: Arte de la lengua baſconcada por manuel de Larramendi. Salamanca, 1729.

Diccionario Trilingue del Caſtillano, Baſcuenſe y Latin por manuel de Larramendi, 1745.

From whence it is evident that the Baſcuenſe is totally different from the Spaniſh, which is the common language of the two Caſtiles, Leon, Eſtremadura, Andaluſia, Aragon, Navarre, Rioxa, and the mountains of Burgos; and is generally underſtood in Aſturias, Galicia, Valencia, and Catalonia, though not the language of thoſe provinces, where they have a dialect varying more or leſs from the Spaniſh, in proportion to their ſituation and proximity to neighbouring kingdoms.

ſides

sides five sorts of birds of passage, called *Chimbos*, which fatten soon after their arrival, and are greatly esteemed.

Amongst the different sorts of fish common at Bilbao, there are two peculiar to that river, which the inhabitants are remarkably fond of; these are a peculiar sort of eels in winter, and the cuttle fish in summer; the eels are small like the quill of a pigeon, of a pale colour, about three inches long, and without a back bone, which they catch at low tides in prodigious quantities. In a word, every thing is in plenty at Bilbao, for besides a well supplied market, their gardens abound in pulse, and fruit of all kinds; so that one can live no where better than here, when we take into the account, the hospitable disposition of the inhabitants, which soon falls off, if you slight their cordiality, or attribute it to motives of adulation or interest. Such is the happy life of the inhabitants of Bilbao, free from the luxuries as well as the ambitious passions, which agitate the minds of their neighbours, they pass their lives in tranquility, governed by wholesome laws; amongst which they are said, even to have one against ingratitude, with a punishment affixed to it.

LETTER XIX.

Reflections on the injudicious method laid down in the Spanish ordinances, for the propagation of timber, being the substance of a memorial presented by Don Guillermo Bowles, to his Excellency Don Julian de Arriaga, Minister of State for the department of the Indies and Marine.

TO judge of the quality of oak, fit for building, the four following circumstances are to be considered; First, the situation; secondly, the nature and depth of the soil; thirdly, the age of the tree, when it is felled; fourthly, the manner of laying it down to dry.

In mountainous countries, the best timber is from about midway, up to the tops of the mountains; its goodness rather decreases, in proportion as it approaches towards the valley. In the lower parts, the trees grow quicker, and are more sightly; but as the roots must always partake of a greater share of moisture, from their situation, which exposes them to the continual flow of water from the heights, the stem is not so vigorous nor solid; thus a tree on the top of the mountain, will not be so large nor beautiful at sixty years of age, as another in the valley at forty; but let the builder be cautious

tious how he trusts to outward appearances, otherwise he will certainly be disappointed.

It appears from various judicious experiments, that oaks arrive at their greatest perfection, at the period of fifty years, when the soil has above two feet depth, and at seventy-five years, when the depth exceeds three and a half; if it is above four feet, they then increase in vigour and strength for upwards of a century. From whence it is evident, that trees, like animals, have their period of youth, maturity, and decay. When they cease to grow, they are come to maturity, the conductory vessels are obstructed, the tubes turn to solid timber, the sap ceasing to circulate, becomes all spine or heart, and the tree remains in a state of perfection, and rest, for a term of twenty or thirty years. This is the proper time, between adolescence and old age, to fell the tree; if it was attempted while the sap was yet in circulation, the timber would be liable to warp in hot weather, besides many other defects. We must not imagine, that though this operation was performed in the winter, or what might be thought a proper season, such as the Spaniards call a good moon, according to the opinion of the antients (*a*), that these inconveniencies would be

(*a*) The antients had a great regard to the age of the moon in the felling of their timber. Pliny orders it to be in the very article of the change, which happening on the last day of the winter solstice, the timber, says he, will be immortal.

removed.

removed. Oaks, reared from acorns, in plantations, prepared for the purpose, near villages, with the utmost care and attention, though afterwards transplanted on a mountain, will never be so perfect as those that have grown spontaneously or even originally sown there. These two allegations will shew, that the Spanish ordinance of 1748, for the planting of mountains, committed two capital errors in its decrees; for it says, " That near every village, a nursery shall be established for the sowing of acorns, manuring them every year; and when they are transplanted, the length of a foot is to be cut off from the root of every plant, while two or three feet of earth is laid round them, to make them grow faster (*a*)!" This may do very well to obtain a fine avenue in a park, or form an agreeable grove, but will never answer the end of yielding good solid timber, proper for the building of houses or ships; for, though it is certain that a tree transplanted, pruned, and well supplied with manure, may flourish, and have a beautiful appearance, yet this is obtained at the expence of its constitution, by a precipitated vegetation. The intention of the ordinance was to lessen the original defect, by transplantation on a mountain; but this expe-

(*a*) The words of the ordinance are as follows: " Que en cada lugar se señalara un vivero para sembrar las bellotas, beneficiandole con estiercol cada ano, y en el mismo año del trasplante se cortara a cada arbol un pie de su planta, y para que crescan con brevedad, se les arrimara dos o tres pies de tierra."—Ordenanza. De la cria y plantio de los montes. Del ano de 1748.

dient

dient has not power enough to correct the error arising from its first propagation; and what is still worse, a further law contributes more fully to its decay, since it ordains that " they should be pruned, in order to shoot up more vigorously, and that the straight trees, which might be converted into beams or knee timbers, ought to be improved, by cutting the points of their principal shoots (a)." This regulation produces the reverse of what was intended, and is the original cause of so many hollow oaks observed throughout Spain. For this reason the white mulberry trees of Valencia, and Murcia, are generally hollow, while the black sort in Grenada is solid and healthy, because the shoots are not pruned. On the road from Tortosa to Valencia, I measured three monstrous olive trees, entirely hollow, having scarce any substance beyond the bark, and yet they bore fruit. One of them was forty-one feet in circumference. I saw others, as large, at Villaviciosa, in Portugal, which were stout and solid, because they had not been so barbarously treated: in a word, every tree used in the manner the king's ordinance directs, may thrive and grow for many years, but it will not attain to that crisis of time, between life and death, when it ought to be in a state of perfection. Cedars and firs I allow, may be excepted from

(a) The ordinance says, " Que las podas de los arboles son para que crescan tinos; y que los arboles derechos que pueden convertirse en vaos, quillas y codastes, deben beneficiarse cortando las puntas de la guia principal."

this

this rule, as their interior parts do not run any risk from such an operation, there being a great difference between trees, whose fibres are impregnated with a balsamic and incorruptible oil, and those which draw their nurture from sap, the superabundance of which, tends to putrefaction; for the root of a tree increases, and grows, in proportion as the stem and principal branches require a greater supply of nurture. It is equally known, that the juices sucked in by the roots, are annually distributed from the stem to the branches, affording life and support to the leaves, flowers and fruit. For this reason the mulberry trees in Valencia, which are pruned every two or three years, begin to decay in five or six years, and the oak and chesnut of Biscay, which are used in the same manner for the purpose of charcoal, begin to decline, the former in ten years, and the latter in twenty, when they ought to be in their prime. On the contrary, those oaks which grow in their natural state, never transplanted nor pruned, nor receiving other ill-treatment, neither rot, nor become hollow, except by some particular accident, but push on to a venerable old age, till the course of nature has at last brought them to their final decline.

It is nevertheless allowed, that the small portion of sap diverted from its course by casual pruning, which falls back into the stem, is not sufficient to rot the tree, or cause any essential prejudice, provided the wound is soon

soon healed, which cannot be done when the branch is large; and if the operation is often repeated, it will infallibly occasion a caries. Let us admire those beautiful elms planted by Charles Vth. at Aranjuez, about two hundred years ago, which now have a most amazing trunk, surprising by their height and bulk, some near six feet diameter, without the least appearance of decay; when the trees of the Prado, at Madrid, from having been pruned, were rotten in less than a century; but at Aranjuez, when any of the trees are pulled up, though the tops are decayed from old age, they afford beams as solid as a walnut-tree, while the old trees of the Prado served only for fuel; the same will happen with those in the walks of the Delicias, near Madrid, though planted only thirty years ago, which from being repeatedly lopped, are already in a state of decay, and will soon totally perish.

The mulberry trees of Valencia yield a second leaf, of equal strength with the first that was stripped off. I once asked a peasant why he did not avail himself of this second leaf, for the use of the silk worms? he answered me, that it would be of infinite prejudice to the tree, and drain it of its substance. He was right as to the fact, though his reason was bad, because the roots with their juices, support the stem, branches, leaves, and fruit. If the branches are lopped, the stem grows hollow; if the first leaves are taken off, the sap reverts, and mixes with what comes forth at a second shoot; but if you take this off likewise, then the sap recoils on the bark, and the heart, and the tree will be glutted by repletion, rather than starved by inanition, as the labourer imagines. With respect to the method of falling of timber, it should be done with particular attention to the trunk, so as to prevent a further effusion of the sap, otherwise a great part of that strength, which it affords to the tree, when it condenses, would be lost. When the tree is felled, it should be carefully placed in such a manner, that the two extremities may rest upon a prop of wood or of stone, two feet, at least, from the ground, that the air may have a free circulation. If it lies on the ground, the moisture would penetrate on one side, and it would dry on the other. Even in its raised situation, it will suffer in some degree, as its own shade will cause some alteration, for which reason the tree should be turned two or three times in the year; concerning which there are excellent instructions laid down by Mr. Duchamel de Monceau, and Mr. de Buffon, the result of philosophical observations and repeated experiments (*a*).

(*a*) While we are busy in finding fault with Spanish ordinances, let us for a moment divest ourselves of prejudices, and examine the glaring impropriety of some of our acts of parliament at home. The cutting down of the oak timber in the spring of the year, when the bark will easily part from the wood, as it is now generally practised in England, is also, according to Mr. Miller, a very great absurdity, for the sap of the trees being at that time in full motion in all their vessels, the timber soon after cutting is cracked and torn in many places when

Many

Many confiderable advantages will enfue from a due obfervation of thefe principles, and may be applied to the purpofe of fhip builders and carpenters ; from thefe premifes we may conceive the reafon, that, of two houfes built by the fame architect, one fhall be folid, and remain in a due perpendicular, while the walls of the other fhall give way by the dilation or contraction of the beams ; from hence we may perhaps be able to refolve that curious problem, which has been propofed to all the geometricians in Europe, to find out, why two fhips, built by the fame perfon, on fimilar principles and menfuration, with timber from the fame place, and cut at the fame time, one fhall go like the wind, and the other fhall be the dulleft of failers. One fhall come home tight, and in good condition, from a long voyage, and the other fo leaky, that the pumps muft be kept conftanly going. For my part, as I conceive that the dilatation of a beam, may throw a wall out of equilibrium, I imagine that the fame effects, acting upon various bodies of

exposed to the air, and will not laft a fourth part of the time, as that, which is cut in winter, when the fap is thickened, and at reft; yet there is an act of parliament to oblige every one to cut their timber at that feafon for the fake of the bark. —See Miller's Gardener's Dict. preface to folio edition, London, 1759.

Does not the following paffage from the fame author, fpeaking of the French, breathe the fpirit of a true patriot, as well as a philofopher. " They do not neglect the culture of their own ufeful timber trees, particularly the oak, for as they feem to be very much in earneft to improve and increafe their marine, they are purfuing feveral fchemes, which in time will enable them to carry their point. Surely then this fhould not be neglected in Great Britain, as the welfare of this country principally depends on its fhipping and commerce."

A a

timber,

timber, of different shapes and dimensions, united together, and their action upon one another (*a*), may give a new position to all the constituent parts, and a certain flexibility or inflexibility, which may have an effect on the swiftness, or slowness of its motion, through the water; and what is still worse, strain particular parts, in such a degree, as to make a ship very leaky. It perhaps may be objected, that these observations are only of moment in the northern, and moist districts, and that they are of no signification with respect to the warm and dry air of the southern provinces of Spain; but I beg leave to assert, that they will hold good in every climate, with more or less effect, and are of course worthy of the notice of the public at large, as well as those individuals whom they may more particularly concern.

(*a*) The late learned Spanish Admiral, Don George Juan, published a very elaborate and scientific treatise on this subject, intitled, " Examen maritimo Teorico, Pratico, o Tratado de Mecanica aplicada a la construccion, conociemiento y Manejo de los Navios, &c."—Madrid 1771.

LETTER

LETTER XX.

Description of the iron mine, and forges, at Somorrostro, in Biscay.

THE famous iron mine at Somorrostro, in Biscay, has all the appearance of being alluvial, and originally composed by the congelation of some fluid matter, increasing by insensible degrees, and reduced into a lamellated state, successively forming plates, or scales, one over the other, thinner than paper; as is evident from the many concavities and crevices, covered over by these plates; which supposing to be the case, we need not be surprized, at what has been advanced by some of the workmen, who assure us, that they have often found broken pieces of pickaxes, mattocks, and other instruments, in places that had been worked centuries ago, and are now replete with new ore; if this is a fact, we may further believe them, when they assert, that the mine increases, though the slow progress of nature, in this operation, does not permit us to calculate its gradation, or determine the number of ages sufficient, to fill up a cavity of any given size.

From the above, it results, that a solution, evaporation, alluvion, and deposition, all exist in this mine; its situation is an undulated hill; which, viewed from the neighbouring mountains, seems almost a plain: its form is regular, and one may go round it in about four or five hours. The ore forms an uninterrupted stratum, whose thickness varies from three feet to ten, and is covered with a coat of whitish calcareous rock, from two to six feet thick. I now proceed to their method of working this mine, where every one is at liberty to dig at pleasure, and transport it by land or water, without being subject to duties or any formalities. The people being generally ignorant, and carrying away whatever comes uppermost, often take ore, which has its matrix of quartz, and is of a brittle kind, full of cracks; but the iron masters, who are the purchasers, are more versed, and know what to buy, and what to reject. It is generally allowed, that no iron in Europe is so easy to fuse, or so soft as that of Somorrostro. When the ore is first taken out of this mine, it has the colour of bull's blood, and when wetted becomes purple; great quantities are carried away by water, to the neighbouring provinces, where they fuse it by itself, or mix it with ore of their own, which generally yields a harder iron; I shall only speak of their process with that ore which is fused without any mixture.

The

The first operation is to roast it (*a*) in the open air, by piling strata alternately of ore, and wood, in order to divide the ore, repel the moisture, and diminish its weight, that it may be more easily fused, and the ferruginous parts separated from the slag: when it is sufficiently roasted, they put it in the forge, with the due proportion of charcoal, and when it appears to have fused, by leaving on the hearth, a mass of four or five arrobes, they lay hold of it with tongs, and place it on an anvil under an immense hammer, of about seven hundred to a thousand pounds weight, and there by force of blows, and moving it about, they square it, and reduce it into bars. The numerous sparks which fly off from the blows of the hammer, are no more than the scoriæ of the metal. The bar thus shaped, may be doubled or lengthened in a less forge, if they please, and even beat cold as if it was silver. In this manner the ore is fused in a few hours, and the bars formed, and sold to the blacksmiths.

(*a*) No general rule can be given, concerning the duration, or degree of fire, for this purpose, these being various, according to the difference of the ores; a few days, or even hours, is sufficient for some ores, while others, such as the ore of Rammelsburg, require that it should be continued for several months. Shlutter enumerates five methods of roasting ores; viz.

First, By constructing a pile of ore and fuel, placed alternately in strata, in the open air.
Secondly, By confining such a pile within walls, but without a roof.
Thirdly, By placing the pile under a roof, without lateral walls.
Fourthly, By placing the pile in a furnace, consisting of walls and roof.
Fifthly, By roasting the ore in a reverberatory furnace, in which it must be continually stirred, with an iron rod.

Formerly

Formerly the iron was beat by mere strength of arm; a proof of which may be gathered from the names of many places in Biscay, situated where there is neither river nor brook, and begin, or end, with the termination *ola*, or *olea*, either of which in the Biscay language, signifies iron works, such as *Mendiola*, that is, " iron works of the mountain."

According to appearance, a quintal of ore will produce about thirty-five pounds of good iron, and the residue about thirty pounds of flag, and dead earth. As this mine neither contains sulphur, nor acids, it is not necessary to mix any calcareous substance to fuse it, in order to absorb those matters, so troublesome in mines, that have the misfortune to be loaded with them, as is often the case in France. However, it would not be amiss to use a little of it, were it only to assist the fusion of the ferruginous earth, accelerate the process, and lessen the flag, as well as the quantity of fuel. These workmen, by constant experience, have acquired the proper method of managing the ore, as well as to know the quantity of coal for the forge, which is seldom larger than that of a considerable blacksmith; so that little improvement can be made on their labours; though by several experiments, made in 1773, by the *sociedad Bascongada*; or Biscay society, it appears that it would answer better to roast the iron, in a close chamber, than in the

the open air. A good forge, well conducted, will yield to the owner above five hundred ducats a year (a); some indeed, hardly produce three hundred, after paying all charges. It is neceffary for them to be good œconomifts, with refpect to fuel, and to ufe fmall forges; for if they were to have fuch large ones, as are common in moft parts of Europe, with all the apparatus of hammers and other implements, they would foon ftrip their mountains of wood, and the forges would be at a ftand for want of materials.

Befides the mine of Somorroftro, there are feveral others, fome of which are worked, and others not. In one near Bilbao, the ore is feen above ground. About a mile from the town, there is a mine in a hill, of a quite different nature from that of Somorroftro, being loaded with vitriol; it is an enormous mafs of iron ore, that attracts the vitriolic acid, which penetrating through the ferruginous rock, diffolves the metal, and exhibits on the furface, fmall laminæ of green, blue, and white vitriol. Oppofite to this hill, on the other fide of the river, another fimilar rock produces a quantity of vitriol folely of a pale yellow, and though the colours green, blue, and yellow, may exift without any vitriolic acid, chemifts are very well apprized from experience, that the common iron diffolved in this acid, cryftallizes into green

(a) A Spanifh ducat, worth about four fhillings and eight pence, Englifh money.

vitriol,

vitriol, which we call copperas, forms blue cryſtals, with copper, and white cryſtals, or allum, when united with argillaceous earth, and of the ſame colour when it diſſolves zinc, and produces yellow, when it coagulates with the phlogiſton of common ſulphur, which abounds ſo frequently in the three kingdoms of nature. The moſt remarkable circumſtance, is to meet theſe colours in the Biſcay mines, which neither contain copper, allum, zinc, nor ſulphur; nor is it an eaſy matter to account for it, without ſuppoſing that the pure elementary water, has a part in compoſing theſe cryſtals, and that its evaporation, either by heat, or air, alters the conſiſtency, and deſtroys the green colour of the vitriol of the iron, taking away that proportion of water, which conſtituted it, and that as ſoon as it loſes it, it begins to change colour, and paſſing through the various tints of green, and yellow, terminates in white, when all the water is gone: when it is come to that ſtate, and has a reſemblance to flour, it is called ſympathetic powder, on account of its ſtyptical quality, ſo readily ſtaunching the blood, in hemorrhages, and curing of wounds. Whoever chooſes to verify this theory, need only to pour water on this white powder, and he will find that it cryſtallizes anew into green. If it be aſked, why theſe matters do not unite, and form ſulphur, when there is ſo much acid, and iron in theſe mountains, and the iron contains ſo much phlogiſton? I anſwer, that for this event to take

place,

place, the vitriolic acid, and the phlogiston, should be perfectly concentred, and dry; whereas the reverse happens in these mountains, where they are so overwhelmed with moisture, that the abundance of this acid, has perhaps been the cause, of many of the mines about Bilbao, being neglected, as of course they would yield so brittle an iron. This then would be the time to use a calcareous substance, to correct this defect. It is for this reason, the Swedish iron is preferred to the Spanish, as the latter is so apt to redsear, that is, to crack, between hot and cold. At a small distance from this great ferruginous rock, an engineer lately cut away a considerable part of the hill, to improve the public walks, near the town of Bilbao, and as he made a perpendicular cut of about eighty feet depth, he discovered a vein of iron ore, lying in perfect strata, which, at times, dipped in a direct line, and at others, obliquely, bearing some similitude to the roots of a tree, occasionally of an inch diameter, or the size of one's arm, with infinite variety of ramification, according to the more or less resistance of the earth, to the passage of water; there being no doubt of this mine being alluvial. Here the very circumstance has happened, which Don Antonio de Ulloa, judiciously imagined, would follow in the great hill of Potosi, were it possible to lay it open and examine its contents.

It appears therefore, that the mines of Biscay are in veins, strata, and masses. The *Hematites* (a), so frequently seen in the hollow parts of the veins, are remarkable for their different sizes and forms; when broken, every grain was found to have the shape of a star, which proves solution, deposition, and a flow crystalization. These hematites are exceedingly heavy, and if calcined give proofs of containing two or three times more iron, than the ore of Somorrostro, but of a brittle and intractable nature. Besides these hematites, there are in this mine, many cavities of different sizes, from two inches to two feet, lined with a great deal of ferruginous matter, from one to three fingers thickness; this coating appears to be a true emery, and from hence, issue cylinders of striped hematites, as large as the feathers of a pigeon, two or three inches long, not unlike a hedgehog; others have various and fanciful appearances, that would make objects of singular curiosity in the collection of a mineralogist, or in a cabinet of natural history. I deduce from the whole, that iron is soluble by pure water, and its vapour, as much as by salts. There-

---

(a) Hematites, or blood-stone, is a hard mineral substance, red, black, or purple. The powder of which is always red, sometimes of an intermediate figure, and sometimes spherical, semi-spherical, pyramidical, or cellular, that is, like a honeycomb, consisting of pyramids generally small, the apices of which, appear in a transverse section in the centre. It contains a large portion of iron; forty pounds of this metal have been extracted from a quintal of the stone, but the iron is obtained with such difficulty, and is of so bad quality, that this ore is not commonly smelted. The great hardness of hematites, renders it fit for burnishing and polishing metals.—Dictionary of chemistry, translated from the French. London, 1777.

fore,

fore, we need not be surprized at meeting even pure iron in some mineral waters. Iron ores vary so much in their forms, that more properly they have no determinate one, as sometimes they are earth, stones, or grains; accordingly those naturalists, who attend only to the external forms and appearances in classing of minerals, have been obliged to multiply the names of the ores, calling them ores in the form of peas, beans, coriander seeds, pepper corns, cinnamon, &c. which Mr. Cramer, not without reason, treats as ridiculous trifles (*a*).

(*a*) Dictionary of chemistry.—As in Navarre, and some of the southern parts of France, they smelt iron ore, in small furnaces, after a method similar to that of Biscay, a description of their works by the ingenious translator of the dictionary abovementioned, may perhaps not be unacceptable.

"The furnace consists of a wide mouthed copper caldron, the inner surface of which is lined with masonry a foot thick. The mouth of the caldron is nearly of an oval or elliptic form. The space or cavity contained by the masonry, is the furnace in which the ore is smelted. The depth of this cavity is equal to two feet and a half. The larger diameter of the oval mouth of the cavity is about eight feet, and its small diameter about six; the space of the furnace is gradually contracted towards the bottom, the greatest diameter of which does not exceed six feet. Eighteen inches above the bottom there is a cylindrical channel in one of the longer sides of the caldron and masonry, through which the nozzle of the bellows passes. This channel, and also the bellows pipe, are so inclined, that the wind is directed towards the lowest part of the furnace. Another cylindrical channel is in one of the shorter sides of the furnace at the height of a few inches from the bottom, which is generally kept closed, and is opened occasionally to give passage to the *Scoriæ*; and above this is a third channel in the same side of the furnace, through which an iron instrument is occasionally introduced to stir the fluid metal, and to assist, as is said, the separation of the scoriæ from it. The greatest height of the channel is at its external aperture on the outside of the furnace, and its smaller height is at its internal aperture, so that the instrument may be directed towards the bottom of the furnace; but the second channel below it has a contrary inclination, that when an opening is made, the scoriæ may flow out of the furnace into a basin placed for its reception. When the furnace is heated sufficiently, the workmen begin to throw into it alternate charges of

LETTER XXI.

Observations on the Copper Mine of La Platilla, in the lordship of Molina.

THE remarkable hill of La Platilla, which name it has had time immemorial, is about two leagues to the north west of the city of Molina, capital of the lordship of that name, on the river Gallo, thirty-one leagues from Madrid. The mountainous country in which it is situated, forms a chain of hills, where an intense cold reigns nine months of the year. Here the waters of rivers divide; the Gallo runs towards the Tagus on one side of the hill of La Platilla, and on the other, the waters fall into the Ebro.

charcoal and of ore previously roasted. They take care to throw the charcoal chiefly on that side at which the wind enters, and the ore on the opposite side. At the end of about four hours a mass of iron is collected at the bottom of the furnace, which is generally about six hundred weight. The bellows are then stopped, and when the mass of iron is become solid, the workmen raise it from the bottom of the furnace, and place it while yet soft under a large hammer, where it is forged. The iron produced in these furnaces is of the best quality; the quantity is also very considerable, in proportion to the quantity of ore, and to the quantity of fuel employed. In these furnaces no limestone or other substance is used to facilitate the fusion of the ore. We should receive much instruction concerning the smelting of iron ore, if we knew upon what part of the process or circumstance the excellence of the iron obtained in these furnaces depends; whether, on the quality of the ore, on the disuse of any kind of flux, by which the proportion of vitreous or earthy matter, intermixed with the metallic particles, is diminished; on the forging while the iron is yet soft and hot, as the Marquis de Courtevron thinks, or, on some other cause not observed."

The

The summit of this hill consists of whitish rock, marked with blue and green spots, and is about half a league to cross over from one valley to the other, the ascent being equally steep on both sides. It appears on further examination to have been formerly a mass of vitrifiable rock, that has decomposed into small stone, pebble, sand, and earth, which with decayed leaves, and roots of plants, form that crust of earth which now covers the rocky part of the hill.

In the mine, there are pieces of white quartz, which rise above ground from thirty to fifty feet, full of fissures in every direction; they gradually decay towards the bottom, and form into fine sand and earth. If any one compares the decomposition of this quartz, with the phenomena of its transformation under ground, it is clearly discovered, that new bodies are formed there; for in the galleries of the mine, perpendicular fissures are not found in any uniform order, but a multitude of them, dividing the rocks without regularity, each division afterwards subdivided into numberless smaller fissures, some of which are scarcely perceptible. The copper ore is formed in the interstices, between these fissures, being blue, green, and yellow, mixed with a white limy earth. The largest fissure I saw was about three inches, and others only the breadth of a hair. Some have the superficies only, covered with a thin blue, or green lamina,

others

others are spotted, partly blue, partly green, with all the gradations and tints from the sky blue to the lapis lazuli, and from a light, to the deepest green. In some parts the aperture of the stone is totally filled, and forms a body equal to the breadth of the fissure; but whatever be the size, it is always composed of parallel lamina, as thin as an eggshell, and successively deposited one over the other, by the water, which makes it indubitable, that this mine is alluvial; first formed by the decomposition of the rocks, their recomposition and moisture.

This lamellated metal is composed of various plates, which I call primeval, some are chequered with small hollow round grains, hardly seen with the lens, which I conceive are formed by bubbles of air, at the time of the decomposition of the rock, and the forming the drivel of the metal. These bubbles impress their figure on the lamina above, and occasion those beautiful grains, from whose variegated waves in the concentrical lamina, results that beauty of colour in the stone, when polished, which surpasses those of the east, and would stand unrivalled, were its hardness, equal to the peculiarity of its shades.

Having examined one of these lamina, of a line in thickness, I found it to consist of three and twenty leaves, the white calcareous earth was formed by the drivel of
the

the copper, at the inftant of decompofition, and always follows it, covering the ore, as well in the green, as in the blue, and yellow, and when this white earth abounds, then the green ore is of a very pale hue. Breaking a piece of the ore, fiffures are feen in the centre full of a green or yellow matter, and if there is any cavity, there are fmall blue cryftals, like fragments of fapphires ; others, green like emeralds, and true rock cryftal, blue, or green (*a*). I broke one of thefe cryftals that was fixed in the hollow part of a rock, and was folid without. It was as green as an emerald, in the centre, without the leaft appearance of crack, or crevice, exteriorly ; which I put into an acid, when all the green matter diffolved, and the cryftal remained perfect and entire, except a fmall cavity in the centre. To explain the forming of this cryftal, it is neceffary to fuppofe, that the copper and calcareous earth were formed by the decompofition of the rock, by fome interior labour, and that the limy part mineralized the copper, and covered its atoms, without any communication of acids, fixed or volatile alkali, fulphur or arfenic, for the matter being calcined does not yield any fmoak, neither emit a fulphurous fmell, and expofed to the air many years, does not decompofe, acquire tafte, or change colour.

(*a*) Mr. Bowles fays, that they are not fapphires, nor emeralds, as thofe two ftones will diffolve in acids ; (*a fact which cannot be admitted*) like the green or blue colouring parts of rock cryftal, and that thofe of this mine will not diffolve.—Introduccion a la hift. nat. &c. page 197.

When

When I find this calcareous earth closed within the fissure of any solid rock, and any part of it mixed with the mineral, while the remainder serves for its matrix, and that there is no other similar earth thereabouts, I conclude that the aforesaid calcareous earth is formed by the decomposition of the rock which it is in. I say the same when I meet quartz mixed, and united with the rock, for on breaking it, the stone may be perceived half decomposed, with some part of clay in the centre. Various stalactites are found in the excavations from this mine, which if well considered, prove the origin and diurnal formation of the copper, and decomposition of the rock; one evidently perceives the mineral begins to be dissolved, and fluid, or at least in a mucilaginous state, as its waves demonstrate its flowing in a very gentle manner; but when rain water has forced a passage through the crevices, and meets with that kind of metallic drivel, before it is thoroughly dry, or acquired a sufficient consistence, it carries it forward, till it comes to some cavity, and there, drop by drop, it deposits it, and forms the stalactite, sometimes like a hollow reed, with bubbles in it, occasioned by the air, but more frequently solid, from the viscosity of the matter. I observed, by analysis, that those stalactites of the most perfect green, contain six eighths of pure copper, and two eighths of calcareous earth; they are smooth, hard, and without smell, and do not decompose either in the air or boiling water;

water; but the green, blue, and yellow stones, found here, are the reverse of the stalactites, dissolving in the weakest acid. I do not call these blue, and green stones, crystals, because they are not so, though they have that appearance, as is proved by experiments; nor do I say, that the green is a *malachite* (a), it not being yet decided, whether this is a green vitrifiable stone.

In the cracks formed by the decomposition of the rocks, there is a great deal of cinereous and yellow clay, particularly where there is the most mineral. These clays seem to precede the formation of the white and yellow calcareous earth, whose quantity is always equal to that of copper; so that if one is abundant, the other is so likewise, and vice versa. This yellow earth deceived me at first, having a notion that its mixture with blue, formed the green ore, remembering to have seen the dyers compose their green colour, by an assemblage of yellow and blue, and that the physical cause of the greenness of leaves, proceeds from the mixture of those two colours; and finally, that there are several plants, indigo, for example, whose juices are destroyed by fermentation, and the blue colour remains in the *fecula*; but in all this I was mistaken, as the blue ore does not mix with the green, they being of different natures; for

(a) Copper mixed with gypsum, or plaster, Green. Is found at Ordal, in Norway, and there called Malachites.—Cronsted, sect. cxvi.

the blue appears, by experiments, to contain a little arsenic, silver, and copper, which, when fused, forms a kind of bell metal; but the green ore has not the least atom of arsenic, and the copper mineralizes with the white earth abovementioned, without having the least part of iron. This mine of Platilla, being of an adventitious nature, has no great depth, and lays in strata. If the miners go deep, they are deceived; for though the mine may dip, in a slight degree, which perhaps in a thousand years might form a rich vein, the ore is discovered, at present, from three, to forty feet depth at furthest.

Many have thought that mines are only found in barren districts; but this is an error, that of La Platilla is a proof of it; for though the ore is so near the surface, the ground is covered with plants. The same happens in the quicksilver mine at Almaden, where they shoot up even within the precincts of the furnaces, in the same manner as in other places, where no mines are to be found. In that of La Platilla, where the veins are arsenical, and not above a foot of earth over the ore, the following trees and plants are constantly seen; the oak, holm, cistus, hawthorn, juniper tree, sage tree, dwarf cistus, base horehound, bell flower, ragwort, cornflag, orchis, Bethlem's star, *muscari*, or fair haired hyacinth, milkwort, and above thirty other species,

cies, which grow in cornfields, or meadows, on the road side, and even on the sea shore. The low lands are covered with the same sort of grass as the rest of the country, and serve for pasture to those numerous herds of cattle for which the territory of Molina is famous.

These observations occur in different kingdoms. The mines of Sainte Marie, in France, are covered with oak, fir, apple and pear, cherry and plumb trees, with good pasture and corn, in a soil, about two feet in depth, covering the most sulphurous arsenical rocks, of silver, copper, and lead mines in Europe, where the very veins are often seen above ground. An equal fertility reigns near the mines of Clonsthal, on the mountain of Hartz, belonging to Hanover, with excellent pasture. The same happens on those of Freyberg, in Saxony, that are covered with barley, in June; it being a singular sight, to see a body of people, reaping the corn over the heads of a thousand miners below, busy in digging out passages, and blowing up rocks, full of arsenic, and sulphur. Some mines, without doubt, are found under bare rocks, though this barrenness does not proceed from any mineral vapour, but from different causes, and chiefly, that, moisture, heat, and cold, have more power on some rocks, than over others. This is the case with the great mountain of Rammelsberg, at the foot of which stands the imperial city of Goslar, so famous for its silver mines, where the loosened stone may be observed to crumble away, and be covered with moss and verdure: insomuch that though the period is not yet arrived, for its entire decomposition, soon, or late, it will happen, and be covered with grass, in the same manner as the mountain of Hartz is at present.

☞ About a quarter of a league from the city of Molina, there is a spring whose waters have a smell like rotten eggs, from being impregnated with sulphur and alkali; those who have analyzed them, assure us, that they are of the same nature with the springs near Gibraltar, and the waters of Cotterets, in France, and equally useful in cutaneous complaints. The river Gallo abounds in salmon trout, from half a pound to four pounds weight. About a quarter of a league from the town, the river contains a fine white earth mixed in its waters, which incrusts the earth and such plants as it touches, with a limy substance, though the water appears clear and limpid.

LETTER

LETTER XXII.

The source of the Tagus and its environs described.

IN going from Molina de Aragon, to the westward, you cross over mountains filled with petrifactions, which appearance lasts for two or three leagues. At the third league there is a salt spring which serves the people of Molina. The ascent is continual, through a wood of fir, and over mountains, till you reach the village of Peralejos on the banks of the golden Tagus, so often sung by the poets, so frequently extolled by historians.

At Peralejos, the Tagus is only fifteen paces wide, and one foot deep. The petrifactions are observed again in the village, and the river runs through a narrow channel it has made for itself, between two lofty mountains of marble, perpendicularly slitted near a hundred feet high. Each mountain is a solid block, without either horizontal, or perpendicular fissure, if we except those casual crevices, occasioned by the enormous pieces which now and then detach themselves, and roll down to the banks of the river. Such as have tumbled down on the

south

south side, have crumbled into good earth, and as the water filters through them, the soil is fertile, covered with grass, and different plants, such as purging buckthorn, service, Spanish cherry, black briony, agrimony, pimpinel or common anise, and butterwort sweating drops of water. The opposite mountain is bare, without moisture, earth, plant, or moss, being a stupendous rock resting on a bed of marble, mixed with white gypsum, veined with red, and prismatical stellated spots.

About three quarters of a league to the southward of Peralejos, you meet the highest hill in those parts called Sierra Blanca; its top is capped with calcareous rock, its body of white stone not calcareous, decomposed in the same manner as the former, with veins of imperfect jet, of the thickness of one's finger, with soft grainy pyrites (a) of the colour and odour of those found in the clays of Paris. Veins of bituminous wood extend from a finger to a foot in thickness, and contain pieces of jet, as large as one's head, others less, but always with vitriolic pyrites,

(a) Pyrites is a mineral resembling the true ores of metals in the substance of which it is composed, in its colour or lustre, in its great weight, and lastly, in the parts of the earth in which it is found, since it almost always accompanies ores. From the property of striking sparks from steel, they have been called Pyrites, which is a Greek word signifying fire-stone; they were formerly used for fire-arms as we now use flints, hence it was called carabine stone, still by some marcasite. Perhaps no other kind of natural body has had so many appellations. Persons curious to know the other names less used, may find them in Henckell's Pyrnologia; we think with that celebrated chemist, that the subject has been perplexed by this multiplicity of names, for before his great and excellent work, the notions concerning Pyrites were very confused and inaccurate.—Dictionary of chemistry.

dispersed

dispersed in the very substance, and interstices of the jet. It seems clearly to be wood, as some pieces have still the bark on, exhibiting the knots, fibres, and other parts, with little alteration, still preserving their ligneous original, mixed with that, which composes the true and solid jet. What is still mor extraordinary, veins of a lead mine are likewise found in it, following the oblique, or direct crevices of the wood, while other veins of lead traverse its fibres, in a perpendicular line, as well as horizontally, and some small lumps are fixed in the very substance of the wood. In a word, the four principal orders in mines, may be observed here in a small compass, as it were in miniature, viz. perpendicular veins, cross veins, strata, and masses. These veins are the more extraordinary, if we consider the manner in which the metal must have introduced itself into the timber, for it cannot be said to have made its way through the pores, when the lead was in a fluid state, because pieces of wood are found, whose exterior parts do not shew the least particle of lead, yet on breaking them, some portion of this mineral is discovered within, which could only introduce itself there, when the sap first formed the wood. The country people in the neighbourhood burn this wood, and make shot of the lead, that runs from it, which serves to kill hares, partridges, and other kinds of game, with which the country abounds. The source of the Tagus is about a league from

from the hill of Sierra Blanca, in the higheſt ſituation of Spain, for the waters of this river run down to the ocean, and thoſe of the Guadalaviar whoſe ſource is contiguous, fall into the Mediterranean. The waters called *Vegas del Tajo*, are at a league and a half from hence, in a valley, formed by the river, which has its ſource in a copious ſpring, called *Fuente de la Abrega*. This brook, for here it deſerves no better appellation, meanders ſo often, that it muſt be croſſed four times in the ſpace of half a league. Many have thought the ſource of the Tagus was at *Fuente Garcia*, which is five leagues higher up, but Mr. Bowles aſſures us to the contrary, adding, that *Fuente Garcia* is a trifling ſpring, which he covered with his hat, being no more, than a ſmall quantity of water, collected in the trunk of a hollow tree, placed there to hold what iſſues from a puddle of ſtanding water, which three paces further, loſes itſelf in the adjacent valley, without a drop of it reaching the Tagus.

Half a league from *Fuente Garcia*, there is a ſalt ſpring which ſupplies the town of Albarracin, and eighteen villages in its juriſdiction, with ſalt. The country from hence to the true ſource of the Tagus, is an elevated plain, rather uneven, with a good carpet of graſs, and a great many brambles, whoſe berries afford an ample repaſt for the black birds. It is alſo well ſtocked with that tree called in Spain *Cedro Hiſpanico*, the juniper thuriſera

of

of Linnæus, a tall stout tree, with berries like the juniper tree of the large sort (*a*). The snow remains on the ground in these cold regions, until June, and the country is a continued chain of hills, known by the name of the *Sierra*, replete with various singularities. From Peralejos hither, different petrifactions are found, sometimes in the rock, and at others in the earth. If the sea deposited them there, it will be difficult to explain how this should have happened in the highest situation in Spain.

To return to the Tagus: this noble river passes by the royal palace of Aranjuez, the city of Toledo, Almaraz, and Alcantara in Estremadura; then enters Portugal, at Abrantes, and rolls its waters with dignity into the ocean at Lisbon. Philip the second opened the navigation of this river; the first boat dispatched by his majesty, arrived at Aranjuez, from Lisbon, on the 19th of January, 1582, and then returned to Toledo, to proceed down the river again (*b*); but successive events, and an alteration

---

(*a*) The juniper thurifera, or Spanish juniper, is an evergreen, little known out of Spain, though it might be of much use; it grows very high, and is similar to the juniper tree, we have in England, but the berries are larger than those of the species we have. I was informed in Spain, by a gentleman to whom I am indebted for many communications in the course of this work, that Dr. Ortega, who has visited this country, had assured him, we have it not in England; probably the climate of Spain is more favourable for its growth. Mr. Bowles calls this tree *Cedro Hispanico*, but makes it synonymous with another tree, by saying *Cedro Hispanico o Alerce*, whereas the *Alerce* is the *pinus larix* of Linnæus.

(*b*) Dichos y hechos de Don Philipe 2do por Balthasar Porreno. Madrid, 1748.

of dominion under Philip the fourth, put a final period to thefe improvements. The antient poets have been lavifh in their praifes of the Tagus; Silius Italicus, fays,

" Ore excellentem et fpectatum fortibus aufis
 Antiqua de ftirpe Tagum, fuperumque hominumque
 Immemor."

Faria de Soufa, in his hiftory of Portugal, relates, that king Dennis made a rich crown and fcepter with the gold found in the bed of this river. Many people are ftill employed near Toledo, in thefe refearches, after floods, and have collected a great number of gold coins and trinkets(*a*); though Don Antonio Ponz infinuates, that he looked in vain there for gold fand, and feems to think, that enough of it, had never been found to purchafe a pair of pigeons in the market.

(*a*) Many of thefe curiofities had been collected by Don Francifco Santiago Palomares, of Toledo, who dying in 1775, his library and cabinet was purchafed by his excellency Don Francifco Lorenzana, and prefented to the public library, lately erected in that city. Another fimilar collection was left by Don Juan Antonio de las Infantas, dean of Toledo, to the college of St. Ildefonfo, at Alcala.—Viage de Efpana, por Don Antonio Ponz, fegunda edicion. Madrid, 1776.

LETTER

LETTER XXIII.

Mine of Cobalt, in the valley of Giſtau, in the Pyrenees of Aragon (a).

THE valley of Giſtau is almoſt on the ſummit of the Pyrenees, for very near it, at *El Hoſpitalet*, the waters of France and Spain divide. The river Cinca has its ſource here, and, paſſing by Plan, falls into a gully, two hundred feet broad, between two rocks, perpendicularly open, above a thouſand feet high, and then paſſes on to the Ebro, which it enters at the loweſt part of Aragon. Theſe two rocks are like walls, where one plainly perceives the waters have forced a paſſage through, as the different coloured ſtrata of ſtone, are ſimilar, and exactly oppoſite to each other, on both ſides.

(*a*) The kingdom of Aragon was formerly united to that of Navarre, and continued ſo till 1003, when Sancho the Great, who had married the heireſs of the county of Caſtile, divided his dominions amongſt his children. Garcias, the eldeſt, had Navarre, Ferdinand had Caſtile erected into a kingdom, and united to that of Leon, by marriage with Sancha, only daughter and heireſs of Bermudo, laſt king of Leon. Gonſalve had Sabrarve and other territories, and to Ramiro, his natural ſon, he gave the kingdom of Aragon, with the conſent of the queen, in recompenſe for his bravery, in offering to ſupport her innocence by ſingle combat, againſt the king's ſons, who had charged her with incontinency; the falſity of which accuſation, was diſcovered by a monk, who revealed their confeſſion to the king, on which the queen's innocence was proclaimed, and the combat laid aſide, as is fully related by Roderic Archbiſhop of Toledo.—" Roderici Toletani de Reb. Hiſp. Lib. v. chap. xxv.

The mountain of Plan is of an extraordinary height, made up of five or six hills, piled one upon another, whose divisions are in proportion to the more or less resistance of the rocks, and the quantities of earth brought down by the rains, or high winds. In the month of June I went into France, through the valley of Aure (*a*), exploring my way over those craggy hills which had then above five feet of snow. There are a great many bears, as well as roe-bucks, which are hunted by the people of the country, and now and then they meet with the linx. The mutton is excellent. I bought a sheep for a dollar, (3s. 6d.) and had it dressed with *chenopodium pirenaeum*, " wild spinnage" which is found in great plenty on these hills, where I shivered with cold, in the dog days, and saw a great many white partridges, but not a single fly.

There are three lead mines and one of copper, in the neighbourhood of Plan, and a good iron mine at Bielsa, which is worked with much judgment: also much lime rock, and gypsum, as white as snow, and large lumps of grey granite, dispersed in the bed of the river Cinca, where there is no sand, but stones of this kind, from the largest to the most diminutive size. One likewise finds grit stone of the same grain and colour, as that on the mountain of Elizondo in Navarre, and a great deal of millstone; the best of these are generally at the top

(*a*) This is Mr. Bowles's itinerary, which is preserved entire in the course of this letter.

of the mountain, being the hardest and most compact, better even than those in the centre. One should always prefer those with visible, and deep pores, and small cavities, as the heat arising from the friction, is by this means dispersed over the whole mass. This is the sort found at Gistau. Those that are smooth grained, generate too much heat, which has an effect on the flour. The soft ones are the worst of all, requiring constant repairs, and soon wear out, besides the inconvenience of rendering the bread gritty.

Having made some experiments at Plan, on some lead ore, I found in a slaty mountain, called Sahun, I discovered it to be mixed with white spar, and so abundant and easy to fuse, that it left fifty pound of lead per quintal, notwithstanding that the plane had not a sufficient declivity, for the metal to run off, as it ought to do.

The environs of Plan abound in fir, oak, and beech, of which they make charcoal for the mines; and here one finds that extraordinary mine of Cobalt (a), which

(a) Ores of cobalt resemble those of antimony; their surface is almost always covered with an efflorescence, of a dingy scarlet. These ores contain a good deal of arsenic, and it is from them that arsenic is usually got; they also frequently contain a portion of bismuth. Those which contain cobalt alone, are very rare: Cobalt mines bring in a considerable revenue to Saxony, where the ores are worked with a good deal of intelligence.——Beaume manual of Chemistry.

☞ In the year 1755, Mr. Bowles was ordered, by the court of Spain, to attend his Excellency Don Joseph Augustine de Llano, to the manufacture of Zaffre, at Gingembach, in the Black Forest, in Germany.

has

has not its equal in Europe, except that famous one at Shoenberg, in Saxony, for whatever is found in other places is mixed in arsenical veins of lead, or silver, and in such small quantities as not to deserve any particular notice. I shall now relate the particular circumstances I was informed of, concerning this famous mine at Giftau.

At the beginning of this century, a person having observed, that some stone, found in a steep mountain, situated to the North East of that, of Plan, was more heavy than usual, it induced him to suspect, it might be silver ore, on which he repaired to Zaragoffa, and shewed it to a person conversant in mines; but after various fruitless essays, no silver was found; at last they discovered it to be a mine of cobalt, and some specimens of it were sent to the manufacturers of Zaffre, in Germany, where, finding it, on trial, to be good, they determined to get possession of it, without apprising the Spaniards of its value. To carry on this scheme the better, a German was sent into Spain, to conclude this business with the simple Aragonian, and it was agreed upon, between them, that the Spaniard should petition his court for a grant of the mines of the valley of Giftau, on ceding to the king, a certain quantity of lead, yearly, at a low price; on which condition the grant was easily obtained; none suspecting that these mines contained

any

any other mineral. A private agreement was further entered into, between the German and the Spaniard, that the latter should yield to the former, all the cobalt they might get out of the mine, at the price of thirty-five *pesetas* per quintal, gross weight (*a*).

The people of Aragon, understanding little of mines, Germans were sent for, and they begun to extract the cobalt, which they found about half way in the mountain, on whose summit there was another mine, called after Philip the IVth, perhaps from its having been attempted in his reign, though I do not know what ore it contained, but suspect it to have been cobalt; which, not being much known, at that time, nor its uses in commerce (*b*), was soon after abandoned, no silver appearing, which, was probably their object; but I am surprized they should have filled it up again, when they left the other mines of copper, and lead, open, which are in the very same place.

(*a*) A *pifeta*, or piftreen, is a silver coin, worth about ten-pence sterling.

(*b*) This ignorance of the value of cobalt is not peculiar to the Spaniards; the same happened in Germany, where we are informed, that, for want of a sufficient knowledge of mineralogical science, quantities of rich ores, and fossile substances, have been formerly thrown away amidst the rubbish. There is scarce a mining country, in which they have not, some time or other, paved their highways with stones, and rocks of value; I know, from very reputable authority, (says a German writer) that, this was formerly the case of the cobalt ores in Hissa, which at present, produce an annual revenue of about £14000. sterling, clear of all expences. "Raspe's preface to his English translation of Baron Born's travels through the Bannat of Temeswar, Transylvania, and Hungary, in 1770. London 1777.

The

The Germans, for a long time, got out of this mine, about five or six hundred quintals per annum, sent it from Plan to Touloufe, where it was embarked on the canal of Languedoc, and then by Lyons and Strafburg, forwarded to their own manufactures. After they had, in a manner deflowered the mine, and got as much ore as they could eafily extract, it was probably no longer an object of intereft, and then they abandoned it, which happened a few years before I arrived there, in 1753.

Impatient to vifit this mine, I went to it immediately on my arrival at Plan, and found many fhafts in all that part of the mountain, for as cobalt does not run ufually in veins, the Germans had tried different places, wherever they thought they could get it moft readily. On examining thefe fhafts, I found feveral pieces of good cobalt, of a finer grain, and the blueifh grey colour, lighter, than that of Saxony. I cannot give an idea of it, to thofe who have not feen it, nor teach them, to diftinguifh it from other metals, of the fame colour, as without ocular infpection, explanations are to very little purpofe; however, I fhall juft add, that moft of the lumps of cobalt I found here, were contiguous to a kind of hard flate, as gloffy as if they were varnifhed, with fpots, of the colour of a dried rofe, without touching the cobalt, though it was as much expofed to the moifture as the flate: nor have thefe rofe coloured fpots, either grown livelier, or paler,

paler, during the many years I have had them in my cabinet. These spotted plates may serve as a direction to such as are employed in search of this mineral; for my part, I could not make any further observations with exactness, as the exclusive charter was still in force, and they watched my motions with jealousy, therefore was obliged to be satisfied with the observations I had made, without excavations, and quitted Spain about that time.

Should the Spaniards ever think seriously of Cobalt, as it exists in this mountain, and probably in other parts of the kingdom, as well as in America, I shall add the following directions for its discovery, not intending it for the use of chemists by profession, who are not in any need of it, but only for miners, who have never seen any Cobalt, or for such, who, having no judgment in ores, conclude that all matter which is weighty, and yellow, must certainly contain gold, silver, or other precious metals.

If the heavy grey stone which they find, is united with the glossy black slate abovementioned, there is no doubt, but that it is cobalt, of which that slate is the blend. If the stone is quite detached from the slate, draw lines on it with a pointed iron, and if the lines appear to be black, it is a strong indication of its being cobalt: for greater security, break the stone, and reduce it into powder, put it into a thin glass phial, for the thinner it is, the less liable to break; then place it in an iron vessel, filled with sand, so that the neck of the phial may be open, and the bottom not in contact, with that, of the vessel, then put it into a common kitchen oven: all the arsenic will evaporate at the neck of the phial, and the cobalt will be purified. After this process, it still preserves its grey colour, and, mixed with sand, and the ashes of soda and barrilla, is what the Saxons call zaffre; this mixture is made, because sand and quartz, are infusible, without the assistance of barrilla, or fixed alkali; but with it, they soon vitrify, and communicate the same property to the cobalt. If this zaffre is melted with a vitreous fritt, it changes into a blue glass, called *smalt*, when in masses, and *azure*, or *enamel blue*, when reduced into a fine powder, used by painters, for that beautiful blue on porcelain, and in other manufactures (*a*).

In the essays made on Spanish cobalt, in Germany, it appeared to be entirely free from foreign matter, and so

(*a*) Mr. Bowles in a note finds fault with the Encyclopedie, and other writers on chemistry for saying, that the cobalt and zaffre of the East, are nearly exhausted, and that we have no foundation for such an assertion, and ought rather to apply the inferiority of their modern colouring, to their craft, on finding us so easily satisfied. But the principal reason given by these writers, is, on account of the considerable quantity of zaffre and smalt now exported from Europe to China, which Mr. Bowles takes no notice of. Zaffre has been thought of such use in England, that the society for the encouragement of arts, manufactures and commerce promised in 1755. a premium of 30l. for making the most and best zaffre, and smalt from English cobalt, not less than 5 lb. weight of zaffre, and 15 lb. of smalt to be produced before the society, with satisfactory certificates.

rich

rich, of the blue colouring earth, that it imbibed three or four times more sand or quartz, than, that of Saxony. About the year 1746, it was a great fashion, in Paris, to make sympathetic ink. I set about making of it, as well as the rest, and gave nine livres (*a*) for a pound of Spanish cobalt, with which I made my ink, which was more esteemed, than any they had seen, the green colour being much more lively, than if made with the cobalt of Saxony. The Spanish mineral has not even the grey colour of the Saxon, but is blue, like melted lead, insomuch that in several manufactures, and particularly that of Count Aranda for delf-ware, at Alcora, in Valencia; they use it without any other preparation than pulverising the stone, as it is taken out of the mine, and with this blue powder in its natural state, they paint the ware without further process (*b*).

(*a*) About seven shillings and six-pence sterling.

(*b*) Cobalt has been found in Cornwall and Scotland, and probably in other parts of Europe, of various colours and hues, mixed with different substances, which mineralists have fully described, particularly Cronsted. Wallerius enumerates six different species thereof. If well calcined cobalt be treated with inflammable matter, and fluxed like other metallic calxes, it will be reduced to a semi-metal, called by Mr. Brandt, of the Swedish academy, who first produced it, *regulus of cobalt*. This regulus, and also the calx of cobalt, amongst other singular properties, makes sympathetic ink, by being dissolved in aqua regia. This ink may be applied to the drawing of landscapes, in which the ground and trees are destitute of verdure, being first drawn with Indian ink, giving an appearance of winter; but those parts covered with this preparation, resemble the spring, on being exposed to a gentle heat, when the green leaves appear on the trees, and the grass in the fields, which idea has been executed in France by an ingenious artist on a fire-screen; and as a solution of regulus of cobalt, or of saffre, in spirits of wine, acquires a reddish colour by application of heat, more variety may still be introduced in the landscape, and fruits and flowers suddenly brought out, by the red solution, at the same time that the leaves and verdure appeared with the green.——Dict. of chemistry.

LETTER XXIV.

Observations on alum, with some account of an alum mine near the town of Alcaniz, in the kingdom of Aragon.

THE method of refining alum, seems at present to be totally neglected in Spain, though they have accounts of such works having been formerly carried on, particularly near Carthagena, of which nothing remains but the name of the village, which is *Alumbre*, the Spanish word for alum; but, supposing them to have been once acquainted with this process, they have now entirely lost it; and notwithstanding they have so rich a mine of it in the kingdom of Aragon, near the town of Alcaniz, belonging to the knights of Calatrava; yet the people of the country content themselves with digging it out of the earth, and selling it to the French in its primitive state, who refine it, and then send it back to the Spaniards, to be sold to the dyers at a considerable profit.

Chemists know very well, that the vitriolic acid is dispersed in most bodies all over the world, and is extracted out of many of them for sale, particularly from sulphur. Every body knows, that, alum is a crystallizable salt, composed of vitriolic acid, united with a white argillaceous earth, which many have taken for the residuum of burned plants, and in support of their opinion, mention Italy, as an instance, where the most alum is found; being a country formed by volcanos, as appears from the number of its calcined stones, sulphurs, pumice, and lavas, and thus attribute the origin of alum to fire, like that of sal-ammoniac: without adopting or refuting any particular systems, I shall only add, that the alum of Alcaniz, is found in a low swampy and blackish soil.

The argillaceous earth, of which alum consists, is weakly united to the vitriolic acid, for the salt of tartar, liquid, or solid, volatile alkali, salt of soda, calcareous earth, &c. dissolved in water with alum, eject the clay from the vitriolic acid, and substitute themselves in their lieu, forming new salts, more crystalline, whiter, harder, and drier, than alum itself, but experience teaches, that they are of no use in the dye-house, as the clay only, has the power of fixing the colouring particles, and giving them that brilliancy so pleasing to the eye; for when it is mixed with any of the other above-mentioned matters, the water grows turbid, the clay precipitates, and becomes visible, the other foreign earth taking its place; for which reason, the purer the alum, and the less impregnated with other bodies, it is the more proper for the dyer, and renders the colour more glossy and lively.

The alum of Aragon has the advantage of being entirely free from any foreign matter; consequently is the

best

best for every purpose, superior even to that of Rome, and only requires to be cleansed from casual impurities. Its salt is found already formed, in the earth like nitre, and other common salts, in the nitreous and calcareous earths of Spain; nothing more being necessary to refine it, than a simple lixivation, to filter, and clear it from the impurities of the earth.

This lixivium is put into boilers, and evaporated over the fire, till a thin scum appears on its surface, like a cobweb; the liquor is then run off into other vessels, where, as it cools, it crystallises into larger or small masses, the form being of no manner of consequence.

After this is performed, to save the salt still dissolved in the remaining liquor, they sprinkle this liquor over the earth, prepared for the lixivium, by which means, none of the alum is lost.——Perhaps if the earth which has gone through this process, was to be heaped up, in the same manner as that, out of which they get saltpetre, it might again produce a fresh stock of alum, by some interior labour of nature, with the assistance of water, and air, for the kingdom of Aragon abounds with nitrous soil, from whence they get excellent saltpetre, as is evident by the gunpowder of Villa Feliche, the most famous in Spain. If any of these workmen would set about making experiments in this manner, with alumineous earth, should it happen to succeed, it would

would be of great service to the people of Alcaniz, who are at present in a starving condition. I shall not enter further into the properties of alum, which have been fully described, by chemical writers, particularly Mr. Maquer, in a memoir read at the academy of sciences, in 1762, and such as are desirous to be fully informed of the nature of these works, will find in the memoirs of the French academy of sciences, for 1750, a description of the famous alum works of Solfatara, in the kingdom of Naples, by the Abbe Nollet: those of Tolfa, near Civita-vecchia, in the Roman state, have been accurately described by the Abbe Mazeas, in the fifth volume of memoirs of foreign members of the same academy. And with respect to the subject at large, Mr. Monet, in his treatise *De la alunation*, has collected every necessary information for a perfect knowledge of the subject: an object of consequence to a commercial people, and has always been attended to, by enlightened nations. England, Sweden, Flanders and Italy, are the countries where alum is principally found; to say nothing of its use in medicine, I shall only add, that it is so material an ingredient in commerce, for dying and colouring, that without its assistance, neither of these branches can be tolerably performed, it being as serviceable and necessary upon stuffs, as gum water and glutinous oil are in painting.

LETTER

LETTER XXV.

Remarkable depository of fossil bones, seen near the village of Concud, in Aragon.

THE village of Concud is about a league distant from the city of Teruel, in the kingdom of Aragon, situated on a hill of calcareous rock, degenerated into hard earth; and though it now appears very uneven, it seems to have been formerly rock which the rains have destroyed by degrees, in proportion to its greater or less resistance. Going out of the village of Concud, towards the North, you ascend three small hills, and then come to the *Cueba Rubia,* "The Red Cave," so called from a species of red earth, which the waters of a gully have laid open. This hill is about two hundred paces long, thirty broad, and eighty in depth. The top of the hill is of calcareous rock, more or less hard, in strata, of two or three feet breadth, full of terrestrial and aquatic shells, which appear to be calcined. In the centre of the same rocks, there are bones of oxen and horses, asses teeth, and other bones of lesser domestic animals. Many of these bones seem preserved in the same state as those found in cemeteries; others seem calcined;

calcined; some are solid; and other sorts are pulverized. The thigh and shin bones of the human race are seen with their cavities full of a cryſtalline matter. The horns of cattle are mixed with theſe, and other bones of different articulations, white, yellow, and black, confuſedly jumbled together, in ſome places there being ſeven or eight ſhin bones of men, without the leaſt regularity or order.

These bones are generally found in a bed of rock about three feet thick, decompoſed, and almoſt converted into earth, with a ſtrata of ſuperincumbent ſtone, from fifteen to twenty feet thick, which ſerves as a cover to the hill, the bed which contains the bones, reſts upon a maſs of red earth, and rounded limeſtone conglutinated with ſand not unlike pudding-ſtone. A ſimilar congeries is ſeen at the bottom of the gully, and the adjacent hills are of plaſter-ſtone. On the other ſide of the gully, and near it, there is a cave blackened by the fires of ſhepherds, where there are bones, in a bed of hard earth, above ſixty feet high, covered with different ſtrata of rock, correſponding exactly with thoſe on the other ſide; which ſhews that, what may have been carried away by the waters, was exactly the ſame as the maſs that remains. The chain of hills at this place, five leagues from Abbarracin, and eight from the ſource of the Tagus, produces the thorny restharrow (a); two species of wormwood, two of santoline, southernwood, French lavender, eryngo, sage, and thyme, and wherever they dig, bones, as well as aquatic and terrestrial shells, are found, in masses of hard rock, four feet broad, and eight long; some firmly fixed and rivetted therein, with so hard and smooth a grain, as to admit of polishing like marble. At a musket shot from the gully, there is a hill of rock, which is crumbling into earth, where an infinite number of bones and teeth is found, at two feet depth, but no further. In some places, the ossified substance is entirely decayed, nothing remaining but the impression of the bones on the stone, in the same manner as it frequently happens with shells. The finding of these bones in hard rocks, and in such different gradations or conversions into earth, of various sorts, and colours, all disposed in regular strata, indicates a decomposition and recomposition, so that the hills in reality consist only of two beds, one of limestone, divided into different strata, and the other of small rounded stone, consolidated with sand and calcareous earth. In this latter part there are no bones, nor shells, which are only to be

---

(a) Ononis spinosa. Linn. Thorny restharrow. Notwithstanding Linnæus makes the thorny restharrow only a variety of the other, and, from the observations of Læsling, in the Flora Prussica, says it becomes thorny in the autumn; yet with us they seem to be a different species; they are seldom found together, and the corn restharrow, without thorns, hath never been observed to become thorny. The smooth sort is sometimes pickled as samphire. A decoction of the roots has been recommended in cases of stone and jaundice.— Dr. Withering's botanical arrangement, vol. 2d, page 444.

found

found in the firſt diviſion, the variety of colours being purely accidental.

It is as ſingular to find ſhells, not petrified, in theſe rocks, as to meet with them, petrified, or the impreſſions of them, near Teruel; but it is ſtill more ſurpriſing to find rocks almoſt entirely compoſed of aquatic and terreſtrial ſhells, confuſedly huddled together, and mixed with ſmall bones, in a thin bed of blackiſh earth, beneath other beds of rock, and yet not to meet with ſuch bones in any other part, either higher or lower, ſometimes above fifty feet deep.

They tell you of an entire ſkeleton having been diſcovered, but this is much to be doubted, for though many bones are white, and well preſerved, none are found that correſpond, or belong to each other, in that whole range of extenſive oſſification. Theſe bones muſt have been ſeparated from their reſpective parts, by ſome accident difficult to be accounted for at preſent: according to their actual poſition one would imagine them to have been conveyed there, by ſome fluid, either water, or mud: ſome ſeem to have ſlided horizontally from thirty, to ſixty feet, which deſtroys all ideas of an earthquake; others have ſtuck faſt in a bed of mud, about two feet from the ſurface, which by degrees has hardened in the air, others have remained on the ſurface, and turned into limeſtone;

stone; finally, many fragments of bones and shells, mixed in this mud, have dried up, and become the most considerable part of the rock.

For many leagues round, the rocks are merely superficial, having always underneath, either soft earth, gypseous, or detached stones, cemented with other matter, which accounts for the facility, with which the waters form so many gullies, and little flat hills, as are seen in different parts of this country. It is probable, however, that those beds of earth were not so soft formerly, otherwise the waters would have made greater ravages, than they actually have done; though at present the destruction is great: there being many living witnesses, who recollect the astonishing progress of some of these gullies, as well as the commencement of others, which at present are small, but may one day acquire a considerable depth (a).

(a) These rocks at Concud seem to contain bones, similar to those, found in the rock of Gibraltar, large pieces of which being examined by the best anatomists in England, no human bones were discovered, and they were supposed to be bones of sheep; many of them were filled with cryftallized matter. It would be an object of no small curiosity to ascertain, if possible, what animals these bones of Concud did once belong to.

Some large bones, supposed to be of elephants, were found in 1778, upon throwing up the new road near the gate of Toledo, at Madrid, and an account of them was inserted in their gazette; they are now placed in the royal cabinet of natural history at Madrid.

See a curious account of some fossil bones discovered in the islands of Cherso, and Osero, by the abate Fortis, in his travels into Dalmatia, translated from the Italian. London, 1778, 4to.

Dr. Mesny, physician to the military hospital at Florence, has lately published a treatise on some bones found on the banks of the Arno, in Tuscany, which are thought to be the bones

Objections

Objections perhaps may be started, to what has been offered, relating to the decomposition and recomposition of matter, and some may even allege, that such bodies were always one, and the same, which is contrary to experience, and ocular demonstration. In such case, they would find themselves obliged to allow that minerals, spars, crystals, &c. do not form anew, and that there is no such event in nature, as decomposition and recomposition: A principle not to be supported by any sound arguments. We need only open our eyes, and examine those enormous oyster shells, seen on the surface of the earth, between Murcia and Mula, where the soil evidently appears, to be formed by the reduction of lime rock, into calcareous earth, these shells having fastened themselves there, when that matter was in a muddy or dissolved state, and become afterwards calcareous earth; it being evident, they were not always in the state they are in at present. Let us then suppose, this earth to have hardened in the course of time, which is not improbable, and to form rock or granite; who will deny, that a decomposition, and recomposition must have happened? It is not possible indeed to produce witnesses of the fact, because the life of man is too short, and the information received from our predecessors, too defective for that purpose; to which may be added the flow and incompre-

---

of an elephant, or some unknown animal. The Doctor told me, when I was at Florence in 1777, that they pretended to have found the skeleton of an elephant entire.

hensible

hensible progress of nature, imperceptible to human observation. We are therefore still very much in the dark, relating to these bones, as well as, with respect to our knowledge of fossil substances in general; having yet to ascertain, a more accurate discovery of their former natural situation, as well as the true origin of the mountains, and strata of earth in which they are found (*a*).

(*a*) "Philosophers, antient and modern, (says a late writer) have hitherto considered mountains, in general, from a point of view, too confined, or entirely different from that of mineralogy and mining; being unimproved by the light of volcanos, and by that extensive knowledge, which they might have reaped, in the deepest mines, or on the highest mountains, and from the instruction of unscientific miners, they stuck only to their libraries, and to the uppermost crust of the earth, which they had an opportunity of examining, without any great trouble to themselves, in the most pleasing countries, and in the most superficial quarries of sandstone, limestone, and slate. We are not to wonder therefore, that orology, or the science of mountains, is so little understood amongst the learned, and that the descriptions of the higher mountains of Peru, Teneriffe, Switzerland, and different parts of Europe, are generally filled with meteorological observations, botany, and other accounts, which leave their very nature, in a mineralogical, and orological respect, full as unknown, as they were before. The consequence was plain, that, general conclusions have been too rashly drawn, from a single kind of mountains, and that, the pretended systems, of the origin of mountains in general, are, for the greater part, so very romantic, and superficial."—Travels through the Bannat of Temesswar, Transylvania and Hungary, by Baron Inigo Born, translated from the German, by R. E. Raspe. London, 1777. See preface, page xxix.

END OF THE FIRST PART.

PART II.

LETTER I.

Don Guillermo Bowles's journey, by order of Government, to inspect the mine of Almaden, in La Mancha, describing his new method of extracting the quicksilver from the ore of that mine; with some account of the use made of quicksilver, by the Spaniards, in the silver mines of Mexico, and Peru.

IN the year 1752, 'I received orders, from the ministry, to inspect the rich quicksilver mine, at Almaden, in La Mancha. Our first stage, from Madrid, was to Getafe, and from thence to Toledo. The waters of the Tagus are very good here, and mix well with soap, though they are bad at Aranjuez, on account of their union with limy and saline particles, in that part of the river. From Toledo I proceeded to Mora, through a well cultivated valley, and from thence to Confuegra, passing forwards by the Puerto Lapiche, Daimiel, and Miguelturra, to the village of Carrascal. Hitherto the country is well cultivated, but further on, the

the plains are filled with holm trees, privet, rosemary, southern wood, and furze with white flowers, as far as Zarzuela, and from thence to Almaden, forty-one leagues, to the westward of Madrid. Here the face of the country is totally altered, and now becomes mountainous.

The quicksilver mine of Almaden is the most curious and instructive, with respect to natural history, as well as the most antient we know of in the world. Theophrastus, who lived 300 years before Christ, speaks of the cinnabar of Spain; and Vitruvius, who lived under Augustus, mentions it likewise.

Pliny says, this mine was in the province of Bætica, as it really is, Almaden being the last village of La Mancha, and only divided by a brook, from the kingdom of Cordova. He further tells us, it was always locked up, by the governor of the province, and never opened, but by express command of the Emperor; and when the quantity wanted for Rome was taken out, was instantly shut again; but since their dominion, every thing has been so altered, and overturned, that no traces are left of their labours.

The two brothers, Mark and Christopher Fugger, of Augsburg, had a grant of this mine, and were to furnish the king, yearly, with four thousand five hundred quintals

quintals of mercury, but not being able to make good their engagements, or for some other reasons, best known to themselves, they gave it up in 1635, as well as the silver mine of Guadalcanal, which was likewise in their hands, yet these Germans made such a fortune in Spain, as to leave great riches to their heirs, who now flourish in Germany, raised to the highest dignities, being counts of the sacred Roman Empire, and possessed of considerable estates in the circle of Suabia (*a*); their opulence was so conspicuous as to become a proverbial expression in Spain, *Ser rico como un Fucar*, "To be as rich as a Fugger," a simile we find in Don Quixote. There is a street of their name in Madrid.

The church, with great part of the village of Almaden, consisting of above three hundred houses, stands upon cinnabar, and the inhabitants are chiefly supported by the profits of the mine, which lies in a hill of sandy rock, forming two inclined planes, with a craggy rock on the summit, studded with specks of cinnabar, which, no doubt were the first tokens that led to the discovery of the mine. In other parts of the hill, small beds of slate appear, with veins of iron which on the surface follow

(*a*) The family of Fugger is descended from John Fugger, a citizen of Augsburg, in 1370, father of Jacob, who, from a merchant, rose to be a councellor to the Emperor. His sons, Ulric and George, were made Barons of the sacred Roman Empire, by the Emperor Maximilian, in 1504, and their descendants were afterwards raised to the exalted dignity of Counts of the Empire. They have immense property in the circle of Suabia, are divided into several branches, and allied to the greatest houses in Germany.

the direction of the hill. Some improperly call thefe fuperficial veins, for there are fuch in the adjacent hills, where no cinnabar was ever fufpected to exift, and all the country abounds in mines of iron; what is more, in the very mine of Almaden, pieces are fometimes found, in which the iron, quickfilver, and fulphur, are fo mixed together, as not to form a different body. This deftroys the common opinion, that iron amongft metals, is the only one, indiffoluble by mercury, the fallacy of which I have further experienced in the quickfilver mines of Hungary, where it is certain there is a mixture of iron ore, and I have feen in the quickfilver mines of the Palatinate, a great deal of ironized mineral ferve as a matrice to cinnabar.

The neighbouring hills are of a fimilar kind of rock to that of Almaden, and furnifh the fame forts of plants, which fhews that cinnabar does not exhale thofe poifonous vapours fome have imagined, nor are they obnoxious either to vegetation or mankind. A miner may fleep in fecurity on a ftratum of cinnabar, and I have counted above forty forts of ufual plants that thrived and run to feed within the precincts of the twelve furnaces where the mineral is roafted.

The felons who work there, feel no inconvenience from it, and do nothing more than wheel about the earth

in

in barrows, yet many of them are so crafty, as to counterfeit paralytic and other complaints, to impose on the benevolent disposition of those, who visit the mine. Each man costs government eight reals per day, (about two shillings) they are better fed, than any labouring man, sell half their allowance, and enjoy good health; yet from a principle of compassion, are only made to work three hours a day, and the public think their condition so infinitely wretched, as to be little short of death.

The very judges on the bench must be of that opinion, when they affix this punishment to the most atrocious crimes, yet they are deceived (*a*), and may be assured, every labourer in Almaden does of his own free will double the work of these felons, and for half the profit.

In this mine, two veins, from two to fourteen feet broad, run the length of the hill, with branches shooting out into various directions. Every one knows that the sandstone is composed of grains of different sizes, the stone of the vein is the same as in other parts of the hill, and serves as a matrice for the cinnabar, which is more or less abundant in proportion to the fineness of the sand stone, on which account some lumps of the vein will contain to the amount of ten ounces of quicksilver in the pound, and others only three.

(*a*) Mr. Bowles follows on this occasion the opinion of Don Antonio de Ulloa, in contradiction to the experience of all ages.—See Dr. Robertson's history of America, vol. 2d, note lxxi.

The two principal veins are attended with those upper and lower strata of rock, generally observed in all veins, to which miners have given the names of the roof, and the floor. At Almaden they are of black and rotten slate, and I have occasionally seen in them a quantity of cinnabar, and large round, or flat pyrites, yellow, and sulphurous, which, being broke with the hammer, exhibit within small particles of cinnabar. The pyrites decompose and dissolve, which occasions that vitriolic moisture which shews itself in yellow spots on the linen of those who enter the mine; and as it comes out with lemon juice, it is evident they are martial pyrites. There was one of these in the King's former cabinet, that weighed sixty pounds; I collected some of three pounds. Besides pyrites, they also find in the mine, pieces of white quartz, richly ramified with cinnabar, and light spar, sometimes even cryftalline, both filled with the same matter, either lamellated or in the form of rubies. There is also slate, full of them, and the chert, or *bernstein* of the Germans (*a*), is studded with cinnabar like nail heads: even pure and native mercury is seen in the crevices of slate and sandstone (*b*).

(*a*) Chert. *Petrosilex. Lapis corneus.* Cronsted, sect. LXIII.

(*b*) Though native cinnabar has ever so lively and red a colour, it has always a mixture of argillaceous, or calcareous earth, or of sand; and these substances are frequently impregnated with an arsenical taint. Even mercury, though with so pure an appearance, may yet be loaded with a pernicious vapour; for which reason, I think that native cinnabar

From

From the best information I could get, the heirs of the Fuggers rented this mine till 1645, when the King took it into his own hands, and the German miners were dismissed. The next year the crown allotted forty-five thousand trees to support the galleries of the mine, but the workmen reaped no advantage from it, the timber having been employed without art or ingenuity. The same year Don Juan Alonzo de Bustamante established the reverbatory furnaces with alludels, the Germans having only used retorts, of which many fragments are still to be seen amongst the rubbish.

The direction of the hill of Almaden is from north east to south west, having about 120 feet elevation. I went its whole length in four and twenty minutes, and its breadth in fourteen. Like most of the hills in La Mancha, it is composed of two plains, whose summit forms a peak of craggy rock, but the upper part has not that perpendicular elevation it seems to represent, for it forms an in-

---

should be banished from the shops. At the foot of a steep mountain, near San Felipe, in Valencia, I made excavations, and at the depth of twenty-two feet, found a hard, white, calcareous earth, containing drops of fluid mercury. This earth, being washed, in a neighbouring fountain, left twenty-five pounds of pure mercury, which was sent to Madrid, and deposited in the royal cabinet of natural history. A little above the spot where the mercury was found, there were petrifactions and gypsum. From exact researches, we know that a bed of cinereous clay, two feet below the surface, extends the length of the city of Valencia, from East to West, replete with drops of mercury, which were discovered after repeated experiments in digging of wells; particularly in the house of the Marquis of Dosaguas. Thus we found it in a white calcareous earth, with petrifactions, at San Felipe, and behold it in the city of Valencia, in a cinereous clay, without them!

clined

clined angle of fourteen degrees, and all the smaller rocks of the hill have more or less the same inclination. We shall next see, that a due observation of these circumstances, constitutes a principal branch of the art of mining.

The stone on these hills, as well on the superficies, as in the centre, is of the same nature as that of Fontainbleau, and the pavement of Paris : on calcining it, and examining it minutely, when it comes out of the furnace, the grains of sand are found to be of the same shape and transparency with those on the sea shore. The enormous pieces of rock which compose the internal part of the mountain, are cut with vertical fissures, and though the rocks seem to have an erect position one over the other, the length of the hill, this is not the case, for they all incline to the south.

Two veins, more or less impregnated with cinnabar, cut the hill almost vertically, and form those strata which we have said were from two to fourteen feet broad; these unite on the most convex part of the hill, stretching as far as one hundred feet, from which happy union arose that prodigious richness of mineral called *del Rosario*, which has given many millions of quintals of quicksilver, and was in my time the occasion of that dismal fire in the mine.

A bed of rock two or three feet broad, runs from north to south, across the hill, and cuts the two veins, so that further on, there is no appearance of cinnabar. This kind of rock being prior to the forming of the ore, stops the mineral vein, which finding it so hard, cannot penetrate that way, and is obliged to turn out of its direct course. It is from this rock to the other extremity of the mine, that I said I went in fourteen minutes. If the veins ran without interruption, and always on a straight line of the same breadth, less trouble and art would be necessary in the working of mines. Let us now speak of the method of working these of Almaden before my arrival there.

The miners had never sunk their shafts according to the inclination of the vein, but had made them perpendicular, letting themselves down by pullies in buckets, from which awkward contrivance arose all the mischiefs that followed, for in proportion as they went deeper, they often lost the vein, and were obliged to open a new shaft with the same inconveniences, and thus went on, continually encreasing their shafts and galleries with similar defects, by which they not only lost a great deal of labour and time, but were deprived of a free circulation of air underneath, as that which rushed in at one part, immediately made its escape at the other, next to it, and the people were suffocated below; the same.

fame would have happened in a stone quarry, as well as in a mine: moreover, the great number of galleries, filled with quantities of decayed and rotten timber, produced obnoxious vapours, and made a hanging vault of the mine, replete with danger, from the large pieces which continually tumbled in; to prevent these inconveniences in future, I laid before the ministry the following proposals.

That a new mine should be opened lower down, and a general shaft sunk obliquely, following the direction of the vein, and leaving a staircase at every twenty feet, to go up and down. That two galleries should be extended on the vein, one to the right, and the other to the left, continuing them in proportion as the shaft went deeper. That a space of three feet should be left on the vein, between one miner and another, in the nature of steps which the French call *travailler en banquette*. By this means a file of workmen, from twenty to a hundred, might be placed commodiously, and go as deep as they pleased without danger, because the new excavations are supported with the stone and rubbish dug out of the mine, the props which serve for this purpose being solid, and not liable to the same inconveniences as timber.

The same should be done in the second vein, and they might continue their labours at pleasure; when they go deeper,

deeper, a gallery for a communication of air, must be made from one vein to another, by which a constant circulation is kept up through the whole, as is always practised in well regulated mines.

My plan was well received by the ministry, miners were sent for from Germany, and the whole was tolerably executed. About this time the Cinnabar mine of Guancavelica, in Peru, had begun to decay, after supplying the mines of that kingdom for above two centuries past with a prodigious quantity of quicksilver (a), that of Almaden only furnishing Mexico, for which purpose they generally extracted five or six thousand quintals per annum, but the ministry finding it was necessary to send more to Peru, ordered a large quantity to be provided, so that from Almaden, and Almadenejos, they extracted about eighteen thousand quintals per annum, but the greatest part came from the mine worked by the Germans.

The Fuggers were the most experienced men of their age, and their shafts and galleries were according to the strictest rules of art; but they never undertook any thing very great, perhaps only considering themselves as occasional tenants, therefore endeavoured to get as much as they could at the cheapest and easiest rate, concluding their

---

(a) The mine of Guancavelica was first discovered in 1563. See Noticias Americanas. Entretenimiento physico historico por Don Ant. de Ulloa. Madrid, 1772, 4to.

harvest would be short. They appear to have directed their views where the ore was richest, which they soon after quitted, to go upon others, for we find above six hundred galleries of theirs, propped by timber, as a temporary support, which they knew could not last.

Let us now speak of those furnaces invented by Bustamante, so perfect that no alteration has been thought necessary to be made in them to this day.

The form of the furnace is similar to that of a good lime kiln (a), only that the chimney is placed on the anterior wall, that the flame may spread itself equally every where. On the lower part of the furnace, they first lay a stratum of the poorest sort of stone, containing the least mineral substance, over this a better sort, with the sweepings and dross, in which they suspect there might be some mercury, to which they add water, making it into a paste, and laying it on the top. Then, a little lower down, they set fire to the furnace, with faggots of terebinthinus, lentiscus, cystus, rosemary, and other shrubs which abound in the neighbourhood. The upper part of the furnace is covered with earth, leaving eight apertures of six inches

(a) In the memoirs of the academy of sciences of Paris for 1719, there is a circumstantial account of these furnaces, by the celebrated Bernard Jussieu, and it will not be amiss to consult the *Dictionnaire des arts & metiers, par Jaubert*. Mr. Bowles, in his dedication to the king, says, that the mine at Almaden had been rendered useless by a conflagration till he put it in repair, which fixed him in the service of that crown, and afforded him the opportunity of visiting so many parts of the kingdom.

diameter,

diameter, where a file of eight aludels are placed, properly luted in an inclined position, and terminating at a square chamber, where the quickfilver is received. The fire penetrates the ftone, and heats the fulphur, by which means the mercury dilates; and as both are fo volatile, they efcape together, through the aludels; but the fulphur, being more penetrating, exhales in the chamber, and even works into the aludels, and the compofition with which they are luted, while the mercury, from its weight, condenfes, and in its paffage cools, when it falls into the tubs placed to receive it. From hence it follows, that if the furnace is good, all the quickfilver in the ftone, muft be found in thefe tubs, there being only this objection againft it, that the fire is not active enough, to burn all the fulphur, rarify the mercury, or extract it out of the ftone; or, that the fire, being too violent, does not allow time for the metal to condenfe, but hurries it, united with the fulphur, fo that it efcapes from the aludels. To try whether either of thefe inconveniencies happened, I made the following experiments, before the governor, and feveral other perfons of rank.

I caufed fome pounds of ftone, burned in the furnace, to be pulverized, and then mixed them with the nitre and charcoal, then fired them, covering them with a veffel, previoufly wetted with water, to receive the vapour. As nitre, and charcoal united, burn with extraordinary violence, it is evident, that if, in this mixture, there had been the least grain of quickfilver, it would necessarily rarify and condense against the sides of the moistened vessel. In effect, we did observe some mercury there, but in so small a degree, that it was hardly perceptible with a lens, and of course of no consequence; for in every fusion of ores, some minute particles will escape in the scoria.

To discover if any grains of mercury were lost in the air, I placed four large copper vessels, not tinned, in four different places, one on the eight inches of earth, which covered the furnace, whose aperture is about three feet and a half diameter, others on the first aludels, which are the hottest, another at the obtuse angle of the same, where the mercury condenses, and the other at the highest part of the chimney, in the chamber, where the aludels lead to: as it is known, with what quickness mercury unites to all metals, except iron, if it exhaled at any of these places, where the copper vessels were fixed, it would have appeared on the copper, for I left them there above twelve hours, at the expiration of which, not the least particle of mercury appeared.

In the precincts of Almaden, there are twelve furnaces, called The Twelve Apostles; each can receive about

TRAVELS THROUGH SPAIN. 245

bout 200 quintals, including good and bad stone, which in three days will produce about 40 quintals of quicksilver. Three days more are required to repair the furnace, and replace every thing properly, so that four out of the twelve, are always in action, the violent heats of the summer excepted, when a suspension from labour is unavoidable.

When we reflect on the advantages of these furnaces, they must be considered as objects of the greatest utility and honour to Spain, foreigners having likewise improved from them. The Hungarians have imitated them in their mines, by which they have considerably reduced the number of workmen, employed in the old method, with retorts. Foreigners are shewn every thing without reserve (a), and are permitted to examine the rocks at their leisure, and even make drafts of the furnaces, and see their method of packing-up the quicksilver in goatskins, which is certainly the best policy, to facilitate the

(a) Mr. Ferber, in his travels through Italy, speaking of the quicksilver mines of Idria, in Friul, belonging to the house of Austria, says, " They consider here their common melting and sublimation of the mercurial ores, as an arcanum, and accordingly do not allow any stranger to examine their sublimation house, though even its exterior form undoubtedly, and at first sight, proves their method being the very same as that which is used at Almaden, in Spain, and has been very minutely described by Mr. Jussieu, in the memoirs of the French academy; this method is far from being perfect, and above any improvements, but probably they do not think so, else there could be no possible reason for this mystery in so common a manipulation: nothing is more opposite to the progress of science, and even to the interest of states, than so singular a reserve." Travels through Italy in 1771 and 1772, by John James Ferber. London, 1776.

operations

operations of a mineral that, perhaps, one day or other we may be in want of ourselves.

    Let us enquire into the five or six thousand quintals of quicksilver, sent yearly from this place to the Mexican mines; though my account should not be entirely exact, it will come as near as is necessary in points of this nature. Many of the mines of New Spain are worked by fusion, but where fuel is scarce, or the ore very poor, they amalgamate it with quicksilver; it must be allowed the Spaniards were the first who undertook this process in 1566; it is true, it was in use in the gold mines of Hungary, but this had no connexion with the works of the Spaniards, because in Hungary, the ore either appears to the naked eye, or is perceived with a lens, and as every body knows that quicksilver mingles with gold, it was natural to suppose, it could be extracted by this method; but none before the Spaniards ever thought of mixing quicksilver with a stone, containing invisible silver, dissolved with sulphur, and arsenic, and oftentimes mixed with copper, lead, and iron. They therefore discovered an ingenious mode of reducing a poor ore to an impalpable powder, and to form a mass of about twenty-five quintals, mixing it afterwards with salt, or green copperas, and with lime, or ashes, reduced to a fine powder.

These

These bodies, however, being of a different nature, would remain in perpetual rest, without a dissolvent to put them in action, for which purpose, they are sufficiently sprinkled with water, throwing in thirty quintals of mercury, at different times, taking care to stir it about constantly, for the space of two months. The fixed alkali of the ashes, and lime, dissolved by this means, works in the acid of the salts and copperas, which intestine action causes a violent effervescence and heat, by which means the sulphur, and arsenic, absolutely dissolve, and destroy the copper, lead, and iron. Then the imperceptible atoms of silver, escape from their confinement, are collected by the quicksilver, which amalgamates with them, and form that substance or paste the Mexicans call *pina* (a).

By this process they collect one and a half, or two ounces of silver from every quintal of ore, from which, according to the method practised in Europe, they would not defray workmen's wages.

(a) The most perfect silver extracted from the ore at the mines is in that form, which the Spaniards call *pinnas*, which is a lump of silver extremely porous, because it is the remainder of a paste made up of silver dust and mercury and the latter being exhaled, leaves this remainder of the mass, spungy, full of holes, and light. It is this kind of silver that is put into different forms by the merchants, in order to cheat the king of his duty, &c.——See the process of the ore from the mine to this kind of cake or mass.—— " Voyage to Peru, performed by the ship *Conde* of St. Malo." Written by the chaplain. London, 1759.

I cannot

I cannot afcertain with precifion the quantity of mercury loft in this operation, as the accounts of miners are fo varied and incorrect on this head; the moft probable conjecture, is, that they lofe as many ounces of mercury, as they obtain ounces of filver, fo that an ounce of mercury delivered at Mexico, becomes nearly of the fame value as an ounce of filver (a).

(a) The 18000 quintals of mercury, mentioned above, are difpofed of in the following manner; 13000 fent to Mexico and New Spain, 1000 to Guatimala, and 4000 to Lima; Peru furnifhed the remainder from its own mine of Guancavelica. According to Barba, who was parifh prieft of Potofi, in 1637, mercury was firft ufed in the mines in 1574, and down to his time, the royal office had received 204700 quintals of mercury, exclufive of the great clandeftine import. Efcalona in another work, declares that before 1638, it appeared by the public accounts, that the produce of the filver amounted to 395,600,000 pefos, which in 95 years, the time it had been difcovered, amounts to 41,855,045 pefos per annum; from whence may be conceived the wealth of the mountain, and though it has not of late been fo productive as formerly, yet it is ftill very confiderable.——See "Voyage to South America, undertaken by command of the king of Spain, by Don George Juan and Don Ant. de Ulloa, tranflated from the Spanifh." London, 1758.

The following is an account of the Spanifh mints in America, as they ftood in 1777.

Mexico coins annually, about	18,000,000 pefos.
Lima	9,000,000
Santiago de Chili, *chiefly gold*	8,000,000
Popayan and Santa Fe together	12,000,000
Guatimala	2,000,000
Potofi	10,000,000
Sonora in California. New mint eftablifhed in 1778, uncertain	....
	59,000,000 pefos.

Fifty-nine millions of pefos, at 4s. 6d. each, — £.13,275,000 fterling per annum.

LETTER

LETTER II.

Itinerary of Don Guillermo Bowles, continued, from Almaden to the city of Merida, in Estremadura.

INTENDING to make a tour into Estremadura, I set out from Almaden towards the north west, as far as Zarzuela, then, instead of continuing the road to Madrid, I went to the westward, crossing a chain of hills which divide La Mancha from Estremadura. These hills are covered with rosemary four or five feet high, privet, several sorts of the cistus with lavender leaves, elm leaves, rosemary leaves, and two other species: Also a great deal of lavender, thyme, and dwarf cistus, and though the cistus is of no use to the bees, they draw so rich a store from the other plants with which the country abounds, that hives are numerous every where in these parts. From these hills you descend to the village of Guabaguela, where the good pasture begins for the Merino sheep, the grass being plentiful and fine. The hills are chiefly covered with oaks, which become hollow by the imprudent manner in which the branches have been lopped; however they produce abundance of acorns for the swine, which are all black hereabouts. The principal revenue of the country gentlemen, confifts in pafture, honey and wax. They have ftuds of brood mares, and a breed of cows, which all over Eftremadura are whitifh or red. It is feven leagues from Guabaguela to Alcocer, over an uneven ground, watered by a great many fprings. You next come to Tallarubia, whofe diftrict is level, and proper for pafture. The rocks of fand or quartz are feen no more, but many loofe pieces of each lie fcattered on the furface of the ground; the rocks have perpendicular laminated fiffures, fome thin, others thick, which feem to demonftrate their fucceffive decompofition into arable land, and the fame happens with the quartz rocks on the hills. The flaty rock is compofed of argillaceous earth, and fine fand, and from them, when they decompofe, comes that fine fand feen in the brooks, and on the fides of the road, the water carrying away all the argillaceous earth, which does not cling faft to the roots of fhrubs, or trees. Some rocks hereabouts, are apparently as hard as the Egyptian Bafaltes, and of the fame colour, and nature; neverthelefs they moulder away like the reft, and turn into earth. In the midft of this vitrifiable country, the calcareous ftone begins to form itfelf, and is feen difperfed up and down, on the furface, like patches.

The paftures called *Debefas de la Serena*, are contiguous, being a depopulated diftrict of nine leagues extent,

tent, reaching to the village of Coronada, confifting of a plain without either trees or plants. At the end of this diftrict, there are rocks of white quartz, veined with a pale red; alfo a great many oaks and wild olive trees, as well as that fpecies of crowfoot, called *ranunculus ficaria* by Linnæus, whofe roots are like barley corns, and from their refemblance to external hemorrhoides, fanciful people have imagined they had the virtue of curing them.

From Coronada, it is a journey of three hours to Villanueva de la Serena, from whence an extenfive plain, entirely of fand, reaches to the village of Don Benito, neverthelefs fertile in corn, vines, pears, figs, &c. owing to the proximity of the water, as appears from the quantities of rufhes fpringing up every where; for, though the furface is covered with a loofe fand, for two or three feet, there is a bed of a more firm and compact fort underneath, which fupports the water, without the affiftance of clay, hard earth, or rock, to impede its filtration; fo that this foil will often produce thirty for one; it being enough to plant a branch of a fig-tree, or a flake of an olive, for it foon to take root, and give fruit; yet, notwithftanding all thefe advantages, great part of the country lies wafte, as far as Medellin, on the banks of the Guadiana, whofe houfes are fmall, and only of one ftory. In the centre of Medellin, they fhewed me an humble manfion, though worthy of notice, as having been the native place of the illustrious Hernan Cortez, the great conqueror of the Mexican Empire. The lintel of the door, is of granite, similar to that of the Escurial, *a small cage indeed, for so considerable a bird!* said a bishop of Badajoz, on viewing this building.

From Villanueva I came, in four hours, to the village of San Pedro, crossing part of a sandy plain, but except what is cultivated, by the inhabitants of Don Benito, all the rest is neglected, and only serves for pasture, the water being at a greater distance. This district is called Torre Campos, and extends four square leagues, to the village of San Pedro, amidst hills, covered with oak, gum cistus, lavender, and white asparagus; from hence it is three hours journey to the city of Merida, descending, after the first league, into a well cultivated country, traversed by several brooks, that empty themselves into the Guadiana, whose beds are dry in the summer, as well as this great river itself, in many places; for, as it meanders so much in the plains, the sands soak up its water, which, by degrees, eats away the hills, converting the granite, sandstone, and rock, into sand; so that the coarse sand, the fine, and the pebble, are seen, decomposed, in the valley, in the same order they were ranged on the hills, from whence they have insensibly rolled down. Thus, for example, if, on the eminence,
there

there was a quarter of a league of granite, the same proportion will be found in the valley, of pebble; if sandy rock, then coarse sand; and, if solid rock, then fine sand, and, at times, all blended together, from their having been so in their former position.

Merida, from its venerable remains, and antiquities, justly deserves the attention of the curious. What is now left of this antient city, is on a small hill, occupying about the circuit of a league, on the banks of the Guadiana, but its ruins extend much further, and shew it to have been the principal colony of the Romans, in Spain.

Examining the remnants of stone, scattered amongst the ruins, I found a great variety of colours, mixtures, hardness, and qualities. To be the better acquainted with their nature, I attentively observed the adjacent hills, and plains, from whence they were most probably dug out; from these researches, I deduced four primitive sorts, which, by various mixtures, constitute the great variety observed here. The first is of a deep red, like bulls blood, and sometimes as brown as chocolate, with a smooth grain; this is the mother of Porphyry; the second is white, and without any grain; the third is of a blueish cast, tending to black; and the fourth inclining to green; all these primitive kinds, when considered singly, are of very little value, from the

dullness

dullnefs of their tints, the white excepted; but, when blended together, have a pleafing effect. The white united with the porphyry, conftitutes an anomalous ftone, which cannot be claffed with any of thofe defcribed, either by the antients or moderns. Pieces of it are found on the furface of the ground, of twenty pound weight, and it is probable there are confiderable beds of it underneath; for, naturally, the antients dug out the beft, and where it was eafieft to be got. The mother of porphyry, appropriated to itfelf in its primitive ftate, divers fragments of white quartz, from the fize of a hazle nut to that of a chefnut, which occafions thofe various fpecks and appearances: when a piece of red ftone is feen, chequered in this manner, it is the true porphyry, fo efteemed by the antients; in a word, this beautiful ftone has no where its equal, and may juftly be ftiled the *Nonpareil of Merida*. Whenever the blue ftone grows darkifh, mixing with a little of the white, and fome glimmer, it forms the grey porphyry; and when the green combines with fragments of white, it becomes the ferpentine ftone, and receives an admirable polifh. Thefe various combinations into one folid mafs, evince, that at fome remote period, they had a feparate exiftence, in a ftate of folution, or foft pafte; but if I am further afked, when this furprifing union happened? I fhall be obliged to anfwer, that this is a circumftance I am entirely ignorant of.

There

There are still to be seen, in the city of Merida, the superb remains of two aqueducts, a theatre, a triumphal arch, a naumachia, a circus, two handsome bridges, one over the Guadiana, and the other over the Albarregas; all which announce its former magnificence, exclusive of the statues, inscriptions, medals, and other antiquities, so frequently dug out of its ruins (*a*). It was made a Roman colony by the Emperor Augustus, after the Cantabrian war, became the capital of Lusitania, and stiled *Augusta Emerita*. But at present agriculture and cultivation are at the lowest ebb; nor do the banks of the river, in its neighbourhood, afford that verdure and pleasing shade, so greatly praised, even in the days of Prudentius, who said of this place,

   Nunc locus Emerita est tumuli
   Clara colonia Vettoniæ
   Quam memorabilis amnis Anas
   Præterit, et viridante rapax
   Gurgite mænia pulcra alluit.

(*a*) The great indolence and negligence of our countrymen, with respect to antiquities, says Don Antonio Ponz, generally engages such travellers as come to Merida, to speak slightingly of our want of taste and little curiosity. In the year 1752, when Don Juan Williamson visited that city, he made no difficulty to declare, that if the King had made excavations at Merida, as Don Carlos had done at Naples, he concluded it would turn out, in a manner, a second Herculaneum.—Viage de España. Tom. 8. Madrid, 1778.—This person here mentioned, was the Rev. Dr. Williamson, chaplain of the British factory at Lisbon, whom Ponz, by mistake, calls the British ambassador, at that court. Our envoy, at that time, was Mr. Castres, who died, in Lisbon, in 1756, where I happened to be, when that city still lay in ruins, in consequence of the fatal earthquake, of the first of November, 1755.

LETTER

LETTER III.

Natural history of the locusts that ravaged the province of Estremadura, in the years 1754, 1755, 1756, *and* 1757, *from the observations of Don Guillermo Bowles.*

THE locusts, of which I am now going to speak, are continually seen in the southern parts of Spain, particularly in the pastures and remote uncultivated districts of Estremadura, but in general are not taken notice of, if not very numerous, as they commonly feed upon wild herbs, without preying upon gardens, and cultivated lands, or making their way into houses. The peasants look at them with indifference, while they are frisking about in the fields, neglecting any measures to destroy them, till the danger is imminent, and the favourable moment to remedy the evil is elapsed.

Their yearly number is not very considerable, as the males are far more numerous than the females. If an equal proportion was allowed, only for ten years, their numbers would be so great, as to destroy the whole vegetative system. Beasts and birds would starve for want of subsistence, and even mankind would become a prey to their ravenous appetites. In 1754, their increase was
so

so great from the multitude of females, that all La Mancha and Portugal were covered with them, and totally ravaged. The horrors of famine were spread even further, and assailed the fruitful provinces of Andalusia, Murcia, and Valencia.

The amours of these creatures are objects of surprise and astonishment, and their union is such, that it is difficult to separate them. When this separation is voluntary, after having lasted some hours, they are so exhausted, that the male retires immediately to the water for refreshment, where, losing the use of his limbs, he soon perishes, and becomes an easy prey to the fish; having given life to his offspring, at the expence of his own. The female, disembarrassed, though not without violent struggles, spends the remainder of her days in some solitary place, busy in forming a retreat under ground, where she can secure her eggs, of which she generally lays about forty, skreening them by her sagacity, from the intemperature of the air, as well as the more immediate danger of the plough, or the spade; one fatal blow of which, would destroy all the hopes of a rising generation.

The manner of her building this cell is equally surprising. In the hinder part of her body, nature has provided her with a round, smooth instrument, eight lines in length, which, at its head, is as big as a writing quill, diminifhing to a hard fharp point, hollow within, like the tooth of a viper, but only to be feen with the lens. At the root of this vehicle, there is a cavity, with a kind of bladder, containing a glutinous matter, of the fame colour, but without the confiftency, or tenacity of that of the filk-worm, as I found by an experiment, made for the purpofe, by an infufion in vinegar, for feveral days, without any effect.

The orifice of the bladder correfponds exactly with the inftrument which ferves to eject the glutinous matter, it is hid under the fkin of the belly, and its interior furface is united to the moveable parts of the belly, and can partake of its motions, forming the moft admirable contexture, for every part of its operations, as fhe can difpofe of this ingredient at pleafure, and eject the fluid, which has three very effential properties: Firft, being indiffoluble in water, it prevents its young from being drowned; next, it refifts the heat of the fun, otherwife the ftructure would give way and deftroy its inhabitants; laftly, it is proof againft the froft of winter, fo as to preferve a neceffary warmth within.

For greater fecurity, this retreat is always contrived in a folitary place; for, though a million of locufts were to light upon a cultivated field, not one would depofit her

her eggs there, but wherever they meet a barren and lonesome situation, there they are sure to repair, and lay their eggs: this difference in the earth they discover by the smell. Those who are of another opinion, surely have not observed the delicacy of those organs in every species of insects, birds, and animals, which govern all their pursuits. I have even seen numbers of wasps come to a piece of meat, placed in an open field, and covered over with a glass, so that their motions, which seem the result of reflection, arise from the emanations and effluviæ in the air, which strike their delicate organs. I have seen legions of insects fly to places where they were bleaching wax; the workmen observe, that the minute they touch it, they become faint, and if they do not, by a sudden exertion, free themselves from that vapour, which exhales about half an inch from the wax, they are suffocated, as we should be by the fumes of charcoal. Every one knows with what sagacity birds of prey fly to such distances, guided by the effluviæ of cadaverous bodies. Thus the locust of Estremadura, distinguishes the tilled land from the barren, and regulates its conduct in consequence, though ignorant of the motive of this preference, nor can it have any idea of the spade, or rejoice at the thoughts of saving its progeny; acting in consequence of that infinite perfection of its nature, given originally by the omnipotent creator. Like other insects, its motions are the consequences of primi-

tive

tive laws, founded on infinite wisdom, and not proceeding from secondary reflection; therefore its behaviour preserves a constant sameness, and uniformity, originally perfect, and not standing in need of alteration, or improvement. The first locusts were as skilled as the present race, and their progeny will tread in their steps. Those who call it instinct, I suspect, do not understand what they mean, nor explain to us the true sense of that word.

Having spent many hours and days in observing the labours of the locust, I shall now proceed to describe them. The female begins, by stretching out her six legs, fixing her claws in the ground, and holding with her teeth to the grass; then expands her wings, to press her chest close to the ground; where, clinging firmly, and raising that part of the belly, where she has the instrument mentioned before, after forming a right angle with her body, she fixes it, with such strength, that it fastens to the hardest earth, and even in stone; she has all the necessary aparatus to make a perforation, but this alone would not answer the purpose, a place being still wanted wherein she may deposit her eggs.

This hollow cavity is made in about two hours; she then begins to shift the earth underneath, and emits the glutinous substance. Having thus kneaded the earth into a substantial paste, and smoothed the floor with her trunk, she lays the first egg, then renews the operation and lays more, with admirable order, and after various repetitions, completes the whole in about four or five hours; next covering the superior aperture with a glutinous composition, the structure is perfect, with every advantage against the inclemency of the weather, or any hostile invasion.

The female is now overcome with fatigue, few having strength, like the male, to seek after refreshing waters; but, exhausted and spent, they expire close to their progeny, exhibiting a melancholy sight to the labourer; who, from their appearance, foretells the mischiefs to follow, without being able to prevent them; forming an idea of the hidden enemies, who are to devour his harvest, from the multitude of carcases he finds dispersed in the fields.

I cannot omit one circumstance, observed by many others, as well as myself; and that is, when the females are busy in laying their eggs, or in turning the earth, a male would immediately fix on her back, another male upon him, and another besides. Sometimes I have seen six males piled upon one another, over one female; the peasants pretended it was to give her more weight and strength to open the ground; but this could not be the reason, it seeming rather a moment of fury, as observed a-

mongst

mongſt animals; the more as I obſerved, that notwithſtanding the great number of females in 1754, that of the males was ſtill greater, even before they took wing, ſo as to be two or three hundred males to one female, and when they ſallied out of Eſtremadura, to ravage La Mancha, I think I can take upon me to ſay, there were twenty males to a female; their ſex is eaſily diſtinguiſhed by their body and trunk, which induces me the more readily to give weight to my conjecture, from the great ſuperiority of numbers in the males, who, luckily for mankind, are ſeemingly diſappointed in their purſuits.

The egg which incloſes the embryo, has the ſame cylindrical ſhape as the repoſitory it is laid in, being a membraneous cylinder, one line long, very white and ſmooth. They are placed aſide each other, rather obliquely, the head, as in others being neareſt the part where it is to come out. The time of hatching varies according to climate, thoſe that are in high and mountainous places, being generally later than thoſe on the plains. I ſaw legions of them ſkipping about at Almeria in February, becauſe the climate is ſo mild there that moſt kind of greens are nearly over at that time. In Sierra Nevada they only begin to appear in April, and in La Mancha they were hardly animated in May, when there were no greens yet in the market of San Clemente. So that they form a certain thermometer to judge of the warmth of the air.

From

From these various situations proceed those immense swarms of locusts which appear succeffively in June, July, and August; but as they always lay their eggs in barren places which require a certain additional warmth, and temperature, to hatch them, it will account for their not appearing so frequently in cold climates, except such casual swarms of them as may have been wafted there by the winds.

When they first come out of the egg, they are black, of the size of a gnat, and gather in great heaps at the foot of shrubs, particularly the *spartum* or matweed, continually leaping upon each other, and occupying a space of three or four feet in circumference, two inches high. The first time I beheld this sight, it surprized me exceedingly, to observe this moving body, like a mourning scarf waving about, as at this period they only live upon dew, and are frisking about to catch it. For a few days they move at a very little distance, their limbs being weak, their wings very small, and their teeth not sufficiently strong to bite the grass. In about twenty days, they begin to feed on the youngest shoots of plants, and as they grow up, they leave the society of each other, and range further off, consuming day and night every thing they fix upon, till their wings have acquired a full degree of strength; in the mean time, they seem to devour, not so much from a ravenous appetite, as from a rage of destroying

ing every thing that comes in their way. It is not surprising, that they should be fond of the most juicy plants and fruits, such as melons, and all manner of garden fruits, and herbs, feeding also upon aromatic plants, such as lavender, thyme, rosemary, &c. which are so common in Spain, that they serve to heat ovens; but it is very singular, that they equally eat mustard seed, onions, and garlic; nay, even upon hemlock, and the most rank and poisonous plants, such as the thorn apple (*a*) and deadly night shade (*b*). They will even prey upon crowfoot, whose causticity burns the very hides of beasts; and such is their universal taste, that they do not prefer the innocent mallow to the bitter furze, or rue to wormwood, consuming all alike, without predilection or favour, with this remarkable circumstance, that during the four years they committed such havock in Estremadura, the love apple, or *lycoperficon folanum* of Linnæus, was the only plant that escaped their rapacious tooth, and claimed a respect to its root, leaves, flowers and fruit. Naturalists may search for their motives, which I am at a loss to discover, the more, as I saw millions of them light on a field near Almaden, and devour the wool-

(*a*) Thorn apple. Datura ferox of Linnæus.

(*b*) Deadly night-shade, or Dwale. Atropa Belladonna. Linn.—Solanum Lethale. Park. 346. Gerard 340. The whole plant is poisonous, and children allured by the beautiful appearance of the berries, have too often experienced their fatal effects.—See a curious account of this plant in Dr. Withering's Botanical Arrangement, &c. vol. 1. pag. 116.

len

len and linen garments of the peasants, which were lying to dry on the ground. The curate of the village, a man of veracity, at whose house I was, assured me, that a tremendous body of them entered the church, and devoured the silk garments that adorned the images of saints, not sparing even the varnish on the altars. The better to discover the nature of such a phænomenon, I examined the stomach of the locust (*a*), but only found one thin and soft membrane, with which and the liquor it contains, it destroys and dissolves all kinds of substances, equally with the most caustic and venomous plants, extracting from them, a sufficient and salutary nourishment.

Out of curiosity, to know the nature of so formidable a creature, I was urged to examine all its parts with the utmost exactness: Its head is of the size of a pea, though longer, its forehead pointing downwards, like a handsome Andalusian horse, its mouth large and open, its eyes black and rolling, added to a timid aspect not unlike a hare. With such a dastard countenance, who would imagine this creature to be the scourge of mankind! In its two jaws, it has four incisive teeth, whose sharp points traverse each other like scissars, their mechanism being such as to gripe or to cut. Thus armed, what can

---

(*a*) Swammerdam tells us, the locust is of the ruminant kind, thinking to have discovered in them a triplicate stomach, like those animals; but he may have been deceived, and ken one thing for another, or examined locusts different from these of Spain.

resist a legion of such enemies; after devouring the vegetable kingdom, were they, in proportion to their strength and numbers, to become carniverous like wasps, they would be able to destroy whole flocks of sheep, even the dogs, and shepherds; just as we are told of ants in America, that will overcome the fiercest serpents.

The locust spends the months of April, May, and June, in the place of its birth; at the end of June its wings have a fine rose colour, and its body is strong. Being then in their prime, they assemble for the last time, and burn with a desire to propagate their species; this is observed by their motions, which are unequal in the two sexes. The male is restless and solicitous, the female is coy, and eager after food, flying the approaches of the male, so that the morning is spent in the courtship of the one, and the retreat of the other. About ten o'clock, when the warmth of the sun has cleared their wings from the dampness of the night, the females seem uneasy at the forwardness of the males, who continuing their pursuit, they rise together five hundred feet high, forming a black cloud that darkens the rays of the sun. The clear atmosphere of Spain becomes gloomy, and the finest summer day of Estremadura more dismal than the winter of Holland. The rustling of so many millions of wings, in the air, seems like the trees of a forest,

rest, agitated by the wind. The first direction of this formidable column is always against the wind, which if not too strong, it will extend about a couple of leagues; they then make a halt, when the most dreadful havock begins; their sense of smell being so delicate, they can find at that distance, a corn-field, or a garden, and after demolishing it, rise again, in pursuit of another: this may be said to be done in an instant. Each seems to have, as it were, four arms and two feet; the males climb up the plants, as sailors do the shrouds of a ship; they nip off the tenderest buds, which fall to the females below. At last, after repeated devastations, they light upon some barren ground, and the females prepare for laying their eggs.

What a dismal sight for a poor farmer, after having been visited by such cruel guests! A sensible man, amongst them, on viewing his corn-fields, where nothing was now left but chaff, thus expressed himself; " If these creatures were not so coy, and would " suffer the embraces of their mates, in the country " where they were hatched, we should not be loaded with " such dreadful misfortunes; but, like us, they fear " death, and strive to prolong life; for which reason, " they shun the advances of the males, knowing, that " afterward nothing is left, but to deposit their eggs " and expire!"

We learn, by tradition, as well as from history, that these locusts have been a plague to the meridional provinces of Spain time immemorial. I remember to have read in an old Spanish novel, the following question, " which was " the animal that resembled most all other animals?" the answer was, " the locust; because he has the horns " of a stag, the eyes of a cow, the forehead of a horse, the " legs of a crane, the neck of a snake, and the wings of " a dove."

However puerile this may appear, it proves the great length of time they have been known as well as dreaded. Many old people assured me, when so much mischief was done in 1754, it was the third time in their remembrance, and that they always are found in the pasture grounds of Estremadura, from whence they spread into the other provinces of Spain. They are certainly indigenous, being of a different shape from those of the north or the Levant, as is evident in comparing them with such, in the cabinets of natural history. The locust of Spain is the only one that has rose-coloured wings: besides, it is impossible they can come from any other part; from the north it is clear they do not, by the observation of so many ages; from the south they cannot, without crossing the sea, which is hardly possible, by the shortness of their flight, and, like birds of passage, they would be known. I once saw a cloud of them pass over Malaga, and

and move towards the fea, and go over it, for about a quarter of a league, to the great joy of the inhabitants, who concluded they foon would be drowned; but to their difappointment, they fuddenly veered about towards the coaft, and pitched upon an uncultivated fpace furrounded with vineyards, which they foon after quitted. When once they appear, let the number demolifhed be ever fo great, the proportion remaining is ftill too confiderable; therefore, the only way to put an end to fuch a calamity, is to attack them beforehand, and deftroy their eggs, by which means they might be totally extirpated (*a*).

(*a*) In the life of Dr. Thomas Moffet, prefixed to a work of his, intitled, "Health's improvement, London, printed for T. Ofborne, 1746;" mention is made of his Theatre of infects publifhed abroad in 1598, where, fpeaking of locufts, he particularly relates, how much the Spaniards were then afflicted with fwarms of them, that flew over from Africa, the news of which was received when he was writing that account. If to this occafional calamity, we add the frequent droughts to which their meridional provinces are fo fubject, and which caufe fuch diftrefs amongft the poor, it will be a great drawback from their boafted fertility.

LETTER

LETTER IV.

Of the barren and wretched district of Batuecas, in Estremadura.

THE territory of Batuecas, situated on the confines of Castile and Estremadura, near Portugal, has given ample scope to the fanciful conceits of different writers, relating to its imaginary discovery, and whether or not as supposed, it was an unknown land, inhabited by Pagans, blinded by ignorance, without the least knowledge of the Christian religion. This district we are now going to explore, is fourteen leagues to the south west of Salamanca, about eight leagues eastward of Cuidad Rodrigo, and twelve to the north west of Plasencia, forming a plain, or more properly, a most dismal and horrid gully at the foot of that famous mountain, where stands the noted convent called *La Pena de Francia*. The situation of this place inspires every idea of gloom and melancholy, closed in by jagged mountains, where hardly a tree is to be seen, or the least appearance of vegetation: on the contrary, numberless precipices, occasionally choaked up by broken masses of stone, detached insensibly from the rocks, form the most frightful scene the mind can conceive;

ceive. Such is the true state of Batuecas, horrid by nature; rendered still more so, by ignorance and folly. The itinerary from Plasencia to the convent of Batuecas, is as follows: Plasencia to Aigal four leagues; Mohedas one; Casar de Palomero one; Cambroncino two; Vegas de Coria two; Las Mestas one; and to the convent of Batuecas half a league.

Between Plasencia and Aigal, the hamlets of Oliva and Gijo de Granadilla, appear on the right, and Santibanez el Baxo, on the left, with woods of oak and cork trees. You cross the river Ambroz, or de Caparra, and pass by the Puerto del Gamo, before you reach Casar de Palomero. Then enter the melancholy district of the Jurdes, being a division of what is generally called Batuecas; but in any part of this wretched country, if you ask whereabout is the Jurdes, some will tell you, a little further on, and when you proceed, another informs you, it is at a small distance behind; nobody being willing to acknowledge himself an inhabitant of the unhappy country of the Jurdes.

The valley of Batuecas, was idly considered as an unknown part of the world, by those who gave into the fabulous accounts invented in the reign of Philip the IId. though an enlightened age in the annals of Spain. As a further proof of the ideas of the times, we have only to
look

look back on the report made by Galarza, bishop of Coria, to whose diocess this country belongs, when he gave leave to the Carmelite friars to build a church there, which document is to be found in the records of that house. " I give thanks to the Almighty (says this prelate) that in so desolated and wretched a country, where it appears from certificates, which I have among the records of my bishopric, that about forty years ago its inhabitants were Gentiles, deceived by the devil with visible apparitions, his majesty has now ordered a sanctuary to be built, to which I give my concurrence with great satisfaction, and shall as far as lies in my power, contribute towards so pious a foundation."

This record being positive, and the good bishop having given ear to the many exaggerations and false reports, obtruded on the public, might have confirmed these fables in the minds of the people, which insensibly spread themselves over Spain, and extended even amongst foreign nations. They were the more easily propagated at Batuecas, amongst ignorant people, in want of pastors and Christian instruction; their neighbours then took the alarm, and would not venture to move forward with their flocks. In more remote villages these reports lost nothing by the way, so that in many places, the poor harmless inhabitants of Batuecas were looked upon as savages,

savages, destitute of all information, beyond their bleak hills, where they lived in the grossest ignorance, and were supposed to worship the devil.

It was given out as an incontrovertible fact, that a certain lady, belonging to the illustrious house of Alba, seduced by her lover, had fled to these parts, and first made the discovery, meeting with a barbarous people, whose manners, and even language, were strange to them, except a few Gothic expressions. Such were the tales believed at Salamanca, the seat of a famous university; at Madrid, the residence of the court, and in many other places of note. It served as a foundation for novels, as well as dramatic performances, repeatedly exhibited on the stage, and propagated all over the kingdom.

Soon after the friars had settled themselves in this place, and spoken to the graver sort of people, concerning these matters, many of them laughed at their simplicity, while others expressed their indignation against the inhabitants of Alberca, whom they reproached with being the authors, through motives of jealousy, of such a ridiculous and invidious report.

The town of Alberca is the principal place in the territory of Batuecas, and not above a league distant from this valley: its inhabitants could not be supposed ignorant of the fallacy of the report, as their flocks were constantly grazing there; yet, so great was the prejudice and ignorance of the people, that Thomas Goncales Manuel, a clergyman of the town of Alberca, thought it necessary to justify his countrymen, and in 1693, published an essay in their defence, under the title of "A true narrative and apologetical declaration of the antiquity of Batuecas;" in which he seriously refutes the illusion by authentic documents and records, belonging to the town of Alberca, and its neighbourhood.

The late father Feijoo said every thing necessary on this subject, in his critical works (a), intended to explode the many vulgar errors that prevail amongst his countrymen, adding his astonishment that they should have been corroborated by national writers, such as Nieremberg (b) and Alonso Sanchez (c); by which means they even got credit abroad, and geographical writers of no small reputation ventured to copy them; particularly Thomas Corneille, and the author of the Great Atlas, as well as Moreri in his Dictionary.

The whole of this district may properly be reduced to an intersected valley of about a league in length, sometimes so confined as just to leave room for the passage of

(a) Theatro critico, tom. 4. Disc. x.
(b) Nieremberg cuoriosa philosophia, lib. 1. cap. 95.
(c) De rebus Hispaniæ, lib. 7. cap. 5.

the river that gives name to the valley: This then was
that unknown country so surprizingly dreaded, where it
is certain no others dwelled but a few wretched shepherds, and some miserable peasants, in forlorn huts,
surrounded by precipices, divested of all intercourse with
their neighbours, in a wild romantic situation, which the
most fanciful pencil would find difficult to delineate, or
the language of Shakespeare to describe.

The other valley called, "of the Jurdes," which may be
about four leagues long, and three in breadth, yields not
to the former in wretchedness and misery. During the
whole journey from Alberca to Batuecas, nothing is to
be seen but a repetition of jagged and illshapen rocks,
with their rugged peaks, like so many turrets and battle-
ments, towering one over the other, as far as the eye can
extend, forming dreadful gullies where the river forces its
way, whose waters are clear, abounding with trout, and
having grains of gold in its sands, which the peasants
know well how to look after, and sell at Plasencia, Cuidad Rodrigo, and Salamanca (*a*), which is a great resource to them in this sorrowful vale; where during winter, the sun's rays can hardly penetrate for above four
hours in the day. To increase still further its horror, the
hills are perforated with dismal caves, one above the o-

(*a*) The same happens in the river Sil, in Galicia, where the poor people are employed in this manner, after floods.

ther, and some so extensive, that three or four hundred sheep may easily take shelter there; to complete this picture of distress, let it suffice to add, that this country is the resort of numerous birds of prey, and affords shelter to bears, wolves, wild cats, and weazles, which destroy all the hares and rabbits, with the addition of snakes, serpents, and many obnoxious reptiles, particularly one sort of serpent, which darts at its prey with great violence, and perhaps may be of that species called *Jacula*, or *Jaculum serpens*, described in the acts of the Leopoldine academy, which mentions one of these to have darted from a ditch, to a considerable distance, and fixed itself upon the arm of a peasant. But why need I enlarge any further on so dreary a spot, or describe so barren a country, where even grass is not to be seen! here and there a solitary cistus, and nothing but furze, the only resource of goats and some bees, who are of service merely on account of their wax, as their honey is neither valuable for its colour nor flavour, having all the bitter taste of their food.

In this wretched country the Carmelite Friars pitched upon a little plain on the banks of the river, and built their convent in 1599, but their house has nothing worthy of description; and though the very sight of a distressed traveller at their gates, should be sufficient to engage the benevolent minds of these holy fathers, they

are

are seldom in a hurry to open their doors, and none are admitted or intitled to hospitality, but such as are provided with letters of recommendation and positive orders from the provincial or General of their order. The hermits who dwell here, practise all the austerities observed by the primitive christians, when living amongst pagan princes under the most violent persecutions, while these good men who deny themseves every blessing of Providence, are in the centre of a christian kingdom, where the truths of its holy religion are acknowledged protected and established, and where notwithstanding their self denial and mortification, the virtues of an active life united with morality must be the primary and essential qualifications in the territories of a powerful and extensive dominion.

LETTER

LETTER V.

The convent of Juste, in the Vera of Plasencia, famous for the retreat of the Emperor Charles.

WERE we to believe the exaggerated accounts which Spanish writers in general give of their country, we should be inclined to imagine the whole kingdom was a paradise flowing with milk, and honey, where nature had lavished her most luxuriant productions; but whenever the traveller happens to pass through the interior parts of the kingdom, and to form his judgment from personal inspection, he will then be convinced that the lofty style and diction of elegant writers, requires a considerable lowering before it is reduced to the simplicity of fact and of truth, for though it must be allowed that the southern parts are fertile, that the plains of Valencia, are delightful, and that the Biscayners have been indefatigable in cultivating their rugged mountains, yet when we take a general survey of the kingdom in the review of a journey through Spain, it will be found that barren hills, and naked rocks and mountains, form a considerable part of the prospect, diversified only here and there with a few scattered spots of imperfect cultivation:

Many

Many districts still remaining uncultivated, and the rivers overflowing their banks without any impediment, in the same manner as they did in the earliest ages of the world; as if they were to receive every blessing from Providence without the least trouble or fatigue (*a*). Amongst innumerable instances which might be alleged in support of this assertion, I shall confine myself to one given by the Spaniards themselves, of the so much celebrated valley of Plasencia, in Estremadura, represented by many as the most delightful place in the world, selected by the great Emperor Charles to finish his days, and supposed to be seated in an enchanting vale, covered with all manner of fruit trees in the highest perfection, where the very air was embalmed with the most delicious odours; but alas! this is far from being the case, as the judicious Spanish writer (*b*), who lately visited that province, informs us, who complains loudly of its most miserable state, and from his authority, therefore, I shall venture to pronounce on its present most wretched and neglected condition.

(*a*) Don Antonio Pons reproaches his countrymen very feelingly for their neglect on this subject in the following lines; " Los rios regularmente corren entre nosotros por donde Dios los encamino a principio del mundo, como si no hubiera dexado con grandissima providencia nada que estudiar en el cultivo de las tierras, sino que todo hubiera de ser facil. No es assi, ni tal quiso, sobre cuyo punto dijo bien uno de los mejores poetas."

Pater ipse colendi
Haud facilem esse viam voluit primusque per artem
Movit agros, curis acuens mortalia corda.   Virg. Georg. I.

Viage de Espana, tomo 3. Madrid 1777.

(*b*) Don Antonio Ponz.—See Viage de Espana, tom 7. Madrid, 1778.

After

After quitting the city of Plasencia, and crossing the river Xerte, you pass over the hill of Galcones, opposite the city, then descend into the territory of the Vega, leaving on your left the villages of Garguera, Barrado, and Arroyo Molinos; you next go through the village of Pasaron, five leagues from Plasencia, and come to a pleasant situation called La Magdalena, where there is a good farm house, which formerly belonged to the Jesuits: you are now at a league's distance from Juste, and to go there you traverse a woody country with a few chesnut trees, and pass several brooks, where they catch excellent trout. The convent of Juste is situated nearly in the centre of the Vera, on the brow of a steep hill, which protects it from the North wind, and with other mountains forms that chain which is called the Puerto de Tornavacas, joining with the hills of Arenas, Puerto del Pico, and others. Neither thec onvent nor church have any thing remarkable, and would have passed on to future ages in oblivion, had it not been for the distinction shewn them by the great Emperor who ended his life in this solitary place. Over the great altar in the church, they have a copy of that famous picture called the glory of Titian, which stood formerly here, and was removed to the Escurial by express command of the Emperor, who ordered that the original should be fixed in the same church with his remains. The following inscription is seen on the wall,

in

in a corner of the garden, underneath the arms of the Emperor.

"EN ESTA SANTA CASA DE S. HIERONIMO DE JUSTE
"SE RETIRO A ACABAR SU VIDA, EL QUE TODA LA
"GASTO EN DEFENSA DE LA FE Y CONSERVACION DE
"LA JUSTICIA, CARLOS V. EMPERADOR REY DE LAS
"ESPANAS CHRISTIANISIMO, INVICTISIMO. MURIO A
"21 DE SETIEMBRE DE 1558."

In this holy house of St. Jerom of Juste, ended his days, he, who spent the whole of them in defence of the faith, and in support of justice, Charles V. Emperor, King of Spain. Most christian, invincible. He died on the 21st Sept. 1558.

These are the only traces left here of that great Emperor, who once filled the world with the glory of his deeds. The ruined decorations of the garden and ponds seem to intimate their pristine state in happier days, and the several plantations in the Vera, watered by numberless brooks, might once have exhibited a more pleasing appearance.

A distinction must be made between the *Vera of Plasencia* and the *Valle de Plasencia*. The valley extends from the city to the Puerto de Tornavacas, upon a straight line from East to North, the length of nine leagues, and so level, that the whole extent lies open to your view, as far as the *Puerto*, closed by high mountains, dividing on the right hand the *Vera* from the *Valle*, and on the left the hills between the valley and the road to Banos, and finally thofe of Tornavacas, whofe high tops are always covered with fnow.

The villages belonging to the valley are Afperilla, Cafas del Caftanar, El Torno, Valde Aftilla, Cabrero el Rebollar, Navaconcejo, Cabezuela, Badillo, and Xerte, which gives name to the river, as Tornavacas does to the *Puerto*, but at prefent every branch of cultivation is at the loweft ftate, without even the appearance of an orange or a lemon tree, if we except two or three blighted ones at the convent of Santa Cruz de Tabilla, where the country is a defart: and what is ftill worfe, the mountains and paffes are filled with affaffins and robbers, to the great terror of the inhabitants and travellers. The *Vera* is no better, and affords the moft melancholy afpect imaginable; amongft the various experiments to deftroy the worms that ruin the chefnut trees, fire was the laft expedient, in fo much, that the trees, fcorched and half burned, now refemble the oaks ftruck by the thunder of Jove, inftead of the golden age of the poets, and their whole agriculture is reduced to the fowing a few peas, with fome miferable fcraps of a vineyard. The villages of the *Vera* are Piornal, Barrado, Garguera, Arroyomolinos, Pafaron, Gargantalolla, Xarandilla, Gijo de Arandilla, Xarais, Robledillo, Aldeanueva de la Vera, Viandar, Villanueva, El Ofar, and Cuacos: This laft being near to
Jufte,

Juste, and distinguished by the savage disposition and ferocity of its inhabitants; to such a degree as to overcome the patience of that great personage who lived in their neighbourhood, by offering him every affront their low station would permit, taking his cows if they happened to stray into their district, and stealing the trout reserved for his use; and to crown all, flinging stones at Don John of Austria, the Emperor's son, whenever he ventured to taste of their cherries.

LETTER VI.

Further observations made in the course of another tour by Don Guillermo Bowles from Almaden to the silver mine of Guadalcanal.

I SET out from Almaden for the village of Alcocer; in the plain there is a lead mine which has never been worked; after an hour's journey we came to the mountain of Lares, where there are ruins of a Moorish castle; here I saw for the first time the true Spanish emery, which before I only knew by specimens in the cabinets of Paris (*a*); the hill where it is found, is of sandstone, mixed

---

(*a*) Emery is a sort of metallic stone, found in most, or all mines of metals, but chiefly in those of iron, copper, or gold, of which three kinds are usually distinguished; the Spanish, red, and common emery. The first sort is found in the gold mines of Peru, and other provinces of Spanish America. It is judged a kind of *Marcasite* of that rich metal, being streaked with little veins and specks of gold, for which reason the king of Spain prohibits the exportation of it, whereby it is rendered exceedingly scarce, to the great regret of the searchers after the philosophers stone, who build great hopes in the transmutation of this precious metal. The red emery is found chiefly in the copper mines of Sweden and Denmark. The common emery is taken out of iron mines, and is almost the only sort used in England, the consumption of which is very considerable amongst the armourers, cutlers, locksmiths, glaziers, lapidaries, masons, and other mechanics, some of whom use it to polish and burnish iron and steel works; others to cut and scallop glass, marble, and precious stones.

The common emery is of a brownish colour, bordering a little on red, exceedingly hard, and of course difficult to pulverize. The English are the only people that have got the art of making it into powder, which is done by mills contrived for the purpose, and in that state they send it to their neighbours. Emery fused with lead and iron hardens them. It increases

with

with quartz: this mineral is blackish, resembles the polish given by the bloodstone, and is so hard that it emits fire when struck with steel. The Moors worked this mine, but more perhaps, for the sake of the gold which it probably contains, than for any other motive; and as their method is not to be found in any Arabic book that I know of, either printed or manuscript, I should think the following trial might be made. Let the ore be first softened by fire and water, then exposed to the air for four or five months or more, that the phlogiston might separate, leaving the matter in a proper state to extract the metal by fusion. I found two sorts of emery in Spain, one in a ferruginous stone, and the other in sand loaded with iron (a).

and heightens the weight and colour of gold. It is usual to mix a little of it with the gold from Madagascar, which is naturally pale and soft. It is brought in English ships from the Levant, particularly from the island of Naxia, where it costs but a crown the twenty-eight quintals; the quintal weighing 140 lb. which is therefore what they usually ballast their ships with.—Rolt's Dict. of Commerce.

(a) Notwithstanding what is said here relating to emery, Mr. Bowles, in page 364 of his work, further informs us, that he found five sorts of emery in Spain. First, That of Reinosa, composed of large grains. Secondly, Of very small fine grains, found at the foot of Guadarrama mountains, and used at St. Ildefonso, for polishing of crystals. Thirdly, The one of Alcocer, mentioned above, worked by the Moors, which has no grain, but on breaking the stone is smooth like an hæmatite, and contains a little gold. Fourthly, A species of emery, as it were, marbled in quartz, found about Molina de Aragon, and in Estremadura, in a district granted by the king, to Don Pedro Rodriguez Campomanez, containing a little gold, but not worth the expence of searching for. Fifthly, Another sort dispersed in many parts of Spain, particularly in the lordship of Molina, between Tortuera and Melmarcos, in loose, black, heavy stones, seeming to be the residue of some rock or mine, and having when pulverized, hard pungent and mordicant particles.

Between

Between Alcocer and Orellana, there is an iron mine in sandstone, with the finest red ocre in the world. A steep mountain must be crossed to arrive at Nabalvillar, where there are blood stones, and a species of black earth, which shines when rubbed in the hand, but is only a *blend* or dead mineral of no use. From hence you go to Logrosan, at the foot of a chain of hills which run from east to west, called *La Sierra de Guadalupe*. In coming out of the village, a vein of phosphoric stone crosses the road obliquely from north to south. It is a whitish stone without any flavour. When pounded and thrown on the fire, it burns, and emits a blue flame, without any smell (a). In the mountain to the north of this village, there is a silver mine in a whitish stone, with white *mica*, and in the mountain of *Guadalupe* to the south, there is a copper mine in a flaty stone, jaspered with blue and green. An extensive uncultivated plain lies half way between Nabalvillar and Logrosan, covered with the kermes oak; but before you reach Logrosan, the sandstone disappears, and the houses of that village are built with granite from the hills of *Guadalupe*.

After having gone out of our road to examine the phosphoric stone, we returned again to Orellana, at which

---

(a) Mr. Bowles says it is the phlogiston of the coal that causes this flame, but this explanation cannot be admitted; for it is well known that the phosphoric stones emit a blue light, when heated, without being exposed, to any substance, supposed to contain phlogiston.

place we crossed the Guadiana, where its bed is very shallow, in order to see a lead mine two leagues further to the southward, on the road to Zalamea (*a*). This mine is found on a small eminence called *Vadija*, or *Valle de las minas*; the vein runs from north to south, cuts the slaty stone, and is seen in a bed of quartz, which is discovered from a brook about two hundred paces from the first shaft, where the vein does not follow as I said above, but strikes off from east to west. The miners lost it by crossing the brook from north to south, when they should have followed it according to the direction of the soft slate as I did, and found it again.

Continuing two leagues further to the southward from this mine towards Zalamea, there is a silver mine without any lead in the spar; this vein is found in a rock of granite, cut contrary to its natural direction, and consists of spar, quartz, white and yellow pyrites, with a shining, black, small pyritous matter. The country, for many

(*a*) The town of Zalamea is six leagues from Aracena, in the very heart of the Sierra Morena. The country people have a tradition, that it was built by those persons sent there by Solomon in quest of the silver mines, who named the place after him, in proof of which they assert that a very antient castle just by, is still called Castle of Solomon. One of the villages in the jurisdiction of Zalamea is named *Obiud*, and the river near it *Odiel*, being Hebrew names, which I was informed of, says a celebrated Spanish writer, by a clergyman, as well as by antient people of the place; but this is not so easy to prove, or for me to give assent to, merely on their traditional relations. If it were true, that the *Tharsis* of scripture was *Tartessus*, then indeed it might be presumed that the treasures were got from hence; for which I refer them to Goropius Becanus L b. 7. Hispanicorum. See Antiguedades de Sevilla par Rodrigo Caro. Sevilla 1634.

leagues

leagues round, is replete with immense pieces of granite; lying above ground, like the rocks of Fontainebleau; the land produces a great deal of corn, and is well furnished with oak.

These two mines being so near to each other, might be reciprocally advantageous, as the lead would be useful for refining the pyritous silver. In the one which is abandoned, the remains of a crucible and reverbatory furnace are still to be observed; they quitted it on being overwhelmed with water, but it might easily be cleared again, it being situated on an eminence, called *Chantre*, as the lead mine is on another, 300 feet higher than a brook, where, in summer, there is seldom any water.

From Zalamea we passed an extensive plain of eleven leagues, called *Vinolas de Zalamea*, and came to the village of Berlanga; where, entering upon the *Sierra Morena* we arrived, in four hours, at the famous town of Guadalcanal, observing great quantities of sumach in these parts, which is cut in the month of August; after which the leaves and flowers are pounded and sold to the curriers of Seville, who use it for dressing of leather (*a*).

(*a*) The best Sumach is that which is greenish and new: Oporto in Portugal, being the place which furnishes the most, and generally speaking, the best. Roh's Dict. of commerce.

LETTER

LETTER VII.

Description of the famous silver mine at Guadalcanal in Estremadura.

THE town of Guadalcanal is the last to the southward in the province of Estremadura, only separated from Andalusia by the small stream of Benalija. The famous and boasted silver mine of Guadalcanal (*a*), so celebrated by historians, and of which such various and uncertain accounts have been published, is situated about half a league distant from the town of that name, belonging to the knights of Santiago, and surrounded with high mountains. The first discovery of this mine, according to the

(*a*) This is not Mr. Bowles's account of the Guadalcanal mine, but I have reason to think it a more perfect one, giving the real state and present condition of the mine from whence a judgment may be formed of Mr. Bowles's conjectures. He says there are about 800 families at Guadalcanal; but they exceed a thousand, besides a convent of friars, three convents of nuns, and sixty ecclesiasticks, who do not enter into the contribution roll, though they have houses and families. He mentions the mine being a league distant from the town, whereas it is only a mile and a half. He tells us, Guadalcanal is a very dry spot, though the inhabitants allege that there is not a more moist and damp town in all Estremadura. In the square there is one of the richest springs of excellent water that can be met with any where, and all the houses have wells at a small depth. There are four fountains in different parts of the town, which have no connection with the principal spring in the square, besides several small spouts of water continually running in the streets, that make the houses so damp, that the lower apartments cannot be inhabited without inconvenience before July. Though he says the galleries of the mine were in perfect good order, he could not have a just notion of them, proceeding no further than 50 feet, for the information of Don Joseph de Carvajal, minister of state at that time.

best

best information, was made by a farmer of the town of Guadalcanal, whose name was Delgado. This man accidentally met with the ore, as he was ploughing his fields: being struck with its brightness, he carried it home, after carefully covering the place, and then set out for Seville, where he was informed it was a valuable ore. This is said to have happened in the year 1509, soon after the discovery of America by Columbus, and is looked upon as the most ancient record of this mine. The surprising accounts which used daily to arrive from America, relating to those new discovered mines, added to the little information Delgado was able to procure at home, inspired him with the same ardour as many of his countrymen, and engaged him to repair thither for further instruction, where, after obtaining all the lights in his power from the American miners, he returned again to Spain, made a discovery to the court of the mine of Guadalcanal, soliciting a grant, and proposing to work it at his own expence. Though it might be supposed, this must have answered his purpose, nothing appears from history, either with respect to himself, or his heirs; and what is still more singular, the mine seemed to be without any proprietor in the reign of Philip the second, which gave rise to the several laws promulgated in his reign, under the title of *Ordenanzas de Minas*, and are to be found in the *Recopilacion*, or code, published by that prince,

prince, which with respect to mines, are the only laws extant in the kingdom.

The Fuggers of Augsburg, obtained a grant of them from Philip the second, after they had been worked for some time on the king's account. Several Spanish writers assert, that immense riches were taken out of this mine, particularly Carranza, in his treatise on Spanish coins (a), affirms, that one week with another, they extracted the value of sixty thousand ducats. The history of the house of Herasti says, that this mine had produced eight millions of *pesetas* (b), which were employed in building the Escurial. Be this as it may, the chief shaft in the mine acquired the name of *Poso Rico*, "The rich shaft", and continued in the hands of the Fuggers and their heirs, until 1635, when they totally abandoned it, after having gone a great depth, and formed ten galleries, though it is surmised they continued it for political reasons, to cover other projects, as they solicited considerable loans to pursue their works, and when they relinquished it, reports were spread, that it contained several rich veins of silver ore, which none could contradict, for in less than a month the mine filled with water within thirty feet of the surface. This opinion however has

(a) Licenciado Alonso Carranza Ajustamiento de Monedas y reduccion de metales. Madrid, 1629.
(b) Valuing the peseta at 10 d. sterling, the eight millions above-mentioned will amount to £. 333.333. 6 s. 8 d. sterling.

been handed down from one to another to the prefent time.

In 1690, Raphael Gomez, a Jew, obtained a grant of this mine from Charles the fecond, and formed a company with fome Portugueze merchants of his tribe. They attempted to drain Pozo Rico, but for want of a fufficient capital, engines, and intelligent workmen, they could not drain further than the third gallery, and failing in their future attempts, were charged with duplicity and fraud; Gomez was arrefted and carried prifoner to Seville, where he underwent a long and fevere confinement, though he printed his cafe and defence, but died before the bufinefs came to an iffue.

The diftracted ftate of king Charles's finances, fuggefted to his minifters the idea of continuing the works of thefe mines; on this account, and to give this operation a more plaufible appearance, the guilt of Gomez was to be made more confpicuous; Don Alonfo Carillo Rueda, of the council of finances, was named fuperintendant of the mines, and ordered to repair thither directly, and carry on the works on his majefty's account; following the directions of a wandering friar lately returned from America, appointed chief engineer, on a fuppofition of his knowledge in mines. Carillo arrived at Guadalcanal in 1695, and Gomez was arrefted as mentioned

tioned before; he then proceeded in his commiſſion with all the deliberation and formality of the law, iſſuing out orders, and multiplying writings at every ſtep; they began to drain Pozo Rico, but never went further than the third gallery; ſickneſs, want of money, and other impediments, baffled all their attempts; this famous mine was once more abandoned, and Carillo and his retinue returned to Madrid.

The death of Charles the ſecond, the laſt Auſtrian monarch of Spain, and the ſucceſſion war which followed, prevented all further purſuits of this kind, till 1725, when a new company was formed at Madrid; with freſh expectations of ſucceſs. The draining of Pozo Riso was once more undertaken, but all their labours were fruitleſs. In this embarraſſed ſituation a new ray of light ſeemed to pierce the receſſes of theſe hidden mines, and revive the drooping ſpirits of the preſent adventurers, raiſing them from a deſponding anxiety, to the moſt ſanguine expectation. The perſonage who was to work this ſurpriſing alteration, was no leſs a character than an Engliſh lady of quality, of very high rank. In 1728, lady Mary Herbert, daughter of the marquis of Powis, arrived at Madrid from Paris, where ſhe had been concerned in the Miſſiſſippi ſchemes, and by her acquaintance with the famous Mr. Law, had improved her talents and natural genius for enterprize, which engaged

her

her to set out for Madrid, and make proposals to the Spanish company for draining the silver mine of Guadalcanal, in which expedition she was attended by Mr. Joseph Gage, grandson of Sir Thomas Gage, Bart. of Hengrave, in Suffolk.

Those who are acquainted with the genius of the Spaniards, and the great deference they pay to the fair sex, will easily conceive what impression such an offer must have made, when, exclusive of the profit it offered, it came from a lady of the most illustrious birth, with the additional advantages of person and talents. Lady Mary proposed to the company to drain the mines, on condition they would allow her two hundred thousand dollars(a), payable at different times as she proceeded, and half the profit of the mine, which was readily accepted, and a formal agreement concluded; the Spanish company having raised a considerable subscription by public authority. Lady Mary set out for the mines, and procured engines from England, as well as miners, engaging her own fortune in the undertaking as well as that of Mr. Gage, and a large sum from the noble marquis her father: Her agents undertook the draining of Pozo Rico, and had tolerable success, receiving punctual payment from the company; but towards the end, disputes began to arise, the Spaniards insisted that lady Mary's agents were obliged to clear away the mud, and remove

(a) £33,333 6s. 8d. sterling, valuing the current dollar at 4od. English.

every

every obstruction from rubbish in the galleries: Her ladyship endeavoured to prove her contract only related to the water: the payments were stopped, and a suit at law commenced. Lady Mary went on at her own expence, and thoroughly cleared the mine to the tenth gallery. Here there was supposed to be a rich vein of mineral, and as no Spaniard had gone to that depth, the opinion was easily circulated: it got further credit, when lady Mary presented a petition to the judge conservator of the mine, requesting in a judicial form, that a quantity of this ore should be brought up and smelted in presence of the court; its value properly ascertained, and attested. The judge issued his decree accordingly, but as all the agents were foreigners, and united in their views, an imposition is said to have been artfully practised, in presence of the judge and officers of the court, as well on the Spanish agents, as on the numerous witnesses present on the occasion. Out of 40lb. of ore supposed to be from the tenth gallery, the produce was made evidently to be ten pounds, thirteen ounces of fine silver; which was handed about in an ostentatious manner, and afterwards shewn to the king, who then resided at Seville, by the marquis de la Paz, prime minister of Spain, which fixed the reputation and riches of this mine beyond all manner of doubt. The law suit had continued against lady Mary for two years, and as the preserving the galleries already drained, was very costly, they soon

filled

filled again with water; but her ladyship, by her high rank and polite addrefs, having been able to acquire a powerful intereft at court, king Philip, out of his natural benevolence and equity, after being informed of all thefe tranfactions, was pleafed to declare, That lady Mary Herbert had fulfilled her engagements: giving a decree in her favour, againft the Spanifh company, excluding them from all their right in the mine of Guadalcanal, and granting the fame to lady Mary Herbert, for the term of thirty years, to her and her heirs, &c. under the fame conditions, and with the fame provifos of continuing the works at her own expence, within the term of two years, of which her ladyfhip afterwards obtained a prolongation, but never appeared any further in this bufinefs, though her agents fpared no pains to procure new adventurers, and profecute their fchemes. In 1736, Mr. Gage obtained, in his own name, from the court of Spain, a grant of the mine of Cazalla, which is called *Mina de Puerto Blanco*, where they continued working till 1746; and though it produced fome very rich mineral, with large quantities of filver, it never anfwered the expence, added to the plunder of agents and fervants, particularly after the death of Mr. Richard Weftley, an Englifhman, on whofe fkill they chiefly depended. Moreover the buildings of both mines were robbed of the timber and materials, by the inhabitants of the adjacent villages, who, living in a remote part

of

of the country, did every thing with impunity, as no effectual methods were taken to prevent it; all these misfortunes contributing to ruin the mine as much as the water; while the event of the *ten pounds thirteen ounces* of fine silver, having been printed by authority and circulated abroad, kept up its reputation in those remote kingdoms, where they were at too great a distance to know the real state of the case, and only saw the favourable side of the question. In the year 1767, Mr. Thomas Sutton Count de Clonard, who is settled at Paris, made his proposals to the court of Spain. The Spanish council of commerce and mines being well informed that lady Mary Herbert, on account of her great age and other reasons, was not in a situation of fulfilling her contracts, was willing to grant the mines on the same terms to the Count de Clonard; accordingly, on the 27th November, 1767, a *cedula* or decree, was issued in his favour, granting him, for thirty years, the royal mines of Guadalcanal, Cazalla, and Galarosa, declaring the former grant to lady Mary Herbert null and void, as well as all her property therein. By virtue of this patent, the Count de Clonard formed a new company at Paris, in 1768, and in August the works were begun. Hydraulic machines were erected, and they drained the shafts very fast; but the ruinous state of the galleries requiring them to be supported anew, great delays ensued, in so much that the draining of the mine was not entirely

entirely compleated till July, 1774. They then made the fatal difcovery, that there never exifted a vein, or any appearance of fuch in the tenth gallery, and that the event alluded to, had been a deception to draw in new fubfcribers to indemnify former loffes. This has been a dear-bought experience to the French, who had erected confiderable buildings at the mine; particularly at Cazalla, where they had built large furnaces, and a machine for grinding inferior ore, at a league and a half diftance, on the rivulet of Guefna. There is no doubt however that the former adventurers muft have obtained great quantities of very rich mineral, as is evident by the excavations from the furface, down to the fourth gallery, which diminifhed towards the eighth, the total depth of the mine being 1200 Caftilian feet. The chief engineers are of opinion the antients had great fuccefs down to the fourth gallery, and that there, as the vein ftruck off more obliquely to the South, they were deceived by a branch of the chief vein, which decoyed them as far as the eighth gallery, where it finifhed; that from thence they proceeded at a great expence in queft of the vein to the tenth gallery without fuccefs, and then gave it up.

The prefent adventurers difcovered a very rich mineral in the eighth gallery, which at firft appeared to run a great length, but they were foon difappointed, and only extracted

extracted 400lb. of mineral, though so rich, that some pieces produced at the rate of 70 to 80 per cent. and on a medium, have been rated at 50 per cent. specimens of which were sent to the court in November 1775, and are to be seen in the royal cabinet of natural history at Madrid, particularly one very curious specimen, like an incrustation of rubies, called *Rosicler* by mineralogists, from its rose-colour appearance.

The present workmen have abandoned the old works at Pozo Rico, taken away their engines, and suffered it to fill up, and have applied towards the North, on the direction of the vein from North to South, and in a gallery undertaken two years ago in that part, have discovered appearances which flatter them with success, when they come to a point where several veins reunite.

Their works at Cazalla, where they have extracted some rich mineral, though in small quantities, deviate from the former operations, and are upon a new plan, proposed by Mr. Duhamel a French engineer, who gives them great hopes, according to all principles of the art; but for the carrying this on, no less a sum is required than 600,000 livres; (£25,000 sterling) the ore which has been smelted hitherto at the new foundery, on the river Guesna, has only produced 4852 ounces of refined silver

silver (*a*), an inconsiderable sum for so great an undertaking, attended with such an extraordinary expence. This is the actual state of the celebrated silver mine of Guadalcanal; how far their future operations will be crowned with success, time only will discover (*b*).

(*a*) 4851 ounces of silver, at the rate of five shillings per ounce, would only be 1212 l. sterling.

(*b*) There is no doubt but that the discovery of mines, and their being brought to perfection, is entirely due to the spirit of enterprize amongst individuals, and that the public is frequently benefited by their labours, though private persons may be prejudiced by injudicious and extraordinary expences. Whatever may happen to the French in this pursuit, the inhabitants of Estremadura however have nothing to fear on this score; nor has the spirit of mining made any great impression amongst them. Don Antonio Pons relates, with much humour, the notions of the country people in those parts about mines, when being in the Sierra de Gat, and speaking to his landlord on the subject, he answered him, " What, Sir, are you also one of those strollers who lately came here in quest of mines in these desert countries ? Ah, Sir ! the only mines here are hard labour, and spare diet. I said as much to those people at the time, though they assured me that they had discovered an iron mine, and that we should all soon be rich ! But alas ! they wore out their cloaths, spoiled the fine silk stockings they brought with them, found out their mistake, and marched off, while I remained quiet at home as before." Viage de Espana, Madrid, 1778.

LETTER

LETTER VIII.

Remarkable objects in the course of a tour from Guadalcanal to the city of Seville.

IN travelling to the eastward from Guadalcanal you come in two hours to the town of Alanis, which gives its name to a lead mine about half a league distant from it to the south east, which at present is entirely abandoned. The vein is perceived in the middle of a field, being about two feet broad, and rising that height above ground. Its direction is from south to north, cutting the hard slate that opposes it, as well as the calcareous stone with which that country abounds. It is of a dark colour, and so tough as to require thirty hours in calcining. The ancients followed this vein with a gallery from south to north, but the moderns have only worked one branch of it which shoots off towards the west. These veins may have flattering appearances, but are generally deceitful, though at first the quartz may contain pyrites, but lower down they generally terminate in lead.

Going forward from this place brings you to Cazalla, where there is a mine about half a league from the town,

at

at a place called Puerto Blanco. The vein does not appear above ground, but a few feet from the surface there is a stratum of extraneous earth, different from the other earth seen hereabout. In this mine they find virgin silver, copper pyrites in the quartz, and a little iron.

Two leagues and a half from Cazalla, there is a high mountain called *Fuente de la Reyna*, where the Constantina mine is to be seen, so called from a village of that name, about two leagues distant, and not derived from the Emperor Constantine, who never was in Spain, nor was the founder of it, according to the popular error which prevails on that subject. In former times this mine was worked with great judgment, as appears from the remains of their shafts and galleries. The vein runs from north to south across the direction of the slate, and as the miners term it, has its hat of iron, with pyrites and blend of silver and lead in the spar. Lower down they found silver, called by the Spanish miners *Plata belada*, "frosted silver", and a mine of lead in a small tessallated form. Some years ago an inhabitant of Constantina undertook the working of this mine, sunk two shafts, and made galleries on the top of the hill, but abandoned it soon after, perhaps for want of skill, or sufficient capital to go on with the works, though it was thought to deserve more attention, as the ore was good, and they had fuel at hand with a brook at the foot of the mountain,

mountain, in a fruitful country, with plenty of vineyards.

Two leagues to the westward of Cazalla, there is a copper mine, at a place called *Canada de los Conejos*, which from its appearance should be rich, the vein running from north to south in a pyritous quartz. Half a league from Cazalla there is a mine of vitriol, at a place called *Castanares*, from the number of chesnut trees growing there. The stone is pyritous and ferruginous with deep efflorescencies, or spots of a greenish yellow, and a kind of white powder, which is vitriol divested of the water that crystalises it.

After crossing a mountain, two leagues in length, to the westward of Cazalla, where there are four sorts of the cistus, the terebinthus and other plants similar to those on other hills in this country, you come to a little village, called *El Real de Monasterio*. Half a league from this place, there is a mine of black lead proper for pencils, a species of the *molybdena*, but not of the true sort of *molybdena nigrica fabrilis*, like that from Cumberland, so famous abroad, that in France it goes by the name of *crayon d'Angleterre*; they give the name of *lapis*, in Spain, to those black lead pencils, a term they likewise apply very improperly, to black chalk used for drawings, which is a soft stone, called *ampelitis*.

The

The country about Monasterio abounds with good oak, of which there is a wood of a league square, with a great many cork trees, from which they strip off the bark every four years, as far as a white sap which they leave on the tree. A liquid humour afterwards issues out again, which thickens with the sun and air, and forms a new bark in about four years more. When the bark is taken off, it is piled up in a pond or ditch, and loaded with heavy stones to flatten it, and reduce it into tables, from whence it is taken to be dried and tied up in bundles for exportation, being then in a proper state for the different purposes for which cork is applied (*a*).

There is a great variety of oaks in Spain, the *roble* is the common English oak with a bitter acorn. The *querigo* is a chesnut-leaved oak, also with a bitter acorn. The *encina* is the ilex, or evergreen oak, and has a sweet acorn, being a stately tree, the wood of which is very solid and hard, but its roots are less so, and are used by turners. The acorns are large and delicate, and so palatable as to find a place at the table in preference to chesnuts.

(*a*) Mr. Bowles, speaking of the cork tree, page 67, says, That every four years they peel off the bark as far as the epidermis, "De quatro en quatro anos se le despoja de su corteza hasta al epidermis," which must be a mistake, as the epidermis is the outward skin or bark. He should have said "hasta la albura," as far as the white sap or sappy part. *Alburnum*. His French translator Le Vicomte de Flavigny has followed him verbally and literally on every occasion. "Tous les quatres ans on le depouille de son ecorce jusqu'a lépiderme, page 95. See Introduction a l'histoire naturelle et a la geographie physique de l'Espagne traduite de l'original espagnol de Guillaume Bowles." Par le Vicomte de Flavigny. Paris, 1776.

chefnuts. Another fpecies of the ilex has a gloffy leaf with fweet acorns, but longer and more pointed than the others; the country people know very well how to diftinguifh the former from the latter, by the fhape of the leaf. Mr. Bowles faw a fpecies of ilex in Catalonia very fingular, being only fix inches high, yet had fifty-three acorns as large as hazle nuts (a). The *mefto*, is fo called as it partakes of the *encina* and *querigo*, and has a bitter acorn as well as the *alcornoque* or cork tree.

From Real de Monafterio it is a journey of three hours to Callero, about a mile from whence there is a round infulated hill, capped with a vein of calcareous ftone running from North to South, where there are both white and grey loadftones, their being of either of thefe colours is of no confequence, as it depends on the iron being more or lefs difperfed in fmall grains; if it is much fo, the loadftone is white, if otherwife, abundant, compact and fo that the air may have difcovered its particles, then it is red without and grey within. There is alfo an iron mine divefted of any magnetic quality. The whole country is covered with oak and cork trees, fome of which are fo bulky as to be 50 feet diameter, but moft of them as well as the oaks, are hollow within, from having been improperly lopped.

(a) Mr. Bowles fays he can give no account of the *Efculus* of Spain, nor its acorns fo celebrated by Pliny, who was intendant of Andalufia, and adds, it is a difficult matter to defcribe thofe acorns which were eaten in the golden age; nor has Don Quixotte defined them in his immortal difcourfe to the fhepherds on that remarkable period. Don Guillermo Bowles, page 136.

Leaving Cazalla and crossing several bleak mountains, it requires nine hours to reach Cantillana, on the banks of the Guadalquivir, the Sierra Morena terminating three leagues before at the narrow pass of Montegil. After crossing the river at Cantillana the face of the country is totally changed; the terebinthus, cistus and lentiscus are seen no more, nor the mountainous plants observed before between Almaden and this place, from whence one may conclude that hitherto the soil was much of the same nature, for in coming from the Pyrenees to the southward, these sierras are common, but going northward towards France, it is just the reverse, and no real mountains are to be seen in the interior parts of that kingdom, the country consisting chiefly of strata of earth one over the other.

An extensive plain reaches from Cantillana to the city of Seville, which requires five hous to pass over, consisting of poor land, without any stones, but producing a great deal of dwarf palm, or palmetto, the *chamærops humilis* of Linnæus, which covers the ground like fern: the leaves being tied together serve to make besoms sufficient to supply the whole kingdom (*a*); two sorts of wild asparagus also grow here with a

---

(*a*) A very accurate modern traveller, having given a curious account of these parts of Spain which he visited, with a very circumstantial detail of the Palmetto, I presume the following extract from his entertaining and interesting work will not be unacceptable: "The Campina of

very

very thin skin, one green and the other white, which before they bud their leaves have a multitude of flowers as white as snow. In this plain there is a great number of olive trees, whose trunks are scarcely any thing better than bark, from their bad method of planting these trees, they doing no more than taking a stake of an olive tree, of the size of one's arm, slit at the bottom six inches into four parts; they put a stone between the slits, and then set it about two feet under ground, making a trench round it to keep in the water; the top of the stake being uncovered, the rain penetrates that way, and by degrees with the warm air rots the inside.

The antient and famous city of Seville has been fully described by modern travellers; its streets are paved

Marvella, he says, produces an amazing quantity of palmettos, with little dates exceedingly good; they grow in clusters at the root of the shrubs of the size and shape of a plumb, of a reddish colour, bearing a large stone like the great palm tree date; the root of the palmetto is very curious, round it are ranged the stamina of each branch of leaves, with a double coating of dry brown fibres, netted like lace, and which are capable of being spun and used as strong thread. Nature, by such extraordinary care in preserving the root of the palmetto dry and free from humidity, shews that a hard sandy soil, little rain, and a hot sun, are necessary to the welfare of this plant; each plant shoots up to the height of ten or fifteen inches, and in a few days after it has attained its growth, divides and spreads itself like a fan into fifty long thin leaves that come erect in the stem. They are of a deep green, exceedingly rough, especially the stalk, which is armed with prickles. They use them as brooms, and eat the fruit which is very delicious, and no way inferior, except in size, to the palm tree date. The root, which is thick and eight inches long, is not only wholesome food, but very palatable, and eat with eagerness by the common people. The inside is tender and sweet, though accompanied with a bitterness, disagreeable to those who are not used to it. The young shoots, pregnant with seeds, are juicy and pleasant." One root may contain two pounds of food. See journey from Gibraltar to Malaga, by Francis Carter, Esq. London, 1777.

with

with pebbles brought from a great distance, for there are none hereabouts. The old Roman walls which are of earth are now so well cemented, that they are become as hard as stone. In the Alcazar, a palace built by king Peter in the fourteenth century, there are baths designed for his favourite Dona Maria de Padilla in a retired situation shaded with orange trees, which still continue to give fruit. The *Solano* wind or South-east, is very troublesome here and all over Andalusia, turning the head and heating the blood in such a manner as to cause various excesses, and were not precautions taken to prevent its effects, they would still be more sensible in youth of both sexes. In the winter season storks are very numerous in Seville, almost every tower in the city is peopled with them, and they return annually to the same nests. They destroy all the vermin on the tops of the houses, and pick up a great number of snakes, so that they are welcome guests to the inhabitants, and looked upon with peculiar veneration. It is said in some parts of Spain, that if they do not appear by St. Agatha's Day, (the fifth of February), the people fling stones at them when they come, and drive them away. The cathedral of Seville is a fine gothic building, with a curious steeple, or tower, having a moveable figure of a woman at top, called *La Giralda*, which turns round with the wind. This steeple is reckoned one of the greatest curiosities in Spain, and is higher than St. Paul's

in

in London (a). The first clock made in the kingdom was set up there in the year 1400 in presence of king Henry the IIId. when the oldest clock we have in England that is supposed to go tolerably well, is in the palace of Hampton Court, and of the year 1540 (b). Nothing can be more delightful than the prospect of the country round Seville, beheld from the steeple abovementioned, its beautiful and fertile plains, with its delightful gardens and orange groves, convey every idea of fertility and pleasure, with the addition of the river Guadalquivir, which brings ships up to the walls of the city. Amongst other fish which this river affords, they catch sturgeon, which is greatly esteemed, and in Lent is sent up to Madrid by the dean and chapter of the cathedral, for the king's table on Good Friday, sturgeon being still considered a royal fish as in the days of the Romans, as the Spanish poet Martial has said:

> Ad Pallatinas accipenses mittite Menfas,
> Ambrosias ornent munera rara dapes.   Lib. 13.

(a) This beautiful tower is 350 feet high. St. Paul's in London, 314. St. Mark's, at Venice, 337 feet. Salisbury steeple, 400 feet; and St. Peter's, at Rome, 432 feet. The traveller who looks on the tower of Seville, will then understand the following passage of Don Quixote, tom 3, page 162. Madrid, 1771. " Una vez me mando que suelse a defiifiar a aquella famosa giganta de Sevilla llamada la Giralda, que es tan valiente y fuerte como hecha de bronze, y sin mudarse de un lugar es la mas movible y voltaria muger del mundo."
" —She once ordered me to challenge that famous giant of Seville, called the Giralda, so vali-
" ant and strong as being of brass, and yet without moving from its place, is the most fickle
" and variable creature in the world".—

(b) See observations on clocks by the Hon. Daines Barrington, in the 5th volume of the Archaeologia.

LETTER

LETTER IX.

Extraordinary qualities of the River Tinto, with some account of the copper mine of Rio Tinto in its neighbourhood.

ABOUT fourteen leagues from Seville on the frontiers of Portugal, and on the banks of the river Tinto, stands the village of Tinto, which has also given its name to a celebrated and very ancient copper mine that is near it. It must have been greatly esteemed by the Romans as may be judged from the considerable remains of their works still to be seen, which Alonso Carranza has fully described, adding that these mines were not worked in his time, though the remains of the furnaces were found capable of containing four or five hundred quintals of ore, being much larger than any used in Spain or the West Indies; the country all round is covered with slag. In the year 1725, a grant of this mine was made by the court to Mr. Liebert Wolters a Swede, who drained the mine of the water, and after that spent large sums of money which he had raised by subscription to very little purpose, and died two years after the grant had been made to him, leaving his interest to his nephew Manuel Tiquet, who continued the works with better fuccefs, difcovered the vein of copper, and eftablifhed a manufacture of vitriol of copper of the beft fort: but Tiquet had not the good fortune to furvive thefe promifing appearances, he died in 1758, and left every thing to his mother and two fifters, the mine being at that time in a flourifhing ftate, producing enough to defray all charges, as well as the engagements entered into for the benefit of the undertaking, having furnifhed annually for the laft ten years about one hundred and forty thoufand pound weight of fine copper, which fold for 4¼ reals vellon, (about 1s. 4d. fterling) per pound, and paid one thirtieth part duty to the king. The heirs of Tiquet not having received any advantage from the mine, have complained to the court, and new orders have been given to make an inventory of the whole, and report its prefent fituation, when the actual value of this mine will be more accurately known. Don Guillermo Bowles did not go there, though invited by the adminiftrator thereof; however he afferts that the copper is difficult to fufe and has a mixture of iron ore, which the miners of Rio Tinto will not agree to; fo far from it, they boaft of its quality, and even flatter themfelves it may contain gold, according to the report of the affay mafter when the contract was made, which is ftill to be feen amongft other papers depofited in the archives of the royal mint at Segovia. Thofe concerned at prefent are all Spaniards, and no foreigner has any intereft therein,.

therein, or any emolument therefrom, except what might have arisen to some few individuals for manual labour in the mine, but now it is entirely worked by Spaniards, and produces excellent copper. A very curious plate of copper was discovered by the workmen in this mine, on the 31st of July, 1762, three feet long, and two broad, which was found buried ninety feet under ground, and has the following Roman inscription.

IMP. NERVAE. CAESARI. AVG.
PONTIFI. MAXIMO. TR...
OTEST. PP. COS. III.
·G. IIII. PUDENS AVG. LIB.
...PROCVRATOR
IO. POSVIT.

The river Tinto is equally one of the great curiosities of this place. It rises in Sierra Morena, and empties itself into the Mediterranean near Huelva, having the name of Tinto given it from the tinge of its waters, which are as yellow as a topaz, hardening the sand and petrifying it in a most surprizing manner. If a stone happens to fall in and rest upon another, they both become in a year's time perfectly united and conglutinated. This river withers all the plants on its banks, as well as the roots of trees, which it dyes of the same hue as its waters, no kind of verdure will come up where it reaches, nor any fish live in its stream, it kills worms in cattle when given them to drink, but in general no animals will drink out of of this river, except goats, whose flesh nevertheless has an excellent flavour. These singular properties continue till other rivulets run into it and alter its nature, for when it passes by Niebla, it is not different from other rivers, and falls into the Mediterranean six leagues lower down at the town of Huelva, where it is two leagues broad, and admits of large vessels which may come up the river as high as *San Juan del Puerto* three leagues above Huelva. This country is remarkable for several events which make a considerable figure in the history of Spain. In the first place, Huelva is said by some writers to have been the place of nativity of Juan Sanchez de Huelva, the person who is supposed to have sailed from the Canaries, and to have been driven by tempestuous weather on the coast of America, and after being out seventeen days, was forced back to the Canaries, where meeting with Columbus, was hospitably entertained by him, and dying soon after of fatigue, communicated his discoveries, by which means that great navigator was further confirmed in his opinions about the new world, and encouraged to pursue them (*a*). The writer who relates this event says, that while he was writing his book,

(*a*) See Antiguedades de Sevilla por Rodrigo Caro. Sevilla, 1634, who does not tell us on what authority he relates this event of Juan Sanchen de Huelva, which would have been an anecdote of some curiosity; for want of which we may join with Dr. Robertson, who says, that the name of the pilot is alike unknown as well as that of the port in which this supposed personage landed on his return. Dr. Robertson's history of America. Vol. 1. Note 17.

a whale having been cast ashore in the night near Huelva, made such lamentable groans, and frightened the people to such a degree, that they imagined these hideous yells could only proceed from the bottom of hell, on which the friars of the convents *Delabella* and *Larabida* at Palos all ran to the churches, fearing every moment to be their last, however they were soon convinced of their ignorance. A description was afterwards published of this whale, from whence it appeared, that it was ninety feet long and thirty feet high, a man could stand upright in its mouth, and there was eight feet distance between its eyes. But these are not objects to perpetuate the memory of Palos or the fryars of Larabida, more striking events have handed down their name to posterity; even the ignorant convent of Larabida was at one time governed by one of the most enlightened characters of the age, and to whom the Spanish monarchs had the greatest obligations; this person was Juan Perez, prior of Larabida, the intimate friend of Columbus, who after that great man had received his final answer from court, ventured to write again to Queen Isabella in his favour, and by his interest, and persuasion, engaged that princess once more to consider his case; the arguments of Perez were drawn up with such strength of reasoning and ingenuity, that he was ordered to attend the court to confer with the ministry on that subject, the result of which was the final settlement of his plan in behalf of his friend,

whose

whose children were at school under his tuition, and the little port of Palos, as most pleasing to them both, was fixed upon for that ever memorable expedition, from whence Columbus sailed in 1492, in quest of a new world for the crown of Castile, verifying that enthusiastic prediction of Seneca,

> Venient annis
> Sæcula feris, quibus oceanus
> Vincula rerum laxet, et ingens
> Pateat tellus, Tiphysque novos
> Detegat orbes, nec sit terris
> Ultima Thule!
>
> SENECAE MEDEA.

LETTER X.

A tour into the kingdom of Jaen, with some account of its lead mines, more particularly that of Linares.

THE little fairy kingdom of Jaen, which now makes part of Andalusia, is in a manner surrounded by a chain of mountains, formed by the Sierra Morena, Segura, Quesada, and Torres, separating it from the kingdoms of Cordova, Toledo, Murcia and Granada, while the river Guadalquivir divides it from the kingdom of Seville. The face of the country is rugged and hilly, with no other vallies but such as have been formed by torrents of water, according to the more or less resistance of the soil, or the hardness of the rocks, for the earth not being divided in strata the heights crumble away in proportion to their moisture, and the tops of the hills not being connected nor contiguous, have decomposed at a variety of periods, from whence those singular gaps and passes have resulted which now form the roads in this petty kingdom, once the domain of a Moorish chieftain, and for a long course of years the theatre of chivalry, honour, and love.

In the centre of this cragged kingdom, about three quarters of a league from the village of Linares, there is a small plain, situated in the highest part of the country, which affords an extensive prospect, closed by barren hills and steep rocks, with a view of the city of Jaen the capital, as well as those of Anduxar, Baeza and Ubeda. At the end of this plain the hills are pierced like a sieve, with numberless shafts and excavations of mines undoubtedly the work of the Moors, for surely the Romans could never have proceeded in so awkward a manner; these Mahometan princes must have struggled hard to extract from the bowels of the earth those revenues which its dreary surface refused them, and probably they supplied the neighbouring states with silver, copper and lead; some of which minerals are always found here, and occasionally all of them together. In ranging the hills it is extraordinary to observe the prodigious number of shafts made in direct lines at four paces distance from each other; there are above five thousand of them, and no doubt the violence of the water gushing through the hills first laid open the veins and led to the discovery of the mines, but when the Moors improved upon these advantages with which nature had favoured them, they did it with all the ignorance and unskilfulness to be expected from their barbarism. I shall only speak of two of those veins, one that begins in the valley on the West side of the plain, and the other

other on the Eaſt. They each have a parallel direction, at about a thouſand paces diſtance, running from North to South and incloſing the plain between them.

There are two other modern mines, but one of them does not enter into the plain, and the other is ſo low, that it will be difficult to work for any time, as there is no iſſue for the water, neverthelefs the former miners extracted from hence the lead which was ſold to the king before his majeſty took thoſe mines into his hands, and one may ſee by their labours that they were exact imitators of their predeceſſors the Moors, following their method, and making the ſame range of ſhafts in purſuit of the vein on the hill, almoſt as far as the village of Linares.

No mine of the kingdom of Jaen is found in calcareous rock, that of lead abovementioned is in common grey granite, at times ſixty feet deep, at others only one; with every gradation between theſe extremes, the ſtratum in which the ore is enveloped is generally clay, though ſometimes it runs through granite which puzzles the miners for want of a regular method to follow it; however they are right in general when they tell us that regular veins have two ſtrata, one lying above called the roof, and the other underneath termed the floor, both together forming the trunk of the vein, it being thought the roof ſerves to cheriſh it, while the floor anſwers the

purpoſe

purpose of a basis : in Jaen they sometimes find the ore in fragments or masses, for which no certain rules can be given; it is fortunate to meet with these masses, Don Guillermo Bowles says that one was found in his time, so remarkably rich that in four or five years it yielded an extraordinary quantity of lead, in a space about sixty feet broad and as many in length; adding that though he did not recollect the exact number of quintals, he could aver that more lead was obtained from that single place, than from the mines of Freyberg in Saxony, or those of Clonsthal in the mountain of Hartz, in the course of twelve years. It is a true *Galena*(a), of a large grain, yielding from 60 to 80 lb. of lead per quintal, and they fuse it in the open air for want of a laboratory at Linares.

The first use made of the lead is to run it into shot of all sizes for sportsmen, which is sold every where in Spain for the king's account. The potters are next supplied, who use it to varnish their wares, another part is pulverized for writing sand, the remainder is sent to France and sold at the fair of *Beaucaire*: though it is a *Galena*, as it only contains three quarters of an ounce of silver per quintal, it is not worth while to copel it.

(a) Galena is the name of a lead ore consisting of cubic particles, and sometimes tessellated. It is the most common ore of lead, if the cubes are large the mineral is richest, and when small and grey, contains a little silver, but in such small quantities, as not to be worthy of notice.

The country produces the same kind of plants as at Almaden, to which may be added the common or wild camomile, a plant generally scarce in the meridional provinces, yet so common here that the whole kingdom might be stocked with it: they have also great plenty of game (a). This little kingdom is famous in the annals of Spain for that memorable victory at *las Navas de Tolosa* in 1212, over the king of Morocco, obtained by Alfonso the IXth king of Castile, assisted by Peter the IId king of Aragon, and Sancho VIIth king of Navarre, in which an incredible number of Moors were destroyed. After the battle the king gave orders to his general Don Diego Lopez de Haro who commanded the van of the army, to dispose of the booty, as the kings of Aragon and Navarre had consented to abide by his decision, upon which the gallant General, knowing the magnanimous disposition of his sovereign, decreed, that the kings of Aragon and Navarre should have whatever was found within the chains and palisades of the enemy's camp, the remainder of the spoil to the soldiers in general, and for the king his master what he thought the most honourable of all, *The glory and honour of the day* (b). This

---

(a) When Mr. Bowles travelled this way, at a miserable venta they gave him an omelette for dinner made with partridge's eggs, and they shewed him five hundred of those eggs in the house for the same purpose. Every peasant is a sportsman and has the use of his gun, for game laws are unknown.

(b) The king of Navarre being the first who broke down the chains of the Moorish camp, altered his coat armour in memory of that day, to a field gules traversed with a chain of gold, commander

commander having been reflected upon for having just before lost the battle of Alarcos, out of jealousy, because the king of Castile had said the nobles of Estremadura were as good as those of Castile; his son Don Lopez Diaz de Haro, came to him the eve of the battle of Tolosa, and said, Sir, I hope you will not suffer me to-morrow to be called the son of a traitor; No, replied the general with warmth. *Llamarte an hijo de puta pero no hijo de traydor* (a), which sharp answer proceeded from the conduct of the lady Maria Manriquez his wife, who fled from her husband with a blacksmith of Burgos, but afterwards repented, and by way of atonement in her last moments ordered her corpse to be placed with her effigy in marble, without the church door of the convent of Huerta, that every one might trample on her tomb, and take warning from her weakness, which being long after observed by the Emperor Charles, he ordered her remains to be removed into the church with her ancestors, saying she had now done penance enough.

having a rich emerald in the centre, being part of the spoil, and a piece of the chain was fixed round his tomb in the church of St. Mary at Roncesvalles. Many Spanish knights did the same, or added chains to their arms from having been present on that memorable day, particularly those of the names of Romeu, Mendoza, Stuniga, Munoz, Peralta, Meneses, Maza, Abarca, Villaseca, Otazo, and Irrazaval de Vergara. The royal standard of the king of Morocco, which is azur with a crescent argent and five stars or, was suspended over the tomb of Don Diego Lopez de Haro, in the choir of the cathedral of Toledo.

(a) "They may call you son of a w—, but not son of a traitor."

S f   A more

A more fatal inflance of love is recorded in the chronicles of Jaen, which the Spanish bards have made a perpetual theme of their ditties, lamenting the fate of that unfortunate lover *Macias* the poet, one of the esquires of Don Henrique de Villena, grand master of the order of Calatrava(a). It seems Don Henrique had a beautiful handmaid who had given great encouragement to Macias, who on his side had improved every opportunity from the fair object of his love, and although the grand master had disposed of her in marriage to a principal gentleman of Porcuna in the kingdom of Jaen, it had little effect on their mutual affection, which being reported by the husband to Don Henrique de Villena, he, finding all admonition vain, cast Macias into prison at Arjonilla, a town belonging to the knights of his order, five leagues from the city of Jaen, where the distracted enamorato had no other alleviation than writing letters to his mistress, and composing love songs in her praise, replete with the most tender expressions, as well as the hardship of his fate, which reaching the jealous ears of her husband, he mounted a fleet courser, and armed with his lance, rode up to the windows of the prison, where fired with resentment on hearing the name of his wife, he darted his lance at him with fury, and pierced him through the heart, then clapping spurs to his horse,

(a) Don Henrique de Villena died in 1434.

fled

fled into Grenada. The unfortunate Macias was honourably interred in the chapel of St. Catharine belonging to the castle of Arjonilla, and the bloody lance was suspended over his tomb, with the following inscription.

  Aquesta Lanza sin falla
  Ay coytado!
  Non me la dieron
  Del muro,
  Nin la prise yo en batalla
  Mal pecado!
  Mas viniendo a ti seguro,
  Amor falso y perjuro,
  Me firio, e sin tardanza,
  E fue tal la mi andanza
  Sin venturo!

LETTER XI.

Journey from Merida to Malaga.

IT is a journey of seven hours from Merida to Talavera (*a*) through a sandy plain traversed by the Guadiana, which has a great many islands covered with flocks of

(*a*) Different from *Talavera de la Reyna* on the Tagus in New Castile, famous for its fine earthenware and silk manufacture: these belonged to the crown till sold in 1762, to a merchant of the name of Ustariz, for 7,410,000 reals vellon, £83361 10*s*. sterling. Their annual consumption is 11000 lb. of silk, 4000 marcs of silver and 60 of gold, having 336 looms and about 1438 workmen, chiefly Spaniards. They make annually 35000 varas of gold and silver lace, 560000 varas of ribbands, 5000 pair of silk stockings, 31000 varas of taffety, 8200 varas of velvet and velvereta, 2300 varas of gold and silver stuffs, 2000 varas of velveretta mixed with silk, 10500 varas of damasks, tabbies, &c. exclusive of gold and silver twist buttons, handkerchiefs and other less articles. The greatest encouragement is given to the raising of mulberry trees for the silk worms; many plants of which have been distributed by the proprietor, at his own expence, to all the villages round him.

They have remarkable processions here at Easter, which go by the name of *mondas de Talavera*, when all the country people assemble and form a procession with garlands of flowers, each division guided by a person carrying a staff covered with flowers at top, and making an offering of them to the Blessed Virgin, according to the custom of the Pagans, who used to do the same to their gods; perhaps the difficulty of abolishing these ceremonies, says Don Antonio Ponz, has engaged the clergy to convert them into obsequious rites to the Blessed Virgin, as the church has wisely done with other heathenish customs equally difficult to eradicate. Viage de Espana tom. 7. Madrid 1779.

Two leagues from *Talavera de la Reyna* you find *Talavera la Vieja*, famous for the remains of a temple as well as several Roman inscriptions and other antiquities, which have been described and published with copper plates, at Madrid, in 1762, by Don Ignacio de Herrozilla of the secretary of state's office for the West India department.

sheep

sheep and numerous herds of cattle, that are often carried away as well as the shepherds by the sudden increase of the river: the plain from Talavera to Badajoz produces nothing but broom. At this last city the soil changes again, and the calcareous earth, stone, and rocks make their appearance once more. Estremadura is the only part of Spain where they have neither salt springs nor rock salt, which obliges the inhabitants to procure those articles from their neighbours. This large and fertile province, reputed about fifty leagues in length and forty in breadth, so happily situated for every branch of culture, and where the Romans seem to have taken such delight, is now thought not to contain above a hundred thousand inhabitants, a number comprised in many capital cities; but if their numbers are small, they value themselves on the quality of their heroes, having furnished a Cortez, a Pizarro, and the unfortunate though great Velasco Nunez de Balboa (a).

The antient city of Badajoz the *Pax Augusta* of the Romans, called *Badaugos* by the Moors, and now Badajoz is the frontier town next to Portugal. The bridge over the Guadiana has twenty-six arches, and was built by Philip the IId. Numerous families of Negroes and Mulatoes are settled in this country between Badajoz and Zafra: this last town with the dutchy of Feria is

(a) See the character of Nunez de Balboa in Dr. Robertson's history of America.

now

now fallen into the ducal houfe of Medinaceli. Joining to the duke's palace, in a church belonging to a convent of nuns, there is an elegant marble monument to the memory of an Englifh lady of the noble family of Harrington, with the following infcription:

AQUI YACE DONA MARGARITA HARRINTON HIJA DE JACOBO HARRINTON BARON DE EXTON, Y DE DONA LUCIA HIJA DE GUILLERMO SIDNEI VISCONDE DE LISLE, BARON DE RENHURST, NACIDA EN INGLATERRA, MUGER DE DON BENITO DE CISNEROS, CUYAS SINGULARES VIRTUDES PUDIERAN HAZERLA INSIGNE QUANDO LE FALTARAN TANTOS TITULOS DE NOBLEZA PARA SERLO. ROGAD POR ELLO A DIOS. MURIO EN MADRID ANNO DE 1601.

DONA JUANA DE FERIA, PRIMA, ALBACEA Y PATRONA, EN CUMPLIMIENTO DE SU AMOR Y DEL TESTAMENTO MANDO HAZER ESTA CAPILLA Y SEPULTURA.

In ENGLISH.

Here lies Margaret Harrinton, daughter of James Harrinton, Baron of Exton, and of Lucy, daughter of William Sidney Vifcount Lifle, Baron of Renhurft, born in England, Wife of Don Benito de Cifneros, whofe fingular virtues would have rendered her illuftrious, even if her many other titles had been wanting. Pray to God for her. She died in Madrid in the year 1601.

The lady Jane de Feria, confin, executrix, and patronefs, as a proof of of her love, and in compliance with the will, ordered this chapel and monument to be erected (a).

Proceeding from Zafra to Sta. Marta the country improves for about five leagues to Zarza del Angel, then you pass by Monasterio to Fuente de Cantos where the Sierra Morena begins: Sta. Olalla is the first village in the kingdom of Seville, it being a dismal and melancholy journey of ten hours over these dreary hills to Castel Blanco, with the same plants as at Almaden, to which may be added the wild germander. Great efforts have

(a) There seems to be some error in this inscription, it was John Harrington, who the first of James I. was created baron Harrington of Exton, in 1613. He died at Wormes in Germany, his issue John survived him but a few months; nor does it appear that Sir William Sydney, of Penshurst in Kent, was ever raised to the peerage, though his descendants might have had the title of Viscount Lisle and Baron of Penshurst.

Dona Juana de Feria was the only daughter of Sir William Dormer by his first wife Mary Sydney, whose youngest sister was mother of Margaret Harrington. She was maid of honour to queen Mary, and when the Conde to Feria came into England as ambassador to the queen in her last illness from Philip the IId, he fell in love with this lady, and married her, and they had a son born at Mechlin, September 18th, 1559. The Conde was made a Duke eight years after, and died in 1571: and the family is now extinct. A picture of the Dutchess of Feria, supposed to be of the hand of Sir Antonio More, is in the possession of the Rev. Mr. de Salis. She is in the dress of a nun, with this inscription on it, D. Jana Dormer Feriæ Ducissa Vidua D. Gomesii Suarez de Figueroa y Cordova Feriæ Ducis æt. 35. A. D. 1578. As she retired into a convent the year after her husband died, perhaps this might be the reason that she did not assume the title of Dutchess on the monumental inscription to the memory of her cousin Margaret Harrington, who probably went to Spain with her. The Jesuit Ribadeneira, who came into England with the Conde de Feria, as his chaplain, but principally with a design to procure a settlement here for his order, continued his attachment to the Dutchess of Feria, and dedicated to her his second volume of lives of saints, which is dated at Madrid June 15, 1608. I am indebted for this communication to my worthy friend the Rev. Mr. John Bowle, of Idmiston.

been

been made to improve the waste lands of this horrid Sierra, and give a new face to the country, for which purpose foreigners have been invited to settle there, and great exertions have taken place for some years past. In the year 1767, eleven towns and five villages were already formed in the Sierra Morena, as well as four towns and fifteen villages in that part which divides the kingdom of Cordova and Seville (*a*), making all together 2446 families, consisting of 10490 persons, of which 8175 were labourers, and 2217 mechanics, exclusive of journeymen and servants. They have built twenty-four parish churches and chapels, 2200 houses and fifteen inns, planted 200,000 olive trees, above half a million of mulberry trees, and as much more of various kinds of fruit-trees, elm, vine, &c. their harvest consists at present chiefly of wheat, barley, peas and beans, producing one year with another five hundred thousand *fanegas*; the vines begin to prosper, and are expected to become a considerable object, and they have moreover established many branches of silk and woollen manufacture.

After traversing the Sierra Morena it is no small relief to enter the extensive and fertile plain of Seville, which leads to that capital city, and makes some amends to the traveller for the scene of desolation he has passed. You

(*a*) See in Mr. Swinburne's travels, a description of the new settlement of La Carolina, one of the principal places of this establishment, which he passed through going from Cordova to Madrid. Many of these people are since dead through intemperance and change of climate.

pass through a beautiful country for three days, till you come to Antequera, situated on a hill at a league distance from a high mountain consisting of an entire block of flesh-coloured marble, which must be crossed on horseback, to go to Malaga; several springs which issue from it form themselves into a rivulet, whose banks are lined with perriwinkle, bulbous iris and the fallow leaved hare's ear: the rocks are mostly covered with the *lichen* called *orchilla* by the Spaniards, but as the sort from the Canaries is preferred both in England and France, the gathering of it is totally neglected in Spain. That sort which has little white specks upon it like warts is thought to be the best; it grows on the highest rocks on the sea coast, and fixes its roots in the cavities of the rock. Its common length is from one to three inches, and makes a considerable part of the commerce of the Canaries, where it is gathered at all times of the year; some goes to the Mediterranean markets, but the largest quantity for England, where they have a particular method of preparing it with human urine and other ingredients, so as to make it of great use in dying fine purples and blossom colours (*a*).

(*a*) The name of *orchilla* was perhaps given it from the island of Orchilla, one of the Leeward islands, near the coast of Terra Firma, in America, where probably it was first discovered. The sort used by the dyers is the *Lichen Calcarius* of Linnæus, being so peculiar to limestone rocks that wherever that stone occurs among others, it may be distinguished at the first view by this plant growing upon it. When dried, powdered and steeped in urine, it is used to dye scarlet by the Welch and the inhabitants of the Orkneys. The warty kind is the

The hills are covered with vineyards, and as you descend into the low lands, the eye is enraptured with the most beautiful objects; the dreary month of January in a northern climate is here a scene of delight, the fields are full of perriwinkle, myrtle, oleander, and lavender, with many other flowers in full blow, at that early season, and this enchanting prospect continues to Malaga, an antient and celebrated city, taken from the Moors, in 1487, by Ferdinand and Isabel, after a most vigorous defence, and having been 772 years in their possession. A city not less remarkable for its opulence and extensive commerce, than for the luxuriance of its soil, yielding in great abundance the most delicious fruits; whilst its rugged mountains afford those luscious grapes which give such reputation to the Malaga wine, known in England by the emphatical name of *Mountain*. These valuable mountains have moreover a peculiar advantage, that the drought which is so prejudicial to corn, contributes principally to the goodness and flavour of the grape, as the surrounding mists afford every necessary refreshment, and are more serviceable than rain, which would rather injure the roots, by washing away that light coat of soil with which they are so sparingly provided.

lichen pertusus of Linnæus. Another sort called *tartareus* by that great writer, is common in Derbyshire, and gathered by peasants who sell it for a penny a pound to the dyers, who use it for purples. It is so plentiful that they can collect twenty or thirty pound a day. See Dr. Withering's botanical arrangement, &c.

But

But before I leave Malaga I cannot omit speaking of those excellent and remarkable potatoes peculiar to that district, and in so great esteem in other parts of Spain; they are sweet and luscious, of an oblong form and of a bright yellow colour like gold, and when roasted eat extremely well with wine and sugar; they are equally an American production though different from the common potatoe which is only known of late years at Madrid, and not in any other part of the kingdom, except Galicia where they are common as having been first brought there by the Spaniards, and from thence conveyed originally to Ireland.

About three miles to the westward of Malaga, there are gardens about a hundred paces from the sea, and on a level with it, inclosed with the Indian fig or prickly pear, and with the aloe, whose sharp pointed leaves serve as an excellent fence against cattle; several plants grow under their shade, particularly two sorts of mallows, spurge, geranium, marsh marigold, borrage, asphodel with onion leaves, bastard dittany, sorrel, clary, goldylocks, goosegrass, avens, nightshade, shepherds purse, fumitory, and white asparagus; many of these even grow in the burning sands on the sea shore, and are in flower in January, also a great deal of celandine the same as in the interior parts of Spain.

Further on to the westward about two leagues from Malaga, there is a cavern where the water forms enormous pieces of calcareous spar (*a*), which takes a beautiful polish, and much of it has been used in the royal palace of Madrid; some pieces are of a white ground, with veins of different colours, but in general the ground is grey, with a pleasing clare obscur happily ramified with white, at other times a dark grey interspersed with veins of a brilliant white. This cave lies immediately under a considerable bed of lime rock, in a plain about a hundred paces from the sea, and half that distance from a chain of limy hills, the decomposition of which produces the spar above mentioned.

(*a*) Mr. Bowles's editor, page 111, very improperly calls this spar by the name of *Alabastro calizo*, " limy alabaster;" as there is no such thing in nature; it must either be a marble, or an alabaster, and cannot partake of the properties of both, but from the mode of its formation it appears to be a spar.

LETTER XII.

Describing the country between Malaga and Cape de Gat.

THE first remarkable place to the eastward of Malaga is the town of Velez Malaga, near which the captive in Don Quixote is supposed to have landed from Barbary, with the beautiful Zorayda. A few leagues further is the little port of Herradura, where a fleet of gallies was lost in 1562 under the command of general Don John de Mendoza who had sailed from Malaga with twenty-four gallies, having 3500 soldiers on board, and finding the wind contrary, put into the Herradura, where he came to an anchor, but it blew so hard that twenty-three of the gallies were driven ashore and lost, and all the crews drowned (a). This port is not laid down on Lopez's map of Spain, but may be seen on the French chart of the Mediterranean, dedicated to the duke of Choiseul in 1764, by Joseph Roux at Marseilles, hydrographer to the king, and is an exact copy from

(a) Vida de Felipe IId. por Luis de Cabrera. Madrid, 1619. Also Guerra de Granada por Hurtado de Mendoza. Valencia, 1776. This event is hinted at in Don Quixote, where Sancho speaks of Don Alonso Maranon, Knt. of St. Jago, who lost his life there. Vol. 3, page 418. Madrid, 1771.

Michelot,

Michelot, who was pilot of the gallies to Lewis the XIVth.

Further on, Motril is another little sea port, and on the road to it, one may see samphire, orache, dock, thorn-apple, and cardomindum growing in the sands on the sea shore, with the Indian fig shooting out amidst the rocks dashed by the waves of the sea. In different parts of this coast almost as far westwardly as Gibraltar there are above twelve sugar mills called *Ingenios*. In Motril only there are four of them, which cost at least eight thousand pistoles each, sugar having been made there time immemorial as perfect according to the opinion of good judges as any imported from the West Indies, which is not so extraordinary when we consider that the first slips of the cane were sent from hence to the Canary islands, from whence Nicholas de Ovando, governor of Hispaniola, introduced them in 1506 into his government, where they thrived surprisingly: but in Spain their cultivation is disregarded, though the soil of the meridional provinces, the temperature of the air, and the glowing heat of the sun are well adapted for the cane and many other productions of South America, which might be brought to perfection, were industry and encouragement in any proportion to the advantages of nature. With respect to sugar it has been neglected through political motives, and the canes have been rooted up to make way for

for the vine: even the pine apple, which was firſt introduced from the Spaniſh ſettlements, was unknown in the royal gardens of their monarchs, till within theſe few years, that Boutelou, the king's under gardener, raiſed them at Aranjuez.

From Motril to Almeria you range along the mountains, many of which are of marble to the very ſummit, the ſtrand is level and ſandy, with very little earth, except near Almeria, which antient city was conquered from the Moors in 1147 by Alfonſo, ſtiled the emperor, aſſiſted by Garcias king of Navarre, Raymond count of Barcelona, and a fleet of Genoeſe; theſe laſt taking for their ſhare of plunder that beautiful veſſel, ſuppoſed to be an emerald, which they ſtill ſo carefully preſerve in their treaſury. They make ſalt-petre of the firſt boiling at Almeria, which is ſent to Granada to undergo a ſecond proceſs, without the aſſiſtance of fixed alkali, nor does the earth from whence it is collected contain any gypſum.

About half way towards Cape de Gat there is a large plain ſo full of garnets that a ſhip might be loaded with them; they are likewiſe to be found in a gully formed by the waves at the foot of a hill in that neighbourhood. The ſea ſometimes throws up worms hereabouts four or five inches long, and one broad near the belly, with circular

cular loins and the body divided into ringlets, which emit a purple liquor flowing from every part when cut into pieces; of this species there are three sorts, viz. the common *murex* which generally remains at the bottom of the sea, the *nautilus* which by help of a fin sails like a ship, and the worm without any shell thrown up by the sea on this coast (*a*).

The famous mountain of Filabres is about three leagues from Almeria, but it takes ten hours in going to it, the road is so turned by the many hills to be passed before one reaches it. This amazing and stupendous mountain is a solid block of white marble about a league in circuit, and two thousand feet high, without the least mixture of any other stone or earth, the marble appearing in many places where neither the wind, rain, or any of those causes which destroy the hardest rocks, have yet made the least impression. On the side towards the village of Machael, lying at the foot of this mountain, a great part of the kingdom of Granada is discovered, which is mountainous, and resembles the waves of the sea in a storm. On the other side the mountain is cut almost perpendicularly, and from its prodigious elevation affords a most awful prospect, with the city of Gandia, which though at a distance, if considered with a bird's eye view, seems only half a league off. The Sierra de Gador

(*a*) Don Guillermo Bowles. P. 316.

Gador is another immense mass of marble, of which they make excellent lime. It dissolves intirely with acids, without leaving the least residue of clay or other matter, whereas the stone in other parts of Spain, particularly in Valencia, has a mixture of clay or sand, of these we are to understand the Spanish proverb, with respect to ore, which is literally true in that kingdom, *Donde hai yeso y cal, no hai mineral*; viz.

"Where of gypse and lime there's store,
"Don't expect to meet with ore."

Notwithstanding the goodness of the marble of Gador, there is a great difference between the solidity of the old houses in the village, and the modern ones, the former being much more durable, owing to the builders having used the sand of the river Rambla, while the present generation, either from supineness, or ignorance, make use of sea sand, which from its saline nature attracts moisture, and dissolves, defeating the union necessary to be supported with the lime, which is not the case with fresh water sand.

Amongst other natural products of this country, the *Esparto*, or matweed (a), grows in great plenty, and deserves particular attention; they not only make cordage with it for boats, but also mats for floors, sackcloth,

(a) Stipa tenacissima. Linn.

baskets for raisins, and above forty other articles in domestic œconomy. They even spin it like flax, which is made into linen, for which secret the inventor has been amply rewarded by his present majesty, and a large sum advanced him to set up his manufactory.

Cape de Gat is a huge promontory, consisting of an enormous rock, of a singular nature, different from any other appearance in Spain, eight leagues in circuit and five broad; the first object that strikes the eye is a rock two hundred feet high, about fifty paces from the sea, all crystalized in large stones of the size of a man's leg, with four or five plates chased one within another, of a cinereous colour, from eight to fourteen inches long, with a large grain that will take a good polish. Precious stones are said to be found in the mountain of Bujo, in a cavern with an entrance about fifteen paces wide and twenty feet high, where the agitation of the waves is very great in bad weather; Mr. Bowles went in there but could discover nothing of consequence. On the outside a large white patch serves as a land mark to mariners, and from thence called *Vela Blanca*. This is what is properly called Cape de Gat. Near the *Torre de las Guardas* there is a bed of jasper of a white ground veined with red, and further on near the *Torre de Neste*, a low rock is seen almost covered with a stratum of white cornelian. They gather a black sand not far from the *Torre de de San Joseph*, which proceeds from the demolition of the rock, added to the constant percussion of the waves, and is sold to throw over writing. They might find another sort of sand very near this place, less angular, which would answer for hour glasses, but they still import it from Germany for this purpose.

In the centre of this promontory there are four hills near to each other, called the Sacristan, the Two Fryars, the Captain, and the White Mountain, but nothing remarkable is to be observed from their outward appearance (*a*). The other side of the promontory, after passing these four hills, is called *El Puerto de la plata*, where the Moorish Corsairs lie lurking for Spanish vessels to intercept them, and carry their crews into dire captivity. There is a rock near this *Puerto*, which extends towards the sea, and called *El monte de las guardas*, where they find amethysts, but still more abundantly in a stratum of quartz of very difficult access, being in a precipice twenty feet high. The true amethyst resembles a pyramid reversed, while the rock crystal has six faces, and is larger at bottom than at top. But there is no probability of further researches for precious stones, or even for marble, as the exportation of this latter has

---

(*a*) Mr. Bowles says that Cape de Gat is the most meridional point of Spain, as may be observed by looking on the map, but such an inspection will convince us of the contrary. Europa Point at Gibraltar is more so, and often said to be the most southern point; but perhaps the *Punta de Carnero*, on the Algeziras side of the Bay is yet further to the southward.

been lately prohibited, by which a total stop has been put to the labour and industry of the inhabitants in that valuable branch. Were we to believe the boasted accounts of the green jasper found in a gully called *El barranco de San Juan*, in that part of the *Sierra Nevada* through which the river Genil passes to Granada, it is an universal remedy for all manner of complaints, and has singular effects if wore over the stomach, or applied to any part of the body where its efficacy is required. There are two sorts of it, some having black veins and very hard, others with white veins, less so, but reputed equally efficacious (*a*).

(*a*) All its supposed virtues are set forth in a paper printed at Granada, without any date, entitled, " Maravillosas virtudes de la Piedra Jaspe verde sacadas de muchos autores y confirmadas con muchas experiencias." It is not only used in the applications abovementioned, but pulverized, and when mixed with milk cures old wounds, the bites of serpents, the piles, and is good for the sight; but what is best of all, an excellent remedy against enchantments and witchcraft! John Fragoso, in his *Cirugia universal*, speaks of it in his index of simple remedies under the word *jaspe* on the authority of St. Epiphanius. Morales also in his " historia medecinal de lo que se trahe de Indias," fol. 181 as alfo Galen, lib. 9, de facultatibus simplicium. Pliny, lib. 36, cap. 7, and lib. 37, cap. 9. Dioscorides, lib. 5, c. 117, and his commentator *Laguna*. According to the paper abovementioned, it has been in great demand since the year 1770.

LETTER

LETTER XIII.

Excurſion from the city of Granada to Cordova and Anduxar, in Andaluſia.

IN going from Granada to Andaluſia, the firſt ſtage is at Loxa, a journey of ten hours, through that beautiful plain called *La Vega de Granada*, and then aſcending a mountain, through another cultivated vale, with wheat, flax, hemp, and pulſe. Loxa is a middling town, pleaſantly ſituated on a high hill of conglutinated ſtone, which forms a kind of *brechia* or pudding-ſtone, in the centre of olive grounds having plenty of fruit, notwithſtanding its elevated, cold and dry ſituation.

From Loxa to the weſtward, the country is fertile, producing wheat and barley, in a limy ſoil well furniſhed with oak. The ſoil of theſe hills ſeems to proceed from the decompoſition of former rocks, many of which appear in broken lumps, intermixed with the arable land. Alameda is the firſt town in the kingdom of Şeville: ſwallows make their appearance there in February, a few corn fields are ſeen in the low lands, but in general the weſtern

western boundaries of Granada are made up of steep rocks and craggy mountains. The *Solano* winds prevail much here, and do a great deal of mischief, destroying the harvest if they blow early in the season. The country people are fond of tobacco, and though they have near them those excellent wines of Malaga and Xerez, they seldom or ever drink them, preferring distilled liquors (a), without any visible prejudice, for the men are robust, and the women have good features, with lively sparkling eyes full of expression and fire. The country is extremely pleasant to Herrera, with a white and red earth which is remarkably fertile, divested of any loose stone, pebble, or flint, so common in other parts of the kingdom. This rich soil is a perfect marl, and under the olive tree yields plentiful crops of wheat and barley. Estepa, about a league from Herrera, stands in a picturesque manner, on the top of a hill surrounded with olive trees. The olive of Estepa is small, but delicious, and gives an oil as clear and delicate as that of Valencia. The Seville olive, though often as large as a dove's egg, does not yield near so good oil, for which reason they are more frequently pickled. Even so far back as the days of Cicero they were in high estimation, for in writing to his friend in Andalusia he compliments him on being intendant of so fertile a province, and re-

---

(a) Called in Spain *rosoli* and *mistela*.

minds

minds him to send him some Seville olives to Rome. They are very careless notwithstanding in making their oil, leaving the fruit a long time collected in heaps, so that it rots before it is ground, part of the oil turns into mucilage, and acquires a rank and disagreeable flavour, and as there are few mills in proportion to the quantity of fruit, each person is obliged to wait for his turn sometimes for months, from whence in this warm climate a fermentation ensues, which of course occasions bad oil. Others deceive themselves through a principle of avarice, for though the olive yields more juice from having lain by for some time, it is at the expence of its quality, such thin fermented matter hardly deserving the name of oil, for which reason, and from their little care in putting it into proper vessels, and carrying it about the country in skins, the oil in general is wretchedly bad at Madrid.

The olives are gathered from the middle of October to the middle of November. If a good year they sell from 20 to 24 reals the arroba (about 5 *s.* 4 *d.* sterling) but in years of scarcity will rise to 36 or 40 reals. A *fanega* of olives will yield an arroba of oil. In the south of France they are not gathered till they are perfectly ripe, and have acquired a reddish hue inclining to black; if this period passes, they wrinkle, moulder, and rot. Those that are green give a bitter taste to the oil, and they carefully separate such as are worm-eaten, which would
vitiate

vitiate the flavour of the found ones, they grind them as in Spain, then the fubftance is laid under the prefs; the firft juice that runs out is called virgin oil, and is the moft delicate for the table, its goodnefs arifing from the frefhnefs of the fruit. The fecond fort is obtained by pouring boiling water on the fubftance remaining in the prefs; but this oil is like that of Spain, acrimonious, and fubject to corruption. In general all oil obtained by fire or hot water, is of a bad quality; much will alfo depend upon its being put into proper veffels, clarifying it with judgment, and placing it in commodious cellars with a proper medium of heat and cold, both extremes being equally prejudicial. In the year 1769, Mr. Sieuve of Marfeilles, prefented a memorial to the academy of fciences, defcribing the beft method to make oil, having invented amongft other improvements, an inftrument to feparate the fruit from the ftone, by which the olive is freed from thofe vifcous, fetid, and fulphureous particles which are found in the ftone, and alterate the juice of the fruit; but thefe hints feem to have little weight with the Spaniards, who continue the old method, implicitly following the cuftoms of their forefathers.

It is five hours journey from Herrera to Ecija, agreeably fituated, but one of the hotteft towns in Spain. The horfes of Ecija are reckoned the beft in Andalufia, and remarkable for the goodnefs of their hoofs, owing to the

dryneſs

dryness of the ground, while at Seville, and in the flat country on the banks of the Guadalquivir, they are spungy, and liable to crack in hot weather; but in point of shape, the beautiful horse of Cordova is the most perfect, though of late their studs are greatly neglected (*a*).

Nothing can be more delightful than the face of the country from Ecija to Cordova, a space of nine leagues, yet without a single village, or even a spring; for which reason they must have a great deal of rain to have any crop, but when they are blessed with plentiful showers their harvest is very great. The city of Cordova is seated on the banks of the Guadalquivir, about a league from the Sierra Morena, and has ever been famous for the magnificence and splendour of its nobles. Even the Jews in former times are said to have vied with the others in pomp and parade (*b*). Its cathedral is famous for its

(*a*) There is a curious Arabic manuscript in the Escurial, marked DCCCXCVII. on horses and horsemanship, written by a Moorish general, and dedicated to Abdalla king of Cordova IIId. of the race of Bennasseret, who reigned A. D. 1301, which if ever made public, might perhaps illustrate what we have already received from the illustrious names of Newcastle and Pembroke. The title as given by Casiri in his catalogue of Arabic manuscripts in the escurial is as follows. "Theatrum equestri Abu Mahommed Abdala Laikamita Cordubensi, viro genere dignitate ac laude bellica præclaro. Is naturas equorum, proprietates, colores, formas, adnotatas etiam multis eorum nominibus credile atque eleganter hoc opere perfectum librum suum Regi Abdalla Mahommed Ben Naffor Almansor dedicavit. Accedit in extremo codice equitandi disciplinæ synopsis."

(*b*) If any credit is to be given to David Ganz in his edition of Verstius, quoted by Sarmiento. Quotidie tunc exibant Kordoba in Hispania Septingenti viri Israelitici qui vehaban-

X x antiquity

antiquity and structure, with numerous pillars of different marble, which seem to have been taken from old Roman structures. The country from Cordova to Anduxar is extremely well cultivated, and beautifully varied with corn, olive and vines; as the ground is in general of a hard nature, and does not give way, the rains have no other effect than gently washing away a small part of its surface, for which reason those deep gullies, so common in Murica and Valencia, are not seen here, where the soil is composed of different kinds of earth, alternately with rock, and easily carried off by the waters. This accounts for their having such plentiful crops in Andalusia after heavy rains, with such deep sloughs; but after a drought they have scarce any harvest, and travellers are smothered with dust. They are famous about Anduxar for making those little pitchers of a white argillaceous earth that preserve water so cool in summer. In other parts of Andalusia they have earth of the same quality of a red colour, with which they make elegant drinking bowls that keep the water equally cool as the others, being light, thin, porous, and having the surface always damp: but they are not so fine and delicate as those earthen vessels from the West-Indies called *bucaros*, nor made with such neatness and art. The Spanish la-

tus septingentis curribus, omnes vestiti indumento regio et redimiti tiaris juxta legem magnarum Homelitarum."—Memorias para la historia de la poesía y poetas Españoles. Madrid, 1775.

dies are so fond of them, that not content with putting broken pieces thereof into their boxes to give a flavour to their snuff, they will frequently eat them with singular pleasure. Besides what is used in this manner, they have boxes reserved for it solely, and their attachment to *bucaro* is so great, that the old ladies pile it up in cabinets like valuable china; in these jarrs and basons they occasionally put water, which diffuses a fresh earthy smell, which they are very fond of in their apartments.

LETTER XIV.

Observations made in a progress from Cadiz to Carthagena.

THE city of Cadiz is built on a peninsula upon rocks stretching out into the sea, composed of a great variety of matter, such as marble, spar, pebble and shells incorporated in the sand, and combined together by a glutinous substance in the sea, which seems powerful in this place, as may be observed by the rubbish thrown into it, insomuch that bricks, stone, sand, shells, &c. after a certain time become consolidated, and form one single mass.

In 1440, John king of Castile gave this city to Don Pedro Ponze de Leon, with the title of Count thereof; his grandson Don Rodrigo was afterwards made Duke of Cadiz in 1484, by Ferdinand and Isabel, but thinking it a place of too much consequence after the discovery of America, they took it from him again, and made him Duke of Arcos. In queen Elizabeth's reign, it was taken by storm by the English forces under the Earl of Essex with a trifling loss, Sir John Wingfield, quarter-master general

general of the army, being the only Englishman of note killed in the expedition (*a*). In old Spanish chronicles it is called *Calis*, from whence our English mariners generally call it Cales.

The *Solano* wind is still more prejudicial here than in Seville, and when it has blown for eight or ten days, in-

(*a*) Sir John Wingfield was grandson of Sir Anthony Wingfield, knight of the garter, vice-chamberlain of the houshold, and captain of the guard to king Henry VIII. immediate ancestor to Sir Mervin Wingfield, Bart. who dying without issue male, the title became extinct, and his only daughter, Mary, married Francis Dillon Esq; late of Proudston in the kingdom of Ireland, and was mother to John Talbot Dillon, who dedicates this note to her memory.

Sir Richard Wingfield of Kimbolton brother to Sir Anthony Wingfield above-mentioned, was appointed marshal of the town and marshes of Calais, by Henry VIII. 14th November 1511. The next year he was one of the embassadors to treat with the pope and emperor. In 1514 he was made a banneret at the siege of Tournay, and joined with Sir Gilbert Talbot in the deputyship of Calais, was sent into Flanders embassador to Charles prince of Spain, and appointed with the duke of Suffolk, to receive the queen dowager of France, and conduct her into England in 1521; he was one of cardinal Wolsey's retinue to meet the emperor in Flanders, was chancellor of the dutchy of Lancaster, and on the 23d of April 1522, having had the honour to be elected knight of the garter in the same scrutiny with Ferdinand afterwards emperor, he was installed the 11th of May at Windsor. That year, with Sir William Sanders, knight of the garter; he led the rear of the English army sent into France; attended on the emperor into Spain, at his return from whence he was present at the burning of Morlaix. In 1525 he was sent embassador into Spain, with Cuthbert bishop of London, and died at Toledo 22d July, where he was buried with great solemnity in the church of the friars observants of St. John, by the directions of Navera king of arms of Spain, assisted by Christopher Barker Richmond herald. He married to his first wife Catherine daughter of Richard Widville Earl Rivers, widow first of Henry Stafford Duke of Bukingham, and after of Jasper de Hatfield Duke of Bedford, by which marriage Sir Richard became great uncle to king Henry VIIIth.

Sir Richard Wingfield, another descendant of this family, was constituted mareschal of Ireland, by queen Elizabeth, and one of the lords justices by king James the Ist, who also on the 1st of Feb. 1618, created him viscount Powerscourt of that kingdom.

troduces

troduces such an acrimony in the blood, and causes such a tension of the fibres, as to have the most alarming effects on the fair sex, with every unpleasing symptom, like the *Scirocco* in Italy.

In the capucin's garden there is a dragon tree, supposed to be the only one in the kingdom, though it grows naturally in the Cape de Verd islands, as well as at the island of Madeira (*a*). Modern writers have fully described the extensive commerce, affluence, and hospitality of the citizens of Cadiz: they are badly supplied with water, and their flesh market is indifferent, but the bay affords them a variety of excellent fish, particularly dories, called here St. Peter's fish (*b*), soals, and red mullets, with many other sorts, of an excellent flavour (*c*).

(*a*) Professor Vandelli, of Lisbon, principal botanist to the king of Portugal has published a treatise on the dragon tree. See " Vandelli dissert. de arbore Draconis Olissp. 1768."

(*b*) So called from a legendary tale of St. Peter, who when he found money in the fish's mouth to pay tribute, left the marks of his fingers upon the fish.

(*c*) Suarez Salazar, a prebendary of Cadiz, has published the antiquities of this city, and has given a design of the famous statue of Alexander the Great, which he saw in his time, and supposes may be the same that stood in the temple of Hercules, visited by Cæsar, which drew tears from that illustrious warrior; but if, says our author, Cæsar was to behold it again, he would weep once more to see it in so bad a condition. This reverend prelate the more clearly to evince the spirit and vivacity of the women of Cadiz, has collected, with the gravity of a schoolman, the most obscene lines of Martial, Juvenal and Catullus, to illustrate their libidinous conduct, and this he dedicates to cardinal Don Antonio Zapata. " Grandezas y antiguedades de la Isla y Ciudad de Cadiz por Juan Bautista Salazar Racionero en la Santa Iglesia de Cadiz." En Cadiz, 1610.

Port St. Mary is a large and handsome city; on the north side of the bay, from whence it is a journey of three leagues to the city of Xerez, remarkable for its excellent wine so well known by the name of *Sherry*. The best and richest sort is called *Pagarette*, from the Spanish word *Pago*, a district, and particularly applied to this vintage. In one *aranzado* (an acre of vineyard) they plant 1800 vines at regular distances. It is reckoned a good year if it gives three butts per acre, middling if it gives two, bad if it gives but one, but some years it yields four or five (*a*).

Medina Sidonia is six leagues from Xerez, then the city of Arcos, seated on a cragged rock, at the foot of which runs the river Guadalete, on whose banks the unfortunate Roderic the last Gothic king of Spain lost his life and dominions; a route of ten hours through a stony country leads to the village of Algodonales lying under a high mountain, pierced through from East to West. The people here have a tradition that this place was built by the Romans who had made this perforation in search of a mine.

(*a*) Names of grapes: - - *Pedro ximenes, palomina, canocoso, alvillo, bejarego, mantudo, perruno, muscadel* large and small, *calona* for eating, *feral* and *molinar* both for eating and wine, *brba*, to eat, *almunnecar* for wine.

The first year the vine is called *sarmiento*, a shoot; second, *grenudo*, little fruit and not good; third, *descoronados*, pruned; fourth, *virote*, much fruit and not good wine; fifth, *majuela*, compleat vine makes good wine. The vines continue ten years in full force, and last a hundred years with proper care.

The

The city of Ronda is six leagues from Algodonales, on a very high situation, it being a continual ascent from Xerez, which continues as far as Gibraltar: the country about Ronda is remarkably fertile and supplies Cadiz with all kinds of fruit and vegetables, the soil is of a reddish colour with pebble and resists the heat of the fire, for which reason it is much used in furnaces for fusing iron. Amongst other curiosities with which the country of Ronda abounds, that little animal called the gennet is one of the most extraordinary, and not to be found in any other part of Europe except Turkey. It is smaller than the civet, has a long body, short legs, a sharp snout, and a slender head: under its tail there is a long bag which emits a perfume. Its fur is soft and glossy, of an ash colour marked with black spots, which unite upon the back and form stripes which run longitudinally from the neck backward, with a long tail diversified with ringlets of black and white: the fur was formerly in esteem, but of late has been counterfeited by tinging grey rabbet skins with black spots, and is now out of fashion (a). The district of Ronda also furnishes

(a) We read in the history of France, that Charles Martel having obtained a compleat victory over the Saracens, at the battle of Tours, in 762, found so many of their helmets, ornamented with the skins of gennets, that he instituted the order of knighthood of the Gennet, in memory of that action. The knights wore the figure of that animal pendant to a golden chain about the neck. This order supported itself till the reign of St. Lewis, when it fell into disrepute. Mr. de Buffon appears to have been misinformed in saying that the gennet could only live in low and marshy spots, when the mountains of Ronda abound with them. See "Journey from Gibraltar to Malaga, by Francis Carter, Esq;" London, 1777.

the

the fierce bull, the ravenous wolf and other obnoxious animals; its rocks serve as a retreat for the eagle, the ofprey and kite; yet notwithſtanding fuch numerous enemies its foil makes ample amends by its unbounded fertility (*a*).

About three leagues from Ronda to the fouth eaſt, and four from the little ports of Eſtepona and Marvella, an attempt has been made fome years ago to erect a manufacture of tin-plates by Don Miguel de Topete, marquis of Pilares, affifted by Benito Berbrungen, a fugitive Saxon, who brought the fecret from Germany. Three hundred thoufand dollars (£50,000 ſterling) have been laid out in buildings and other acceffories relating to this manufacture to very little purpofe. On the road to the manufactory, there are iron mines where the ore is found in little pieces like comfits, fimilar to that of Befort in France. Four leagues from hence to the South Eaſt, nearer the fea, there is a famous mine of black lead, the true *molibdena*, being a perfect mine, not divided in lumps in the fand-ſtone, like the other mentioned before, yet even this is totally neglected. A few years ago, a foreign conful had the king's leave to extract two hundred and

---

(*a*) See Natural hiſtory of Ronda in Mr. Carter's journey, who fays that the diſtrict of Ronda is fo fertile that the druggiſts ſhops are fupplied with medicinal herbs from thence both in Spain and the Indies. An account of theſe plants has been publifhed in Spain by Don Macario Farinas, who died in 1663, under the title of "Virtudes nuevamente deſcubiertas de las hierbas medicinales de la Sierra de Ronda."

fifty quintals per annum, but it is presumed he got four times that quantity. Near the town of Ximena they are building a cannon foundery. They get the ore in the *Sierra* at about two leagues distance, and it is said to be very good : they also find loadstones. The revenues collected at Marvella, Estepona, Manilva, &c. are applied to the expences at Ximena, which is five or six leagues from the sea with very bad roads.

The *Sierra Vermeja* is a range of hills which run westwardly towards Malaga, and afford a singular curiosity, for though they run parallel, and so close that their bases join, yet one is red and the other is white ; snow will not remain on the highest, while it constantly covers the other. The white hills produce the cork tree and the *Encina* oak ; the red has no oaks, but is covered with firs. The white has iron ore in little lumps ; the red has several ores but no iron. The waters of the white hill are martial and vitriolic; those of the red sulphurous, alkaline, and with a strong smell like those of Cotterets in France. Near this place is the last village on the Carthagena side ; the Granada hills are covered with the golden saxifrage, which the Spaniards call *doradilla*, and hold in repute in calculous cases.

The plains of Lorca abound with oleander, which on account of the bitterness of its leaves is named *amarga adelfa*,

adelfa, and serves as a constant comparison in Spanish sonnets and novels. Near Lorca there are two antient mines of lead and copper, and in the *Sierra* towards the sea near Carthagena, the village of Almazarron is famous for its fine red earth without any mixture of sand, and is a principal ingredient used in Spanish snuff, to give it that fine colour and softness to the hand, and to fix its volatility. It is sometimes called after the name of the village, but more commonly *almagre*, and is likewise used in the glass-house of St. Ildefonso instead of *tripoli*, to give the last polish to glass, as others use *colcothar of vitriol*, the caput mortuum, or residue left at the bottom of the vessel after the distillation of vitriol. Spain also furnishes *colcothar nativa rubra*, which is a red martial earth loaded with vitriol, but this is a scarce article in commerce. The neighbourhood of Almazarron moreover affords another singularity, and that is the white stone called plume alum, or *pseudo asbestus*, which is a matter truly saline, tasting and dissolving in water like alum, and crystalizing in form of feathers, from whence its name, being found thus in grottos, where aluminous minerals pass. The other matter to which the name of plume alum has been given, is nothing else but a friable *amianthus*, or *asbestus*. Near Almazarron the remains of a silver mine are to be seen, which in former times is reported to have yielded great quantities of silver. A plain of six leagues, with reddish soil, like the

neighbouring

neighbouring hills, leads to Carthagena, and is so fertile in corn, in rainy seasons, that it produces sixty for one; but this seldom happens, as the country is frequently scorched up, and they suffer from droughts; however their plentiful harvest of *barilla* (a) makes them ample amends, requiring little water, and being in great demand in England, Ireland, and France, for making crystal glass, hard soap, and for bleaching. Besides these advantages, the kingdoms of Granada and Murcia, yield together, annually, 700,000 lb. weight of raw silk, which is now totally consumed in the manufactures of Spain, which must have increased to an immense degree, as formerly the exportation of raw silk was very great; whereas, of late years, upon short crops, they have sometimes been under a necessity of importing it from Italy. The famous harbour of Carthagena has been lately described by an ingenious traveller (b). They make cables in the arsenal of Carthagena with hemp from the kingdom of Aragon, the use of which was introduced under the direction of the late celebrated admiral Don Jorge Juan, and they imagine them to be equal in goodness to any imported from abroad. Amongst the stone at the bottom of the harbour, the fishermen bring up the *Pholades*, which a few years ago were not known there, the people not suspecting they could subsist in the cen-

(a) Salsola soda. Linn. Glass wort.
(b) Travels through Spain in 1775 and 1776, by Edward Swinburne, Esq. London 1779.

tre

tre of these rocks, without any visible aperture to get in at; at present they are searched after as a delicate morsel, and are to be found in most places on the Mediterranean coast.

Being now in the kingdom of Murcia, I should not forget the baths and waters of Archena, whose virtues are so extolled as to be thought an universal remedy for every disorder, concerning which Don Francisco Cerdan a physician of Villena, published a dissertation in 1760. A professor of poetry having found great benefit from the warm baths, has also sung their praises in a poem (a). These baths were frequented by the Romans, as appears from an inscription on a very hard stone, almost black, and roughly cut, found in the men's bath in 1757, which is now fixed as a resting place at the door of a principal house near the river; the inscription is as follows.

    C. CORNELIVS CAPITO. L. HEIUS LABEO
    II. VIR AQVAS. EX D. D. REFICIENDAS
    CVRARVNT. IQ. P.

        THAT IS

Caius Cornelius Capito, Lucius Heius Labeo
Duumviri aquas ex Decreto Decurionum reficiendas
curarunt iidemque posuerunt.

(a) See Thermæ Archenicæ, por Don Ignacio Ayala, professor de poesia en San Isidro en Madrid. Impresso en Murcia en latin y Espanol, 8vo, 1757.

The other hot baths of Spain are Ledesma in Castile, Trillo, Hardales in Anḍaluſia, Alhama in Granada, Villavieja, Busot, Sacedon, Graa, Fortuna, Azaraque, Mula, and others of less note.

LETTER

LETTER XV.

The face of the country described between Carthagena and Alicant.

IN going from Carthagena to Alicant, you cross the rich vale of Murcia, covered with mulberry trees, and pass through a delightful country to Orihuela and Elche (a), remarkable for its numerous groves of palm trees, the branches of which are a lucrative article of trade. The fertility of this country, particularly round Orihuela, exceeds all description, their harvests of wheat are very great, and they are reckoned to have the best bread in Spain. At Orihuela they make those curious snuff-boxes with the roots of the terebinthus, called *cornicabra* in Spanish, which are so much admired on account of their beautiful shades, representing landscapes, &c. they are chiefly useful for Spanish snuff, as they preserve it moist and cool, and for this purpose are in great estimation at Rome. As a further proof of the great abundance and plenty at Orihuela, it is said that the tythes

---

(a) The antiquities of Elche have been lately illustrated by Don Antonio Mayans, canon of Valencia, brother to Don Gregorio Mayans y Sifcar, the celebrated writer. See "Ilici hoi la villa de Elche illustrada con varios difcurfos, por Don Juan Antonio Mayans y Sifcar." Valencia, 1771.

of *Pimenton* and *Tomates*, "guinea pepper and love apple," paid to the bishop of Orihuela, amount to £1600. sterling per annum.

The castle of Alicant stands on a limy rock above a thousand feet high, having shells half petrified on its summit. The plants of the vallies grow also on its top, the seeds of which were probably dropped by birds, or brought by the winds. The eastern side of the hill contains red wavy flint, with pieces of agate fixed in the rock, and on the west side there is plume alume in the crevices of the rock, and lower down beds of *tripoli*, which is used by the silversmiths in these parts. Going from the city towards the north-west about half a league distance, the fields are full of those stones called *numulariæ*, and by the people of the country *moneda de las bruxas*, "witches coin." Likewise *lenticulares*, some of which are as small as a pin's head. This country also produces the *scinus molle*, or Peru pepper, whose fruit grows in bunches of a handsome rose colour (a).

The *huerta de Alicante* is a beautiful plantation, about one league long and two broad, full of vineyards, which they

(a) In Gerard's herbal mention is made of a tree called *molle* or balsam tree, "This tree, says a learned physician, Johan Fragosas, grows in the king of Spain's garden at Madrid, which was the first he had ever seen; since which time Juan Ferdinando, secretary to the king, did shew unto the said Fragosas in his own garden, a tree so large and of such beauty, that he was never satisfied with looking at it, and meditating on the virtues thereof." See Gerard's herbal, and Lobel's description of it.

are

are sometimes obliged to water; the grape nevertheless affords that excellent wine so well known, to which must be added an amasing quantity of mulberry trees, almond trees, fig, and *algarobas*, or carob trees, the *ceratonia edulis* of Linnæus, which requiring little moisture, succeeds in dry soils, and thrives equally in every situation, whether on hills or in plains (*a*).

The city of Alicant forms a crescent, on the sea side, and is well known for the luxuriancy of its environs, as well as its extensive and lucrative commerce. That part of the shore nearest the city forms a bed of limestone mixed with sand, in which the triple-hinged oyster shells are found, with *buccinæ, molæ, tellinæ,* and *ursini*, half petrified, the shells often preserving part of their natural varnish, and the oyster shells their scales, by which the commencement of their petrifaction may be perceived. In that part of the beach next the sea, the sand is the same as in the neighbouring rocks, washed from the limy earth, which the water has dissolved, leaving only the

(*a*) The fruit grows in a husk like a bean cod, inclosing four or five beans, and is given to cattle shell and all. It is sweet and palatable, and often eaten by poor people: it is a tall sightly tree, and in a manner peculiar to the kingdom of Valencia. The pods are green on the tree, but grow brown when dry. According to Miller, they are apt to loosen the belly, and cause gripings of the bowels. He says, these pods are directed by the college of physicians to enter some medicinal preparations, for which purpose they are often brought from abroad. The tree is preserved as a curiosity in England among other exotics, as the leaves always continue green, and being different in shape from most other plants, afford an agreeable variety, intermixed with oranges, myrtles, &c. in the green-house.

pilla

pilla marina formed by the fibres of the roots of the *alga*, or sea moss.

A chain of hills are discernable at Alicant, extending from Murcia, forming a semi-circle of two leagues extent from the city, and close in with the sea about four leagues from each other, shutting in a fine vale, and inclosing the part we have spoken of before, which it shelters from the north winds, and enables it to partake more effectually of every benign influence of the south. The western side is uneven, full of stone, and consists of a white calcareous soil, whose surface is covered with large shells more perfectly petrified than those on the sea shore, particularly two sorts of *ursini*, the large and small, the former of the size of an orange, found still larger in the interior parts of Valencia, of a distinct species, and so perfectly petrified as to receive a polish like marble, being different from those generally seen in cabinets of natural history. The oyster shells between Murcia and Mula are also distinct from those of Alicant, having only one hinge, are about eight inches long and five broad; which opens a field of speculation for naturalists, with respect to these various petrifactions and their period of antiquity.

Two leagues to the south west of Alicant, there is an insulated calcareous mountain, at the eastern foot of which

which they find small crystals, red, yellow and white, with two points like diamonds as regularly cut as if done by a lapidary. The red and yellow are hyacinths. A spring called *Fuente Caliente* issues from that side of the mountain, and waters the lands belonging to the house of the late admiral Don Jorge Juan (a), so well known to the learned world, who was born at Novelda, in this neighbourhood.

(a) Don Jorge Juan died in 1773, and is buried in the church of St. Martin, in Madrid, where a monument is erected to his memory, with his bust in profile, by Philip de Castro, and the following inscription.

Ex D. D. *Georgius Juan & Santacilia Noveldae apud Valentinos natus, melitensis ordinis Eques, Bellicae classis agmini Praefectus, nobilis scholae nauticae cohortis Dux et Regii matritensis seminarii moderator: Demite uvvas structurae navibus mari, lustrata Legatione at Marocbium Africa, peragrata ad telluris figuram asserendam America, literariis laboribus Europa ejusque academiis, Hispana Divi Ferdinandi, Gallica, Anglica, et Borusa illustratis, quam a Deo acceperat vitam, pietatem optimisque moribus excultam, past annos LX. Deo reddidit Matriti Kal Jul. A. M. MDCCLXXIII. carissimo fratri Bernardus et Margarita maerentes annuente Ill. D. D. Joannes Zapata, Marchione S. Michaellis de Gros corpus bic condi et monumentum poni curarunt.*

Don Jorge Juan published the following works.

Compendio de la navegacion para el uso de los Caballeros Guardias Marinas. Cadiz, 1757.

Examen Maritimo Teorico Pratico; o Tratado de Mecanica aplicada a la Construccion, conocimiento y Manejo de los navios, &c. Madrid, 1771.

Relacion historica del a la Viage America meridional y observaciones astronomicas y Physicas en el reyno de Peru por Don Jorge Juan y Don Antonio de Ulloa, 5 tomos, 4to. Madrid, 1748. The historical part of this work was written by Don Antonio de Ulloa, now an admiral in the Spanish fleet, and has been translated into English, of which there has lately been a third and improved edition. See " A voyage to South America, describing at large the Spanish towns, provinces, &c. on that extensive continent, undertaken by command of the king of Spain, by Don Geo. Juan and Don Ant. de Ulloa, F. R. S. &c with copper plates, and a preface by Dr. Campbell, 2 vol. 8vo."

On

On doubling the firſt point of land to the eaſtward of Alicant, the bay and harbour of St. Paul preſents itſelf, with a view of the antient caſtle of the duke of Arcos. Here the ſhips come to an anchor and load ſalt from the *Mata*, a great lake by the ſea ſide, but without any viſible communication with it. The quantity of ſalt collected here is immenſe, and is the property of the king, coſting little more than the labour of heaping it, being in a manner produced naturally. The high bank which ſeparates the ſea from the *Mata* appears natural; the lake is bounded on the land ſide by mountains, and is formed by the torrents of rain water that guſh down in winter, which evaporating gradually by the heat of the ſun, added to the nature of the ſoil, become a maſs of ſalt, ſo plentiful that ſome years the exports have amounted to near one hundred thouſand tun weight, chiefly for Holland and the Baltic; conſiderable quantities alſo are in demand for curing of fiſh, particularly for Newfoundland and New England. The coſt is about eleven ſhillings ſterling per tun, on board; and the king, in order to encourage the export, lets the price always remain the ſame (*a*). The ſoil and air in general, on the coaſts of Valencia, Murcia, and Granada, is im-

---

(*a*) The iſland of Ivica alſo produces immenſe quantities of ſalt with as little trouble and expence as that of the *Mata*, and they have a conſiderable exportation, much on the ſame footing, it being equally the property of the king. This is ſalt alſo ſold for home conſumption, at a price equal to about four ſhilling ſterling per cwt. Engliſh.

pregnared

pregnated to a very uncommon degree with salt, and considerable salt-petre works are carried on in many parts, particularly at Murcia and Lorca, collected from the earth in the fields, the very dust on the roads and in the streets; from which, after extracting the quantity of salt-petre, the same dirt, thrown up in large heaps, serves again in four or five years, for the like purpose, and furnishes a fresh supply. This circumstance renders the soil so peculiarly favourable for the culture of *barrillas*. There are eight or ten different sorts of plants in the plains of Alicant, whose ashes serve for making glass and soap; but the *barrilla* (a) is the principal and best sort: the method of making it is well described in Miller's gardener's dictionary, and is much the same as is used in the North of England in burning kelp. An acre may give about a tun.

I close this letter with the further observations made here by Don Guillermo Bowles, relating to a cinnabar mine, which I shall give in his own words, as they relate to particular researches of his own: "About two leagues from Alicant there is a mountain called *Alcorai*, composed of lime-stone. On digging in that part next

---

(a) The four principal plants for the purposes abovementioned are distinguished by the names of *barrilla*, *gasul*, *sosa*, and *salicor*, and are difficult to be distinguished except by good judges. They have been fully described by Mr. Swinburne.

the

the valley, I discovered a bed of mineralized mercury with sulphur and calcareous earth, of the shape and colour of cinnabar; however as this bed disappeared at a hundred feet depth, I suspended my pursuits. I found thirteen ounces of heavy sand, of a beautiful red colour, in a crevice of rock; I essayed one ounce, and found it to contain more than eleven ounces of quicksilver per pound; it perfectly resembles the sea sand in its hardness and angular form. The colour becomes livelier when pounded, which shews that every grain was possessed of sulphur and mercurial vapour, in the same manner as the sand is with iron at Cape de Gat.

On the top of this mountain, and not far from a bed of red gypsum, I found different marine bodies petrified, such as *telenites* and pieces of *madrepores* mineralized with iron as well as other petrifactions: and about fifteen feet under ground I discovered pieces of mineralized amber, fixed in the rock, being of the same sort as those on which the late Don Joseph Sunal, the king's physician, published a treatise. There is of this amber in Asturias, near Oviedo, but not so beautiful as the specimen shewn to me by that physician. I also found, in the same place, a lump of rock bigger than my fist, having a petrified shell, and a piece of dark amber, like colophony, with a vein of cinnabar, like a thread, running between. On considering

ing the nature of thefe materials, that is, the gypfum, the petrifactions, and the cinnabar, I am of opinion this laſt is of a later date (a)."

Cloſe to the Port of St. Paul there are ruins of a Roman edifice, and a few years ago a brick oven was difcovered, containing feveral coins of Auguftus, about a mufket fhot from the fea, which confirms the little it has retreated on this fide.

(a) Don Guillerme Bowles. Page 34.

LETTER

LETTER XVI.

Road from Alicant to the city of Valencia.

THE beautiful objects which crowd in upon the eye of a traveller, as he moves towards Valencia, are such, and the hand of nature has been every where so profuse, that a writer must be possessed of uncommon abilities to do justice to so animated a picture, or describe in its proper colours so enchanting a vale, enriched with every valuable production. In going from the city of Alicant towards this fertile kingdom, the first observation that occurs is at the pleasant village of Ibi, where there are numerous plantations of the garden almond, grafted on the wild tree, which from the mildness of the air produce the best almonds in Spain, and will keep very well for eight or ten years, when the others soon grow considerably rancid. The neighbouring hills are covered with the kermes oak and the common mastick tree, or *lentiscus*(a), the savin, restharrow, rosemary-

(a) Mr. Bowles says, he knew an apothecary at Alicant, who used to boil the leaves of the *Lentiscus*, and collecting the scum which was left to dry, sold it for male incense, which he imagined to be the same as the *olibanum* or frankincense, imported from the Levant. The Spanish *Lentiscus*, however, is different from the true mastic-tree of the Levant, and from which

leaved.

leaved ciſtus, and great quantities of roſemary, which contributes ſo much to the excellence of the honey, that it is ſent even to Rome.

Between Ibi and Biar the mountains are of a calcareous nature, though half way up, they contain flint, which is in requeſt for muſkets. Striking off to the ſouthward towards Villena, ſeveral ſtrata of alabaſter are ſeen on the road cloſed in beds of limeſtone. There is a mine of ocre in theſe rocks, and they frequently find iron. Near Villena a lake of two leagues circumference furniſhes the neighbouring villages with ſalt, and two leagues further, an inſulated hill conſiſts entirely of ſal gem, covered with a gypſeous coat of different colours. After paſſing Villena, a pleaſant and well cultivated vale extends to Caudete and *Fuente La Higuera*, at the foot of a high mountain covered with mithridate. Two fine ſprings iſſue from the hill of *La Higuera*, and form the brook of Rambla, whoſe ſides have ſtrata of red and white earth, which ſhew themſelves and diſappear alternately in proportion as the waters force their way deeper. Following

---

the maſtic is gathered, which is well explained by Mr. Miller in his dictionary, who complains of theſe trees having been confounded by moſt botanic writers, and that even Mr. Tournefort, who was on the ſpot where the maſtic is collected, had not diſtinguiſhed the ſpecies. The Spaniards ſtill follow the old cuſtom of making toothpicks with the *Lentiſcus*, the ſame as the Romans did, of whom Martial ſays,

Lentiſcum melius, ſed ſi tibi frondes cuſpis
Deſuerit, dentem penna levare poteſt.

this

this brook for four hours you come to Mogente, and in three more to Montesa, opposite to which a towering mountain terminates in a pointed rock, on which stood the convent belonging to the military knights of the order of Montesa. On the 23d of March, 1748, a dreadful earthquake overturned this rock, demolished the convent, and buried its inhabitants under its ruins. An unfortunate man in endeavouring to make his escape through a crevice of the rock, it suddenly closed and crushed him in so terrible a manner that when the body was afterwards found, there were hardly any remains seen of the skull or bones. It is remarkable that in a chain of hills opposite to Montesa, there is a steep hill with an old moorish castle on its summit, which never has suffered from earthquakes, though frequent in Valencia, owing perhaps to its very perpendicular position, being one solid and compact mass, having its root, as it were, deeply fixed under ground, whereas the mountain of Montesa consisted of various strata of stone in a horizontal direction, not sufficiently combined to resist such a violent impulse.

Near San Felipe the country gradually opens in a most rural and fanciful manner; while the eye is struck with new objects; an old ruined castle and shattered fortifications, on the summit of the hill recall to one's mind all the horrors of war and devastation, which are soon effaced by a chearful valley worthy the pencil of a Claude or Pouſſin; you inſenſibly find yourſelf encircled with mulberry trees, which gives to the whole country the appearance of a pleaſure ground, where a rich cinereous ſoil yields three crops a year, owing to excellent culture, as well as its natural quality, beſides the advantage of water at pleaſure at ſix feet depth, independent of the ſurface being amply ſupplied by the river Xucar.

Three leagues to the eaſtward of San Felipe, there is a high mountain entirely of marble of three ſpecies, without any fiſſure, white, red, and yellow, which all admit of a very good poliſh, and the fields are covered with plantations of rice far ſuperior to that of the Levant, though yellower, but will keep much longer without acquiring any acrimony(a).

(a) Mr. Swinburne having given ſo accurate an account of the culture of rice on this ſpot, I cannot offer a more exact deſcription thereof than related by him; which correſponds with Mr. Bowler's information: "In winter they plough out a piece of land, and ſow it with beans that come into bloſſom about March, when they plough them in for manure; water is then let in upon the ground, about four inches deep. It next undergoes a third ploughing, after which the rice is ſown; in fifteen days it comes up about five inches out of the earth, and is pulled up, tied in bundles about a foot diameter, and carried to another well prepared field, covered with water to the depth of four inches. Here each planter ſets the plants of his bundle in the mud in rows at about a foot diſtance one from another. Every ſtem ought to produce from ten to twenty-four fold and grow ſo cloſe that the ears may touch. When ripe it is gathered in ſheaves, and put into a water mill, where the lower grinding-ſtone is covered with cork; by which means the chaff is ſeparated from the grain without bruiſing."

I come

I come now to speak of the plain of Valencia, but where shall I find words expressive of its beauties, such as none can conceive who have not been on the spot, and beheld this lively scene of natural magnificence. This plain is composed of two strata of clay, having a sandy soil or pure sand between them. On removing the first stratum, which may be from fifteen to twenty feet deep, they infallibly find water running between these two beds; the clay not suffering it to filter through: whenever the upper stratum is wanting it of course overflows that part of the country. This accounts for so many lakes in those plains, and for that considerable one called *Albufera de Valencia*, which is no more than an extended portion of such a situation, where the upper stratum has failed, and occasioned that great lake of fresh water, four or five leagues in circumference, receiving also the waters of the river Xucar, and many springs and brooks without any visible increase, because its surface is so extensive that it loses by evaporation as much as it receives, and thus always preserves an equal depth of about two or three feet.

This lake supplies the markets of Valencia with fish, particularly eels ; at certain seasons of the year it is greatly resorted to by sportsmen, and covered with boats, as numbers of aquatic fowls delight in this place, and sometimes

times they see the flamengo (*a*); but neither the excrements of so many birds, nor the putrefaction of so many dead fish, afford the least symptom of volatile alkali when analyzed, no more than the water of the sea, notwithstanding the numbers of fish that die in it. The bottom of the *Albufera* is a bed of pure clay, and if by any accident the waters should run off, we should find it without any mixture of stone, sand, or iron, and perfectly similar to the fuller's earth of England.

Amongst the beautiful spots in this country, none exceed or can be compared to a district in this neighbourhood, called the *Huerta du Gandia*, yet this enchanting place, so near to the city of Valencia, is little known to travellers, as it lies on the sea coast out of their track, at a small distance from the road, hemmed in by a circular chain of hills, forming an inclosure of about a league and a half diameter. Near the sea the city of Gandia,

---

(*a*) This singular bird is so called on account of the red or flame-colour of its wings, and feet; it is a scarce bird in Europe, and always frequents lakes. They have a tongue not much less than a kid's tongue, and which was reckoned a delicious morsel by the voluptuous Romans. When Mr. Peiresc received his friend Le Vayer at his house, he entertained him with this dish, repeating those lines of Martial,

> Dat mihi penna rubens nomen sed lingua gulosis
> Nostra sapit.

Le Vayer wondered why Apicius and the emperors Caligula, Vitellius, and Heliogabalus, had reckoned it so dainty a dish, for instead of being exquisite, he found it rather unpleasant, with a fleshy taste, like that of all water fowl. Therefore the inhabitants of Provence generally throw away the flesh, and only make use of the feathers as an ornament to other birds at particular entertainments. See "Life of Peiresk, by Gassendi. Translated into English by William Rand, M. D." London, 1657.

capital

capital of the dutchy of that name, offers a new point of view, and from the church steeple, you have a noble prospect of the *Huerta*, and may see above twenty villages dispersed amidst an infinite variety of verdure and foliage, enriched by a diversity of fruits. Amongst the rest, the blue fig, the glowing pomegranate, and the verdant olive vie with each other in excellence; even the very beach seems desirous of adding a share to this plentiful store, for the prickly pear shoots out every where amongst the clefts of the rocks, and its fruit is free to all who choose to partake of it. In this seat of bliss, simplicity and perfection fill the mind with delight, and all the laboured powers of invention are outdone; for nature here, as Milton says,

> Wantons as in her prime, and plays at will
> Her virgin fancies, pouring forth more sweet,
> Wild above rule or art.

LETTER

LETTER XVII.

Observations made in the city of Valencia and its environs.

FAIR Valencia! how shall I describe thy transcendant beauties, or speak of those infinite glories that adorn thee? If celebrated architects have not graced thy capital city with sumptuous palaces, or given a more pleasing form to thy streets, be contented that the great Architect of the universe has poured on thee blessings innumerable to render thy happiness compleat, and make thee the admiration of the world, inspiring at the same time thy sons with the most exalted talents to sing perpetually thy praise (a)!

The city of Valencia is happily situated about three miles from the sea on the West side of the river Guadalaviar, with five stone bridges over it, which afford a variety of agreeable outlets from this pleasant city, exultingly rising out of a forest of mulberry trees,

(a) An account of the writers of the kingdom of Valencia only, makes a work of two volumes in folio. See " Escritores del reino de Valencia, chronologicamente ordenados desde el ano 1238 de la Chriſtiana conquiſta de la miſma Ciudad baſta el de 1748 por Vicente Ximeno Preſbitero, &c. Valencia, 1749. 2 tomos en folio.

which bring an immense wealth to its citizens. The branches of these trees are made to grow horizontally, in order to pick the leaves more easily, and the trees are pruned every two or three years, to preserve the leaves soft and tender, that the silk may be finer, cleaner and lighter than that of Murcia, where the trees are only pruned once in four years, which renders the leaf woolly and tough. In Granada they do not prune them at all, and yet suppose their silk is the finest in Spain; but their trees are of the black sort, and those of Valencia and Murcia are of the white mulberry, for which reason the worms of these two last provinces when carried to Galicia, where they have none of the white sort, never succeed, while the worms of Granada thrive admirably well, in meeting with a similar leaf to that of their own country.

I shall not enter into a detail of the manifold branches of cultivation in the environs of Valencia, where nature always smiles, and where the very air is constantly embalmed with the fragrant perfume of an infinite number of fruit trees and odoriferous herbs. The cedrats are so large as sometimes to weigh more than six pounds, when the tree that produced them is not above two or three feet in height: as to flowers and plants, their beauty and variety are wonderful, as well as the amazing quantities of pomegranates, figs, cherries, pears, and grapes the most delicious imaginable,

ginable, with bunches fourteen pound weight, and every grape as large as a nutmeg. To heighten still more this boundless fertility, the intermediate spaces between the trees are filled with melons, artichoaks, caulyflowers, and almost every species of pulse supplied with constant and copious streams of water, which in a kingdom blessed with an eternal spring, and where the grim frost is unknown, seems to unite every idea of the golden age of the poets.

The grapes of Valencia and Granada have the preference to all others in Spain. They cannot, it is true, from their distance, be sent fresh to England like those of Portugal, but they ship off large quantities of raisins at Malaga. They prepare them in Valencia with the lixivium of seeds whose salt augments the heat of the water in boiling. The grape is dipped for a moment in this lixivium, when the skin bursts on every side, and the juice gushing out candies in the air, after which the bunches are hung to dry in the sun. The cold weather afterwards perfects this crystalization, so that when they get to England, they become so many cakes of sugar, infinitely better than when first shipped off. The raisins *of the sun*, as they are called, are still more delicate, having the stalk half cut through, while the bunch remains suspended on the vine, and partakes of the heat of the sun, as the sap cannot penetrate after they are dried; they

are

are packed up in boxes. This is the method used in Granada, which makes them more luscious and delicate, and justly gives the preference to the Malaga raisins.

As the river Guadalaviar empties itself into the sea, about three miles below Valencia, it is said a plan has been proposed to deepen the channel of the river, which would be of great advantage to its commerce, as the ships lie in an open road in a dangerous situation. Much might still be done to enliven and give activity to this agreeable city, formerly known to the British army, having opened its gates in 1705 to the earl of Peterborough, but after the defeat at Almanza, the duke of Orleans at the head of the Spanish forces recovered it again.

There is a pleasant village about two leagues from Valencia, consisting of four streets inhabited chiefly by potters, who make a pretty earthen ware of a copper colour with gilding, that serves the country people both for ornament and use, it is made of an argillaceous earth, very similar in quality and colour to that of Valencia, in which virgin mercury is found: this earthen ware is very glossy, and remarkably cheap, but is far from being the best ware in Valencia; another manufacture has been lately set up at *Alcora*, by the count de Aranda, a grandee of Spain, which for the fineness of the clay might vie with

with other manufactures of the kind, were its varnish less liable to crack and scale off (*a*).

The famous marble quarry of *Naquera* is three leagues from Valencia; the village is on an eminence, and the quarry is on one side near the surface in beds of a few inches, formed seemingly by the waters. The marble is of a dark red ground, with black capillary veins like a *mocha*, which have a very good effect. Though the beds do not sink deep, it is hard enough to make solid tables, which take an excellent polish, and are greatly valued in Spain. Two leagues to the eastward of the city there is a quarry of alabaster, at a place called *Ninerola*, of which substance many curious pieces of workmanship may be seen in the house of the marquis of Dos Aguas in the city of Valencia. At two leagues distance from the city, on the banks of the river, the ruins of the antient city are discovered; near them they find monstrous petrifactions of oyster shells, like those of Murcia, mixed with rounded sand stone; but nothing of one or the other is found in the river.

It is an agreeable tour of five leagues from Valencia to Morviedro, famous for the remains of the antient *Saguntum* and its Roman theatre, described by dean

(*a*) It goes by the name of Count Aranda's ware, and is sold at Madrid.

Marti

Marti (*a*) as well as by such English travellers as have passed that way. The plants on the hill of Morviedro and its neighbourhood, are prickly pears, henbane, stinking orache, mithridate, capers, marshmallow and thyme. The view from the top of the hill is most beautiful, with an extensive prospect of the vale and city of Valencia and the Mediterranean. At a few leagues distance from hence to the South East, beyond a chain of hills, consisting of red marble and lime rock, the Carthusian Monks have a convent situated in a perfect paradise, where they make excellent wine. The gullies and fields are filled with pudding-stone of different sizes, firmly conglutinated together; their church is built with a stone of this kind, veined with white spar; but who will inform us whether this spar existed before or after the conglutination of the stone with its natural bitumen? The stone is undoubtedly of use to the vine, preserving to its root in the night, the genial heat of the day, while it shades it at noon from the scorching rays of the sun. There are two copper mines near this convent.

To return to the plains of Valencia, it would be an endless theme to enlarge upon its products; they culti-

---

(*a*) The best edition of Dean Marti's letters " Aloisi Martini epistolæ," with a plate of Saguntum, in 4to, was printed in Holland from an edition 2 vol. in 12mo, and the life another volume by Mayans, printed at Madrid by Sir Benjamin Keene. This edition is now scarce and dear in Spain, and the Dutch edition is better.

vate great quantities of medick or lucern (*trifolium Hispanicum*) which is acceptable to horses, and makes excellent hay. The Spaniards call it *alfalfa*. Its roots make little brushes for the teeth, that are sought after by dentists. The *chirimoya*, a very fine fruit from South America, thrives and bears fruit in Valencia; in a word, every production of nature may be said to prosper in this kingdom(*a*), for here we find corn, wine, oil, honey, flax, fu-

(*a*) The following sketch exhibits the value of the principal products of Valencia.

Silk crop annually about 2,500,000 lb. of 12 ounces, which sells on the spot, at a price equal to 10 s.		£. 750,000 sterling.
400,000 lb. wt. English, or 10,000 ton of rice for home consumption, at 16 s. per pound;		300,000
150,000 lb. Barilla,	at 10 l.	75,000
80,000 Raisins	7 l. 6 d.	30,000
10,000 Kernels of almonds } For exportation	40 l.	20,000
10,000 Pipes of brandy	10 l.	100,000
10,000 Wine	4 l.	40,000
		£. 1,315,000 sterling.

Besides great quantities of wool, oilseeds, cummin seeds, and many other smaller articles, and a large quantity of oil for home consumption. Nothing is mentioned in this account, of cotton, which is a considerable article. I shall now state the whole, as given us by Mr. Swinburne, and reduce it into English money, as it makes the annual revenue much more considerable.

Silk crop of 1775, one million of pounds at 4 dollars per pound, (though a good deal of it sells for 3 dollars.)	4,000,000 dollars.
Fruit of different kinds	2,000,000
Hemp at 3 dollars per arrove	300,000
Rice at 10 dollars per load	1,400,000
Cotton 450,000 arroves	1,350,000
Vintage of 1767 wine, at 3 reals per measure	861,133
	9,911,133 dollars.

Which sum of 9,911,133 dollars, at 40 d. sterling per dollar, is £. 1,655,855. 10 s. sterling.

gar,

gar, cotton, rice, silk, besides fruits, and plants, producing all together near ten millions of dollars per annum. Few cities enjoy a more temperate air, or have more beautiful environs. The *Alameda*, or public walk, is one of the most pleasing in Spain; if we add to the variety of its beautiful trees, the gaudy equipages and numerous concourse of people that resort there, it forms so picturesque a scene enlivened by the fields, with a view of the city and bridges, as seems to surpass the utmost powers of description; and were public spirit equal to its natural blessings, would nearly resemble the marvellous scenes of romance! Such is the beautiful Valencia, like the garden of Paradise in Milton:

> A happy rural seat of various view;
> Groves whose rich trees wept odorous gums and balm,
> Others whose fruit burnish'd with golden rind
> Hung amiable! Hesperian fables true,
> If true, here only, and of delicious taste.

LETTER XVIII.

Journey from Barcelona to the mountain of Montferrat.

THE city of Barcelona is generally reckoned one of the moſt agreeable places in Spain. Its pleaſant ſituation, its commerce, with the activity and induſtry of its inhabitants, contribute to make it a place of ſplendour and affluence (*a*). In this city the traveller will find a curious cabinet of natural hiſtory belonging to a private citizen, Mr. Salvador, an eminent apothecary, who ſhews his collection to ſtrangers with the utmoſt urbanity.

The celebrated mountain of Montferrat, nine leagues from Barcelona, has of late been ſo fully deſcribed by Britiſh travellers, a fine print having been lately exhibited of it (*b*), that the ſubject is become exhauſted, and

---

(*a*) The Engliſh merchants ſeem to have ſettled later at Barcelona than in other commercial towns in Spain. Mr. James Howel, in a letter from Barcelona, dated 24th Nov. 1620, to Sir James Crofts, ſays, "In this place there lives neither Engliſh merchant nor factor, which I wonder at, conſidering it is a maritime town, and one of the greateſt in Spain, her chiefeſt arſenal for gallies; but I believe the reaſon is, that there is no commodious port for ſhips of any burthen but a large bay." The new mole however has rendered this port more convenient, and immortaliſed the memory of the late marquis de la Mina, captain general of the principality, under whoſe orders it was erected.

(*b*) In Mr. Thickneſs's travels into Spain.

words seem feeble to describe this awful mountain, raising its exalted crest towards the skies, with all the powers and majesty of nature; yet as it makes so capital a figure in the geography of Spain, we shall once more ascend its jagged rock, and explore its wondrous form.

The first stage from Barcelona leads to the town of Martorel, at the conflux of the rivers Noya and Lobregat; here you are sensibly struck with the tremendous appearance of this grand and solemn mountain, impressing on the mind the most exalted ideas, in viewing this wonderful effort of nature. You seem quite close to it, but have still three hours in the usual method of travelling in Spain to approach its basis, and as many more after to climb up to its summit. There is a famous bridge over the Lobregat at Martorel, with an arch at its foot; it has been lately repaired, as appears by the following modern inscription placed on it.

POR LOS ANOS DE 533 DE LA FONDACION DE ROMA FUE CONSTRUIDO ESTE ADMIRABLE PUENTE POR EL GRANDE ANIBAL CAPITAN CARTAGINES Y HIZO EREGIR EL ARCO TRIUMFAL QUE AUN EXISTE A SU SALIDA EN HONOR DE SU PADRE AMILCAR. DESPUES DE 1985 ANOS DE DURACION SE HALLAVA ESTA FABRICA MUY MALTRATADA Y EN ESTADO DE ARRUINARSE ENTERAMENTE PERO AFIN DE CONSERVAR UN MONUMENTO DE TAN RARA ANTIGUEDAD LO MANDO REES.

REESTABLECER EN ESTE AÑO DE MIL SIETE CIENTOS Y SECENTA OCHO, LA MAGESTAD DEL SEÑOR DON CARLOS REY DE ESPAÑA A SOLICITUD DEL EXMO SEÑOR DON IUAN MARTIN DE ZERMEÑO COMANDANTE GENERAL DEL CUERPO DE INGENIEROS, &c. &c.

In ENGLISH.

This admirable bridge was erected in the year 533 of the building of Rome, by the great Hannibal, a Carthaginian captain, and he raised the triumphal arch which still exists at its foot, in honour of his father Hamilcar. This fabric, after having stood 1985 years, was greatly damaged and in a ruinous state, but his Majesty Don Carlos King of Spain, in order to preserve so rare a monument of antiquity, ordered it to be repaired in the year 1768, at the entreaty of his excellency Don John Martin de Zermeño, commandant general of engineers, &c. &c.

Martorel is a large town, replete with industrious inhabitants, all employed and constantly at work; the women in making black lace, and the men in various useful and laborious occupations; a little farther on, at the village of Espalanguera there is a manufactory of cloth, which maintains numbers of families; the same spirit of labour and application is universal every where in Catalonia; but we now draw near to the lofty mountain of Montserrat, the most singular perhaps in the world for its appearance, composition, and productions; as much the admiration of the naturalist, as revered by the natives in general, from the renown of its sanctuary, famous

for

for miracles and the extraordinary favours granted by our lady of Montserrat to its numerous votaries.

The whole extent of this mountain may be about eight leagues in circumference, its chief materials consisting of round limestone, firmly conglutinated with a yellow calcareous earth and sand, not unlike the *Brecbia* or pudding-stone of Aleppo, only that the grain is coarser and the stones larger than that of the Levant, with a further addition of round white quartz streaked with red, as well as touchstone, all firmly cemented together, forming one perfect solid mass; and according as the natural bitumen which united all these together, has occasionally given way in the course of fleeting years, various torrents of rain water have rolled down and washed away the earth, the result of their decomposition, and have split the mountain into an infinite variety of shapes and singular appearances, forming in some places the most amazing clefts and frightful precipices: in others huge pieces of blanched and bare rock shoot up into sharp cones, pillars, and jagged forms, from twenty to a hundred feet high, exhibiting wonderful aspects that strike the eye with surprize and the mind with astonishment! its wildness increasing in proportion as you advance higher, insomuch that on reaching the summit of this enormous pile, human reason is lost in conjecture; but the sight is gratified with the most splendid

did profpect, looking down on an extenfive kingdom beneath you as on a map, exhibiting a fertile country to the South, ftudded with villages and watered with rivers; the eye ftretching out further over the Mediterranean, the landfcape is rendered ftill more ftriking from the contraft on the North and Eaft, bounded by the bare and dark mountains of the Rouffillon, and the fnowy tops of the Pyrenees. On thefe inhofpitable cliffs of Montferrat, amidft the conftant inclemency of jarring elements, dwells the pale hermit, with hairy gown, wrapt up in filent contemplation. Here he has hewn a folitary dwelling and offers up his fervent prayer, and takes his lonely walk, lifting up his eyes, mufing

> Of every ftar that heav'n doth fhew,
> And every herb that fips the dew.

But though the elements have wreaked their fury upon thefe elevated peaks, the indulgent hand of nature has not been fparing in her gifts to this furprifing mountain, as numberlefs evergreens and deciduous plants ferve to adorn the various gaps and breaks which its fingular fhape admits of, rendering it a curious repofitory of the vegetative kingdom. The lower part of the mountain has decompofed much fooner than the upper parts and turned into foil, productive of corn, vineyard and olive, while the fhelving rocks facilitate a paffage to the fummit, and

exhibit

exhibit to the botanist a view of above two hundred sorts of trees, shrubs, and plants, that shoot up spontaneously, gracing this hoary and venerable pile; amongst others the scarlet oak, three different kinds of juniper, bastard alaternus, mock privet, the lote or nettle tree, the scorpion sena, the perennial strawberry tree, rosemary, gorze, thyme, fern, and towards the top the stinking trefoil of the sea shore of Valencia, and the rough bind weed of Andalusia and Biscay, proving that these plants grow equally in cold and warm climates.

Here we find the touchstone, or *lapis lydius*, known to Theophrastus the disciple of Aristotle, who says it was found in the river Tmolus in Lydia, and that the upper part was better for essaying gold than the lower, adding, that these stones appeared to be pebbles, and as they were not round, it was inferred they were fixed in the earth, and were never washed away by the rivers. The moderns make use of acids with greater advantage for the essaying of gold, by comparing a line drawn on the stone with gold of a known standard, to another line which they want to essay, for as aqua fortis has the property of dissolving all metals except gold, the colour and diminution of the lines compared together, will shew what allay they have, with little danger of error. From hence it is plain the touchstone is not limy, otherwise it would dissolve in the acid, and the only quality required is to receive the line

line drawn on it, and not diffolve in aqua fortis, nor is its colour of confequence, though the blacker is preferable, as fhewing the gold better. This is the colour of that found in the Tmolus, the Bafaltes or cryftalized rocks, in many parts of Saxony, in the mountain of Uffon in Auvergne, the Giants caufeway in Ireland, and thefe of Montferrat. They are all indiffoluble in acids, and of a different nature from marble, which being limy would not anfwer the purpofe, as the aqua fortis would carry away the ftone jointly with the metal it diffolved; thus true touchftone being of a very hard nature, all vapour and moifture condenfe on its furface; it muft therefore be carefully rubbed and wiped dry before it is ufed, that the adhefion of gold may be perfect. Theophraftus, though a great man, reafoned according to the philofophy of his age, which made him imagine that marble would fweat, when the dampnefs proceeded from the fmooth texture and coldnefs of it, condenfing, and rendering vifible the moifture diffolved in the air.

The direction of this great mountain is from eaft to weft, with a vifible inclination to the weft. Thofe who adopt the fyftem of the formation of mountains, from a fucceffive depofit of fediment from the fea, will find it difficult to reconcile their hypothefis with the ftructure of the mountain of Montferrat, as it is no eafy matter to difcover how the fea could give a round fhape to the ftone,

or

or how quartz, fandftone, or touchftone, could conglutinate fo firmly together; but this muſt be left to more able pens to difcufs: I fhall only add, that it is impoſſible to view this amazing mountain without the utmoſt admiration; its name has been extended to one of the Britiſh iſlands in the Weſt Indies, and its fame is univerſal: its prodigious clefts impreſs the mind with ſuch wonder, that it has given rife to the opinion in common with Gaeta in Italy (*a*), that thefe tremendous rocks were fuddenly rent in this manner when our Saviour gave up the ghoſt on the crofs, when " *The earth did quake, and the rocks rent.*" *St. Matt. c.* 27, *v.* 51.

(*a*) The fingular rock of Gaeta in the kingdom of Naples, has an amazing cleft from the top to bottom, and is totally rent afunder, which they tell you happened at the death of our Saviour; a large block of marble has fallen in between, on which they have built a little chapel, dedicated to the Trioity, and ſhips paffing near falute it; this place is held in great veneration, particularly in Spain; during the wars in Italy, *La Santiſſima Trinidad de Gaeta* was greatly reforted to, and a conftant invocation. There is a good plate of this rock in the " remarks on ſeveral parts of Europe by John Breval, Eſq; author of the former remarks. London, 1738."

LETTER

LETTER XIX.

Singular mountain of fossil salt, near the town of Cardona, in Catalonia, as described by Don Guillermo Bowles.

THE town of Cardona is sixteen leagues from Barcelona, at no great distance from Montserrat, and near the Pyrenees. It stands at the foot of a rock of salt, which on the side of the river Cardonero appears cut perpendicularly, forming a mass of solid salt between four and five hundred feet high, without the least crevice, fissure, or strata, nor is any gypsum to be found in the neighbourhood. This amazing rock is about a league in circumference, and much about the same height as the adjacent mountains, but its depth being unknown, it cannot be ascertained on what basis it rests. The salt is commonly white from the bottom to the top, though in some parts it is red, which the people of the country cut into pieces like bricks, and think it of use for pains in the side, by applying it to the part after being moderately warmed; sometimes it is of a light blue, but these colours are of no importance, as they disappear in grinding, the salt remaining white, and being eatable, having no flavour or taste either of earth or vapour.

This

This prodigious mountain of falt, divefted of any other fubftance, is unparalleled in Europe; philofophers have an ample field to ftudy its formation; it will not be fufficient to fay, it proceeds from an evaporation of the fea, as this will not be deemed fatisfactory.

In the fhop of a fculptor at Cardona, I purchafed feveral figures, candlefticks, cafkets, and other toys cut out of this falt, as tranfparent as cryftal: when one of the workmen was carving a candleftick, I obferved he wet it with water, then rubbed it dry with a towel, and wiped off the white powder which enfued on the working of it, and gave it a greater tranfparency. The falt is fo hard and compact that water will not diffolve it if it is foon rubbed dry again.

This mountain has a confiderable furface, neverthelefs the rain does not diminifh the falt (*a*). The river which runs at its foot is briny, and when it rains the faltnefs of the water increafes, and kills the fifh; but this effect does not extend above three leagues, beyond which fifh live as ufual.

After many experiments which I made with the water of this river by evaporation diftillation, and various

(*a*) Perhaps not fenfibly; but how fhall we otherwife account for the addition of falt to the water mentioned in the next fentence.

different procefses, I never could difcover in it, the leaft grain of falt, which perfuaded me that the falt was entirely decompofed by motion, and diffolved into earth and water. The water of the Tagus, which paffes between hills of gypfum and fal gem, at Aranjuez, is bad in that fpot, but at Toledo it is good; foap eafily diffolves in it, and a little lower down, if it is diftilled, not the leaft particle of gypfum or falt is to be found (a). If we burn fulphur, arfenic, pitch, or other combuftible matters at the foot of a tower, none of thofe that are near it can bear the ftench, while thofe above will not perceive it; becaufe it entirely decompofes into water and earth before it reaches them, and the inflammable principle which is inodorous rifes anew to form frefh combinations, and occafion thunder and lightning. I fhould think the emanations of malignant fevers, and of the plague, follow the fame laws.

It is commonly faid, that of the three acids of nature, the nitrous, which is the fecond in ftrength, ejects the marine, which is the third and the weakeft, but experience is contrary to this doctrine, fince in Spain the fal gem ejects the nitrous acid from its bafis: grind twenty-four ounces of this falt with twelve of falt-petre, let them be diftilled in the ufual manner, and the refult will be a,

---

(a) Thefe curious facts merit a further examination, as the prefent illuftration is by no means fatisfactory.

very

very good aquafortis, which will readily diffolve filver, and have no effect upon gold. The filverfmiths of Madrid ufe no other. To clear up more fully this fingular phenomenon, and fee whether the chemifts are miftaken or not, nothing is left but to afcertain whether this fal gem contains a vitriolic acid, becaufe in fuch cafe it would not be the marine acid that was more powerful than the nitrous, but the vitriolic: however as it has not been demonftrated, or known, that any fuch vitriolic acid exifts in common falt, the difficulty ftill remains. This fingularity of the Spanifh fal gem merits the attention of chemifts and repeated experiments; as this fyftem feems to militate againft the received opinions concerning the nature of the three acids, the mafter-key of chemiftry, and overturns the theories now in vogue (a).

What rhapfodies have been publifhed with refpect to the phyfical caufes of the faltnefs of the fea, fome faying that immenfe beds of falt exifted at its bottom; others, finding this argument deftroyed itfelf, had recourfe to the idea of rivers bringing down falt enough to the fea to impregnate its waters, which fuppofition is as falfe as the former, as we are pofitive that fea water is at prefent as briny as it was in ancient times in proportion to its fitua-

(a) Mr. Bowles feems to have drawn his conclufions rather too haftily, without reflecting that nitre when divided to a certain degree and kept divided, may by the force of heat alone be deprived of its acid; whilft common falt can fuftain a much greater degree of heat without any decompofition.

tion, temperature, evaporation, or quantity of fresh water running into it; besides this, I have made several experiments, but never found salt at the mouth of rivers, where they disembogue into the sea. It is true, that sometimes after distillation and evaporation I have found a thousandth part of common salt, and I once discovered as a *residuum*, a little nitre; but this proves nothing, and with respect to the nitre, I consider it to be a *residuum* of common salt, being persuaded that this may change its acid and alkaline basis, and become nitre with motion and ebullition, and reciprocally nitrous, and the alkaline basis change into common salt (*a*).

(*a*) It would have been acceptable to the chemical readers, if Mr. Bowles had favoured us with any sufficient reason to support this belief.

LETTER

LETTER XX.

Observations made by Don Guillermo Bowles, on the roundness of pebbles in the beds of rivers.

THE pebbles of which I am now going to speak, are those which are commonly found in most places without angles, or points, and though not perfectly round, have yet more or less that form, with a smooth surface. They are composed of various matter, and the first idea which occurs of their having acquired this smoothness, is from their rubbing against each other, or some harder body; this being the method we use in order to give such a polish to any substance, and as these stones are frequently found in large quantities in the beds of great rivers, it is very easy to say they have been brought down by the waters, and become smooth by their constant friction. For my part, I was always of this opinion till my arrival at Aranjuez, where I discovered the fallacy of this reasoning, for I clearly perceived that the stones in the bed of the Tagus never moved from their places. This of course staggered my former belief; I was confirmed in my new principles by a variety of observations, but to avoid being prolix I shall only offer

offer a few of them, which have all the appearance of being decisive in favour of my system (a).

There are no pebbles more singular than those crystalline ones found in the bed of the river Henares, near San Fernando; now if these pebbles had any progressive motion, let it be ever so small, they ought certainly by this time, after so many ages, to have reached the bed of the Tagus so near them, yet none are to be found there.

The Tagus is full of calcareous stone at Sacedon; a little lower, at Aranjuez, not one of these is to be found in its bed.

In the kingdom of Jaen near Linares, there is a hill chiefly composed of round smooth stones, about the size of an egg; the smooth polish of these and their roundness cannot be attributed to rains, because they are not exposed to them, nor dispersed on the surface of the hill, but buried underneath at a considerable distance: nor much less can it be attributed to any river, for I do not know from what system, or by what chronology, it may be conjectured that any river ever run over that eminence.

(a) Mr. Bowles tells us, he looks upon this as one of the happiest discoveries he ever made, as striking him in a forcible light, and serving as a key tending to illustrate the true physical theory of the earth; but in what manner it had this effect he has not informed us.

In the village of Maria, three leagues above Zaragoſſa, there is a broad gully full of quartz, ſandſtone and limeſtone, and gypſum of a perfect white, yet at Zaragoſſa the Ebro contains none of theſe ſorts.

I believe no body has ever ſeen in the bed of the Ebro large or ſmall round granite ſtone, nor blueiſh ſtone veined with white, but the Cinca before it empties itſelf into that river is full of them: in ſo much that it carries no other ſand but theſe ſtones reduced very ſmall, near San Juan in the valley of Giſtau.

The river Naxera is full of ſmall ſandy ſtone, and of white quartz reſembling little almonds, mixed with others of a red colour. This river runs into the Ebro, in whoſe bed when it paſſes by Zaragoſſa, none of theſe ſorts of ſtones are to be ſeen.

The bed of the Guadiana has in its different parts the ſame kind of pebbles as are found on its banks, and on the adjacent hills, without being mixed with thoſe that are found a league higher or lower; and at Badajoz, where the country is without any ſtone, none are to be found in the bed of the river.

This holds good not only in Spain, for I have taken notice of the ſame in other countries; not to multiply

ply examples, I shall only offer what has fallen under my observation in France; the river Alier at its source, about half a league from Varenne, contains a great variety of pebbles, of red and yellow quartz, of the same nature as those in the fields in its neighbourhood; but I could not discover one of these pebbles in this river, when it passes by Moulins, where nothing is seen but coarse sand.

The Loire at its source runs over an immense quantity of small pebbles, lower down, none are to be seen when it passes by Nevers, where the bed of the river consists of sand and large pebbles the same as the adjacent fields.

There is a great deal of pebble and flint in the river Jonne, before and after it passes by Sens, because its banks are covered with it from Joigny. The Jonne enters into the Seine above Paris, and yet I do not believe any body has ever seen one of these pebbles go through the *Pont neuf*, and what is more, nobody has ever seen the Seine bring any sort of limy pebble along with it in passing through Paris, either round or of any other shape.

What happens in the Rhone is still more conclusive, and as several writers have spoken of it, and of the Lake of Geneva in a manner which is incomprehensible to me,

I shall

I shall briefly relate what I have seen. A valley flanked on one side in part by the Alps, and on the other by Mount Jura, forms the Lake of Geneva, which is about eighteen French leagues in length: a small river with a great many brooks falling from the mountains on its sides fill the cavity of the valley, and the water which overflows, forms the river Rhone near the city; as its depth there, is less than in the centre, and the water extremely limpid and transparent, the pebble is seen at the bottom covered with moss; the waters even with the highest winds never moving them from the first spot where they fell in. The Rhone after it has quitted the lake runs for some leagues over a bed of pebble, and then enters a narrow gorge formed by two rocks cut perpendicularly, then passes by the mountain of Credo, at whose foot the river disappears, for reasons very different from those with respect to the Guadiana.

The Credo mountain is a composition of sandy earth full of round stone, from its summit to a considerable depth. There is another similar mountain opposite to it in Savoy, likewise full of sandy, limy pebble, granite, and flint; the Rhone passes between these two mountains: as the basis of the Credo consists of strata of limy rock of different degrees of hardness, the waters in course of time have eaten their way through such beds as happened to be of a softer nature than those above and below,

low, and made themselves a passage between them. I crossed the upper rock, which penetrates the basis of the two mountains, and over the river, went from France to Savoy in less than a minute, as it is not forty paces from one shore to the other. This singular vault is pierced in some places, and the water gushes out at the apertures, foaming like boiling water amongst those enormous pieces of broken rock. This is what is commonly called *La Perte du Rhone*, and may be about sixty paces in length. At another place it is less, about a musket shot higher up, from a similar cause, of the river meeting with a strata of less resistance, where it has formed a passage which it enters with no inconsiderable violence.

This phenomenon being explained, I reason in this manner: If stones were carried forward by the motion of the rivers, these cavities through which the Rhone passes should be full of them, for though the strength of the current would hurry them forward, there are so many holes at the bottom, and so many detached pieces of rock to stop them, that some would inavoidably be interrupted in their passage, and many be found there, but I could not discover the least appearance of such, notwithstanding that the bed of the river from Geneva to this place is in a manner crouded with them. I therefore conclude that these pebbles never move from their place; and what is still more convincing, there is not a
single

single pebble in these vaulted places, excepting such as are found on the banks of the river, in the long course of which there are many of all shapes and sorts, at least as far as Lyons; nevertheless I do not believe any one has perceived such stones at its entrance into the sea, nor in the gulph of Lyons, where this river loses itself.

I will add one observation more, though perhaps I have given too many already. A few paces from the occultation of the Rhone you cross the river Valseline, which has its source near Nantua, in the high Bugey. The bed of this river is full of pebble, because the hills and plains through which it passes are equally so. There is a place where it forms a cataract with great violence, when the water runs into a cavity; now if it brought any pebbles along with it, they would certainly be found in this cavity, but it is a fact that none are to be found there. When I went to Geneva I threw some remarkable stones into the river above this gap, and at my return I found them in the very identical spot without having been moved in the least.

If I am asked how all these pebbles come to be so round and smooth, and to have lost their sharp points, I shall freely acknowledge that I do not know the reason, that I have ideas of my own concerning them, but do not venture to insist on them. Any hypothesis would have more weight with me than the common one, that the motion of waters or rivers has been the cause of the roundness of stones, for who can have resolution to embrace a system which would engage him to hold that the Rhone for instance had traversed the summit of the mountain of Credo, one of the highest in the world, all composed of such pebble; and the same reasoning must be allowed to many other mountains with similar appearances in different parts of the world.

Sometimes, it is true, stones and pieces of rock are hurried forward in rivers, and brought down by torrents after storms; the same may happen in streets and cities, but this is not extraordinary, when the declivity of the situation is considered, which gives additional power and force to the water, occasioning a natural effect, which ceases when such bodies come to a place where they will be at rest. This will account for such stones as have been rolled down into the beds of rivers by their natural weight, when the earth which supported them has given way.

Supposing then this notion to be exploded, the difficulty still remains to account for their smoothness and roundness, which is no easy matter to explain, being involved with many perplexing circumstances, which I shall leave to be elucidated by others more intelligent than myself. It is certain that water and time are two powerful

ful agents that can bring about furprifing effects. The world is full of thefe round ftones of various fizes and appearances, they are found in vallies, on hills, and at a confiderable depth in the earth, as well as on the fummit of the higheft mountains. I have feen round diamonds covered with a light fcurf, fapphires and oriental topazes round like cornelians. The cryftal of the Rhine never becomes round, becaufe in its natural ftate it is not angular, and forms a mafs already round, the reverfe of common rock cryftal, compofed of *laminæ* of a regular fhape. Many of the learned have been deceived by thefe cryftals of the Rhine, thinking, becaufe they found them at two leagues diftance from Strafburg, in the midft of the fields, that the river has altered its bed, entertaining that fond notion, of the waters carrying them along; at the fame time, they did not confider that they are not to be found a few leagues above Dieux Brifac, nor any where below Strafburg. Therefore if thefe rivers carried fuch pebbles in their courfe, they would have them at their mouth, where they enter the fea, and there would be no fand banks at thefe places, for the ftones would fill up the cavities, and the waters would roll over them, which certainly is not the cafe. The very bottom of the fea would fuffer fome change from the great quantities of ftones brought down by fo many rivers, and forced into its bed, from whence it would follow, that the

obfervations

observations of the sounding line would no longer be of use to the mariner, who always finds the same bottom when he heaves the lead at one time as at another (a).

(a) True with respect to the British Channel, and of which I have been often an eye witness, and seen the same kind of sand, small shells, and pebbles, brought up at the bottom of the lead as were described in charts published many years ago, by which the mariner on entering the channel in a dark winter night can know in what part he is in; but this is not the general use of the sounding line, which is thrown out occasionally, to know the depth of water, and number of fathoms, when approaching the coast, or amidst shoals, and in every situation of danger. Will Mr. Bowles persuade us, contrary to ocular conviction, that great quantities of pebble are not daily thrown up upon the beach by the waves, and choak up the mouth of harbours, while others are brought down by rivers with similar inconvenience?

LETTER

LETTER XXI.

Describing the hot wells at Caldas in Catalonia, and those of Caldelas, near the city of Mataro.

AS I had not an opportunity of visiting the hot wells and baths of *Caldas* in Catalonia I was favoured with the following account of their situation and present state, by my worthy friend William Gregory, Esq; his majesty's consul at Barcelona.

" There are several hot wells in the neighbourhood of Barcelona, but the principal spring is at Caldas de Monbuy, about five leagues North of Barcelona. The town takes its name from the waters, but at present is much decayed and dwindled into a very inconsiderable place, with a few priviledges to support its rank as a town, though it was once the capital of a district inhabited by a people known in the earliest periods of the annals of Catalonia, under the denomination of *Aquicaldenses*, of whom frequent mention is made during the contest between Rome and Carthage for the dominion of that part of Spain, sometimes taking part with one side, sometimes with the other. The greatest part of a flight antient

antient wall remains, as alfo its four gates, which are ftill kept in repair; but the caftle of the lord of the manor, though of a late date in comparifon with the reft, feems to have been abandoned for fome years, and is in a moft ruinous condition. Caldas is fituated in a very romantic part of the country, which rifes into abrupt hills all round, and in a manner encircle it. Thefe hills, or rather mountains, are for the moft part covered with olive groves, which yield a confiderable quantity of oil, for the extraction of which the hot water that flows fo plentifully in the town is of infinite ufe. As this place is at prefent in no wife recommendable, either for its elegance or accommodations, you may well imagine that the baths are not much frequented with a view of diffipation or pleafure, but numberlefs are the votaries of health that vifit it from all parts of the country in fpring and autumn, and they are accommodated in the beft manner that a Spanifh country town can afford. Some of the apothecaries, and many of the private houfes at Caldas have neat baths for thofe that choofe to hire them ; and there is an hofpital where the poor are admitted gratis. Various are the virtues that this water is faid to poffefs, and many the cures that it daily performs, in fcorbutic, fcrophulous, as well as rheumatic complaints, ftiffnefs in the joints proceeding from old wounds, &c. I cannot however pretend to defcribe to you any of its particular qualities, fuch as what mineral it is chiefly impregnated with,

with, or the cause of its extraordinary heat, or any part of its analysis, having had but little time during my residence in that country for the investigation of things of that sort, and I never found any of the inhabitants that could give me any satisfactory account about the matter; all that I know of from my own observation, is that it rises much hotter that either the spring near Aix la Chapelle, or those of Bath or Bristol; it is boiling hot, and the people of the town come constantly there to boil their eggs, cabbage, and all sorts of vegetables, by simply suspending them under the spout of the fountain in a basket, and yet make use of no other water, when sufficiently cooled, for drinking either alone, mixed with wine, or cooled with snow in orgeats, sherbets, &c. Some years ago there was a short treatise written on the qualities of these waters, by some well-disposed and intelligent person; a few detached sheets of this work once fell into my hands, when I was at Caldas, but the whole edition has now some how or other disappeared. The general opinion is, and I believe not without foundation, that some invidious persons after the decease of the author, made a point of buying up the work, and have secreted or destroyed every page of it, except here and there a few copies that fell into the hands of ignorant people who tore them to pieces without consideration.

Another

Another hot spring flows in the village of *Caldetas*, which likewise takes its name from the waters, like the former, though expressive of a less degree of heat in the water, as well as the inferiority of the place in respect to the other. This village is about two miles from the city of Mataro, near the sea side, and is also frequented by persons afflicted with the above-mentioned complaints in a slight degree, for the water being only tepid, it has not the efficacy of the hot water at *Caldas*. Those of Caldetas are also taken as a purgative, and are not fit for any culinary purpose. You will easily conceive that those watering places differ widely from what are so called in other countries, being solely frequented by the infirm out of *pura necesidad*, and are therefore indifferently supported; was the beneficial improvement of England to take place, it would in a short time extend the reputation of these salutary waters, and make them rival, if not out-do Spa, Aix la Chapelle, Bareges, and most of the noted places on the continent, over all which the famous baths of Caldas have such an undoubted superiority in point of climate and situation.

LETTER

LETTER XXII.

Remains of ancient volcanos in Spain.

IT is not my intention to advance or add any new hypothetical theories to the many that of late years have been offered relative to the grand subject of volcanos, and how far in conjunction with earthquakes they have been the powerful causes of the great inequalities and shattered condition of the surface of the earth. Varieties of specimens of rock, stones, and earths, bearing evident marks of a former fusion or calcination, have been collected, though found in places where no volcanos at present exist, yet leaving no doubt of their having formerly existed, and that ages have elapsed since their extinction: this subject of late years has more particularly engaged the attention of curious travellers, and ingenious writers of different nations. Sir William Hamilton, his majesty's envoy at the court of Naples, has not only given a more perfect account of the eruptions of Vesuvius, but has considerably enlarged the field, and brought to light new and important discoveries, with respect to the volcanic eruptions of Italy. Those of France and different parts of Germany have been likewise laid before the public, but those of Spain remain still unobserved,

observed, and Mr. Bowles appears undoubtedly to be the first who has discovered any remains of volcanos in that kingdom, which is the more remarkable, in a country where they have so many individuals that must have seen those famous ones of Pinchina, Cotopaxi and Chimboraso in Peru, the most extraordinary and amazing volcanos in the world; with respect therefore to the Spanish volcanos, I shall confine myself to such facts regarding their appearance as are stated by Mr. Bowles, and for the consequences to be drawn from them, must refer to what has been already said on this subject, and to the great book of nature that lies open before us. " I have seen, says Mr. Bowles, many mountains in Spain with evident signs of volcanic conflagrations, no account of which is handed down by record, or even any tradition remaining: between Almagro and Corral in La Mancha, near the river Javalon, on the road to Almaden, pieces of rock may be seen with evident marks of fire, and many stones rather weighty may be seen lying in the fields of a sooty colour inwardly and outwardly, with all the appearance of having once been in a state of fusion.

There is a great mountain near the sea, between Carthagena and Murcia, where there has been a volcano, the aperture of which still remains, and is looked upon by the country people as an inchanted cave; there are five similar ones in the territory of Murcia, there is one near Carthagena, with visible remains of an alum mine, having

having this additional circumstance for the more readily finding it, that there are four springs of hot water near it. The red earth, of Almazarron used in the glass-house at St. Ildefonso, as well as the other species of red earth in various parts of Spain, employed for different purposes, are undoubtedly produced by volcanos. At the entrance of Cape de Gat there is a mountain towards the sea, on the side next Almeria, consisting chiefly, in one part, of stone larger than ones arm, cryſtalized in equal layers, delicately fixed to a certain height, of a cinereous colour, as iron was wanting to give them another hue in the fusion, for their shape evinces the effect of having cooled by degrees, according to the laws of cryſtalization; it is true nevertheless, that there are ores of a pale colour, with cryſtalized bodies of a perfect white, which are of the class of vitrescents; I have not seen them, but Mr. Godin informed me, that he had observed such not well cryſtalized, in the high and stupendous mountain near Quito, covered constantly with snow and its bowels in combustion, the result of a horrible volcano. In Catalonia, between Gerona and Figueras, near the sea, there are two pyramidical mountains of equal height, whose bases touch, having every appearance of a former volcano; and though at their bases impressions of shells are frequently seen, they are of a later date than the volcano; when these petrefactions are found near volcanos they are proofs of their antiquity.

These

These revolutions in our globe are no where more plainly seen than in the mountain of Montferrat. The small touchstones seen there, in a mountain of a calcareous nature and amidst those elevated and conglutinated pyramids, being of a black colour and of the same grain as the others found in Catalonia, are all from the effects of fire, and have the same ferrugineous nature, as the high columns of the extraordinary mountain of Usson in Auvergne. These pillars of basaltes were probably in a state of fusion with the iron, when they mixed with it, and their irregular shape proceeds from having cooled by degrees, like the white basaltes, if I may be permitted the expression, of Cape de Gat. The small round grains, blue and green, found in the fields near the mountain of Usson have been iron. I have seen some that were metal within, and were formerly like iron shot. Their shape may be explained from the practice observed in iron forges, when the workmen throw a ladle full of fused metal on the ground, which runs into a globular shape, and is purchased by sportsmen instead of shot.

The globular iron ore is therefore the product of volcanos as those certainly are near to Ronda and Befort in France, both are, as well as those of Germany, with a superficial coat, and give a very soft iron. Touchstones might be made of the pillars of Usson, as the Germans do with the basaltes in different parts of Hesse and Saxony,

Saxony, whose forms are more irregular than the pillars of Usson. The Giant's causeway and other places in Ireland have innumerable pillars of irregular basaltes, similar in colour and form to those of Usson, which serve also for touch-stones; the black soft slaty stones, found in the Pyrenees of Catalonia, and commonly called *lapis*, are likewise the result of volcanos long since extinguished.

I think I perceived the remains of a volcano on the mountain of *Serrantes*, near Bilbao, adjacent to the sea at the entrance of the river of Bilbao; its figure is like a sugar-loaf, and it has been mistaken for the mine of Somorrostro, which is a low uneven hill, at some distance from this pyramid. Pliny fell into this error, perhaps from not having seen it, or from the reports of some mariners who traded in Andalusia, where Pliny was writing his history.

I never perhaps should have known that the quartz of many mountains of Spain had been calcined, if previously, at Gingenbach, in the Black Forest in Germany, I had not seen them calcine the *Kieſſelſtein* to soften and mix it with cobalt, and make zaffre; this *Kieſſelſtein* is a true white quartz of the antient volcanos of Spain, but to know and understand these matters clearly definitions are not sufficient, they must be seen."

LETTER

LETTER XXIII.

Return to Valencia and Castile. Mine of sal gem at Mingranilla. Source of the river Guadiana. Mine of antimony near Santa Cruz de Mudela in La Mancha.

IN going from Barcelona towards Valencia you cross a fine bridge, lately built, over the Lobregat, at Molino del Rei (*a*); further on, another bridge over a deep valley has been attempted with a triple row of arches at an immense expence, the foundation has given way, and a long time must pass before it is compleated. The new road was finished in 1778, as far as Villa Franca de Panades. The country is hilly and affords a variety of rural prospects. The antient city of Tarragona stands near the sea, on an eminence that commands a fine prospect over a beautiful vale. The city exhibits several remains of Roman antiquities and inscriptions. The learned Don Antonio Augustin archbishop of Tarragona is buried in the cathedral (*b*); proceeding from Tarragona the next

---

(*a*) In the second volume of the Spanish translation of Muller's fortifications, there are views of the bridges of Molins, Martorel, Acantara, Almaraz, and Aranjuez.

(*b*) Don Antonio Augustin, archbishop of Tarragona, born in 1516, son of Don Antonio Augustin, vice-chancellor of the kingdom of Aragon, was famous for his writings on canon and civil law and antiquity. All the great men of his age were unanimous in their

town

town is Reus, a commercial place, which of late years has greatly increased in buildings and population. Here the merchants of Barcelona have their factors and warehouses, and ship off their wines and brandies as the ships come to an anchor in the road of Salo, about three miles from Reus. Catalonia furnishes annually thirty-five thousand pipes of brandy, which require a hundred and forty thousand pipes of wine to make them, besides which near two thousand pipes of wine are also annually exported: and of fruit about thirty thousand bags of hazle nuts every year chiefly for England, and worth about twenty shillings a bag on the spot.

It is a few hours excursion across the country to the northward, through Monblanc to the royal convent of Poblet, founded by Alfonso first king of Aragon, in the twelfth century, for monks of the Cistercian order; the abbot is a temporal baron and has an extensive jurisdic-

praises of his learning and virtues. He came over to England with Cardinal Pole, and assisted in such regulations as were then drawn up for the purpose of ecclesiastical discipline. Of all his works, none were more eagerly sought after than his dialogues on antient medals and inscriptions, "Dialogos de medallas inscriciones y otras antiguedades ex bibliotheca Arr. Augustini archiepiscopi Tarracon, en Tarragona, por Felipe May, 1587, 4to. This edition is so scarce, that Padre Feijoo relates in his *Theatro critico*, that an English gentleman travelling through Spain offered thirty pistoles to any one who would bring him a copy, which being complied with, he offered thirty pistoles more for another. I saw this edition in the library of Don Gregorio Mayans at Valencia; there are only plates to the two first dialogues; it has been translated into Latin and Italian; a new edition of it was printed at Madrid in 1744, in the same form as the Tarragona edition, and may be had for about five shillings. The life of this archbishop has been written by the learned Don Gregorio Mayans.

tion,

tion, with a confiderable revenue. Several of the kings and queens of Aragon are buried in the church with ſtately monuments, as well as ſome of the dukes of Medina, celi, and Cardona: on viewing theſe tombs the emotions are only to be felt by an Engliſhman, that occur when he perceives in an obſcure corner, on an humble ſtone, the name of an Engliſh Peer, Philip duke of Wharton an unhappy nobleman; at the pinnacle of glory in the dawn of life, but alas! whoſe evening was clouded with miſery and ſcorn. After leaving his native country, he meanly crouched to the pretender, aſſumed the inſignia of the order of the garter, bore arms againſt his country: abandoned and deſpiſed by all, he was kindly received in the laſt moments of his wretchedneſs, and was interred by the hoſpitable abbot of Poblet. Thus ended Wharton, an exile and an outcaſt, ſhewing how little availed the higheſt dignities, fortune and talents, without virtue and love for his country. His line is extinct, and the faint inſcription on his tomb, at preſent nearly effaced, will ſoon be totally obliterated, while the energetic lines of Pope, ſo deſcriptive of his character, will hand down his failings as an example to poſterity (*a*).

(*a*) The inſcription on his tomb in the church of Poblet is as follows, and ſaid to be of the duke's compoſition.

Hic jacet Exs. Dom Philipus Warton, Anglus, Dux, Marchio et Comes de Warton, Marchio Malbuiſiæ et Carloſh Comes Rathcaſrem, vicecomes de Wincheſter Baro de Tramlon Eques S^{ti} Georgii alias de la Geratera, obiit in fide Eccleſiæ Catholicæ Romanæ Povuleti, die 31. *Maii,* 1731.

It

It is a tedious journey from Reus to Tortofa, on the banks of the Ebro, where there is a bridge of boats that is croffed in paffing to Valencia. I fhall now refume the itinerary in going from Valencia towards Caftile; the ground continues to rife gradually as far as the chain of hills that divide that kingdom from La Mancha, with a very fteep afcent at the *Puerto de Bunol*. Near Utiel the country is covered with dwarf furze called *Erizo* by the Spaniards, from its fimilitude to the prickles of a hedge-hog: it is a beautiful plant, and at the proper feafon of the year is covered with blue flowers, which give it the appearance of a prodigious amethyft, forming a cup of three feet diameter, fo clofe and firm withal, that a man might ftand upon it. Clufius was the firft who defcribed and gave a plate of it. It is the *Anthyllis erinacea* of Linnæus.

The afcent ftill continues to Villagorda, through a rugged country, broke up every where by gullies occafioned by torrents that gufh from the mountains. On the higheft of them there is a quarry of grey marble, veined with red; the river Cabral runs at its foot. At its fummit there is a briny fpring, where they make falt with a boiling heat. It is a conftant defcent from thefe hills to the village of Mingranilla: half a league from the village, there is a diftrict of limy foil, with fome hillocks about half a league in circumference, having below this bed of lime, a solid mine of sal gem, equal to the superincumbent stratum; its depth is not known, for when the excavations exceed three hundred feet, it becomes very expensive to extract the salt; the mine frequently gives way and fills with water, which obliges them to abandon the shaft and work another near it, the whole country being an enormous body of salt, sometimes mixed with a limy substance, and at others pure or reddish, mostly crystaline. Those who have seen no other mine might be inclined to think that the limestone forms the fossil salt of Spain, but this will not be the case, if it is found to be free from lime at Cardona, yet crystaline enough to be carved into figures, being much harder than that of Mingranilla, which is brittle like spar (*a*).

The ground has been perceptibly carried away by torrents that have discovered the mine, for pebbles and hyacinths are dispersed in the gullies which are now seen firmly conglutinated in the lime, forming hard rock, yet leaving no doubt of their having fallen, at some pe-

---

(*a*) Mr. Bowles says, that as the fossil salt of Mingranilla has less watery particles in its crystallization, it therefore attracts little of the moisture of the air, and does not dissolve in a humid atmosphere like that of springs, but this cause is hardly admissible: salt that is crystalized with a boiling heat undergoes more or less of a decomposition, is therefore less perfect and more disposed to diliquesce, than that which is formed in circumstances more favourable to its crystallization.

riod, from the hills, by what may be obferved on their
fummit.

From hence an eafy defcent for about four hours, leads
into the extenfive plains of La Mancha, thofe regions of
fancy which Cervantes has rendered immortal. They
have plentiful crops of faffron at San Clemente, and the
beft that grows in La Mancha. The onion remains four
or five years in the ground, producing annually flowers;
then the roots are taken up and tranfplanted, and the
foil becomes excellent for corn, but twenty years muft
pafs before any faffron is cultivated again. Caftile alfo
abounds with the deadly carrot, the *Thapfia villofa* of Linnæus, which according to Clufius is in great requeft
amongft old women at Salamanca (*a*).

La Mancha produces great quantities of lavender
cotton, faid to be the fame with the famous *moxa* from
China, imported conftantly by the Englifh and Dutch;
while the Spaniards, if this is the fame plant, have it at
home and know nothing of the matter (*b*).

(*a*) Its ufes may be feen in Dr. James's Englifh difpenfatory.

(*b*) The *fantolina chamæcyparissus* of Linnæus. Mr. Bowles fays it is an excellent fpecific
for the gout, by being burned, on the part. It would have been of fervice if he had given
us any further proof of its efficacy, for whatever they may tell us of the practice in India,
and notwithftanding the praifes of Sir William Temple, it does not feem to be in ufe in
England.

The greatest part of La Mancha may be considered as one continued plain, as far as the eye can extend without a single tree; as the villages are large, and the churches have lofty steeples, they make a good figure at a distance, but when you draw near, their mud walls with many houses in ruins convey a quite different idea. The inhabitants, for want of wood, burn thyme, southernwood and wormwood, and though they have few springs they console themselves with drinking good wine: when one considers their manner of living in these silent villages, added to their natural simplicity, they seem to have lost little of their original character. At Socuellanos they get water about two or three feet from the surface; but at Tomilloso, four leagues further, the wells are a hundred feet deep. From hence it is an hour's journey to Lugar-nuevo on the banks of the famous Guadiana, and only three leagues from its source; there are many lakes hereabouts which communicate with each other, produced by springs whose waters form a river, which having run for some leagues disappears in the meadows near Alcazar de San Juan. In summer this river is trifling, but in winter it is necessary to go over the bridge at Villarta. The river disappearing there, shews itself again a few leagues off, in other lakes called *Ojos de Guadiana*, " The eyes of Guadiana;" from whence the proverbial

verbial expression of a bridge where many herds of cattle are constantly grazing. To form an idea of such a phenomenon, we must suppose that all the ground in those parts consists of some loose substance, replete with fissures and crevices, to a considerable depth, without any solid materials to resist the pressure of the water, by which means the river has less water at Lugar-nuevo than within a league of its source: after great rains it sinks so much the deeper, and fills all the cellars of the village without any visible cavity, or passage where it might penetrate. On this spot called *The Bridge* they have sunk wells for travellers and cattle, and always find water. When the Guadiana issues out of the lakes, it turns several mills, is a hundred feet broad and about four in depth. It passes afterwards by Calatrava, Ciudad Real, Medellin, Merida, Badajoz, and Ayamonte, where it enters the ocean dividing Spain and Portugal. Its singular qualities are alluded to in the following epigram of Don Juan de Yriarte, whose poems were lately published at Madrid.

Ales et amnis Anas sociant cum nomine mores :
Mergitur ales aquâ, mergitur amnis humo.

Before.

Before I quit the territory of La Mancha, whofe fame will never perifh as long as wit and humour remain, I muft once more inveftigate the bowels of the earth, and fpeak of a mine of antimony near Santa Cruz de Mudela, at the foot of the *Sierra Morena*, which fince 1774 has been fuccefsfully worked by Don Antonio Sancha, an eminent printer at Madrid, who after having been at a confiderable expence, now gets lumps of regulus of antimony of an enormous fize, one weighing a hundred and fifty *arrobas*, and many of twenty or thirty, the fmalleft of four or five, for which he has a confiderable demand: he has eftablifhed a manufacture of *regulus* of antimony, and has wrought up above fix hundred *arrobas*, fo white and cryftaline, as to look like filver, being fuperior to that of France and Hungary; it is a valuable article in different manufactures, particularly amongft printers for making types, and is in great requeft at Madrid, where the art of printing is now brought to a remarkable perfection: they are provided with good letter founders and no foreign types were made ufe of in the elegant edition of Salluft, tranflated by the Infant Don Gabriel, his catholic majefty's brother.

Senfible as I am that much more remains to be faid, yet I now clofe my labours, though not a thoufandth part has been mentioned of what the fubject affords: moreover

moreover the kingdoms of Leon, Navarre, Galicia, and the principality of Asturias, remain yet to be treated of, which perhaps may be brought forward hereafter, at a more favourable opportunity.

THE END.

APPENDIX.

PART I.

LETTER I.

WHEN Spaniards speak of a *peso* only, they mean 15 reals vellon, or a current dollar, an imaginary coin, and not the *peso fuerte*, or *duro* of 20 reals vellon, an effective coin both in gold and silver. This distinction however holds good, merely in Spain, for in America they know only the *peso fuerte*. The dobloon, or pistole, is also an imaginary coin of 60 reals vellon, or three hard dollars, but the *doblon de oro* is a gold piece, worth 75 reals vellon. In currency you find as much American coined money as Spanish, particularly silver and old gold. In Spanish America they have no copper money. Gold and silver is coined at Madrid and Seville, copper at Segovia. The new coinage consists of

GOLD.	Reals vellon.
A Gold piece of four pistoles worth	300
The half, or double *doblon*	150
The *doblon de oro*	75
The gold crown	20

SILVER.	
Madrid silver crown, or *peso duro*	20
The half	10
Peseta	4
Real de plata	2
Realito or *real de vellon*	1

COPPER.
Piece of — Two *quartos*
One *quarto*
One *ochavo*
One *maravedi*, the least coin in Spain.

N. B. A *real de vellon* is worth 8 *quartos* 2 *maravedis*, or 17 *ochavos*.

According to the old coinage, the par of exchange between England and Spain was settled at 40 pence sterling for a Spanish current dollar of 15 reals vellon, and this varies in proportion with the balance of trade between the two kingdoms. According to the new coinage, the par may perhaps be less. In speaking of the hard dollar in the course of this work, I have followed the example of Dr. Robertson, and fixed it at 4s. 6d. sterling, which will answer every purpose of an historical enquiry.

LETTER V.

Since my return to England, an ingenious correspondent in Spain has favoured me with the following observations relating to the salt given to the *Merino* sheep. "I cannot think Mr. Bowles's account of the quantity of salt given to the sheep exact, for I have two or three times met these flocks of *Merinos*, and always asked the question: sometimes the answer was *Conforme* (a Spanish mode of speech when a direct answer is not ready) but that meant only with respect to weather and the kind of soil the sheep happened to be feeding in. I never found the quantity of salt any thing like what Bowles says; I understand that in the northern parts of Spain they give salt in small quantities to their oxen, and sometimes to their horses."

LETTER VI.

The quantity of land necessary to sow a *fanega* is called a *fanegada*. The fanega measure, besides corn, is further used for chesnuts, beans, acorns, various kinds of seeds, fruit, and salt. Half a *fanega* is called an *almud* in many parts of Castile. 12 *celemines* make one *fanega*, four *fanegas* one *cahu*. A *fanega* of good wheat weighs from 90 to 100 lb. A Spanish lease cannot exceed 9¼ years.

LETTER VII.

It is a difficult matter to ascertain the exact population of Madrid; for its size it is populous, perhaps may contain about 150,000 souls, something more or less.

The longitude of Madrid, according to Don Thomas Lopez, geographer to the king, is found by the most accurate modern observations to be 13°. 49'. 30". reckoning

koning from the island of Ferro, or 12°. 47'. 30". from the peak of Teneriffe, from whence Spanish navigators reckon their longitude. The Spanish astronomers who followed the Alfonsine tables, drew their first meridian at Toledo. Don Thomas Lopez justly censures L'Abbé Vallemont, a French writer, for saying in his *Elements de l'histoire*, that the Spaniards drew their first meridian at Toledo, because Adam was the first king of Spain, and that God placed the sun over Toledo at the creation; when in fact they only imitated the example of other nations, in drawing their meridian from the place where the first observations were made, as Ptolomy did at Alexandria, and amongst the moderns, the English at the observatory at Greenwich, and the French academy at their observatory near Paris.

When Mr. Bowles says, Madrid is supplied with provisions at all hours, *a todas horas*, it seems rather an exaggeration: early in the morning, it is. Madrid is well lighted, but the lamps are not lighted on moon light nights. With respect to the invention of Joseph Lucatelli, mentioned in the philosophical transactions, his machine is called a *sembrador*, or seed box, and at once ploughs, sows, and harrows, whereby the sower's labour is saved, and the grain falls in order, and in the bottom of the furrow, and remains at the same distance under ground. There is a plate of it in Mr. Duhamel de Monceau's treatise on husbandry, but as it is liable to many exceptions, particularly in stoney countries, and that other improvements have since been made of more general utility, it is deemed needless to enlarge any further concerning it, as a full description of it is given in the work above-mentioned. See " Practical treatise of husbandry, by Mr. Duhamel de Monceau, translated by John Mills, 1759."

Three or four years ago there was a *zebulo*, or *cibolo*, alive at Aranjuez. In the gardens there are two basons of water, in one of which a small elephant has water falling out of his trunk, in the other bason there is a figure of the *zebulo*.

The following description of the Crested Falcon may be added to what has been already said of that bird. " Falco Cristatus.—Corpus magnitudine gallo-pavonis, caput crista verticali ornatum, temporum genarumque pennis erectis cinereis, rostrum aduncum, cera nigra, mandibula inferiore rectiuscula, dorsum, alæ, gulaque nigræ, abdomen album, cauda fasciis quatuor cinereis transversis : ob animalis ferociam rectrices numerare non licuit. Habitat in *Carracas*. Nulla hujus novæ speciei mentio facta est a Cl. Linnæo."

APPENDIX.

LETTER VIII.

The expedition againſt the wild cats at Cuerva, about fourteen leagues from Aranjuez, beyond Toledo, is uſually made when the court is at Aranjuez, at a very great expence, perhaps little ſhort of £1000. a cat, as the Rev. Mr. Clarke has related. They are a large mountain cat, not very fierce, and do little more harm than deſtroying ſome game.

A few camels breed at Aranjuez, and many buffaloes, the camels carry burthens, and the buffaloes draw in the carts. The king has a ſtable for his ſtallions called *Caſa de Monte*. The famous jack aſſes called *Burros padres*, are kept at Villa Mayor, about three leagues from Aranjuez, on the road to Toledo.

There are 21 *depoſitos*, or magazines for corn, at Aranjuez; theſe are inverted cones under ground, the earth only cleared out, which will hold 1000 or 1500 *fanegas* each, and preſerve corn dry for ſeveral years.

Amongſt the many fine trees in the gardens of Aranjuez, the lote or nettle tree, the *Celtis* of Linnæus, is one of the moſt beautiful, and is a large tree which has a moſt pleaſing effect.

LETTER X.

St. Ildefonſo gardens, are ſaid to have coſt between ſeven and eight millions ſterling, a great deal of which was expended by the late king Ferdinand the 6th, to perfect the improvements of his royal father.

Amongſt the pictures of St. Ildefonſo, are two Claude's, the drawings of which are in the Duke of Devonſhire's collection, and have been lately publiſhed by Boydel.

Ice to be found in hot weather in moſt parts of Spain, very cheap at St. Ildefonſo, for a farthing a pound. Water ſellers are very numerous every where, always Frenchmen, from Bearne, and Gaſcony, who drive aſſes about with barrels of water, the pooreſt Spaniard thinking it beneath him to follow ſo mean a livelihood; but if water is wanted in a glaſs for immediate refreſhment here, the Spaniard ſtretches out his hand, and helps you, and preſents a few carraways to give it a reliſh.

APPENDIX.

relish. Others sell barley water, and likewise a nasty sweet composition called *aropé*.

The method of cooling water, and preserving it in cellars or caves, was first introduced into Spain at Valencia, by Don Lewis Castelvi, a gentleman of the household of the emperor Charles Vth; on this account the people of Valencia gave him the name of Don Lewis de la Nieve. In the reign of Philip IIId, Pablo Jarquies first invented a mode of laying a tax upon preserved snow.

The storks leave St. Ildefonso about the 12th, or generally before the middle of August, and they come to Madrid about the beginning of February. There are many of them at the escurial, not above one or two nests at Madrid. The swallows begin to assemble for their departure by the middle of September.

The new altar of fine marbles in the cathedral of Segovia was a present from Charles the IIId, and cost about £8000. sterling.

LETTER XI.

The *Garvanzo* from Old Castile, is a large yellow pea, but not a delicate pea, and never used green; is always boiled, and makes part of the *puchero* or *olla*, the favourite dish which all Spaniards dine upon. This dish is called *olla podrida*, when it consists of beef, mutton, fowl, ham, pig's feet, garlic, onions, &c. so called as every thing is boiled down for a long time; though Andreas Bacio, a Roman physician, in his book de *Natura vinorum*, says that *podrida* is the same as *poderida subftantial*. Such might perhaps have been that *olla* of Vitellius, mentioned in Suetonius, and named *Clypeus Minerva*. See Covarrubias *Tesoro de la lengua Castellana*.

The *Berengena* is an esculent fruit, greatly cultivated in Castile, and is also a favourite part of the Spanish *olla*. They are so fond of it at Toledo, that the people there are called *Berengeneros*. This plant produces a fleshy fruit, about the size of a swan's egg, of a dark purple on one side and white on the other. That sort which is white is sometimes called the egg plant. It is the *solanum melongena* of Linnæus; in English, the mad apple. It is said to have several bad qualities, and that they

shew

shew themselves in the face by giving it a livid and dark green colour. It is humourously introduced in Don Quixote, speaking of *Thomas Cecial*'s nose, which besides being full of warts, was also *de color amoratado como de berengena*. It grows naturally in Asia, Africa, and America and is commonly eaten by the inhabitants, and was probably introduced into Spain by the Saracens, according to its Arabic name.

LETTER XVI.

The peaches called *pavies* are of the sort named *amygdalus persica* by Linnæus, but for a more particular account of them see Duhamel on fruit trees.

All fruits grafted though upon their own stocks of the same kind of fruit improve, as is evident in the grafted chesnuts of Spain. The Spanish *castano* is the *fagus castanea* of Linnæus, they graft upon that species of the family of chesnuts which Linnæus calls *fagus castanea sativa*.

LETTER XVII.

In the lordship of Biscay no troops are raised in time of peace; in war, every inhabitant without distinction is a soldier, so that the custom of *Quintas*, every fifth man, as in other parts of Spain is not in use. They have public armouries in the three provinces of Biscay, and the arms are delivered out to the men who are exercised by experienced officers. They have moreover erected twenty batteries on the coast at their own expence, and raised the regiment of Cantabria. According to the laws or *Fueros de Biscaya Ley 5. tit* 1. the Biscayners are to serve his majesty at their own charge, they also furnish considerable drafts for the navy, and present the king with a free gift, in consequence of which, and their extraordinary courage and fidelity they are freed from taxes, though they pay a patronage to the king as their sovereign lord, besides other royalties and tythes; so that when every thing is considered, the nature of their country requiring the utmost spirit of industry, to cultivate, they contribute a full proportion towards the state as well as their neighbours.

In antient times, when the Cantabrians were taken prisoners and tortured by their enemies, they would sing under the most excruciating pains, and bid defiance to their captors as the savages still do in North America. At present they are a brave and hospitable people, famous in peace and in war, as statesmen and soldiers, never yielding to fatigue, as Silius Italicus has described them;

> Cantaber ante omnes hyemisque æstusque famisque
> Invictus.

Thus they held out 70 years against the Romans in the zenith of their power, and only submitted when Augustus came in person with his victorious legions, to whom the whole world, known at that time, had submitted, as Horace tells the emperor.

> Te Cantaber non ante domabilis,
> Medusque et Indus, te profugus Scythes
> Miratur, o tutela præsens
> Italiæ Dominæque Romæ!   Lib. 4. Od. 14.

According to Brantome, the Spaniards were the first who were armed with muskets, and if we believe that writer, they were considered as the best infantry in Europe. Muskets were first used by the English at the siege of Berwick in 1581.

LETTER XXV.

The following article was inserted in the Madrid gazette of the 15th of January 1779: "Many petrifactions of elephants bones are continually found in the excavations made near the bridge of Toledo at Madrid. Two elephants teeth were lately dug up intire, the one about 33 inches long, and the other about half that length. Large pieces have likewise been discovered which by their size seem to have belonged to six different elephants, of whose teeth there are nine pieces and part of the jaws, as also the teeth of some unknown animal, all which are deposited in the royal cabinet of natural history at Madrid."

PART

APPENDIX.

PART II.

LETTER III.

THE love apples mentioned in this letter, which escaped the rapacious tooth of the locust, were of the second species, as described by Miller, called by the Spaniards *Tomates*, commonly cultivated for soups, and used in many sauces, giving them a very agreeable and pleasing flavour. The *solanum lycopersicum* of Linnæus.

LETTER VIII.

No English built ship of more than 150 tun burthen can go up to Seville. Several English vessels go there every year to load oranges. Some go out fully loaded with English manufactures, others are chartered by the fruit companies in London, and sail in ballast, or take any goods that are ready, without waiting for a cargo. They most commonly come to an anchor at *La Puebla*, a few leagues below Seville, and the fruit is sent down to them in boats; others go no higher than the Red Cliff, and some ships load fruit at San Lucar de Barrameda, at the mouth of the Guadalquivir where there is a dangerous bar, and no ships can enter without a pilot, some ships are loaded with Seville oil for the London market, which sells from £30. to £40. sterling per tun of 236 English gallons. The island of Majorca also furnishes about 7000 pipes of oil annually.

Mr. Guthrie, in his new edition of modern geography for 1780, says, that Seville, next to Madrid, is the largest city in Spain, which is just the reverse; Seville is larger than Madrid, and this last is not a city but only a town, where the royal family principally reside.

In the cathedral of Seville there are said to be ninety painted windows that cost 1000 ducats each (about £125. sterling each) valuing the ducat at eleven reals vellon. The first pearls brought from America were presented to this cathedral, and serve to adorn a complete set of rich vestments.

LETTER

In the snuff manufacture about 12000 people are said to be employed at five reals vellon per day. They import tobacco from England and work it up with their own, colouring it with red earth called *almogre*, as has been already described. Their own tobacco costs them five reals vellon per pound, and is sold in snuff at 32 reals vellon, by which the king is said to clear annually about 600,000 dollars.

Great numbers of bustards frequent the banks of the river of Seville, the Spaniards call them *abutardas*. Pliny says the Spaniards called them *aves tarda*, from whence it is conjectured that the Spanish appellation was their original name, which was given them on account of their slow pace and very heavy flying, being large birds; in Scotland they call them *gustards*.

In the spring, they catch great quantities of a fish near Seville, called *savalo*. The savil, which at that season is reckoned delicate, however the Spaniards think them a moist and cold food, as they have a proverb concerning them, *Si no te quieres casar, come savalo por san juan*; "If you do not choose to marry, eat savil at midsummer."

LETTER IX.

Old writers are obscure in speaking of the river Tinto. Covarrubias, in his *Tesoro*, says, it is also called river *Azeche*, signifying black earth found on its banks, which serves to make ink, and is called *Tierra de Sevilla*; Rodrigo Caro, who wrote the antiquities of Andalusia says, a great deal of *azige* grows on its banks, "*Criase en sus orillas mucho azige*."

LETTER XIII.

Spanish horses have ever been admired for their beauty and agility. The horse we call a Gennet owes that denomination to the Spanish school of horsemanship, where the rider, mounted in the Moorish stile, with short stirrups and a high saddle, is said to ride *a la gineta*. The word *Ginete* is applied to the cavalier and means a horseman. Thus in the captive's tale in Don Quixote, " Apenas uvo dicho esto el Christiano cautivo quando el ginete se arrojo del cavallo y vino a abrasar el mozo." With these swift horses and accoutred *a la gineta*, the Spaniard encounters the bull. See the following books :

Discursos para estar a la gineta con gracia y hermosura por Don Juan Arias de Avila. Madrid, 1590. 8vo.

Libro de exercicios de la gineta por Bernardo de Vargas Machucha. Madrid, 1600. 8vo.

Exercicios de la gineta por Don Gregorio de Tapia. Madrid, 1643.

Manejo Real por Don Manuel Alvarez Oforio y Vega Conde de Grajal. Madrid, 1733.

The great fwiftnefs of the Spanifh horfes perhaps gave rife to their fabulous origin, which was humouroufly alluded to by Mr. Addifon, in one of his papers, in the fpectator, N° 127, vol. 2. where fpeaking of the ladies drefs at that time, he fays, "Were they like Spanifh gennets to impregnate by the wind, they could not have thought on a more proper invention."

LETTER XIV.

Mr. Bowles informs us, that after the moft diligent obfervation in that fingular range of hills of the *Sierra Vermeja*, he could find nothing which feemed to confirm the opinion relating to the faliant and reentrant angles of Bourget, and other modern philofophers, which the Abbate Fortis, in his late travels through Dalmatia feems further to have ingenioufly refuted. "That fyftem, fays he, feems to have found more partizans than it deferved, and feveral of them have gained themfelves no honour by adopting it. It was fufficient indeed to ftay in their chambers, and to theorife at their eafe on good geographical maps, concerning the truth of the propofition, *That the fides of the large vallies, as well as thofe of the fhores of the fea correfpond with one another*, and I, who have taken the trouble to examine many of them, am perfuaded, that *neither the fides of the fea fhores, nor thofe of the large vallies conftantly correfpond with each other*."

Mr. Bowles affures us, in his introduction, page 13, That though England, France and Germany abound with chalk hills, he never obferved the leaft appearance of any fuch in Spain, of that fort defcribed by Cronfted, under the title of *terra calcaria, pura folida friabilis*. Sect. vi.

I could have wifhed to have laid before my readers a more exact account of the fifh on the different coafts of Spain, but this requires a fixed refidence in the fea ports; moreover all communication being at prefent interrupted, it has prevented

APPENDIX.

vented me not only on this occasion, but on some others, from giving more accurate information. Don Bernardo de Ulloa says, they catch a species of fish, on the coast of Galicia, like our cod, which would be as useful as that from the banks of Newfoundland, if any encouragement was given to the fishermen (a). The best scallops are catched on the coast of Galicia near Compostella, insomuch that on account of their luscious taste and other properties, they are said to be in high esteem with the pilgrims of both sexes, who resort to the shrine of Santiago at Compostella. In former times the Tunny fishery was very considerable on the coast of Andalusia, near Conil; but when Don Bernardo de Ulloa, was writing, he complains, that the fisheries that used to bring in a revenue of eighty thousand ducats to the territory of Medina Sidonia was then reduced to eight thousand. The places where they catch the fish, are called *Almadravas*.

Our wine trade with Spain is so considerable, that it has induced me to enumerate the various sorts of wine which that kingdom produces:

Biscay,	Chacoli,	See page 156 of this work.
Castile,	Vino de guindas,	A wine made with cherries.
	Foncarral,	A light red wine, and one of the best drank at Madrid, from the village of that name near Madrid.
	Valdepenas,	A most excellent light red wine, with a very pleasing flavour.
	Ciudad Real,	In La Mancha. The wine from this place praised by honest Sancho Panza, who loved his bottle.
	La Mancha,	The light red wine common in La Mancha, and very good.
	Ribadavia,	An agreeable white wine from the district of Rioja.

(a) Restablecimiento de las fabricas y comercio Espanol por Don Bernardo de Ulloa. Madrid, 1740. This gentleman was father to the present admiral of that name, Don Antonio, de Ulloa, of whom mention is made in page 326 of this work.

Aragon,	Saragoſſa,	A rich red wine, very ſtomachick.
	Cariñena,	Another growth with the ſame quality.
Navarre,	Peralta,	A choice ſtrong white wine.
	Tudela, Tafalla, Falces, Villa Franca, Puente de la Reyna,	Theſe are all choice wines; there are many others of a more indifferent quality.
	Eſtella,	A very indifferent wine, which will not keep.
	Arandillo,	This wine is made with bilberries. It is alſo called *Raſpana*.
Andaluſia,	Xerez,	Our ſherry of the dry ſort.
	Pagarete,	A more choice ſort of ſherry wine, and very ſtomachick. A moſt excellent wine.
	San Lucar,	Good wine, but not ſo delicate as the ſherry, though the vineyards of each diſtrict join, owing to its not being made with ſo much attention as by the people of Xerez.
	Tinto de Rota,	The wine we call Tent, from Rota, near Cadiz, the word *tinto* uſed for red wine, in oppoſition to white, as with us, the word tint implies colour.
	Montilla,	A light white wine, in much eſteem in Seville.

Granada,

APPENDIX.

Granada,	Malaga,	Our mountain.
	Pedro Ximenes,	A richer sort of Malaga wine.
	Malvasia,	Malmsey, a rich wine so called, in imitation of that luscious wine from Malvasia, a city of Peleponesus, in Greece, the antient Epidaurus, from whence this precious wine was first imported. This name is given to different growths of wine from Alicant and the Canaries, called sack in English, from the Spanish word *zaque*, a skin to put wine in.
	Marvella,	A lighter wine than the mountain Malaga; this growth is near the sea in the vallies.
Valencia,	Tinto de Alicante,	Sweet red wine.
	Benicarlo,	Strong thick red wine; much of it goes to Bourdeaux, and is mixed with low priced clarets.
	Villa Nova,	A red wine between the quality of Benicarlo and Mataro.
Catalonia,	Sitges,	A most excellent white wine from the place of that name.
	Garnacha,	A sweet red wine.
	Tinto de las Montanas,	Sweet red wine.
	Vals,	A light sweet wine, which with age becomes dry.
	Mataro,	A coarse red wine from the town of that name, near Barcelona, something like port. It is often sold in London.

LETTER

438   APPENDIX.

LETTER XV.

The culture of Barrilla feems to be of a very old ftanding at Alicant; Mr. James Howel gives a particular account of it in a letter to Chriftopher Jones, Efq; dated from Alicant, 27th March, 1621; wherein he tells him, "I am now (thanks be to God) come to Alicant, the chief rendevouz I aimed at in Spain, for I am to fend hence a commodity called barrilla, to Sir Robert Manfel, for making of cryftal glafs. This barrilla is a ftrange kind of vegetable, and it grows no where upon the furface of the earth, in that perfection as here. The Venetians have it hence, and it is a commodity whereby this maritime town doth partly fubfift, for it is an ingredient that goes to the making of the beft Caftile foap. It grows thus;, it is a round thick earthy fhrub that bears berries like barberries, betwixt blue and green; it lies clofe to the ground, and when it is ripe they dig it up by the roots, and put it together in cocks, where they leave it to dry many days like hay; then they make a pit of a fathom deep in the earth, and with an inftrument like one of our prongs, they take the tuffs and put fire to them, and when the flame comes to the berries, they melt and diffolve into an azure liquor, and fall down into the pit till it be full; then they dam it up, and fome days after they open it and find this barrilla juice turned to a blue ftone, fo hard that it is fearce malleable; it is fold at one hundred crowns a tun, but I had it for lefs. There is alfo a fpurious fort called *gazul*, that grows here, but the glafs that is made of that is not fo refplendent and clear. I have been here now thefe three months, and moft of my food hath been grapes and bread, with other roots which have made me fo fat that I think if you faw me you would hardly know me, fuch nurture this deep fanguine Alicant grape gives."

LETTER XVII.

From what I have faid of Valencia, it may perhaps be thought a picture drawn from imagination, but to fhew I am not the only writer who has founded forth the praife of that country, I fhall add the account given of it by Mr. Howel, in a letter to Dr. Fr. Manfel, dated Valencia, 1ft March, 1620.

"I am now in Valencia, one of the nobleft cities in all Spain, fituated in a large *vega*, or valley above fixty miles compafs. Here are the ftrongeft filks, the fweeteft wines, the excellenteft almonds, the beft oils and beautifulleft females of
                                                                                                                        all

APPENDIX. 439

all Spain, for the prime curtifans in Madrid and elfewhere are had hence. The very brute animals make themfelves beds of rofemary and other fragrant flowers hereabouts; and when one is at fea, if the wind blows from the fhore, he may fmell this foil before he comes in fight of it, many leagues off, by the ftrong odoriferous fcent it cafts. As it is the moft pleafant, fo it is alfo the temperateft clime of all Spain, and they commonly call it the fecond Italy, which made the Moors, whereof many thoufands were difterred and banifhed hence to Barbary, to think that Paradife was in that part of the heavens which hung over this city."

Amongft other gay flowers which adorn our parterres, we are indebted to Spain for the mufk rofe, or *rofa fempervirens*, thus defcribed by Linnæus:

Rofa fempervirens. Germinibus ovatis pedunculifque bifpidis caule petiolifque aculeatis.

Seed buds egg fhaped, covered with ftrong briftly hairs, as are likewife the fruitftalks. Stem and leave ftalks prickly.

The plants of thefe and fome other kinds of rofes were found growing naturally in Spain, by the late ingenious Robert More, Efq; of Lindley in Staffordfhire, who fent the feeds to Mr. Miller, who raifed them in England; the flowers are fingle, white, and have a ftrong mufky odour; they appear in Auguft, and if the autumn proves favourable, will continue in fucceffion till October. Miller's gardener's dict.

The Spanifh arum, is the *arum maculatum* of Linnæus, " Wake Robin, cuckow pint, lords and ladies." It is a fmall plant, common in moft parts of Spain, particularly in Bifcay. The roots and leaves when recent, are extremely acrid. The root has been employed in medicine as a ftimulant, but when reduced to powder it lofes much of its acrimony. The French make ufe of the root dried and powdered to wafh their fkin with, it is fold at a high price, under the name of cyprus powder, and is an innocent cofmetic. When the acrimony of the roots is extracted, either by boiling or baking, they certainly will afford a mild and wholefome nourifhment. Many nations prepare the only bread they have from plants as acrimonious as this, firft diffipating the noxious qualities, by force of heat. Starch may be made from the roots. It grows in England in fhady places,

ditch.

ditch banks and rough grounds. "See Dr. Withering's botanical arrangement, &c." There are eighteen varieties of this plant mentioned by Miller, five of which have mild roots, and are eaten by the inhabitants of the hot countries where they grow naturally; sometimes the leaves are boiled and supply the want of other greens, and are esteemed wholesome food, in places where the common European vegetables are with difficulty found; but these do not include the Spanish sort which Mr. Bowles conjectured might in years of scarcity serve as a succedaneum to bread.

The *Anchusa* mentioned by Mr. Bowles is the lithospermum of Linnæus, with a red root. The alkanet. In Spanish *orcaneta*. The bark of the root tinges wax and oil of a beautiful red. In the northern parts of Europe, girls paint their faces with the juice of the root upon days of festivity. We have it in England. The gromewell. "See the variety of it in Dr. Withering's botanical arrangement."

I am informed that some plants of the *Chirimoya* are now growing in England, raised from seeds brought from Peru. Fruit cannot be expected from them, but should they flower their exquisite odour will make some amends for that deficiency.

LETTER XVIII.

The Spanish poem entitled *Montserrate*, by Christopher de Virues, a poet of Valencia, is praised by Cervantes, in his review of Don Quixote's library, as one of the best in that language, equal to the *Araucana* of Don Alonso de Ercilla, or the *Austriada* of Juan Rufo; to all which the Curate gives the following praises, "These three poems are the best that ever were composed in heroic verse in the Spanish language, and may vie with the most celebrated poems of Italy; let them therefore be carefully preserved as the choicest specimens of poetry that Spain is possessed of." Don Quixote, part I. chap. 6.

LETTER XXIII.

Gassendi, in his life of Pyresc, tells a laughable tale of a shepherd of Tarragona, of whom he gives the following account, "He reasoned moreover, touching the engrafting of animals after the manner of plants, upon occasion of a floe

or

or bullace tree growing out of a man's breast-bone. A shepherd of Tarragona had fallen upon a floe tree, and a sharp point thereof having run into his breast, it took such a root in ten years time, that after many branches had been cut off, there sprung up some at last which bare both flowers and fruit. Now he (Peyresc) would never be at rest till Cardinal Barbarini procured the archbishop of that place to testify the truth of the story, and the Chevalier Dupuy not only received letters testifying the same, but also certain branches thereof which he sent unto him. Whoever shall see such things as these, says Gassendi, may surely believe them! Natural history, in those days, lay yet enveloped in fable; it is to the present age we owe so many discoveries and experiments, which have elucidated and ascertained the different parts of that useful and admirable science. If our neighbours were not enlightened in those days, we also came in for our share of their ignorance. When Sir Robert Dudley and Mr. Thomas Cavendish sailed on an expedition to the West Indies, we are told that as soon as the English went on shore in the night, observing an infinite number of moving lights in the woods, they mistook them for Spaniards coming upon them unawares, with their firelocks and match-lights; on which they fled in haste to their ships, though it turned out to be nothing else but a number of those harmless insects called lanthorn flies. See Hackluyt's voyages, vol. 3.

Travellers have observed, that there are no swans in Spain, and that you may go for many days together and never see a goose: if we reflect on the national abhorrence of the Spaniards to the Jews, and to their manners and customs, it may perhaps afford some new light to this singularity, and account for the want of the latter of these birds, from what Dr. Moffet says of them from Jason Pratensis, "That the Jews have so hard a flesh, so foul a skin, so loathsome a savour, and so crooked conditions, because they eat so many geese." Swans flesh was forbidden the Jews, because by them the hieroglyphical sages did describe hypocrify; for as swans have the whitest feathers and the blackest flesh of all birds, so the heart of hypocrites is contrary to their outward appearance. This latter however, being a prejudice of an innocent nature, might have gained a more general admittance, being merely symbolical.

In a review of the most remarkable parts of the animal kingdom in Spain, we shall find that they possess the noble Andalusian horse, the large ass, the bear, the lynx, the ravenous wolf, the wild cat, the gennet, the fleet greyhound, and the

Kkk staunch

staunch pointers; also the wild boar, whose flesh is so dainty, that Strabo says, The *Carietes* of Spain, were the best makers of sausages and wild meats in the whole world. Rabbets were so numerous, that they gave their name to the whole country. It has been hinted by Arabic writers, that even the zebra belonged originally to Spain (*a*). They seem to have been well known in the days of Cervantes, who frequently alluded to their swiftness. The *Cebrero* cheese has nothing to say to this animal, but takes its name from the village of *Cebrero* where it is made, in the bishopric of Avila, as a corruption of the word *Mons Ciperius*. Perhaps the fine English spaniel came originally from Spain; what shall we say of the young Spanish puppies, a food once much esteemed, if any credit is to be given to that writer, who after praising the moose deer in America adds, "Their flesh is an admirable dish beyond that of an ass's foal, so highly esteemed by the Romans, or *of young Spanish puppies, so much cried up in our days in England and France* (*b*)."

With respect to birds we shall find the golden eagle, the vulture, the stork, the flamengo, the bee eater, the hoopoe, the bustard, the beautiful partridge, the becafigo, the solitary sparrow, and others of less note. As for insects the silk worm affords them immense revenues, the bee yields excellent honey; the insect from whence they get the kermes has been treated of, and the cantharides, or Spanish flies, are well known in our shops. Moschettoes and flies, it is true, are very troublesome in the day-time, particularly in the southern provinces; but to make amends, the nights are reviving, the stars shine with infinite brightness over your head, while numberless glow worms glisten under your feet. If you walk out in the evening the fields appear enamelled with a variety of flowers, and at every step the green lizard escapes from your sight, as Virgil has said,

Nunc virides etiam occultant spineta lacertos.

(*a*) See Casiri's bibliotheca arabica Hispan. Escurialensis. 2 vols. folio, printed at his Catholic Majesty's expence.

(*b*) New England's rarities discovered in birds, beasts, fishes, serpents and plants, by John Joselin, London, 1672. Dr. Moffet likewise says, As for the flesh of young puppies, commended by Hippocrates and afterwards by Galen, however in the Isles of Corsica and Malta they are still esteemed as good meat, yet Cardan confiders them, in his history, as bad meats, which neither use nor reason hath confirmed.

The following List of Vegetables, growing upon Mount Calpe, or Hill of Gibraltar, is given by Way of evincing the Fertility of that Climate.

A.

ACACIA	June	Back of the hill
Adder's tongue	Dec.	----
Alder black	Nov.	front
Ale hoof	Dec.	back
Alexander	Nov.	----
All heal	Dec.	front
All clown heal	----	on the top
Almond tree	----	front
Aloe black	----	----
Amomum, the true,	April	
and common	----	back
Apple	April	town
Archangel, red and white	----	back
Arrach, garden stinking	Dec.	back
Arse-smart, hot and spotted	----	common
Artechoke	Nov.	front
Asarabacca	Dec.	common
Asparagus	----	----
Assa-fœtida	----	back
Avens	----	front

B.

Balm, garden	Dec.	front
Balm of Cappadocia	April	----
Balm Peru	----	----
Barbary bush	Dec.	front
Barianas, garden	----	----
Barley	Dec.	----
Bay tree	----	----
Bay of Alexandria	----	common
Bean, garden	Oct.	front
---- horse	----	----
---- Malacca	----	----
Bears breech	Dec.	back
Bears foot	----	----
Bed, ladies straw	----	common
Beets white and red	Nov.	front
Behen	Dec.	----
Benjamin	Nov.	----
Betony, Paul's	Dec.	----
---- water	----	----
---- wood	----	----
Bindweed, green	All the year	
---- rough	----	common
Birdlime	Dec.	front
Birthwort long	----	----
---- round	----	----
---- wooded running	----	----
Bishops weed	Dec.	----
---- cand-weed	----	----
Bitter sweet	Nov.	front
Blackberry bush and bramble	Dec.	common
Blites bush	----	front

Blue bottle the greater — front
Blue bottle the small Dec. — —
Boxtree, garden — — —
Borage — — — common
Briony, black — — — —
Brook lime — — — front
Broom Spanish — — common
Buckthorn plantain — — —
Buglofs, wild garden — front
— — viper — — — —
Burdock, gr. garden — back of the hill
Burdock, small gar. — — — — —
Butterbur — — — common

C.
Cabbage, garden — Oct. front
Calamint, mountain — common
— — — water — Dec. front
— — — common — garden
Calabashes — — garden
Calthrops — — over the hill
Carduus benedictus — front
Cammock — — back of the hill
— — wild, all the year, common
Camphorata — — Dec. — — —
Campions — — — — — —
Carota — — — — garden
Caffia purgens — Oct. front
Carrots — — Dec. garden
Catmint — — Oct. common
Centaury, the great, Mar. front
— — — small — — — —
Chervil — — Dec. common
Chickweed — — — —
Citron — — — front
Citrul — — — April — —

Clevers — — Dec. common
Clove gilliflower — garden
Clover grafs — — front
Clown's mustard — — —
Coleworts — — — garden
Columbine — — — — —
Comfrey — — — — — —
Cucumber, garden and
  wild cauch grafs — front
Cranebill — — common
— — — musty — — — —
Crefies — — — July garden
— — — water — Dec. front
— — — wild — — common
Crowfoot — — Nov. — —
Cuckow flower — Dec. front
— — — tree — — — —

D.
Daify, great — Dec. common
— — — small — — — —
Dandelion — — — — —
Danewort — — — — — —
Date tree — — — front
Devil's bit — — common
Dill — — — — — —
Dittany, white — — —
— — — Crete — — —
Dock, common — — —
— — — sharp — — — —
Dodder and thyme — — —
Dog's grafs — — — — —
— — rofe — — — — —
Dropwort — — — — —
Ducks meat — — front

Elder

GIBRALTAR PLANTS.

E.
Elder - - - Feb. common
Elder, dwarf - - Dec. - - - - -
Endive - - - - ——— garden
Eye bright - - March front

F.
Fennel - - - Dec. common
——— flower - ——— gardens
- - - - hogs - - ——— common
- - - - giant - - ——— - - - - -
Feverfew - - - ——— - - - - -
Fig tree - - - Feb. - - - - -
- - - water - - - ——— - - - - -
- - - wort, common ———
Fetch - - - - Dec. - - - - -
Flagsweet - - - July - - - - -
Flax toad - - - Dec. - - - - -
Flax, mountain - ——— - - - - -
Flower de luce - - ——— garden
Foolstones - - - March, front
French lavender - ——— - - - -
Fumetory ——— - ——— - - - -

G.
Garlick - - - - Dec. front
Garvanzas - - ——— garden
Gentian - - - - ——— front
Gilliflower, stock ——— garden
Gladwyn - - - March, front
Goats rue - - - Dec. common
Ground pine - - ——— - - - - -
Groundsel - - ——— - - - - -
Gum Arabic - - ——— - - - - -

H.
Hare's foot - - Dec. common
Hart's tongue - - ——— - - - - -
Hartswort - - ——— - - - - -
Hartsthorn - - - ——— - - - - -
Hedge mustard - ——— front
Hellebore, black - ——— common
- - - - - - white - ——— - - - - -
Helmet flower - - ——— back
Henbane - - - - ——— common
Herb Robert - - ——— front
Holly, sea - - ——— - - - -
Holly oak - - ——— garden
Honeysuckle - - ——— common
Horehound - - - ——— back
Horse-tail - - ——— - - - -
- - - - - tongue - - ——— front
Horehound, stinking——— common
Hound's tongue - ——— - - - - -
Houseleek, great - ——— - - - - -
- - - - - - small - ——— - - - - -

I.
Jacinth - - - - Dec. garden
Indian corn - -
Jejube tree
Jerusalem cowslips July front
Jew's ears - - - Dec. common
St. John's wort - ——— front
St. James's——— - ——— - - - -
Jointed grass - - ——— - - - -
Ivy

K.
Kidney wort - - Dec. common
King's spear - - ——— - - - - -
King's broom

GIBRALTAR PLANTS.

King's broom - front
Knot grafs - - Dec. common

L

Lady's bed, yellow Dec. front
- - - - - mantle - - May common
- - - - - smock - - ——— - - - -
Larkspur - - - Dec. - - - - -
- - - - spike - - - ——— - - - -
- - - - cotton - - ——— - - - -
Laurel, spurge - - ——— - - - -
- - - - - Alexandrian ——— - - - -
Leek - - - - ——— - - - -
Lentils, garden
Lemon tree - - July - - - - -
Lettuce - - Dec. - - - - -
Lime tree - - ——— back
Locuſt tree - - ——— common
Looſe ſtripe, yellow May back
Lovage - - Dec. front
Limewort - - ——— - - -
- - - - - spotted - ——— - - -
Lupine - - ——— garden

M.

Maidenhair tree - Dec. front
- - - - - - English ——— common
Mallow, common ——— - - - -
- - - - - marſh - ——— - - - -
- - - - - vervain - ——— - - - -
- - - - - muſk - ——— - - - -
- - - - - garden - front
Mandrake - - ——— - - -
Marjoram, sweet - ——— garden
- - - - - - wild - Jan. common
Marygold - - Dec. garden

Maſterwort - - Dec. front
Maſtick - - - ——— - - -
Maudlin, sweet - ——— - - -
Mary weed - - ——— common
Melon, muſk - - garden
Melon, water - - ——— - - -
Mill mountain - Dec. common
Mint, eat - - ——— - - - -
- - - ſpear - ——— - - - -
- - - water - - ——— - - - -
- - - horſe - - ——— - - - -
- - - pepper - ——— - - - -
Myrtle - - ——— garden
- - - - wild - - ——— back of the hill
Moonwort - - ——— common
Moſs tree, all the year, - - - - -
- - - ſea - Dec. - - - - -
- - - ground - - ——— - - - -
- - - of a dead man's
ſcull - - ——— - - - -
Mother of thyme ——— front
Motherwort - - ——— common
Mouſe ear - - ——— - - - -
Mugwort - - ——— - - - -
Mulberry tree - Feb. garden
Muſtard - - Dec. common
Muſhroom - ſouthward and meadow
- - - - - - wild - - garden

N.

Navelwort - - Dec. front
Nettle - - - ——— - - -
- - - - dead - ——— - - -
Nettle dead ſtinking Dec. front
Nightſhade - - - ——— - - -

Nightſhade

GIBRALTAR PLANTS.

Nightshade deadly —·····
Nightshade woody Dec.··,·.

O.
Olive tree · · July front
Onion· · · · Dec. · · .
Opium · · · ——— · · ·
Orange tree · · July. · · · ·
Ox eye · · · ——— · · ·

P.
Palm tree · · July front
Parsley · · · Dec· · · ·
Piast · · · · · —— back
Parsnep · · · —— garden
Parsnep wild · —— back
Peach tree · · July front
Pease · · · Feb. garden
Pellitory of the wall of Spain, common
Pennyroyal · · Dec. front
Pepperwort · · ——— · · ·
Pimento · · ——— · · ·
Pilewort · · —— common
Pine ground · · —— back
Ploughman's Spikenard Dec. front
Poley mountain Dec. common
Polypodium · ——— · · · ·
Pomegranate · July front
Pomegranate poppey Dec. common
——— wild Dec. common
——— white ——— · · · ·
Primrose · · ——— · · · ·
Purslain · · —— garden

Q.
Quincetree · July front

R.
Raddish · · Dec. front
Ragwort · · —— common
Rocket · · garden
Rose red · · ——— ·
Rose white · · ——— ·
Rose damask · ——— ·
Rue wild · · —— common
Rue goats · ——— · · · ·
Rupture wort ——— · · · ·

S.
Saffron · · · Dec. garden
Saffron bastard ——— · · · ·
Sage of virtue ——— · · · ·
Sage · · · ——— · · · ·
Sage·wood · ——— · · · ·
Samphire · · ——— · · · ·
Sabin · · · ——— · · · ·
Savory · · · —— garden
Sanders · · · —— front
Seagreen houseleek Feb. · · ·
Shepherd's purse Dec. common
Sloe tree · · · ——— · · · ·
Snake weed · · ——— · · · ·
Solomon's seal · —— garden
Sopewort · · —— front
Sorrel · · · —— common
Sorrel wood · ——— · · · ·
Southern wood · —— garden
Sow thistle · · —— common
Spignell · · · ——— · · · ·
Spinage · · · ——— · · · ·
Spikenard · · —— front
Spurge . · · · —— common
Starwort · · · ——— · · ·
  Starthistle

Sarthistle	Feb.	Trefoil	Dec. all over
Swallow-wort	———	Turnep	——— front

T.

Tansey	Dec. common	Vine	Feb. common
Tares	———	Violet	Dec. garden
Thistle blessed	Feb.	Viper grass	——— common
Thyme mother of	———	Vervain	——— front
Thyme	———		
Toad flax	———		**W.**
Tobacco	Dec.	Wall flower	Dec. garden
Tomates	——— garden	Woodbine	——— common
Tormentil	——— front	Woodroof	Apr. ....
Thorn	———	Wormwood roman	——— front

They have extraordinary mallow trees, (the seeds of which they had from Spain) about 2 years old, and are now (1778) 14 feet high. They are always green, and flower in April, May and June, supposed to be unknown in England.

☞ Just as I am closing this work, I find the following article inserted in the foreign newspapers, dated Oviedo, April 11, 1780. The Count de Torena and Father Ignatius Buenaza have been employed upwards of a year, by orders of the council of Castile, in examining several mines of ocre and various coloured alum. They have since discovered an exceeding fine quarry of alabaster, abounding with the most beautiful stones, held by the connoisseurs to be equal in whiteness to those of Mount Taurus. Ours are however larger and more proper for columns and statues. They have also examined a mine of jet, the stones of which much resemble those of Calcite. Great quantities of pit coal are found in the neighbourhood of Coboalles. In the district of Cangas they have discovered a mine of stones resembling agate and alabaster; and in the hamlet of Carrotin they found a crystal which has the brilliancy of a diamond. These expert naturalists have sent specimens of all these stones and minerals to the council.

INDEX

INDEX of CONTENTS.

A.

ACIDS,	Three in nature compared	392
Agreda,	Town in Castile	13
Air of Madrid,	Fables relating thereto.	68
Alava,	Province of	130
Alanis,	Town of	301
Albufera,	De Valencia	371
Alcanis,	Town of	220
Alcora,	Manufacture of delf ware,	219
	Established there by Count Aranda.	377
Alcala,	De Henares, city of, and university founded by cardinal Ximenes.	15
Alcocer,	Iron mine between that place and Orrellana.	296
Alfalfa,	Or medick, plentiful in Valencia.	380
Algaroba,	Or carob tree.	359
Alicant,	City of	—
	Huerta de	—
Almaden,	In la Mancha, its famous quicksilver mine described.	231
Almagre,	Used at St. Ildefonso instead of Tripoli.	355
Almazan,	On the banks of the Duero, singular appearance observed in that district.	13
Almazarron,	Town of, singularities observed there.	355
Almeria,	City of	355
Alum	Mine near Alcanis, described.	220
	Plume	355
Amber,	- - - - - -	365
Amianthus,	Or asbestus	355
Anduxar,	Curious earthen ware made there.	346
Angora,	Goats from, introduced into Spain by Charles IIId.	58
Antimony,	Mine of, near Sta. Cruz de Mudela.	422
Ant bear	From Buenos Ayres, described.	76
Aquafortis,	Its use with silversmiths of Madrid.	395
Aranjuez,	Gardens and palace described	81
Archena,	Baths and waters of	357
Arcos,	City of	351
Arrobe,	Spanish weight.	13
Asphaltos,	Or Jewish bitumen.	12
Artists,	Name of Spanish, famous for making fine blades.	137
Atienza,	Hill of, confines of the two Castiles.	13
Augustin Antonio,	Some account of that prelate.	414
Azure,	Or enamel blue	218

Badajoz,

INDEX OF CONTENTS.

B.

Badajoz,	City of	315
Barcelona,	City of	381
	Cabinet of natural history	—
Barrilla,	Harvest of	356
	Different sorts of that plant	364
Bafcuenfe	Language, spoken in Biscay, some account of	175
Batuecas,	In Estremadura, barren and wretched district of	170
Bilbao,	Town of, and manners of the inhabitants.	178
Biscayners,	Their genius and character	161
Biscay,	Lordship, and its products.	153
Bridge,	A place so called, where the Guadiana disappears.	421
Burgensis Paulus,	A converted Jew, bishop of Burgos, his remarkable elevation.	193
Burgos,	City of	115
Bostamante,	Don Juan de, establishes furnaces with alludels at Almaden.	137

C.

Cabinet,	Royal, of natural history at Madrid some account of	75
Cabral,	River	417
Cadiz,	City of	348
Caldas,	In Catalonia, baths there	405
Calderas,	Baths of	408
Canal,	Of Castile, intended	146
Cardona,	Town of, in Catalonia, singular mountain of fossil salt there	390
Carthagena,	Port and harbour of	356

Cervantes,	Miguel de Saavedra born at Alcala, author of Don Quixote.	16
Chacoli,	Wine in Biscay.	156
Cinnabar,	Native, found in Spain.	336
Clocks,	First in Spain, at Seville.	309
Coals,	Not considered as constantly produced from trees, plants or forests.	18
Cobalt,	Mine of, in the valley of Gistau, in the Pyrenees of Aragon.	211
Colcothar,	Nativa rubra.	355
Columbus,	Sails from Palos	313
Commerce,	American extension of	74
Concud,	Village of, in Aragon.	114
Copper mine	Of la Platilla.	196
	Of Rio Tinto.	310
	Near Plan.	212
Cordova,	City of	343

D.

Diaz,	Rodrigo Diaz de Bibar, called Cid Campeador, some account of him.	112
Dories,	Or St. Peter's fish, why so called.	350
Duenas,	Singular proverb relating to that place.	118

E.

Ebro,	River, source of	140
Emery,	Different sorts of	284
Emigrations,	Of Merino sheep, inconvenience attending thereon	37

Erizo,

INDEX OF CONTENTS.

Erizo,	Or dwarf furze, first described by Clusius.	417
Estepa,	Town of, famous for olives.	342

F.

Falcon,	Crested from the Carraccas, at the Buen Retiro, described.	80
Feria,	Doña Juana de, erects a tomb for her cousin Margaret Harrington, at Zafra.	326
Felipe San,	Description of its situation.	369
Filabres,	Mountain of	336
Flamengo,	Seen on the Albufera de Valencia.	374
Flint,	Used to pave the streets of Madrid.	69
Fossil bones,	Remarkable depository of	114
Fossil salt,	Mountain of, near Cardona, see Cardona.	
	At Mingranilla	418
Fruits,	Variety of, in Valencia.	375
Fuente Garcia,	Salt spring near it	106
Fugger,	Family from Germany, enrich themselves in mines of Spain.	233
Full throat,	Observations on that complaint.	131

G.

Gage, Mr.	Grandson of Sir Thomas, Bart. attends lady Mary Herbert to the silver mines of Guadalcanal.	294
	Obtains a grant of the mine of Cazalla.	296
Gaeta,	In Italy, notion of its rock same as at Montserrat.	389
Gandia,	Huerta de, its delightful situation.	373
Gat,	Cape de, described.	338
Gayuba,	Spanish plant, described.	145
Genoet,	Animal peculiar to Spain.	352
Giants Cause-way,	Basaltes there, compared with that of Montserrat.	383
Giralda,	Moveable figure on a steeple, so called	309
Gold,	Found in the Tagus near Toledo,	110
	In the river Jurdes	275
	In the river Sil	—
Gonsalez, Fernan	Triumphal arch to his memory.	111
Grana Kermes,	Or scarlet grain, natural history of	18
Guadalupe,	Sierra de	236
Guadalcanal,	In Estremadura, its famous silver mine	289
Guadalaviar River,	passes by Valencia; project of deepening its bed.	377
Guadiana,	Its source	410
Guipuscoa,	Province of	150

H.

Haro,	Don Diego Lopez de, Castilian general, gains the battle of Las Navas	310
Harrington,	Margaret, her tomb at Zafra	326
Herbert,	Lady Mary, goes to Madrid, engages to drain the silver mine of Guadalcanal.	295
Herradura,	Port of, gallies of Spain lost there.	533
Herrera,	Town of	312
Huelva,	Town of	313
	Juan Sanchez de, supposed to have first discovered America.	—

L

Jaen,	Petty kingdom of	316
Jasper,	Green, of Granada, its virtues.	310
Jews	Of Cordova, their magnificence.	315
	First banished England by Edward the first.	125
	Permitted to return to England by Oliver Cromwell.	
Ildefonso St.	Royal seat and gardens described.	108
Iron	Mine and forges at Somorostro, in Biscay.	187
	Forges, near Plan.	118
Jet,	Discovered in bituminous wood.	106
Juan,	Don Jorge, his monument.	362
Iviza,	Island of, produces immense quantities of salt.	363

K

Kermes,	See grana kermes	

L

Lapis Lydius,	Or touchstone, found on the mountain of Montferrat	187
LælingPeter,	A Swedish botanist, recommended by Linnæus, goes to Spain and enters into the service of that crown.	107
Lead,	Mine of, at Plan.	112
	——— in the kingdom of Jaen	317
	Vein of, in Sierra Blanca.	107
	Black, mine of	307
Lentiscus,	Leaves of, boiled and scum sold for male incense.	361
Lichen,	- - - -	109
Locusts,	In Estremadura, natural history of	256

Lorca,	Plain of	351
Loza,	Town of	311

M

Macias,	The poet, his tragical end	322
Malaga,	City of, its environs	330
Madrid,	Observations made there.	60
Manna,	- - - -	128
Manriquez,	Lady Maria, remarkable story of her.	321
Marble,	Curious, at Merida.	253
Malachite,		201
Marrorel,	Town of, and antient bridge, lately repaired.	384
Mata,	Lake, where they make salt.	367
Medellin,	In Estremadura, Cortez born at	252
Medina	Sidonia, Town of	351
Merida,	City of, its antiquities	253
Merino sheep,	Method of treating them.	46
Mints,	Spanish, in America, state of them.	118
Mines,	Not always in barren countries.	108
Mingranilla,	Mine of sal gem there	414
Minuart,	Don Juan, professor of botany, relieved by the gayuba plant, when on the mountain of Montferrat.	151
Molibdena,	Or black lead	353
Mondragon,	Famous iron ore of	118
Montesa,	Convent of military knights destroyed by an earthquake.	369
Montferrat,	Famous mountain of, in Catalonia.	183
Morviedro,	Remains of antient Saguntum	378
Mountains,	Reason for the uncertain accounts of their origin.	330
Mulberry-trees,	Method observed with them in Valencia.	375
		Murcia,

Murcia,	Rich vale of	358
Mudela,	Santa Cruz de, mine of antimony near it.	428

N.

Navas de Tolosa,	Battle of	320
Navarre,	Description of furnace there for smelting iron ore,	195
Niquera,	In Valencia, famous quarry of marble	338
Negroes,	Families of them between Badajos and Zafra.	185
Ninerola,	Quarry of alabaster there.	—
Nitre,	Basis of, exists in the earth and plants.	33
Nopal,	American name of a plant found in the Mexican woods.	30
Novelda,	Estate of Don Jorge Juan	361

O.

Oak, scarlet,	Near Merida, celebrated by Pliny.	22
Oak,	Varieties of, in Spain.	304
Oak,	Propagation of oak timber in Spain, memorial thereon.	178
Oil,	Spanish method of making it.	344
Oñate,	Town of	131
Orchilla,	See lichen	
Orihuela,	Boxes made there, and plenty of that country described	358
Oyster shells,	Remarkable ones, between Murcia and Mula.	361

P.

Palos,	Port of	313
Pagarete,	Wine	331
Paintings,	At Madrid, some observations on	78
Pamplona,	Plants observed in the plains of	8
Paquet boats,	First appointed at Coruña, when	74
Pebbles,	Remarks on them, found in bed of rivers.	195
Perez,	Prior of Larrabida, the great friend of Columbus.	313
Pheasants,	Island of, Pyrenean treaty concluded there.	133
Phlogiston,	What it is	33
Pholades,	— — — —	116
Plants,	In the neighbourhood of Trillo.	97
Plasencia,	Vera de, and convent of Juste, where Charles the Vth died.	118
	Valley of	179
Plough,	New, with seed box, introduced by Don Joseph Lucatelli.	73
Poblet,	Royal convent of	415
Population,	Sketch of, in Madrid, for 1758.	67
	Of Spain	5
Port St. Mary,	City of	331
Potatoes,	Introduced from America.	331
Puerto,	This word implied to mean a pass, from one province to another.	1
Pyrites,	That mineral described.	206

Q.

Quicksilver	Mine at Almaden, new method of extracting it from the ore, introduced by Don Guillermo Bowles.	140

R.

Rice,	Cultivation of, in Valencia	270
Rivers,	Of Spain	3
Reinosa,	Environs of	110
	Rabbet-skins,	

INDEX OF CONTENTS.

Rabbet-skins tinged,	} Imitate the beautiful skin of the gennet	359
Revenue to,	Crown of Spain on exported wool.	16
Rhone	River, its disappearance	400
Rhine,	Crystal of the,	403
Ripperda,	Duke of, confined in Castle of Segovia, but escapes.	174
Rioja,	Province of, supplies Biscay with wine.	157

S.

Saffron,	Near St. Clemente, the best in La Mancha.	419
Salinas,	Hill, so called from its briny spring.	130
Sailing.	Of vessels, problem relating thereto.	185
Saltpetre,	Method of making it in Spain.	12
Saltpetre	Works, in Paris.	40
	Of first boiling, at Almeria.	115
Scarlet caps,	Dyed with the Kermes exported from Tunis annually	51
Segovia,	City of	113
Seville,	City of	328
Sea,	Its saltness considered	395
Sierra Blanca,	High hill so called	106
	Singular veins of jet observed there	—
Sierra Morena,	New colonies established there.	318
Simancas,	Records of the kingdom deposited there, by Philip the second.	117
Sheep Spanish,	} Or Merino flocks. See Merino	
Smalt,	- - - -	218
Spar,	Beautiful, near Malaga.	331

Solano winds,	Dangerous effect of.	308
	On young people	319
Sounding line,	Its use.	101
Statue,	Equestrian of Philip the fourth, at the Retiro, described.	72
Storks,	Return every year to their nests, many of them at Seville.	308
St. Paul,	Bay and harbour of	363
Sunal,	Don Joseph, published a treatise on amber.	365

T.

Tafalla,	City of, cultivation observed in its neighbourhood.	9
Tagus,	River, its source and environs described.	105
Talavera,	Near Merida de la Reyna, in Castile.	—
	La Vieja.	—
Tinto River,	Extraordinary qualities of	310
Tin plates,	Manufacture of, established near Rooda, by marquis de Pilares.	353
Toledo blades,	Particular account of them.	135
Tarragona,	City of, its antiquities and pleasant situation.	414
Tortosa,	City of, bridge of boats over the Ebro.	417
Touchstone,	Found in the mountain of Montserrat. See lapis lydius	
Trillo,	Baths and mineral waters of, particularly described.	89
Types,	The elegant translation of Sallust by Infant Don Gabriel, with Spanish types.	411
	Valladolid,	

INDEX OF CONTENTS. 455

V.

Valladolid,	City of	117
Valencia,	Plain of	371
	City of	374
	Annual products of	380
Valtierra,	Village of, mine of sal gem near it.	10
Velez Malaga,	- - - - -	333
Venary,	Curious book on, and forest beasts, written by Alfonso king of Castile.	23
Venice,	The kermes still used there, in the dye house, for scarlet	82
Venta de Belate,	Plants observed near that place	8
Vermeja,	Sierra de	354
Villagorda,		417
Volcanos,	Remains of antient, in Spain.	409

U.

Urinal,	Found in Valencia, different from those seen in cabinets.	365

W.

Wharton,	Philip duke of, his character, buried at Poblet in Catalonia.	416
Williamson,	Rev. Dr. chaplain to the British factory at Lisbon, his opinion of Merida and its antiquities.	255
Wingfield,	Sir John, the only Englishman of note, killed at Cadiz, when taken by the English.	319
Wingfield,	Sir Richard, knight of the garter, Embassador in Spain, buried at Toledo. —	

X.

Xerez,	City of, famous for its wine	151
Xixona,	Revenue to the inhabitants from the kermes.	53

Y.

Yaquerlat,	Arabic word, softened afterwards to *escarlata*, in Spanish, our word scarlet.	81

Z.

Zafra,	Town of	383
Zaffre,	Described	114
Zalamea,	Town, and its environs.	287

Index of Plants mentioned in this Work.

A DELFA 330, 354
Agrimony 8, 106
Alaturnus, bastard 387
Alfalfa, see trifolium Hispanicum
Alga 361
Algaroba, or carob 360
Almond ———
       Garden 367
Aloe 331
Anis common, see pimpernel
Anthyllis erinacea 417
Apple love, see tomates
Arbutus uva ursi 130, 145, 387
Archangel 7
Argoma 136
Arsmart 7
Artichoaks 376
Asparagus, white 164, 310
       wild 306
Asphodel 331
Avens 320

B.

Barrilla 356
Beech 7
       mast bearing 113
Bell flower 102
Bethlem star ———
Bilberry wort 141
Bind weed, rough 387
Birthwort, round 143

Borrage 331
Box 8, 110
Briony black 106
Broom 315
       butchers 9
Buckthorn, purging 106
Bullace 8
Butterwort (sweating drops of water 106

C.

Camomile 164
Cantabrian heath 156
Cardemindum 334
Carrasca 11
Carob tree, see algaroba
Carrot deadly 419
Cauliflower 376
Cedrati 371
Celandine 7, 310
Ceratonia 360
Cinquefoil 8
Cistus, gum bearing 187, 191, 249
       dwarf 101
       rosemary leaved 368
Clary 306
Cascora, vide carrasca
Coccus ilicis, ibid.
Colquilla 113
Cork tree 304, 354
Corn flag 102
Cornicabra 318
       Coxcomb,

INDEX OF PLANTS. 457

Coxcomb	141
Crowfoot	2, 8, 151, 164
Cuckow flower	7

D.
Devils bit	8
Ditany bastard	331
Dock	7, 334
Dock weed	8
Doradilla, see golden saxifrage	
Dragon tree	350

E.
Elder	7, 8
Elm	116
Encina oak	354
Eringo	8
Erino, see anthyllis erinacea	
Esparto, see matweed	

F.
Fern	387
Figwort	7
Fig	375
Flax	311
Fumitory	119
Furze thorny	130
bitter	164

G.
Garlic	264
Garbanzo	115
Carul	164
Geranium	331
Goldilocks	106
Goosegrass	310
white	8
Gorse, fine	156, 387
Grapes	375 and 6

H.
Hare's ear	389
Hawthorn	7, 8, 202
Hemlock	164
Hemp	311
Henbane	8
Holm	7, 202
Horehound, white	8
base	202

I.
Jerusalem oak	116, 117
Iris bulbous	389
Indian fig	331, 334, 373
Juniper tree	102, 387
Spanish	206
Judas tree	83

K.
Kermes	18, 130

L.
Lavender	14, 118, 119, 160, 370
cotton	14, 419
Lead wort	118
Lentiscus	367
Lichen	319
Lichnis	116
Liquorice	87
Lote, or nettle tree	387
Love apple	264
Lucern, see trifolium Hispanicum	

M.
Mallow	164, 331
Marigold, marsh	304
Mastick tree, common, see lentiscus	
Matweed	331
Meadowsweet	120
Medick, see trifolium Hispanicum	
	Melons

458   INDEX OF PLANTS.

Melons	326
Milkwort	105
Mint	7
Molle, or balsam tree	359
Mulberry tree, black	174
White	—
Muscari, or fair haired hyacinth	202
Myrtle	310

N.
Nightshade	164
deadly	310

O.
Oak	10
Variety of	164
Oleander, see adelfa	
Olive	8, 249
Opuntia	10
Oracbe	114
Orchilla, see lichen	
Orchis	130, 202

P.
Palm	128
Palmetto	161
Pear prickly, see Indian fig	
Penny royal	143
Perriwinkle	319, 330
Peru pepper	359
Pilla marina	361
Pimenton, or guinea pepper	359
Pimpinel, or common anis	206
Plantain	7
Pomegranate	273, 375
Poplar	116
Poppy	8
Privet	143, 249
Mock	287

R.
Ragwort Meadow	115
Ragwort	202
Restharrow	8, 367
Thorny	130
Ribes	151
Rice	370
Rose, wild	8
Rosemary	149, 264, 368, 387
Rue	264

S.
Sage	14
Jerusalem	118
Tree	202
Salicor	364
Samphire	114
Santolina chamæ cyparissus, see lavender cotton	
Saxifrage golden	354
Service	206
Savin	164, 367
Scorpion sena	387
Scinus molle, see Peru pepper	
Shepherd's purse	310
Sorrel	306
Sofa	361
Sowthistle	7
Spanish cherry	206
Spinage wild	211
Spurge	331
Squinancey berries	143
Shumac	116

T.
Tamarisk	10
Teasel	8
Thyme	14, 117, 249, 264, 387
Thymus Hispanicus	117
Thistle, wild, with yellow flowers	119
Thorn	

INDEX OF PLANTS.

Thorn tree	8	W.	
Thorn apple	264, 334	Wormwood, green	217
Tomates	359		
Thapsia villosa	419	Y.	
Trefollum Hispanicum	380	Yellow weed	143
Trefoil, stinking	387		
Tulip	37		
Tuna	30		
Tutsan	8		

V.

Vipergrass	8
Vervain, parsley leaved	143

N. B. As the list of plants growing in the environs of Trillo, with the Linnæan names of them, may be found at page 97, they are not inserted here.

ERRATA.

Page 11. In Note line 5, as also a fine black varnish, *read*, also for a fine black varnish.
    204. Line 1, Querono Ilex, *read*, quercus ilex.
    207. In Note line 21, for chriftoval velez, *read*, chriftoval velez.
    232. Note (c) line 5, a tenacious taste, *read*, tenacious paste.
    257. Line 2, for Orunda, *read*, Ordura.
    264. Line 8, may, even upon, dele *even*, *read*, feed upon.
    407. Line 7, for hotter that either, *read*, hotter than either.

www.ingramcontent.com/pod-product-compliance
Lightning Source LLC
Chambersburg PA
CBHW051848300426
44117CB00006B/307